— The Unofficial G
to the Great Smoky and
Blue Ridge Mountains —

Also available from Macmillan Travel

The Unofficial Guide® to the
Great Smoky and
Blue Ridge Mountains

Bob Sehlinger
Joe Surkiewicz

MACMILLAN • USA

Macmillan Travel
A Prentice Hall Macmillan Company
15 Columbus Circle
New York, New York 10023

Produced by Menasha Ridge Press
Design by Barbara E. Williams

ISBN 0-02-860079-7

Library of Congress Catalog Card Number: 94-73808

Manufactured in the United States of America

10 9 8 7 6 5 4 3 2 1

First edition

For Steve Garrison and Gary Barton, old friends who never stopped showing me new things in these mountains.

—J. S.

For Mary Whetsell and Ann O'Bryan, raise hell on the mountaintop, but let there be peace in the valley.

—B. S.

Contents

x — *Contents*

List of Illustrations

Acknowledgments

The Southern Appalachians cover a huge chunk of geography that starts just outside Washington, D.C., and goes all the way to Northern Georgia—so putting this book together was a big job. Luckily, we got some help along the way.

Big thanks to Blue Ridge Mountains native—and renowned chronicler of the backroads of Tennessee and North Carolina—Carolyn Sakowski for helping a research team that, in the early going, didn't know Sliding Rock from Blowing Rock.

Hats off to freelance writer Debra Shore, a frequent contributor to *Outside* magazine, for opening up her little black book and providing the names of quotable experts for our section on crime in the mountains.

Kevin Padgett, a freelance writer and staffer at Nantahala Outdoor Center in Bryson City, North Carolina (official title: Bike Guy), drew on his 20 years of experience in the back country of Georgia, North Carolina, Tennessee, and South Carolina to give us the *best* places to hike, bike, swim, and watch the mayhem on a Class V rapid . . . from a safe distance.

Randy Porter, outdoor columnist and co-author of *A Cyclist's Guide to the Shenandoah Valley,* offered us his years of expertise in Virginia's Blue Ridge for the best places to hike, ride a bike, and fish. Ken Howell and Mark Singleton at Nantahala Outdoor Center in Bryson City, North Carolina, gave us the inside scoop on downhill skiing in the Southern Appalachians.

Sue Bland and Julia Scott at the Virginia Division of Tourism came through with maps, information, and hotel reservations on appallingly short notice, while Lee Whitaker at Price/McNabb, the PR folks in Asheville, North Carolina, filled us in on what's new in that vibrant town . . . and the latest back-country craze: llama trekking.

In Tennessee, thanks to Barbara Parker at the State Department of Tourist Development, Kay Powell at the Pigeon Forge Department of Tourism, and Gatlinburg receptive tour operator Abbie Bales for helping us sort out attractions, restaurants, and lodging.

North Carolina tourism pros Christine Mackey and Karen Parker came through with valuable info and last-minute hotel reservations. Mark Ruso at Rock & Roll Sports, a bike shop in Boone, North Carolina, gave us the lowdown on the best places to spin the cranks in North Carolina's Blue Ridge. And Ann Lembo was always there with the right combination of moral and editorial support.

To fulfill their task, the hotel inspection team, Holly Brown and Jennifer Walker, endured sore feet, August downpours, high humidity, and high cholesterol meals.

We would like to thank the following people for their help in compiling the dining chapter: John Burton, Jim Greiner, Cindy Griffin, Mark Hunt, Dolores Kostelni, Hilda Lee, Jan LeTendre, Kevin Padgett, Bob Pastorio, Ray Robinson, Mary Bob Rowe, Carolyn Sakowski, Karen Serba, Tina Skinner, Mark Todd, Kitty Turner, Margo Turner, Lee Whitaker,

Finally, many thanks to Barbara Williams, Tim Krasnansky, Ann Cassar, Sherry Roberts, and icon graphics, the pros who managed to transform all this effort into a book.

*— The Unofficial Guide®
to the Great Smoky and
Blue Ridge Mountains —*

Getting Beyond the Numbers

Expressed in numbers, Great Smoky Mountains National Park is, quite simply, a place without peer. At 517,000 acres, Great Smoky is the largest wilderness area in the eastern United States. The park, which straddles 60 miles of the state line between North Carolina and Tennessee, is within one day's drive of the major urban centers of the East Coast and the Great Lakes—two-thirds of the entire U.S. population.

More numbers: Sixteen peaks inside Great Smoky rise above 6,000 feet, making them the highest mountains east of the Rockies. The region's near subtropical climate—almost 80 inches of rain fall each year—creates a hot-house environment: The park is home to over 100 tree species and more than 1,400 flowering plants. More than 200 species of birds, 50 species of fish, and 50 kinds of mammals call the park home.

Yet Great Smoky's biggest number surpasses all the others combined: ten million, the number of people who visit Great Smoky Mountains National Park each year.

Why do visitors from around the world come to this park—and at a rate nearly three times that of Grand Canyon National Park?

To understand the near-mystical attraction of the Smokies for so many people, you've got to get beyond numbers. You need to visit the park on a morning in June.

Whispering conifer forests cloak forest ridges that recede toward the horizon like waves on a gray-green sea. A bluish mist clings to the mountainsides and fills the valley—and gives the mountains their name. A Tennessee warbler sings from a tree branch, and Catawba rhododendron decorate the woods with huge flowers. Hawks soar at eye level on thermals rising from the valley floor.

Then you'll realize that the Great Smokies is a destination that offers intense beauty, quiet, and solitude.

Yet for many visitors who drive to this park, the Smokies are something less—a lot less: Bumper-to-bumper traffic on the park's narrow and winding roads. "Gateway" towns outside the park full of tacky souvenir shops on narrow streets choked by traffic jams worthy of midtown Manhattan. And beyond Great Smoky Mountains National Park, a massive, confusing region of millions of acres of mountains and forests stretching from Northern Georgia to Shenandoah National Park in Virginia.

For others, another set of numbers presents a problem: The sheer quantity of ways to enjoy the outdoors . . . and deciding what to do. In the Smokies, visitors can enjoy walks, hikes, and whitewater rafting trips, visit breathtaking waterfalls, take a scenic tour from a helicopter, ride bikes, fish for trophy trout, go horseback riding. . . .

Throw in the massive crowds that besiege the Smokies and other popular destinations during the peak tourist seasons, and it's all very confusing—especially for first-time visitors.

But it doesn't have to be that way for you.

This book is the reason why.

We'll tell you when the Great Smokies is the least crowded, when wildflower blooms turn mountain paths into fragrant back-country gardens, and when the fall colors create a crazy-quilt pattern of red, yellow, and gold on the mountainsides.

You'll get the lowdown on the best things to do in the mountains, from the best scenic drives in and around Great Smoky to great day hikes—from half-mile strolls along paved walkways to an all-day scramble leading to a 100-foot waterfall deep in the forest.

We'll also tell you where the biggest trout lurk, the best places to ride a bike, and how to get an adrenaline high on a raging whitewater river.

And if you've never taken a raft trip? Or gone on an overnight hike? Or fly-fished in a tumbling mountain stream? Relax. We give you the straight skinny on exciting outdoor activities like these and more . . . and tell you how to get more information that will open up new ways of enjoying the mountains and make your vacation more fun.

We'll also introduce our secret resource: the national forests that surround Great Smoky and, in Virginia to the northeast, Shenandoah National Park. These millions of acres of mountains are where the locals go when crowds choke the national parks—and so should you.

The hiking, fishing, mountain biking, and rafting is as good—often better—than what the crowds enjoy in the national parks. And what about things to do after a long day enjoying these beautiful mountains? We deliver the lowdown on how to have a good time—from a dinner theater that thrills the crowd with a rodeo featuring more than 30 trick riders to quiet campgrounds where you can set up camp next to a pristine trout stream. *The Unofficial Guide* reveals sides of the Smokies most visitors never see . . . but should: the Ocoee River in Tennessee's Cherokee National Forest, the site chosen as the venue for whitewater canoe races in the 1996 Atlanta Olympics; Asheville, North Carolina, a town boasting the largest private home in the United States and a restored Art Deco downtown with a vibrant restaurant, club, and arts scene; and Charlottesville, Virginia, a hip college town famous for Thomas Jefferson, a diverse restaurant scene, and a gorgeous countryside dotted with wineries.

We also give you the practical stuff you need to know to enjoy a visit to the Smoky and Blue Ridge mountains. You'll find suggestions on how to avoid getting blisters on a hike, tips on how to protect valuables from car thieves, and advice on how to avoid an unplanned confrontation with local wildlife.

That's not all. *The Unofficial Guide* offers a critical analysis of the traditional attractions that have made the Smoky and Blue Ridge mountains a legendary vacation destination for decades, including Dollywood, a Dolly Parton–inspired theme park that draws two million visitors a year; the boyhood home of novelist Thomas Wolfe; and Luray Caverns, an underground wonderland less than two hours from Washington, D.C.

We'll also tell you the best way to enjoy a scenic vacation along Skyline Drive and the Blue Ridge Parkway, almost 600 miles of winding two-lane highway that follows the crest of the Blue Ridge Mountains from Front Royal, Virginia, to Cherokee, North Carolina.

You'll also discover the best seasons to visit the mountains, how to save a few bucks on a hotel room, and where to shop for genuine Appalachian crafts. We also include comprehensive lists of the best dining spots around. You'll also uncover tons of information that will save your feet and your wallet, not to mention your temper.

We also include plenty of information on Shenandoah National Park—a vacation destination only 70 miles from Washington, D.C.

that draws two million visitors a year—and the nearby Shenandoah Valley, one of the most beautiful places on the planet.

Armed with this book, you'll uncover the Smokies and Blue Ridge that most people miss. You'll also discover, as we did in researching this guidebook, another important number about the Southern Appalachians: Why they're the Number One vacation destination for tens of millions of people each year!

About This Guide

—— How Come "Unofficial"?

Most "official" guides to the Smoky and Blue Ridge mountains of eastern Tennessee, western North Carolina, and Virginia tout the well-known sights, promote the local restaurants and hotels indiscriminately, and leave out a lot of good stuff. This one is different. Instead of pandering to the tourist industry, we'll tell you if it's not worth the wait for the mediocre food served in a well-known restaurant, we'll complain loudly about over-priced hotel rooms, and we'll guide you toward the best sights and recreational opportunities to be found throughout the Smoky and Blue Ridge mountains.

Because these mountains sprawl across a huge amount of real estate, it's an area that can bewilder first-time visitors. We sent in a team of evaluators who toured its best-known attractions, ate in the area's best restaurants, performed critical evaluations of its hotels, and sampled a wide range of its outdoor recreational opportunities. If a museum is boring, or if stopping at a roadside tourist attraction is a waste of time and money, we say so—and, in the process, we hope to make your visit more fun, efficient, and economical.

—— Creating a Guidebook

We got into the guidebook business because we were unhappy with the way travel guides make the reader work to get any usable information. Wouldn't it be nice, we thought, to make guides that were easy to use?

Most guidebooks are compilations of lists. This is true regardless of whether the information is presented in list form or artfully distributed through pages of prose. There is insufficient detail in a list, and with prose the presentation can be tedious and contain large helpings of nonessential or marginally useful information. Not enough

5

wheat, so to speak, for nourishment in one instance, too much chaff in the other. Either way, these guides provide little more than departure points from which readers initiate their own quests. Many guides are readable and well researched, but they tend to be difficult to use. To select a hotel, for example, a reader must study several pages of descriptions with only the names of the hotels in bold type breaking up the text. Because each description essentially deals with the same variables, it is difficult to recall what was said concerning a particular hotel. Readers generally have no alternative but to work through all the write-ups before beginning to narrow their choices. The presentation of restaurants and attractions is similar except that even more reading usually is required. To use such a guide is to undertake an exhaustive research process that requires examining nearly as many options and possibilities as starting from scratch. Recommendations, if any, lack depth and conviction. Such guides compound, rather than solve, problems by failing to narrow travelers' choices down to a thoughtfully considered, well-distilled, and manageable few.

—— *How* Unofficial Guides *Are Different*

Readers care about the author's opinion. The author, after all, *is* supposed to know what he is talking about. This, coupled with the fact that the traveler wants quick answers (as opposed to endless alternatives), dictates that authors should be explicit, prescriptive, and, above all, direct. The *Unofficial Guide* tries to do just that. It spells out alternatives and recommends specific courses of action. It simplifies complicated destinations and attractions and allows the traveler to feel in control in the most unfamiliar environments. The objective of the *Unofficial Guide* is not to have the most information or all of the information; it aims to have the most accessible, useful information, unbiased by affiliation with any organization or industry.

An *Unofficial Guide* is a critical reference work that focuses on a travel destination appearing to be especially complex. Our authors and research team are completely independent from the attractions, restaurants, and hotels we describe.

The *Unofficial Guide to the Smoky and Blue Ridge Mountains* is designed for individuals and families traveling for the fun of it, especially those visiting these mountains for the first time. The guide is directed at value-conscious, consumer-oriented adults who seek a cost effective, though not spartan, travel style.

—— *How This Guide Was Researched and Written*

While many guidebooks have been written about the Smoky and Blue Ridge mountains, few have been evaluative. Some guides come close to regurgitating the hotels' and tourist offices' own promotional material. In preparing this work, nothing was taken for granted. Each museum, park, national forest, hotel, restaurant, shop, and attraction was visited by a team of trained observers who conducted detailed evaluations and rated each according to formal criteria. Interviews were conducted to determine what tourists of all ages enjoyed most *and least* during their visit to the mountains.

While our observers are independent and impartial, we do not claim to have special expertise. Like you, they visited the region as tourists, noting their satisfaction or dissatisfaction. The primary difference between the average tourist and the trained evaluator is the evaluator's skills in organization, preparation, and observation. The trained evaluator is responsible for much more than simply observing and cataloging. While the average tourist is gazing in awe at fantastic formations in Luray Caverns, for instance, the professional is rating the tour in terms of pace, how quickly crowds move, the location of rest rooms, and the placement of handrails and stairs. The evaluator also checks out things such as other nearby attractions, alternative places to go if the line at a main attraction is too long, and where to find the best local lunch options. Observer teams used detailed checklists to analyze hotel rooms, restaurants, and attractions. Finally, evaluator ratings and observations were integrated with tourist reactions and the opinions of patrons for a comprehensive quality profile of each feature and service.

In compiling this guide, we recognize that tourists' age, background, and interests will strongly influence their taste in a region's wide array of activities and attractions and will account for a preference of one over another. Our sole objective is to provide the reader with sufficient description, critical evaluation, and pertinent data to make knowledgeable decisions according to individual tastes.

—— *How Information Is Organized: By Subject and by Geographic Zones*

To give you fast access to information about the *best* of the Smoky and Blue Ridge mountains, we've organized material in several formats.

Hotels. Because most people visiting the mountains stay in one hotel, motel, or lodge for the duration for their trip, we have summarized our coverage of hotels in charts, maps, ratings, and rankings that allow you to quickly focus your decision-making process. We do not go on for pages describing lobbies and rooms which, in the final analysis, sound much the same. Instead, we concentrate on the variables that differentiate one hotel from another: location, size, room quality, cost, and value.

Restaurants. We provide several choices when it comes to restaurants. Because you probably will eat a dozen or more restaurant meals during your stay, and because not even *you* can predict what you might be in the mood for on Saturday night, we provide extensive suggestions for the best dining in and around Great Smoky Mountains and Shenandoah national parks, as well as big towns such as Asheville, Charlottesville, and Gatlinburg.

Geographic Zones. Once you've decided where you're going, you will be interested in where to stay and what there is to do. To help you plan your trip, we have divided the mountain region into geographic zones.

- Zone 1. Great Smoky Mountains National Park
- Zone 2. The Northern Foothills of Tennessee
- Zone 3. The Southwest Foothills of Tennessee
- Zone 4. The Southern Foothills of North Carolina
- Zone 5. The Tri-State Mountains of North Carolina, Georgia, and South Carolina
- Zone 6. Asheville and Brevard
- Zone 7. The Blue Ridge Mountains of North Carolina
- Zone 8. The Blue Ridge Mountains of Virginia

All of the information in this guide is organized by geographic zones. If you plan to visit Asheville, North Carolina, you can flip to the Zone 6 (Asheville and Brevard) chapter and access complete descriptions of all the attractions, scenic drives, hiking, rafting, fishing, and biking in the Asheville/Brevard geographic area. While hotels and restaurants are discussed in separate chapters on Lodging and Dining, each hotel and restaurant entry provides the geographic zone number of the hotel or restaurant listed. If you are staying at the McAffee Inn in Pigeon Forge (Zone 2), for example, and are interested in barbecue for dinner, scanning the restaurant chapter for restaurants in Zone 2 (the Northern Foothills of Tennessee) will provide you with the best choices in the area.

—— Letters, Comments, and Questions from Readers

We expect to learn from our mistakes, as well as from the input of our readers, and to improve with each book and edition. Many of those who use the *Unofficial Guides* write to us asking questions, making comments, or sharing their own discoveries and lessons learned in the Smokies. We appreciate all input, both positive and critical, and encourage our readers to continue writing. Readers' comments and observations frequently are incorporated in revised editions of the *Unofficial Guide*.

How to Write the Authors:

Bob Sehlinger, Joe Surkiewicz
The Unofficial Guide to the Smoky and Blue Ridge Mountains
Box 43059
Birmingham, AL 35243

When you write, be sure to put your return address on your letter as well as on the envelope—sometimes envelopes and letters get separated. And remember, our work takes us out of the office for long periods of time, so forgive us if our response is delayed.

Reader Survey

At the back of the guide you will find a short questionnaire that you can use to express opinions concerning your visit to the Smokies or Blue Ridge mountains. Clip the questionnaire along the dotted line and mail it to the above address.

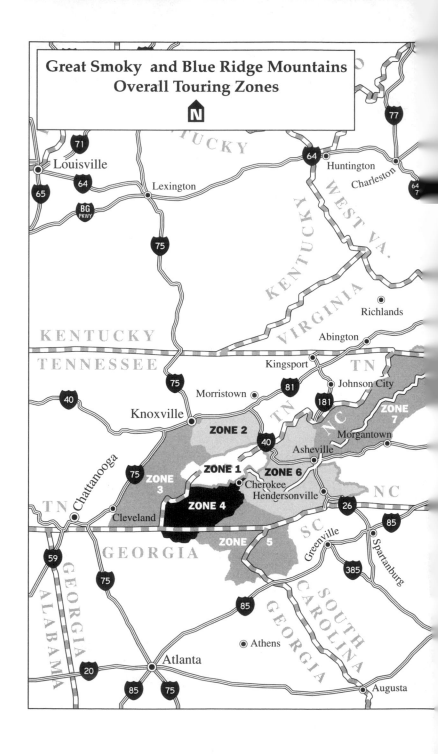

Great Smoky and Blue Ridge Mountains Overall Touring Zones

N

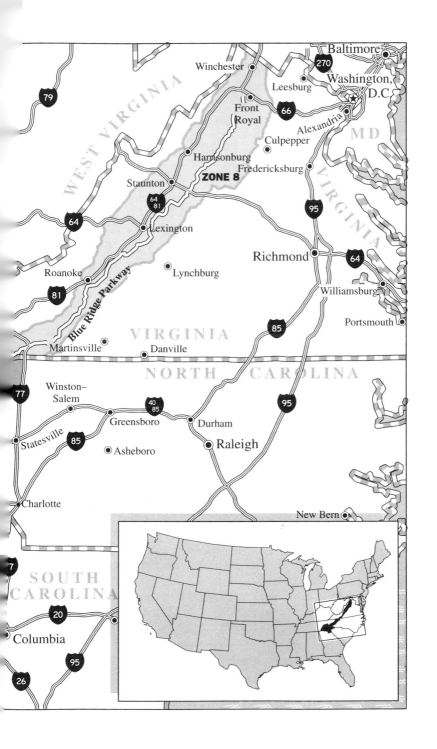

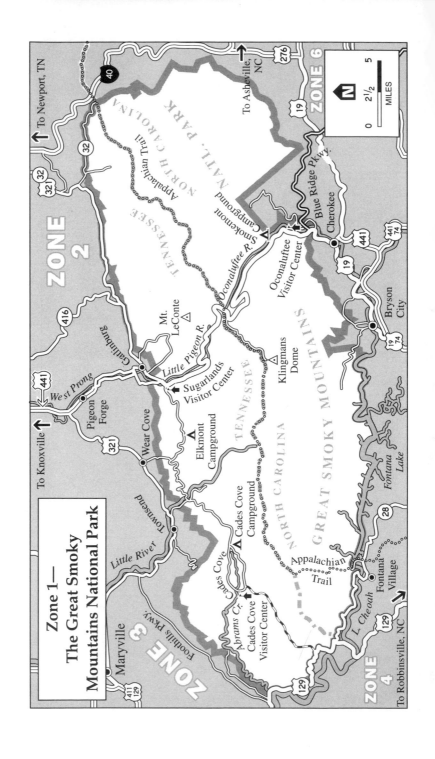

Zone 1—
The Great Smoky
Mountains National Park

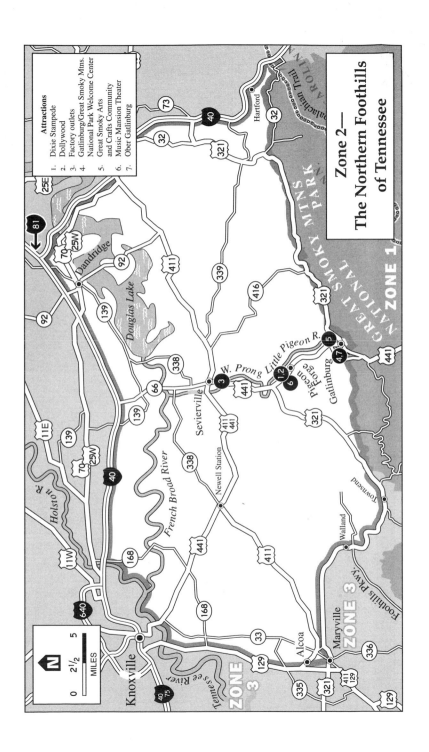

Zone 2—
The Northern Foothills
of Tennessee

Attractions

1. Dixie Stampede
2. Dollywood
3. Factory outlets
4. Gatlinburg/Great Smoky Mtns.
   National Park Welcome Center
5. Great Smoky Arts
   and Crafts Community
6. Music Mansion Theater
7. Ober Gatlinburg

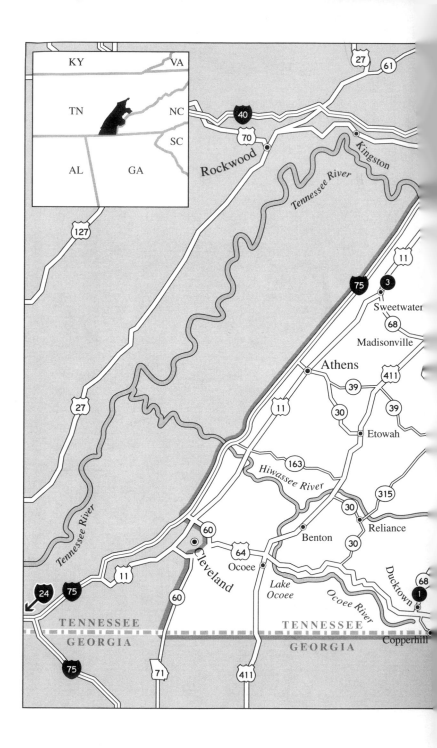

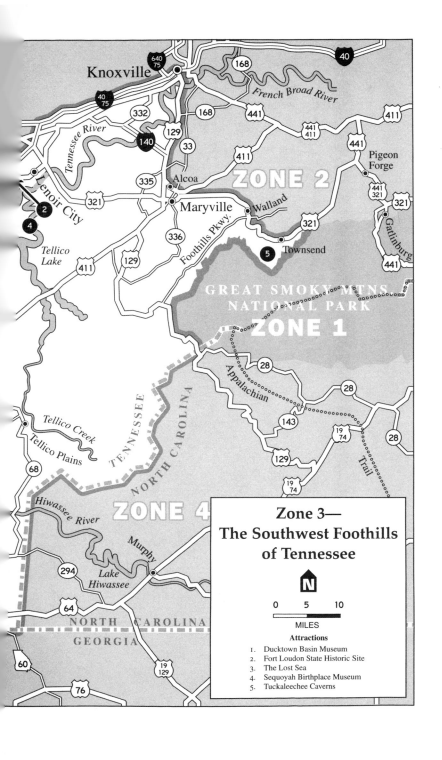

Zone 3—
The Southwest Foothills of Tennessee

N

0   5   10

MILES

Attractions

1. Ducktown Basin Museum
2. Fort Loudon State Historic Site
3. The Lost Sea
4. Sequoyah Birthplace Museum
5. Tuckaleechee Caverns

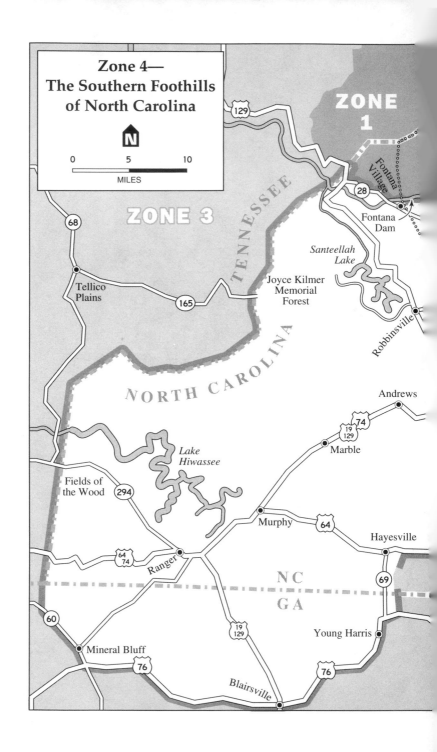

Zone 4—
The Southern Foothills
of North Carolina

N

0   5   10
MILES

ZONE 1

129

28

Fontana Village

Fontana Dam

Santeellah Lake

ZONE 3

TENNESSEE

68

Tellico Plains

165

Joyce Kilmer Memorial Forest

Robbinsville

NORTH CAROLINA

Andrews

74
19
129

Marble

Lake Hiwassee

Fields of the Wood

294

Murphy

64

Hayesville

64
74

Ranger

NC

GA

69

60

19
129

Young Harris

Mineral Bluff

76

Blairsville

76

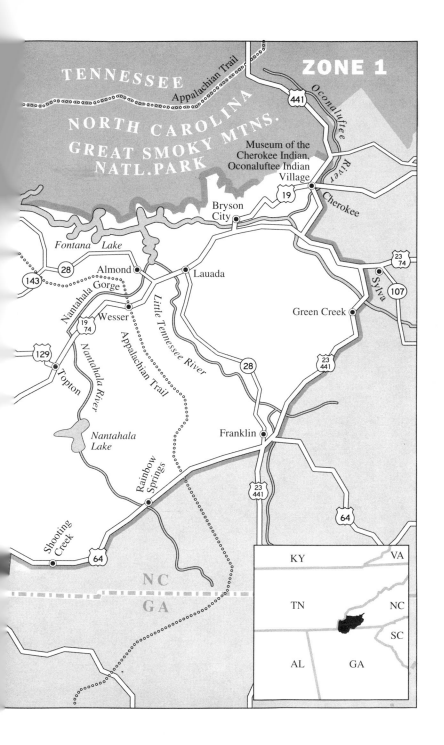

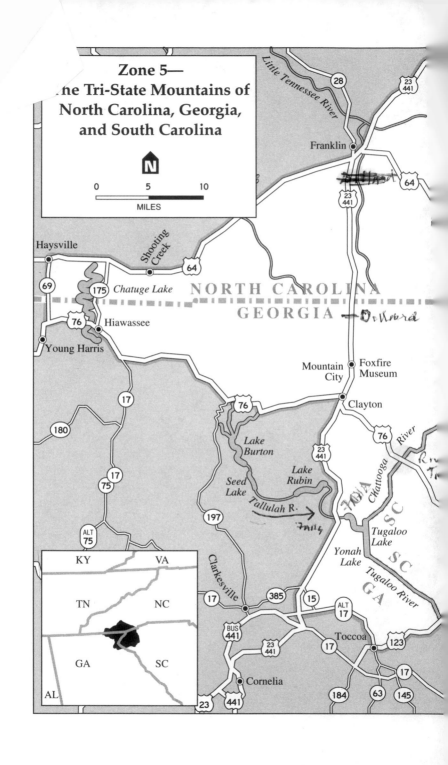

Zone 5—
The Tri-State Mountains of North Carolina, Georgia, and South Carolina

N

0   5   10
MILES

Little Tennessee River

28
23 441

Franklin

23 441

64

Haysville

Shooting Creek

69

175   Chatuge Lake

64

NORTH CAROLINA

GEORGIA

76   Hiawassee

Young Harris

Mountain City

Foxfire Museum

17

76

Clayton

180

76   River

Lake Burton

23 441

Chattooga

17

75

Seed Lake

Lake Rubin

197

Tallulah R.

ALT 75

KY   VA

TN   NC

GA   SC

AL

Clarkesville

17

385

15

ALT 17

Tugaloo Lake

Yonah Lake

Tugaloo River

SC

SC

GA

BUS 441

23 441

17

Toccoa

123

Cornelia

17

23   441

184   63   145

SKy VAlley Resort
Dillard

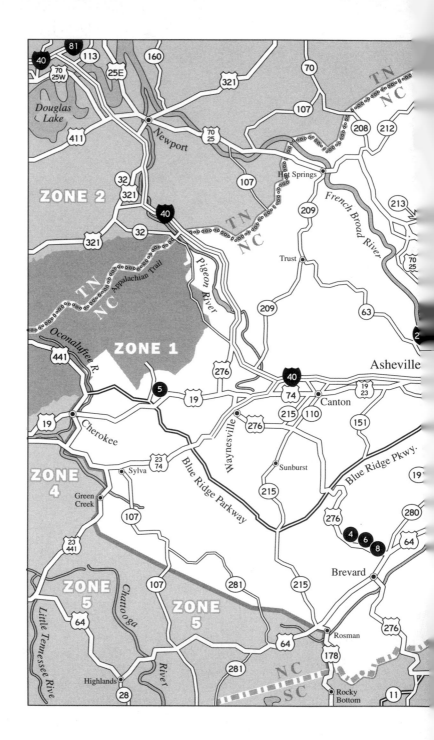

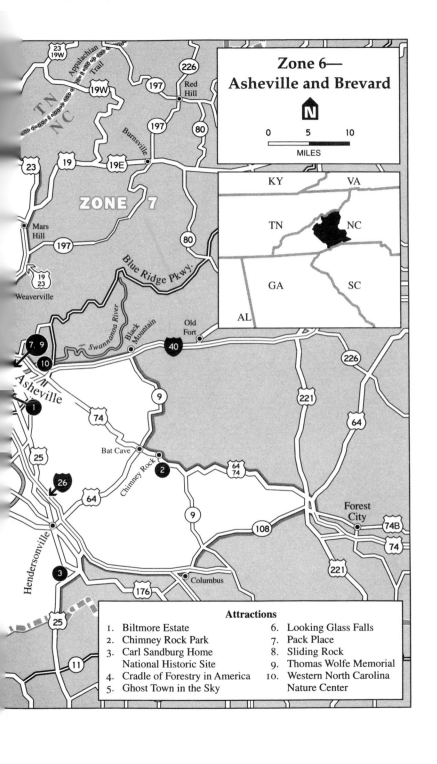

Zone 6— Asheville and Brevard

N

0   5   10
MILES

KY   VA
TN   NC
GA   SC
AL

Attractions

1. Biltmore Estate
2. Chimney Rock Park
3. Carl Sandburg Home National Historic Site
4. Cradle of Forestry in America
5. Ghost Town in the Sky
6. Looking Glass Falls
7. Pack Place
8. Sliding Rock
9. Thomas Wolfe Memorial
10. Western North Carolina Nature Center

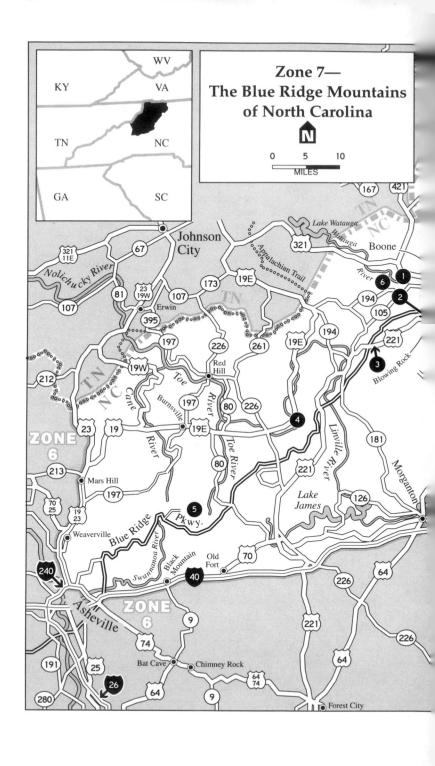

Zone 7—
The Blue Ridge Mountains of North Carolina

N

0   5   10
MILES

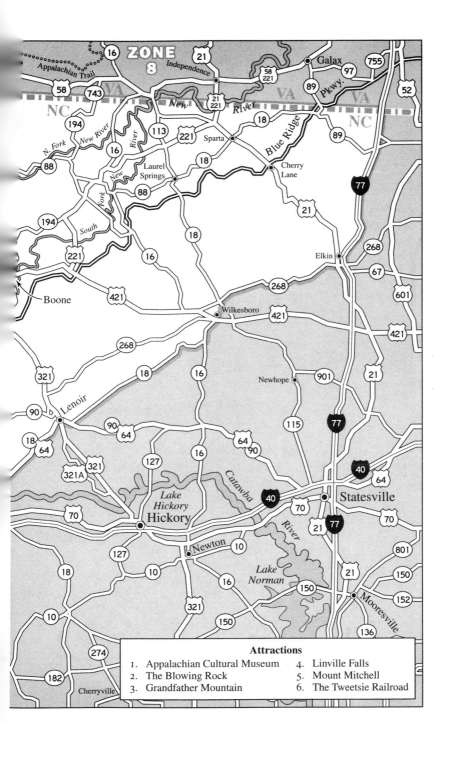

Attractions

1. Appalachian Cultural Museum
2. The Blowing Rock
3. Grandfather Mountain
4. Linville Falls
5. Mount Mitchell
6. The Tweetsie Railroad

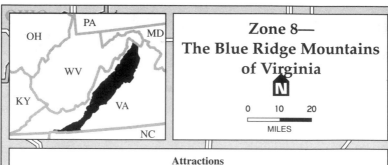

Zone 8—
The Blue Ridge Mountains of Virginia

0   10   20
MILES

Attractions

1. Ashlawn—Highland
2. Center in the Square
3. Luray Caverns
4. Monticello
5. Montpelier
6. Museum of American Frontier Culture
7. Natural Bridge
8. New Market Battlefield Historical Park
9. Old Rag
10. Stonewall Jackson House
11. Stonewall Jackson's Headquarters
12. Virginia Museum of Transportation
13. Woodrow Wilson Birthplace and Museum

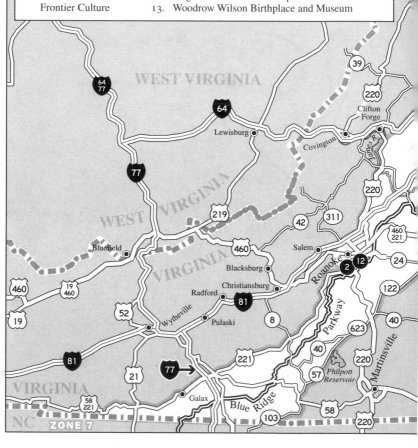

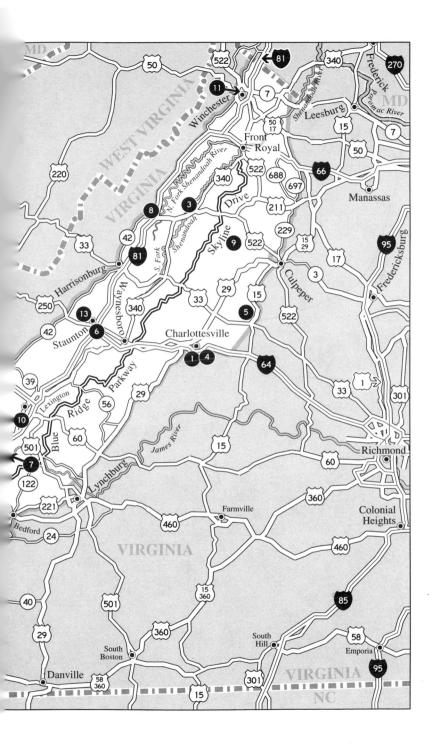

PART ONE:
Planning Your Visit to
the Great Smoky and
Blue Ridge Mountains

A Geographic—and Geologic—Overview of the Southeast Mountains

—— The Lay of the Land

The Great Smoky and Blue Ridge mountains are, respectively, the southern end and the eastern rampart of the Appalachian Mountains, the great, ancient system of ridges that extends 1,600 miles from Québec Province to Alabama. It's a region best described in superlatives.

Great Smoky Mountains National Park, with more then ten million visitors a year and the highest mountains in the East, is the logical centerpiece of the Southern Appalachians—and *The Unofficial Guide*. But this huge, mountainous region stretching from Virginia to Georgia is easier to describe starting several hundred miles northeast of the park, in the Blue Ridge Mountains of Virginia, and then moving southwest toward North Carolina and Tennessee.

The Blue Ridge Mountains

Rising in southeastern Pennsylvania and running to northwestern Georgia, the Blue Ridge Mountains separate the Shenandoah Valley of Virginia from the Piedmont and form the eastern edge of the Appalachian chain in Virginia, North Carolina, South Carolina, and Georgia.

Shenandoah National Park (Zone 8), located in Virginia only 72 miles from Washington, D.C., straddles the Blue Ridge Mountains from Front Royal to Waynesboro. The long but narrow park varies in width from one mile to 13 miles and encompasses nearly 200,000 acres of forested ridges and valleys.

Skyline Drive, a two-lane highway that follows the crest of the Blue Ridge Mountains through the park, is spectacularly scenic as it

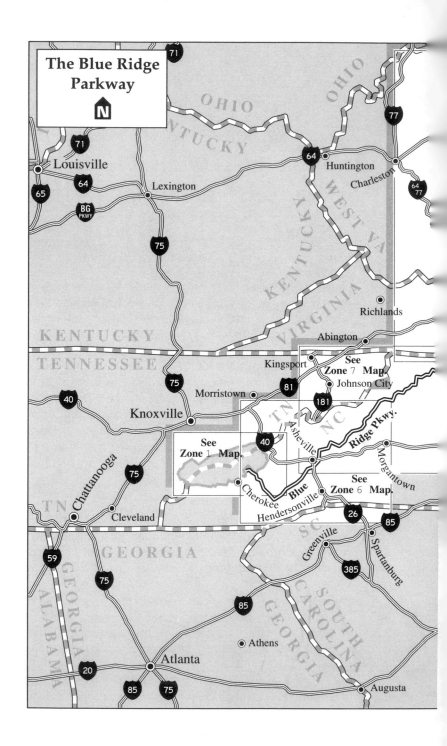

The Blue Ridge Parkway

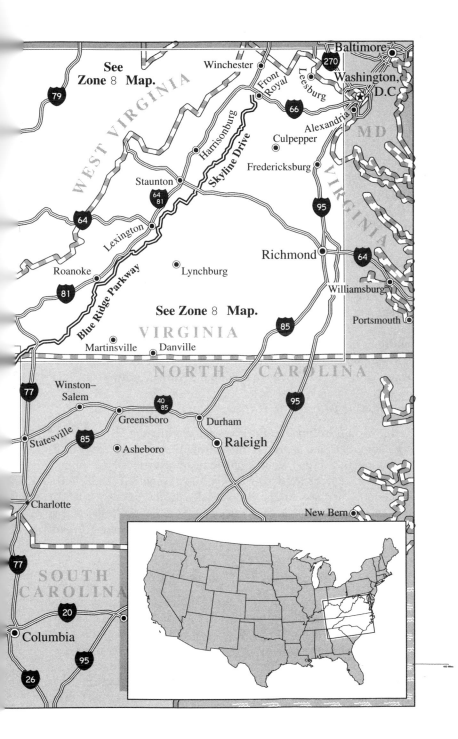

winds for 105 miles at an average elevation of 3,000 feet. The scenic drive provides more than two million visitors a year with easy access to many park sights and visitor centers.

Below Shenandoah National Park and linking up with Skyline Drive is the Blue Ridge Parkway, another 469 miles of scenic, low-traffic roadway. The Parkway winds along the crest of the Blue Ridge Mountains through Virginia to Cherokee, North Carolina, the southern entrance to Great Smoky Mountains National Park.

The Blue Ridge Parkway

The establishment of the two great parks in the 1930s (during the administration of President Franklin D. Roosevelt) is regarded by many historians as one of the great accomplishments of the Depression Era. The Blue Ridge Parkway, an engineering marvel begun in 1935 and not completed until 1987, was built to provide jobs in economically ravaged Appalachia, to furnish easy access to the parks for millions of visitors, and to serve the recreational needs of motorists. In Virginia, the scenic highway starts in Waynesboro and threads its way southwest past Roanoke toward the North Carolina state line.

The Blue Ridge Mountains of North Carolina

In North Carolina, the Parkway helped breathe economic life into a poor and isolated stretch of the Blue Ridge Mountains northeast of Asheville. Today, visitors flock to some of North Carolina's oldest and best known tourist attractions only minutes from the Parkway: Grandfather Mountain, Blowing Rock, the college town of Boone, and Linville Falls and the spectacular Linville Gorge are just a few. The highest peak in the eastern United States is here—Mount Mitchell, with an elevation of 6,684 feet.

The Southern Highlands of North Carolina

Between Great Smoky Mountains National Park to the west and the Blue Ridge Mountains to the east lies the Southern Highlands— a large plateau marked by high ridges and carved by deep river valleys. The Blue Ridge Parkway swings west through the region south of Asheville on its way to its southern terminus in Cherokee.

Once an exclusive refuge for the rich and famous, today the Southern Highlands (Zone 6) are a vacation destination *par excellance*.

Dominated by Pisgah National Forest, it's a region of spectacular waterfalls and mountains with names such as Black, Craggy, and Blue Ridge mountains that provides virtually unlimited opportunities for hiking, fishing, backpacking, camping, canoeing, and mountain biking. The center of the region is Asheville, a hip, bustling small city that lends an air of sophistication to the mountains. The town boasts a restored Art Deco downtown, museums, a classy zoo, restaurants, night life, and Biltmore Estate, the largest private home in the United States and a major tourist attraction that draws thousands of visitors each year.

Other popular visitor destinations in the Southern Highlands include Chimney Rock, a mountaintop park where *The Last of the Mohicans* was filmed; Hendersonville, a popular retirement spot; Shining Rock, a quartz-topped mountain; and Brevard, a pretty town popular with outdoors lovers, retirees, and music lovers, who flock to its internationally renown music festival each summer.

The Tri-State Mountains

South of Asheville, the tri-state area of North Carolina, Georgia, and South Carolina (Zone 5) is a well-defined destination for well-heeled tourists that's centered around Highlands, North Carolina. (With an altitude of more than 4,000 feet, Highlands is aptly named.)

Across the state line in Georgia, Chattahoochee National Forest stretches from west to east across the Blue Ridge Mountains and borders the Chattooga Wild and Scenic River (where *Deliverance* was filmed). In nearby South Carolina, the rolling terrain of the Blue Ridge foothills is defined by a series of low valleys and ridges, huge granite escarpments along the border with North Carolina, as well as Lake Keowee and Lake Jocassee. The Cherokee Foothills Scenic Highway gives motorists an unusual, from-the-bottom-up view of the Blue Ridge Mountains.

Great Smoky Mountains National Park

Located about 40 miles west of Asheville, the Great Smoky Mountains National Park (Zone 1) sits astride the border of eastern Tennessee and western North Carolina. It's the largest wilderness area in the East, with more than a half-million acres and 16 peaks above 6,000 feet. In 1934, when the park was established, it encompassed nearly 150,000 acres of virgin forest, the largest stand of untouched woods in the eastern United States.

Here's another big number: These mountains receive about 80 inches of rainfall a year—almost as much as a tropical rain forest. As a result, it's one of the most biologically diverse regions in North America, with over 1,400 flowering plants, 100 kinds of trees, 50 species of mammals, and 200 different birds. The United Nations designated Great Smoky an International Biosphere because of its tremendous diversity of life.

Not surprisingly, with its spectacular scenery and wide variety of plant and animal life, the park is a tourist mecca, attracting more than 10 million visitors a year—making it by far the most visited national park in the country. What surprises most first-time visitors is the almost total absence of amenities inside the park, which means that most folks stay in "gateway" towns on the park's periphery.

The Northern Foothills of Tennessee

In Tennessee, the resort towns of Gatlinburg, Pigeon Forge, and Sevierville (Zone 2) serve as principal gateways to Great Smoky Mountains National Park from the west and north. Commercial development along US 441, which links the three resort towns to the national park to the south, is dumbfounding: The road offers a nearly endless procession of amusement parks, electronic arcades, goofy mini-golf attractions, fast-food restaurants, outlet malls, souvenir stands, T-shirt emporiums, and the constant roar of helicopters overhead as tourists take off on sightseeing trips over the mountains. For most visitors, a trip through the congested gateway resort towns is a "love it or hate it" kind of thing.

The defining geographical feature of the region west of the national park is the Cumberland Plateau, which rises up from the Tennessee River Valley to the west. To the northeast and southwest, Tennessee's Cherokee National Forest straddles the North Carolina state line.

Southwestern North Carolina

Directly south of Great Smoky Mountains National Park, Nantahala National Forest (Zone 4) and many huge Tennessee Valley Authority lakes and dams help define the southwestern corner of North Carolina. Fontana Dam, 480 feet high, is the highest dam east of the Rockies. Huge Fontana Lake divides the national park and the national forest.

The Appalachian Trail (a 2,000-mile footpath from Maine to Georgia), the Slick Rock Wilderness, the Joyce Kilmer Memorial Forest, and the Nantahala Gorge (offering some of the best whitewater rafting and canoeing in the United States) draw visitors from around the world. Some folks say these mountains are the most unspoiled part of the Southern Appalachians. Unquestionably, this is the place to come to avoid massive doses of tourist hype.

The Southwest Foothills of Tennessee

Cherokee National Forest (Zone 3), which stretches along Tennessee's eastern border with North Carolina, contains a total of 625,000 acres in northern and southern sections divided by Great Smoky Mountains National Park. The forest is the major outdoor recreational draw to this region.

Outdoors lovers find almost limitless opportunities for hiking, fishing, camping, and canoeing. Townsend is a low-key "gateway" town at Great Smoky's western entrance; while to the southwest, Tellico Lake, the Hiwassee River, and several wilderness areas inside the national forest are major outdoor recreation draws.

But the major attraction in the region is whitewater rafting on the Ocoee River, the venue of the 1996 Atlanta Olympic Games' whitewater slalom events. Many commercial outfitters are located along US 64, the scenic highway that parallels the river; they offer visitors guided trips through the river's famous rapids.

—— A Quick Geology Lesson

Complex forces at work over hundreds of millions of years created the Blue Ridge and Great Smoky mountains. While it's beyond the scope of the *Unofficial Guide* to provide a full explanation of how these mountains were created and formed, a brief description of the area's geology can help visitors appreciate these beautiful ridges and valleys.

The Great Smoky Mountains

The building of the Smokies (part of the Unaka Range, a subrange in the Appalachian chain) began more than a billion years ago with the deposition of the base rock, laid down as sediment in a great trough in the earth's crust. After the sediment accumulated to several thousand feet, the trough closed (possibly due to a collision of continental plates that make up the earth's surface). Then the rocks were compressed, broken, folded, and heated by molten rock from the earth's interior. The rock eventually was changed into a hard crystalline mass.

Next, the area was lifted up (again, possibly due to the collision of continental plates) and started to erode, with rocks deposited as sediment in a large marine basin to the west. This new deposit solidified about 600 million years ago into rock known as the Ocoee Series. This is the rock that makes up the Great Smoky Mountains.

About 450 million years ago, folding and faulting occurred as the rocks of the Ocoee Series were pushed up over younger rock to the northwest. About 375 million years ago, a period of heat and pressure was followed by more folding and faulting, with masses of rock once again being pushed to the northwest. Then 250 million years ago the last episode of great mountain building occurred when the whole region rose above sea level.

Erosion. Since then, the Great Smoky Mountains took shape. The mountains we see today were not created by the folding and faulting episodes, but by subsequent erosion. At one time the Smokies may have been higher than the Rocky Mountains (which are, geologically speaking, much younger).

From 500,000 to 20,000 years ago—very recent history in geologic time—glaciers from the north created colder temperatures in the Smokies region. Alternate freezing and thawing caused rock to crack and split into huge boulders that found their way down to the valley floors. These are the rocks you'll see sitting in stream beds, much too large to have been placed there by the action of fast-flowing mountain streams. Once the glaciers retreated, the process of boulder creation ceased.

Ancient Rivers. Old as these mountains are, some of the rivers within them are older. During the upheavals and folding which thrust the mountains up, these ancient rivers were blocked from their westward course to the prehistoric sea that once covered North America. During the ensuing millennia these rivers sculpted the landscape of the eastern United States, carving new routes to the sea and in the process creating the spectacular canyons and gorges that make these mountains so popular with whitewater rafters and canoeists.

There's another element at work that outdoor recreationists who flock to the rivers and streams of the Southern Appalachians should know about: The thin soil of these mountains means there's little water retention capacity. When it rains, streams flow; when it doesn't, they don't. The fast runoff, steep slopes, and rocky terrain make these mountains famous for the small, seasonal, highly technical whitewater streams that attract whitewater paddlers from around the world.

The Appalachian and Blue Ridge Mountains

The Appalachian Mountains and the Blue Ridge Mountains (one of many subranges in the Appalachian system) are believed to be among the oldest on earth. Their geologic history began a billion years ago, when molten magma slowly solidified over millions of years to become the "basement rock," or core, of what is today's Blue Ridge Mountains.

For the next 500 million years, the rock was folded and uplifted, exposing the granitic basement rock. Oddly enough, this older rock is often exposed on higher peaks; in the rest of the mountains, the granite is buried beneath younger rocks.

The uplift formed deep cracks in the granite, leading to volcanic activity. Molten basaltic lava burst forth and formed a smooth, flat plain called the Catoctin Formation. Next, about 600 million years ago, the Americas separated from the continents of Europe and Africa, forming a broad, shallow depression. An ancient sea flooded the area that is now the Appalachian Mountains for the next 300 million years. Layers of waterborne sediments, as well as limestone sediments made of fossilized marine animals and shells, accumulated on the ocean floor.

Continental Drift. Then 200 million years ago, eastern North America collided with what was to become Africa, causing the sea floor to fold, lift, and break apart. The older underlying layer of rock tilted upward and slid over the younger layer, creating a towering mountain range, the Appalachians. The two giant continents fused for perhaps 50 million years, then split apart, with the Atlantic Ocean filling the void.

Once lofty and craggy like the Himalayas, the Blue Ridge Mountains were eroded by wind and water over millions of years to today's soft, rounded ridges. Water runoff also carved the mountains' distinctive alternating patterns of ridges and valleys.

The Blue Ridge Mountains get taller to the south. The highest point in Shenandoah National Park in Virginia is at Hawksbill Mountain (4,051 feet). The mountains top out at Grandfather Mountain in North Carolina (5,964 feet).

Flora and Fauna

—— Biological Diversity in the Smokies

The tremendous diversity of life in the Smokies is one of its great attractions. Consider: This vast forest contains over 1,400 species of flowering plants; 100 kinds of trees; 600 kinds of mosses, liverworts, and lichens; 2,000 different fungi; 50 species of mammals; 80 kinds of snakes and amphibians, including 22 kinds of salamanders; over 50 kinds of fish; and 200 different birds.

Origins

Why all the variety? The reasons are ancient. During the Ice Age, northern species of plants gradually moved southward ahead of advancing glaciers. As the temperatures dropped, the various northern species invaded as far south as the Smokies. When the periods of glaciation ended, the northern plant species didn't retreat with the ice. Instead, as temperatures rose, these northern species simply moved up the slopes to higher (and cooler) elevations. As they moved up the mountainsides, the southern plant species returned to take their place at the lower elevations.

Forests

As a result, the Great Smoky Mountains are home to both northern and southern plant species. The great forests that cover the mountains can be divided into five groups. The *cove hardwood forests* of basswood, magnolia, white ash, sugar maple, American beech, and silverbell occupy the land between the ridges. These are the trees responsible for the Smokies' spectacular fall foliage.

Hemlock forests, usually with an understory of rhododendron and mountain laurel, stand along the streams and banks and on moist shady slopes. The *pine-oak forests* grow on exposed ridges, which are usually dry. *Northern hardwood forests* of beech and yellow birch grow on protected slopes at higher elevations. At the highest elevations, which get double the rainfall of the lowlands, stand the *Canadian spruce-fir forests*, consisting of red spruce and Fraser fir. It's these tremendous forests that gave the Smokies their name.

Through transpiration (the passage of water through a plant to the atmosphere), the trees give off hydrocarbon molecules that break down in sunlight and recombine to form molecules large enough to refract light, as well as react with each other and various pollutants in the air to create a blue haze—which looks like smoke rising off the mountains.

The floor of the forest is covered with ferns and mosses—and a profusion of wildflowers in the spring. Shrubs create the next level of plant life in the forest. In the spring and early summer, rhododendron, wild azalea, and mountain laurel bloom, creating fantastic displays of multicolored blossoms.

Animals

The diversity of plant life results in the wide variety of animal life in the forest: muskrat, black bear, red fox, southern flying squirrel, white-tailed deer, the northern spring peeper, as well as the chickadee and Carolina wren, the wood thrush, yellow-throated vireo, and hooded warbler—just to name a few.

Streams in the Smokies provide habitat for rainbow and brown trout, native brook trout, sculpins, dace, hogsuckers, chubs, shiners, stoneroller, bass, and darters. Animals that once lived in the region but are no longer found include bison, elk, and mountain lions.

Red wolves, once hunted to extinction in the area, were recently reintroduced into Great Smoky Mountains National Park and are making a tentative comeback. The wolves, larger than coyotes but smaller than gray wolves, once ranged throughout the southeastern United States, but are now an endangered species. Officials say the animals are shy and pose virtually no threat to humans.

The Blue Ridge Mountains

Trees and Plants

While not as biologically diverse as the Smokies to the south, Shenandoah National Park and the Blue Ridge Mountains boast more species of plants than all of Europe. Moreover, since the park was founded in the 1930s, many trees, plants, and animals that were once native have returned and now flourish.

Today, more than 1,100 species of flowering plants (including 18 varieties of orchids), 100 species of trees, 47 species of ferns and mosses, and hundreds of different fungi are found in the park. The vegetative regeneration of the park is so complete that in 1976 Congress designated two-fifths of the park as wilderness.

The mountains originally were dominated by the American chestnut and a variety of oak trees. The chestnut blight earlier in the century resulted in oak and hickory becoming the most common trees in Shenandoah; by the early 1930s, the American chestnut was almost extinct. Old stumps of the giant trees are still a common sight in the woods. Occasionally sprouts grow from the stumps and produce a few chestnuts before succumbing to the blight.

Animal Diversity

Animals in Shenandoah range from the elusive bobcat to the more common raccoon. More than 200 species of birds have been observed in the park. The population of black bears is between 500 and 600; visitors, however, aren't likely to see one.

Why? The park's wildlife management policy works to keep the bears wild and unaccustomed to food brought into the back country by visitors—a much healthier situation compared to the 1970s, when confrontations between bears and people were more common. Still, it's strongly recommended that visitors keep food locked in the trunk of their car or suspended from a tree when camping in the back country.

Deer, however, seem to be everywhere in Shenandoah. Reintroduced from other parts of Virginia and New York state, they commonly are seen along Skyline Drive in the early morning and late afternoon. In the woods, they prefer semi-open spaces where the browsing is good.

Other animals living in the Blue Ridge Mountains include the meadow mouse, the groundhog, gray fox, rabbit, owl, and beaver. The park is home to two poisonous snakes, the timber rattlesnake and the copperhead. Rattlers vary in color from black to gray; the rattler's skin shows a faint diamond pattern. The copperhead is smaller and thinner than the rattlesnake and is usually the color of a penny. Both snakes are shy, and few visitors ever see one.

Gypsy moths were first discovered in the park in 1983 and the pests have defoliated many trees in the following years; it's not a pretty sight. The biggest victims are oak trees, the moths' favorite food. In one growing season, the gypsy moth caterpillars can strip a healthy tree of its leaves—and kill it. As the oak trees die, other species less preferred by the moths replace them. Park managers continue to work to reduce the gypsy moth population in developed parts of the park, while letting nature take its course in other parts.

Human History

Since about 1000 A.D., the Cherokee, believed to be a break-away band of Iroquois, lived in a 40,000-square-mile area that included the Great Smoky Mountains. They lived in villages along streams and rivers and enjoyed a settled, sophisticated life based on agriculture.

The first encounter with Europeans occurred in 1540, when Spanish explorer Hernando de Soto passed through Cherokee territory. In the late 18th century, the area increasingly was being settled by Scotch-Irish, German, and English farmers.

As encroachment continued, battles took place between the Cherokee and settlers, and a series of treaties were signed. But after 1819, the Cherokee were forced to withdraw from the Smoky Mountains to the south and west of the Little Tennessee River.

Coexistence, however, was a lost cause. The discovery of gold in northern Georgia in 1828 was the beginning of the end for the Cherokee in the Smoky Mountains region. In 1830, President Andrew Jackson signed the Removal Act, calling for the transfer of all Native Americans east of the Mississippi River to Indian territory in present-day Oklahoma.

The Trail of Tears

In 1838, the U.S. government forced 13,000 Cherokees to march to Oklahoma along what was to become known as "The Trail of Tears." About 4,000 Cherokee died of malnutrition and disease on the forced march.

A handful of Cherokee, however, evaded U.S. forces and hid out in the hills between Clingmans Dome and Mount Guyot in Great Smoky. In 1889, the 56,000-acre Qualla Indian Reservation was chartered with a population of about 1,000. Today, about 10,000 of their descendants now live on the reservation centered around the town of Cherokee, located on the park's southern border.

White Settlers

The settlers who transplanted the Cherokee lived as "hardscrabble" farmers on the steep slopes and valleys of the Smokies, growing their own food, raising their own livestock, and making their own clothes. The legacy of the mountain folk lives on in legends, music, and the wide array of crafts sold throughout the region.

Around the turn of the century, logging radically changed the face of the Smokies—and the lives of people living in the mountains. As technology allowed logging firms to increase the scale of their operations, company towns sprung up throughout the mountains (15 alone in what is today's Great Smoky Mountains National Park). Many mountain people abandoned their farms for the company towns and a steady paycheck.

By the 1930s, all but the most inaccessible areas were logged, and the companies moved west. Some of the mountain people returned to farming, while others migrated out of the area in search of jobs in industry.

An Idea for a National Park

The idea of preserving the Smokies originated in the early years of the century. By the 1920s, the National Park Service was searching for a site for a park to serve the recreational needs of the populous East. (Previously, all national parks had been established on public lands in the wide expanses of the West.) In 1934, Great Smoky Mountains National Park was established with the help of a $5 million grant from philanthropist John D. Rockefeller, Jr.

—— The Blue Ridge Mountains

Native Americans

Early Native Americans who lived in the Blue Ridge Mountains in what is today's Shenandoah National Park were primitive hunters and food gatherers, nomads who moved with the seasons and stayed in temporary encampments for months at a time.

By 7500 B.C., however, the Ice Age ended and the region saw the return of deer, bears, turkeys, elk, and woods bison from the south. The Native American population increased substantially and maintained a stable, healthy community. By 1000 B.C., agriculture and pottery began. But it wasn't until about 900 A.D. that farming contributed to more than a small fraction of the people's food needs.

Early Settlers

The first contact with white explorers and fur traders resulted in the spread of disease, and by 1700 most of the Native Americans had died or moved on; no known descendants of the people who lived in the Blue Ridge remain.

In the early 1700s, white settlers began to move into the Shenandoah Valley, east of the Blue Ridge. They were mostly Germans from Pennsylvania and Scots-Irish from Tidewater Virginia. Over the decades, many of them moved up the slopes of the Blue Ridge Mountains and farmed the thin soil.

By the late 1800s, much of the mountain's natural resources were depleted, the soil was eroded, and the fortunes of the people living in the mountains declined. In the early 20th century, about 2,000 mountain people lived in Shenandoah on hundreds of small subsistence farms on land often stripped of timber, badly eroded, and increasingly unproductive.

By 1925, nearly half of the mountain folk had left, and plans to establish a national park on the Blue Ridge were begun. Shenandoah National Park was dedicated by President Franklin D. Roosevelt on July 3, 1936.

The federal government relocated most of the 465 families who lived in the mountains to several settlement areas in the Shenandoah Valley to the west and the Piedmont to the east. Some elderly residents, however, were allowed to live out their lives in the park. The last resident, Annie Shenk, died in 1979.

In the decades since the park was established, wilderness returned quickly as forests regenerated and wildlife proliferated. Shenandoah today is a "recycled" park, recovered from overuse to become one of the most beautiful and popular natural areas in the national park system.

When to Go: A Three-Season Destination

The Great Smoky and Blue Ridge mountains are located in the Southeast, a region of the United States infamous for hot, humid summers and relatively mild winters, with temperatures only occasionally dipping below freezing at night—and very little snow. With their higher elevations, the southern mountains are usually 10 to 15 degrees cooler than the lowlands. (A rule of thumb: Air temperatures drop about three degrees for every 1,000 feet of elevation gain.) As a result, summer temperatures along high ridges are often quite comfortable—which is why each summer many affluent people from Florida and the coastal regions of the Southeast come to these mountains.

In the winter, it works the other way around: Higher altitude and increased wind often produce wind chill factors that plunge the apparent temperature on exposed skin into the subzero range. Except for downhill skiers (who flock to resorts with snowmaking equipment), hardy backpackers, hammerhead mountain bikers, and other cold-weather aficionados, the Smoky and Blue Ridge mountains don't attract many winter visitors.

—— Spring

Late spring—approximately mid-May through early June—brings mild days and cool nights, with daytime temperatures ranging from the low 70s to the mid-80s, and nighttime readings from the mid-40s to the high 50s.

Spring is usually wet, and hiking trails in the mountains are often muddy—especially if it snowed at higher elevations during the winter. Early spring—say, mid-March through mid-April—is often raw, windy, and cold, with the threat of snow anytime, especially at higher elevations.

Two other factors, however, make spring one of *The Unofficial Guide* researchers' favorite seasons in the southeastern mountains: a profusion of wildflowers and the absence of crowds. Spring wildflower blooms usually peak in mid- to late-April, although late March and early April feature good showings of springbeauty, hepatica, and other flowers. Flame azalea, a wild shrub, blooms at low- and mid-level elevations in April and May as the white blossoms of the dogwood tree brighten the forest understory. Rhododendron blooms reach their peak in June at the lower elevations and at higher elevations in July. Everywhere you look is a profusion of colorful, beautiful, fragrant wildflowers.

Spring also features an absence of crowds in normally packed tourist destinations such as Gatlinburg, Pigeon Forge (both in Zone 2), Asheville (Zone 6), and visitor centers on Skyline Drive in Shenandoah National Park (Zone 8). Room reservations are easy to get, lines in restaurants and popular tourist attractions are virtually nonexistent, and the level of stress—at least compared to that in July and October, the most crowded months—is virtually zero.

Our recommendation: Visit the Smokies and Blue Ridge during late May to early June, when the weather is mild (if a bit wet), wildflowers are in bloom, and traffic jams are nonexistent.

A Spring Bloom Calendar

The best place to view wildflowers is often through the window of your car: The break in the woods created by the roadway allows enough light in to make conditions perfect for wildflowers. Check the following list of the most easily seen spring flowers; bloom times may vary according to elevation.

Flower	*Color*	*Bloom Time*
Trailing Arbutus	white/pink	February–April

Note: A low-growing perennial with evergreen leaves one to two inches long and fragrant blooms.

Trout Lily	yellow	March–May

Note: Look for nodding yellow flowers with strongly recurved petals. The leaves are a distinctly mottled green and brown. They often appear in colonies in open deciduous woods.

Birdfoot Violet	lavender, rarely white	March–May

Note: Leaves are segmented and look like a bird's foot. Inch-wide blooms, two upper petals are deep purple, three lower petals are lavender.

Trillium	white, yellow, or crimson	April–May

Note: While there are many species, they all have three petals and a single stalk with three leaves.

Bluets	blue	April–May

Note: Tiny, delicate, four-petaled flowers with a yellow center. Bluets grow in clumps along road shoulders. The plant and flower stalks are about three inches high.

Lady Slipper	yellow, pink	April–July

Note: The lower petal is inflated, creating a pouch. The leafless bloom stem of the pink lady slipper rises from two leaves. The yellow lady slipper is taller, ranging from 12 to 24 inches, with three to five alternate leaves on the flowering stem.

Rhododendron	pink	April–June

Note: Look for large clusters of pink blooms on large evergreen shrubs with leaves three to six inches long.

—— *Summer*

By mid-June, heat, haze, and humidity are the norm in the Southern Appalachians. While it's true that cooler temperatures prevail at higher altitudes, not many people spend their entire vacation at 4,000 feet or higher—which is where the cooling effects of elevation really kick in. At 2,000 feet of elevation on a July afternoon, it can feel nearly as hot and humid as a coastal beach. Mid-summer daytime temperatures range from a low of 65° (at 6,000 feet) to a high of 90° at lower elevations.

Most precipitation occurs in afternoon thunderstorms, which can be fearsome, appear suddenly, and are often accompanied by lightning and sometimes hail. July is one of the wettest months of the year.

At popular tourist destinations such as Gatlinburg, Tennessee (the western gateway to Great Smoky Mountains National Park), July through mid-August is also one of the busiest times of the year (the other busy time is the month of October): Families with school-age children arrive in droves. Traffic slows to a crawl on Gatlinburg's main drag, room reservations are tough to get, and campgrounds are filled. Shops, restaurants, and tourist attractions are jammed to overflowing.

Our recommendation: If at all possible, schedule your trip to the Smokies before mid-June or after mid-August. And while the situation isn't nearly as bad in Virginia's Shenandoah National Park, it's still quite crowded in the middle of the summer and services are stretched to capacity. If you must visit the mountains during this crowded time of year, try to avoid weekends.

Our Secret Resource: The National Forests

But what if you can't schedule your vacation before or after the mid-summer crush? We offer this alternative: Consider a visit to one of the national forests that surround the national parks.

Most visitors to these mountains drive through the national forests and don't understand exactly what they are: huge expanses of federally owned land managed for multiple use, including recreation and timbering. Yet most people pass right through them on their way to better-known destinations such as Great Smoky and Shenandoah.

They're missing a lot. While it's true that some parts of the forests are regularly logged, there are huge sections that are managed for recreation. Other sections, called wilderness areas, are like mini–national parks where a back-country character is preserved by banning all uses except foot travel. Unlike national parks, however, national forests are a crazy quilt of public and private land. Like national parks, the forests are free. But they also are less restrictive: For the most part, back-country camping permits aren't required and you can car camp anywhere you find a place to set up your tent or park your trailer that's not posted "No Camping."

Here's a quick rundown on the national forests in the Southern Appalachians: In Tennessee, *Cherokee National Forest* (Zone 3) offers more than 600,000 acres of forest, rivers, streams, trails, and lakes for outdoor recreation—including world-class rafting on the Ocoee River.

In North Carolina, *Pisgah* (Zones 6 and 7) and *Nantahala* (Zones 4 and 5) national forests, while not as high in elevation as the nearby national park, feature spectacular waterfalls, world-class whitewater canoeing and rafting, mountain and road cycling, and other outdoor activities. Amenities? Lodging, restaurants, campgrounds, and wilderness regions are scattered throughout the Southern Highlands of North Carolina. Together, the two national forests total more than a million acres.

In Northern Georgia, *Chattahoochee National Forest* (Zone 5) stretches from east to west across the southern Blue Ridge Mountains with more than 430 miles of trails, 1,000 miles of trout streams, 400 campsites, and many roadside scenic overlooks inside its 749,463 acres. In South Carolina, a section of *Sumter National Forest* (Zone 5) provides access to the Chattooga National Wild and Scenic River, trout fishing, camping, hiking, and scenic drives.

In Virginia, those seeking an alternative to crowded (at least on weekends) Shenandoah National Park can head south to the less-visited Blue Ridge Parkway and *George Washington* (Zone 8) and *Jefferson* (Zone 8) national forests, where a total of more than 1.5 million acres of natural beauty awaits them. (Shenandoah, on the other hand, is just under 200,000 acres.) The scenery is just as good—and, unlike Skyline Drive, the Parkway is toll-free.

The moral: There's really no reason to fight large crowds, stand in long lines, and sit in endless traffic on a summer vacation to the southeastern mountains. Just look at a map: Great Smoky Mountains National Park is surrounded by national forests that offer scenic beauty that rivals—and sometimes surpasses—their better-known neighbor.

—— *Fall*

During the last two weeks of August, the crowds decline at major tourist destinations as children get ready to return to school. While late August and early September can be hot and humid, by mid-September a pattern of warm, sunny days and crisp, clear nights often begins. This is another time of the year that's high on the list of *Unofficial Guide* researchers.

But in October, the crowds return with a vengeance—led this time by retired folks from across the United States who trek to the mountains to enjoy the legendary fall foliage. October, say those employed in the tourist industry around Great Smoky and Shenandoah national parks, is every bit as jammed as July.

Our recommendation? Avoid popular tourist hot spots such as Gatlinburg, Pigeon Forge, Cherokee, and, in Virginia, Skyline Drive. Instead, head for the less-visited national forests mentioned above. The foliage is just as pretty—and the traffic is much lighter.

Fall Colors

One last note: Most people who come to the Smokies assume that the fall colors appear like clockwork on October 15. They're usually wrong. The leaves often burst out in shades of red, yellow, and gold a little later in the month (but before November 1). It's farther north along the Blue Ridge Parkway and Skyline Drive that the leaves start to turn in the middle of October.

In the Smokies, the foliage will begin changing in the high mountains in late August and move downward to the valleys through October. Yellow leaves include flowering beech, birch, black gum, buckeye, hickory, mountain ash, and yellow poplar trees.

Scarlet leaves indicate red maple trees, while red indicates dogwood, maple, pin cherry, sourwood, and sumac trees. Crimson leaves indicate blackberry and blueberry bushes. A mixture of colors indicates sugar maple (yellow, scarlet, orange), sweet gum (red, yellow, dark purple), red maple, northern red oak, pin cherry (orange, red), buckeye, and witch hobble (yellow, red) trees.

—— Winter

By early November, the leaves are off the trees, revealing vistas of ridges and valleys hidden all summer by the thick foliage. Yet daytime temperatures are usually moderate, and the crowds are gone. We think early November through mid-December is an excellent period to visit the Smoky and Blue Ridge mountains.

Be warned, however: A dusting of light snow, especially at higher elevations, is a possibility beginning in mid-November. And we recommend that hikers and backpackers stay out of the woods during deer hunting season, which traditionally begins around Thanksgiving.

While Great Smoky and Shenandoah national parks don't allow hunting inside their boundaries, poaching occasionally occurs—plus, the sound of incessant gunfire from outside the parks is often unnerving to people seeking peace and quiet in the woods. But during gun season, there are better destinations than the national forests, where hunting is allowed.

January and February are usually the coldest months of the year. But winter in these mountains can be fickle. Many days are sunny with highs in the 70s. (On the other hand, a lot of days are snowy with highs in the 20s.) In the low elevations, snowfalls of one inch or more occur, on the average, one to five times a year. Lows of −20° are possible at higher elevations.

In addition, many tourist attractions, hotels, and restaurants close over the winter or only open on weekends. However, this is the season that draws thousands of downhill skiers to the region's many ski resorts, which make their own snow.

When hefty snowfalls do occur, watch out: Roads are often closed for long periods. In fact, Skyline Drive and the Blue Ridge Parkway are often closed during rough winter weather. The philosophy in these southern mountains seems to be: Let it melt.

To give you an idea of the temperature swings at different altitudes in the mountains of the Southeast, here are the average monthly temperatures (in Fahrenheit) and precipitation (in inches) for Gatlinburg, Tennessee (elevation 1,462 feet), and Clingmans Dome (elevation 6,642 feet, 22 miles from Gatlinburg, and the highest point in Great Smoky Mountains National Park):

	Gatlinburg:			Clingmans Dome:		
	High	Low	Precipitation	High	Low	Precipitation
January	51°	28°	4.8"	35°	19°	7.0"
February	54°	29°	4.8"	35°	18°	8.2"
March	61°	34°	5.3"	39°	24°	8.2"
April	71°	42°	4.5"	49°	34°	6.5"
May	79°	50°	4.5"	57°	43°	6.0"
June	86°	58°	5.2"	63°	49°	6.9"
July	88°	59°	5.7"	65°	53°	8.3"
August	87°	60°	5.3"	64°	52°	6.8"
September	83°	55°	3.0"	60°	47°	5.1"
October	73°	43°	3.1"	53°	38°	5.4"
November	61°	33°	3.4"	42°	28°	6.4"
December	52°	28°	4.5"	37°	21°	7.3"

Outdoor Recreation and Activities: An Overview

People from all over the world come to the Smoky and Blue Ridge mountains—and for many different reasons. Some like to cruise in the family car along their scenic byways; others enjoy hiking on thousands of miles of trails that honeycomb the valleys and ridges (850 miles of trails in Great Smoky Mountains National Park alone); some come to fly-fish for trout in fast, tumbling mountain streams; while others prefer to launch a boat and angle for trophy bass on a forest-lined lake.

Many people just prefer to loaf.

To put it another way: There's much to do in the Southern Highlands. Whether you're a dedicated hiker looking for new trails to explore or a whitewater novice looking for advice on the ins and outs of rafting down a world-famous river, the *Unofficial Guide* provides accurate, concise advice for people who enjoy all kinds of outdoor recreation—from beginners to experts.

Part Four (beginning on page 199) contains specific and detailed information on the wide range of outdoor activities to be enjoyed, presented on a zone-by-zone basis (described later on in this chapter). But to give you an idea of what you'll find in the zone descriptions, we present here an overview of the most popular outdoor recreational activities in the Southeast's mountains.

We don't stop there. You'll also find the information to get started if you're tempted to try out a new activity; valuable tips if you've never, say, hiked in the lush, wet Southern Appalachians; and, for folks on a tight schedule, specific recommendations on the *best* things to do on a visit to the Smoky and Blue Ridge mountains.

—— Common Sense

A glance at a map reveals that the chunk of geography that encompasses the Smoky and Blue Ridge mountains is huge—and a lot of it, from a population standpoint, is empty. For most visitors, that's a major attraction to these mountains: A visit here is an opportunity to unwind and regain some personal space as you listen to the wind stirring the trees on a remote mountain ridge.

The temptation, of course, is to park the car at an inviting trail head and take off. And that's fine. But novices who have never explored the mountainous back country of the Southern Appalachians need to keep a few things in mind before embarking on a hike, backpacking trip, mountain bike ride, fishing trip, or any other nonguided outdoor excursion that takes them off the beaten track. It's just common sense. Yet thousands of people suffer the consequences of a ruined vacation—or even worse—by not following some simple rules.

Before You Leave

On day hikes or any other foray into the woods that takes you away from roads, private residences, and other outposts of civilization that can provide access to emergency help, check at park headquarters or a ranger station for the latest trail information before you leave.

Here's why: Occasionally, trails are closed or weather conditions create hazards that, had you known about them in advance, could have made the difference between a memorable back-country experience and a death march against a setting sun. Rangers and volunteers staffing the information desks also can make recommendations on hikes that match your abilities and give realistic estimates of how long it should take.

Always leave word with a responsible person about where you're going (say, the manager of the motel or campground where you're staying). Tell that person how long you expect to be gone, and what time you plan to return. In a worst case scenario—say, you get lost or injured in the woods—you'll at least know that you'll be the object of a search if you don't return; don't leave word, and you may have to face a long night in the woods—or worse. When you *do* return, let that person know you're back.

Never hike alone. Getting lost or injured on the trail is much more serious—even life-threatening—when you're by yourself; having another person along could save a life. More common sense: When out on the trail, keep your group together at all times.

Unless you're taking a stroll on a self-guided nature trail, always take a trail map on a hike. The lush woods of the Southern Appalachians often look the same, and even experienced hikers occasionally get disoriented. Not only that, trail signs have a way of disappearing or getting damaged by animals, making a map of the trail system invaluable.

It's beyond the scope of *The Unofficial Guide* or any guidebook to provide the timely, detailed information provided in hiking guides and topographic maps, which graphically depict trail locations and elevation contours. A good, up-to-date map can save you hours of time and effort in the back country.

In the Woods

One more thing: *Never leave the trail.* Most inexperienced hikers get lost by taking "shortcuts" through the forest. If you get hopelessly lost, searchers will scour the trails before setting off cross-country. During the busy summer months, rangers in Great Smoky and Shenandoah national parks perform searches almost weekly for inexperienced hikers who venture off the trail and get lost. Don't be one of them.

It Sounds Corny, But . . . Be Prepared

Never trust the weather, no matter how nice it is when you start your hike. In the mountains, clear skies and warm sun can suddenly give way to threatening clouds, cold winds, fog, and precipitation—rain, hail, sleet, or snow. In the summer, always bring along waterproof rain gear, and in other seasons carry extra warm clothing in case the weather turns colder half way through your hike.

On the Trail

On the trail, use extreme caution crossing streams. In fact, just walking near a stream on moss- and spray-covered rocks can be hazardous. Never attempt crossing a stream unless you are sure you can make it; use a stout stick for support and loosen your pack so it can be discarded quickly if you slip. And note that climbing on waterfalls has resulted in many fatalities. Don't do it.

Wildlife

Consider yourself lucky if you see a bear—but observe it from a distance. Don't throw food or leave food behind for a bear or any other wild animal. If a bear approaches, gather *all* your supplies and retreat (but don't run) along the trail. Report all bear incidents to a ranger. For more information on how to avoid unplanned confrontations with wildlife, keep on reading.

Food and Water

Finally, carry along plenty of food and water on a hike, fishing trip, horse or mountain bike ride, or any other activity that takes you away from civilization. You'll burn up a lot of calories on the trail, and not being able to replace them is both uncomfortable and unsafe. It's always better to carry a little extra than not have enough.

Hint: Stash a couple of extra high-energy food bars in a corner of your day pack or fanny pack—just to be on the safe side. If a hike takes longer than you planned or you're delayed for any reason, you'll be glad you brought the extra food.

Get drinking water from a safe source and carry all that you think you'll need (typically two quarts a day). Don't be tempted to drink water from a stream: All water in the back country is suspect and should be treated to avoid health hazards, no matter how pristine the water looks. Either boil water for at least one minute (using a backpacking stove), treat it with chemicals, or use a water filter (both are available at back-country outfitters).

—— More Things to Know About the Mountains

Dressing for the Outdoors

Weather conditions can change rapidly at higher elevations, so always be prepared by dressing in layers that you can adjust as you warm up and cool down, and by taking rain gear on any outdoor excursion. During the late fall, winter, and early spring, make sure you've got enough warm clothing—say, an extra sweater or a synthetic pile jacket—to throw on when the sun gets low in the sky or the temperature drops. Most people caught unprepared by the weather are wearing jeans or other cotton apparel and do not have appropriate rain gear. Wet cotton robs your body of heat. Wool and synthetic garments, in contrast, wick moisture away from your skin and keep you reasonably warm even when wet. When you pack rain gear, don't forget about your head, feet, and legs. Keeping your upper torso warm is only half the objective.

Listen to weather forecasts before leaving for a hike or a day outdoors. If thunderstorms are in the forecast, keep an eye on the sky and be prepared to get off ridge lines and mountaintops if a storm blows in. Also, avoid open areas during electrical storms; getting struck by lightning is no joke.

Hypothermia

Hypothermia, called the number one killer among all outdoor injuries, is the lowering of the body's core temperature beyond the point where you can maintain your own heat. While most people think of hypothermia as a danger only in frigid winter weather, they're wrong: You're most susceptible in wet weather around 40° F.

Symptoms of hypothermia are uncontrolled shivering, slurred speech and memory lapse, stumbling, fumbling hands, and drowsiness. The cure? Since the condition is caused by getting wet and cold, the solution is to get dry and warm—quickly. If it's raining, get under some shelter, change into dry clothes, and drink warm fluids (but not alcohol). Pay special attention to covering the head and the back of the neck, where the greatest amount of heat loss occurs.

If you or someone in your party starts to exhibit symptoms of hypothermia, get that person into a sleeping bag. Another alternative is exercise: After changing the patient into dry clothes, get him or her walking, with support if necessary, to generate some internal body heat.

Sometimes the body becomes so cold that it cannot rewarm itself. In this event, warmth must be applied externally. Car heaters, fires, hot water immersion, and even hugging can work until professional medical assistance is available.

To prevent hypothermia, stay dry, eat often (even if you don't feel hungry), and drink water so your body can digest the food.

Insects, Snakes, and Other Things That Bite

The list of bugs that bite or sting in the Southern Appalachians includes bees, wasps, hornets, and fire ants, not to mention spiders, chiggers, and ticks. The chances of encountering a wasp nest along a trail is much greater than meeting a poisonous snake or a bear.

Fortunately, for most people a bee sting is only temporarily painful. If you are allergic to bee or wasps stings, however, know what to do and have the appropriate medication at hand for use immediately.

Chiggers, mosquitoes, and other biting insects are at their worst during the summer months at twilight and after dark. The most effective repellents contain DEET, which also repels ticks, carriers of Lyme disease and Rocky Mountain spotted fever.

The safest way to avoid ticks on the trail is to apply repellents before the hike and to examine yourself carefully after a hike. Deer tick nymphs are tiny and, unfortunately, the most active carrier of the Lyme disease bug.

It's important to remove a tick within eight or ten hours after it attaches itself. Do not pull the tick off or apply heat because the head will stay in the skin. Instead cover the tick thoroughly with petroleum jelly, lip balm, or heavy oil to close its breathing pores. Most of the time the tick will drop off. If it has not dropped off after 30 minutes, use clean tweezers to turn the tick onto its back. Grasp firmly near the head and pull very slowly from the skin. Carefully examine the site to make certain that the head has been removed. Wash the site well with soap and water and apply a topical disinfectant, such as alcohol or hydrogen peroxide. Watch for signs of infection. If infection occurs, or if you suffer unexplained symptoms such as fever, rash, or severe headaches within ten days of the bite, seek professional medical care immediately. A prophylactic course of oral antibiotics once a year is often recommended by doctors for outdoors lovers who are exposed to ticks frequently.

Snakes. Most hikers fear snakes more than other hazards in the woods. In reality, the chances of being bitten by a poisonous snake are slim—in fact, consider yourself fortunate if you see a timber rattlesnake or a copperhead, the two poisonous snakes that inhabit these mountains. (Just don't get too close.) Both species, by the way, are extremely shy.

To avoid an unplanned encounter with a snake, be careful stepping over logs and don't put your hands and feet where you can't see. Rattlesnakes prefer warm, rocky outcroppings on sunny, southfacing slopes up to 5,000 feet. Copperheads also like warm rocks, as well as stone fences, log piles, and abandoned buildings. They're also sometimes found near water. Copperheads are rare above 2,500 feet. While rattlesnakes frequently buzz when approached, copperheads don't.

If you should be bitten by a poisonous snake, don't panic: Unless the victim is a small child or elderly, fatalities from a poisonous snakebite are extremely rare. Also consider this: many poisonous snakes, and most particularly copperheads, do not always inject venom when they bite.

Definitive identification of the snake aids proper treatment. If you are familiar with the poisonous snakes of the southeastern mountains and can make a positive identification, fine. If not, then you or a member of your group should kill the snake, *but only if you can do so without further risk.* Even when the snake is dead, avoid any contact with its head. Place the dead snake in a container using a long stick. If the container is cloth, keep it well away from your body. Make the dead snake available to the physician who examines the bite.

Try to remain calm and still after a snakebite because movement accelerates the distribution of the venom. If you are by yourself on the trail, however, and the chances of encountering others is remote, your best bet is to treat the bite as described below and make your way to help. If you are with others, you will have to make a determination (based on your location, the time of day, the location and apparent severity of the bite, and the capabilities of those with you) whether to walk or be carried to help, or to sit tight while you dispatch a member of your party to bring help back. The variables to be considered are many, and there are no easy answers.

Treating a Snakebite. Remaining as still as possible, remove all rings, watches, and bracelets. Wrap a light constricting band two inches above the bite. The operational adjective here is light: Do not apply a tourniquet and do not restrict blood flow. If you have a mechanical suction device, apply it at once to the bite. Do not attempt to make incisions or otherwise enlarge the bite wounds as this will only decrease the amount of venom that can be extracted with the device. Begin suction as soon as possible, preferably within five minutes of the bite, and continue until 30 minutes have lapsed from the time of the bite. Suction attempts beyond 30 minutes from the time of the bite are not effective.

If you do not have a suction device, refrain from "cut and suck" or other invasive treatments. Apply cold applications, such as ice packs, as soon as possible. Do not administer alcohol or pain medications. Treat for shock. During evacuation, avoid exerting any more energy than is absolutely necessary. When you reach a telephone, consult local law enforcement authorities, or national park or national forest rangers, to ascertain the closest medical facility experienced in treating poisonous snakebite.

Poison Ivy

A good dose of poison ivy can produce huge splotches of irritated, itching skin that can ruin a vacation. Unfortunately, this low, bushy plant is common along many trails and along the banks of rivers and streams; it's most obvious in the late spring and throughout the summer. Poison ivy is easy to identify because of its shiny luster and distinctive cluster of three leaves. But if you've never seen any, ask a ranger at a visitor center to point some out.

If you suspect you brushed up against some poison ivy, wash the affected skin as soon as possible with soap and water. Several commercial lotions are on the market that can reduce the itching and irritation, which often results from a brush with poison ivy (calamine lotion is the best known.) But the best protection is to recognize the plant, stay on trails and out of brushy areas, and avoid the plant.

Wild Animals

Seeing animals in the wild is one of the great rewards of visiting the Smoky and Blue Ridge mountains. The most frequently spotted animal is the white-tailed deer, which is most active at dawn and twilight along roadsides, and in picnic areas and campgrounds.

But don't attempt to liven up the action by offering deer or any other wild animals food. Giving human food to wild animals is not only bad for them, but dangerous to you. Raccoons, for example, often will bite or scratch well-meaning people to get at handouts—which means a trip to the doctor for a series of rabies shots. In case you glossed over it, a scratch is as serious as a bite.

Bears

The black bears of the Southern Appalachians are not the huge, fearsome brown or grizzly bears found in the Northern Rockies and Alaska: You don't have to worry about being attacked as you walk down a trail in Great Smoky or Shenandoah national parks or carry heavy weaponry (which is illegal anyway). Most sightings in the woods are only a glimpse as these large, powerful, and intelligent animals melt into the forest. If you're driving in a car and see a bear, pull over (if it's safe) and enjoy the view. Just make sure to roll up the windows if the bear should approach your car.

Don't Feed the Bears. Bears aren't animals that you want to mess with or encourage with food. They're powerful and dangerous if provoked. That's not all. Feeding bears makes them more comfortable around people, which in turn makes them susceptible to getting hit by cars and poaching.

Bears with a yen for human-style fare also can wreck a camp in their search for food and have been known to break into cars. In a few rare cases, black bears have attacked and killed people. Feeding bears is a bad idea for all parties.

Be sure to "bear proof" your food, toothpaste, and cosmetics if you're car camping or backpacking. Store food and anything else with an aroma in the trunk of your car; if you must leave food in the passenger compartment, cover it up so that a bear can't see it. Bears have been known to pry open car doors to get objects that they think is food—even if it's a can of tennis balls that looks like a container of Pringle's potato chips. Bears are smart, but they can't read.

Bear-Proofing a Back-Country Camp. If you're backpacking, tie your food *and* trash between two trees that are at least 10 to 20 feet apart and have branches 15 feet high. (A basic skill quickly mastered in bear-country backpacking is tossing a rock or small log tied to a length of rope over a high tree branch.) Whether you're car camping or backpacking, keep your tent, sleeping bag, and other gear clean and free of food odor.

If you encounter a bear—or any other animal that's intent on getting your food—keep a safe distance and try to use good judgment: It's better to give up a picnic lunch than lose a tangle with a wild animal. Don't advance toward an animal or try to retrieve food or belongings.

Avoid Confrontations. For campers and picnickers, the best way to avoid an unplanned confrontation with bears is not to provide an incentive for them to visit your camp. Don't make food or garbage available, clean up dishes immediately after a meal, and put leftover food into the trunk of the car as soon as possible. Finally, keep eating and sleeping areas separate.

If a bear comes into your camp, sometimes making noise will scare it off. If it doesn't, get into the car. (If you're backpacking, get up a tree; you can't outrun a bear.) By no means "argue" with a bear. You'll lose any dispute over what's sitting on the picnic table or inside a cooler.

In the woods on a hike or backpacking trip, keep food and snacks close to you at rest stops and snack breaks while keeping an eye peeled for animals. If a bear should approach, quickly gather *all* your equipment and food, then slowly retreat. Stay calm and don't run—you'll only excite the bear and you can't outrun these fleet animals.

On a rare occasion, a surprised, approached, or threatened bear may charge. Females with cubs can be very aggressive, so don't get between an adult and her cubs. If a slow retreat doesn't stop a charge, experts recommend climbing a tree to at least 15 feet off the ground. If a tree isn't available, drop to the ground and play dead; curl up into a ball to protect your stomach.

—— Outdoor Ethics

Conscientious walkers, hikers, campers, bicyclists, whitewater enthusiasts, and other folks who enjoy the outdoors only need to follow a few simple rules to make their visit to the forests of the Smoky and Blue Ridge mountains more enjoyable for themselves—and for other people out to enjoy the back country.

- "Leave No Trace": In other words, make it difficult for others to see or hear you in the woods. Limit your group size to no more than ten people. Also use earth-colored equipment and clothing that blend with the environment and lessen your visual impact. And carry out all trash.

- Repackage food from glass and aluminum to plastic containers, which are lighter and can be used to pack out waste and litter.

- If you're camping and must build a campfire, use an existing fire ring and only use small, dead, downed wood. Make sure your fire is dead before you leave.

- Bury solid human waste using the "cat-hole" method. Cat holes should be at least 200 feet from camp, trails, and water sources, dug six to eight inches deep, and completely filled in with soil after use.

- Never bury your trash. Pack it out.

- Don't take rocks, wildflowers, antlers, and artifacts from natural areas (which is often illegal in national parks). As the saying goes, "Take nothing but pictures and memories."

- Keep noise level to a minimum while hiking or camping in the forest. You'll see more wildlife, and other hikers you may encounter will appreciate the quiet.

- Stay on established trails and don't cut across switchbacks.

- Leave pets at home. If you do bring Fido, keep the dog on a leash at all times.

—— Camping

The statistics are impressive: There are upwards of 60 million campers in the United States, and about one in every four households is active in camping. On a hot July afternoon, it looks as if a sizable percentage of them are looking for a site at Cades Cove Campground in Great Smoky Mountains National Park (Zone 1). There are all kinds of campers, ranging from RV-ers to back-country explorers pitching a tent miles from the trail head. And the Smoky and Blue Ridge mountains can accommodate them all in the large number of national parks and forests, state parks, and private campgrounds.

Many members of *The Unofficial Guide* research team like to camp, too—and our preference is quiet, wooded campgrounds in public (national or state) parks that attract tent and car campers.

Which are the best? We didn't sample them all, but high on the list are **Elkmont Campground** in Great Smoky Mountains National Park (Zone 1), **Parksville Lake Campground** on Tennessee's Ocoee River (Zone 3), **Standing Indian Campground** in the Nantahala Wilderness (Zone 5), **Davidson River Campground** outside Brevard

(Zone 6), **Mount Mitchell Campground** (Zone 7), **Lake Sherando** in George Washington National Forest (Zone 8), and **Loft Mountain** in Shenandoah National Park (Zone 8). We've included information on these and many more campgrounds in each zone description that follows.

—— Walks

While the tallest peaks in Great Smoky Mountains National Park soar toward 7,000 feet, you don't have to be an Edmund Hillary to enjoy an uppermost view: For example, the top of Clingmans Dome, the highest point in the park, is a half-mile stroll on a paved path from the parking area. While the walk is steep, it's one of the most popular destinations in the Smokies.

At Great Smoky, casual walkers can explore quarter-mile-long paths along the roadsides called "Quiet Walkways," while all along Skyline Drive and the Blue Ridge Parkway gentle paths lead to scenic overlooks.

Other popular walks (not all of them in the woods) include the University of Virginia campus in Charlottesville (Zone 8); downtown Asheville, North Carolina (Zone 6); and the paths and roadways at the Carl Sandburg Home National Historic Site, three miles south of Hendersonville, North Carolina (Zone 6). To sum up: There's plenty of easy, scenic walking throughout the Smoky and Blue Ridge mountains.

The Best Walks

What are the quintessential easy walks in the Smoky and Blue Ridge mountains? Since a beautiful stroll is as much a factor of the time of day, weather, and the chance sighting of a trio of deer disappearing into the forest, that's a tough call. But we do have some favorites that should be on any visitors "not-to-be-missed" list that offer spectacular views and show off the mountains at their best. For more details—and for information on additional walks—see the appropriate zone.

In Shenandoah National Park, **Stony Man Nature Trail** (Zone 8) is a one-and-a-half-mile ramble to one of the best views in the park. South of Waynesboro, Virginia, off the Blue Ridge Parkway (Zone

8), **Crabtree Falls Trail** leads to five major cascades that tumble for a total of 1,200 feet.

Mount Mitchell in North Carolina (Zone 7) is a remarkably easy stroll to the highest point in the East, while the easy, two-mile hike to **Whiteside Mountain** outside Highlands (Zone 5) overlooks a cliff to a valley 2,000 feet below.

In addition to **Clingmans Dome** in Great Smoky Mountains National Park (Zone 1), don't miss **Laurel Falls Trail**, a paved walkway lined with wildflowers in the spring leading to a beautiful waterfall. **Wayah Bald** outside Franklin and **Big Tree Cove Trail** in Joyce Kilmer Memorial Forest (both in Zone 4) are two places well worth a special trip.

—— *Hiking*

All you need is a broken-in pair of boots, comfortable old clothes, and a day pack or fanny pack stuffed with lunch, granola bars, and a water bottle—and you're all set to enjoy some of the virtually endless day-hiking opportunities found in this mountainous region. Yet if you've never hiked before—or this is your first excursion to the Southern Appalachians or Blue Ridge Mountains—keep a few things in mind before hitting the trail.

Weather

Actually, there's more to it than old clothes and broken-in boots. Weather—and the possibility that it can change suddenly—is a primary consideration when hiking in the mountains. Ridges can be as much as 15° cooler than trail heads, so dress in layers that you can remove or replace as temperatures dictate.

Don't forget rain gear, even if the sky is clear when you start a hike: A waterproof rain jacket, poncho, or anorak not only will keep you dry, but it will keep you warm in windy conditions. If you get caught in a thunderstorm—they're common on summer afternoons—get off ridges and away from open areas immediately to avoid getting struck by lightning.

What to Wear

Comfortable clothing and broken-in footwear will do more to make a hike pleasurable than just about anything else. Dress in layers, starting with a light, inner layer next to the skin made of material that will wick perspiration away. Wool is the old standby, but newer synthetics such as polypropylene don't itch and do the job better. Silk is the ultimate inner layer.

The next layer should be a warm, porous layer that can be removed easily, such as a loose shirt or a roomy sweater; over that, wear an outside layer that's wind and waterproof. Many people wear cotton jeans or cut-offs when hiking, but best are hiking shorts or pants with a roomy fit and big pockets that aren't made of cotton. Cotton is *the* worst material for strenuous outdoor wear. Once it gets wet, it offers no warmth and takes forever to dry. Wool and nylon are a better bet.

Footwear is even more subjective. Sturdy, waterproof (at least in cool or cold weather), and supportive are the key words when it comes to hiking boots. And make sure they're well broken-in before heading out on a long hike. If you think your feet may get a dunking while crossing a stream, bring along an extra pair of socks.

Blisters

If you're susceptible to blisters or haven't done much hiking, take along some precut "moleskin" bandages. When you feel a hot spot develop on your foot, stop, air out your foot, and place a moleskin over the area before a blister forms. Moleskin is available by name at all drugstores. Pack the stuff in a small first-aid kit and place it in your day pack or fanny pack.

Maps and Choosing a Trail

Don't attempt hikes that are beyond your physical abilities or will keep you out after sunset. Take along a trail map (preferably a U. S. Geological Survey seven-and-a-half-minute topographic map that shows elevation). Leave an itinerary of your hike with someone before you leave, including where you'll be hiking, where you'll park the car, your estimated time of return, and who to contact if it becomes necessary. And don't hike alone.

Some hikers take along lightweight survival kits that include a compact space blanket (NASA technology that can be turned into an emergency sleeping bag), a whistle, waterproof matches or a butane lighter, a compass, a high-energy food bar, 10 or 20 feet of strong nylon rope, and a small flashlight. While a kit like this is essential on a multiday backpacking trip, we think it's optional for folks out for a day hike.

Water

Should you drink water from springs and streams? The answer is no, regardless of how clear and pristine they look—unless the water is first treated by boiling, filtered through a reliable filter/purifier (available at outdoor outfitters), or treated with chemical purifiers. The best bet for day hikers is to carry water from a reliable source. Figure on two quarts of water a day.

Water and Altitude. If you're from a lower elevation and come to the Smokies, you're likely to experience shortness of breath on higher—and steeper—trails. Take it easy for the first few days when hiking, and you'll slowly acclimatize. With its lower altitude, acclimatization usually isn't a problem in the Blue Ridge Mountains.

The exertion of hiking also will make you more susceptible to dehydration. Carry plenty of water—*and drink it.* You may not always feel thirsty, but thirst doesn't always accompany the body's need for water. So don't wait until you're dehydrated before drinking some water. Plan on at least two quarts of water per person per day when hiking.

Crossing Streams and Waterfalls. Heavy rains can swell streams in the back country unexpectedly, making them difficult to ford (although it's rarely a problem on paths close to paved roads that have foot bridges). Never attempt to cross a stream unless you are positive you can safely reach the other side. A stout walking stick can aid your crossing by giving extra support; loosen your pack so you can easily slip out of it if you fall. If you should slip and begin an unscheduled whitewater journey (sans boat), float with your feet pointed downstream to protect your head. Change into dry clothes as soon as possible to prevent hypothermia.

Mossy, spray-drenched rocks often make crossing a stream a slippery and difficult maneuver. Be careful to avoid a fall or twisted ankle. And climbing on waterfalls? Don't—it's just plain dumb. Fatalities are common.

Getting Lost

Virtually all trails in these mountains are marked with paint marks on trees called "blazes" or metal trail markers nailed to trees, as well as trail signs. In addition, sudden changes in direction of a trail are marked with two blazes or markers, one above another on the same tree.

Keep in mind, however, that rangers are called out almost every week during the summer to search for lost hikers who were looking for a "shortcut." Never stray from designated trails, don't hike alone, and keep your group together.

If You Lose the Trail. What should you do if you've lost the trail or if you're not sure what direction you need to go to finish your hike? The first rule is to stay calm. If you're on a trail, *don't leave it.* Searchers will cover trails first before setting off through the woods to find a lost hiker.

Remember that no one is completely lost until hysteria sets in. Although the most common reaction is to *do* something by rushing off in one direction or another, the best thing to do is to stop and think things over. Talk to your companions (never hike alone, remember?) and get out maps and a compass (if you brought one). The best approach to the problem is to apply what knowledge you have to the issue at hand: finding your way.

Other things *not* to do: Don't forge ahead down a trail you're not sure of (or through the woods if the trail suddenly gives out). And don't separate the group: Keep everyone within sight and earshot. Often, the best course of action is to retrace your steps to a place that you can identify on a map.

And what if you're really lost with no practical hope of finding a way back to the trail head? Stay in one place and concentrate your energy on staying as warm and as comfortable as possible until a search party comes (that's why you left word with someone about when you planned to return). Find a protected spot and wait for morning; the experts say hiking at night is too dangerous.

Take solace from the fact that if the situation merits drastic measures, national parks such as Great Smoky and Shenandoah have almost limitless resources and manpower to draw on for rescue operations: trackers, dog teams, and sometimes helicopters.

How* Not *to Get Lost. Experts advise that hikers embarking on a long day hike take along food and extra clothes to get them through a night—just in case they get lost. And use common sense. Most lost hikers either strayed from the trail or incorrectly judged the time needed to complete a hike.

Be conservative when estimating how long you think it will take to complete a hike: Terrain and steepness of most trails results in most hikes taking a little longer than you may have planned. Again: *Stay on the trail.*

Hikers in Shenandoah National Park who get lost are helped by its long and skinny configuration, if they remember one thing: If you head down the side of a mountain in any direction, you're bound to come out on a state road, where you can flag down help.

Serious Injuries

If someone in your group gets seriously injured while on the trail—say, a broken bone or a sprain—make the patient as comfortable as possible and go for help. Get to a main road and flag down a motorist, or find a phone and dial 911.

Again, don't give in to panic. If you must leave someone alone, make the patient warm and comfortable, and go for help: Wild animals aren't going to attack injured hikers waiting on the side of the trail. But it's preferable to leave someone with the injured hiker.

If the group is large enough, send two people for help, just in case one of them gets injured on the hike out. Keep in mind, however, that with long distances in the back country, an injured hiker can expect at least a two-hour wait for help to arrive.

Most accidents in the woods are a sprain or fracture in an arm or a leg—not a dangerous injury under normal circumstances. They usually can be handled without great danger to anyone's life—providing the situation is dealt with in a calm and sensible manner.

As an aside, evacuation on a nonambulatory person, even with the proper equipment, is arduous beyond belief and should be left to experts if at all possible.

Great Day Hikes

Here's a hit parade of some of the best day hikes in t
and Blue Ridge mountains. For more details—and for information
on other great hikes—see the listing in the appropriate zone. Check
the trail conditions with a ranger before leaving on a hike, and take
along an up-to-date map. Keep in mind that it's beyond the scope of
this or any other guidebook to provide the timely, accurate information you'll need to navigate the back country.

In Zone 1 (Great Smoky Mountains National Park), the most popular trail in the park is the 68-mile segment of the **Appalachian Trail**
that crosses the park from north to south along the North Carolina–
Tennessee border. One of the most popular—and scenic—stretches
is **Newfound Gap to Charles Bunion**, an eight-mile round-trip hike.

In the Southwest Foothills of Tennessee (Zone 3), the **Bald River
Trail** is a delightful hike along a mountain river loaded with scenic
spots perfect for camping, trout fishing, and enjoying the mountain
scenery. The Nantahala Wilderness (Zone 5) features a hike along the
Appalachian Trail from Deep Gap to a bald called the **Standing Indian**; or go the other way on the Appalachian Trail and explore Whiteoak Stamp, a unique highland bog. They're both high-altitude, relatively easy hikes.

South Carolina (Zone 5) features **Raven Cliff Falls Trail,** a strenuous hike to an observation deck with views of five major waterfalls.
In Pisgah National Forest, an eight-mile hike off the Blue Ridge Parkway leads to **Shining Rock** (Zone 6), a quartz-topped mountain that
the Cherokees said talked. You can camp at the summit.

Linville Falls and Linville Gorge (Zone 7) provide views of—
and hikes into—the deepest gorge this side of the Grand Canyon.
Roan Mountain Gardens (Zone 7) in Pisgah National Forest features trails passing through the world's largest natural gardens of
crimson-purple rhododendron; the peak blooming period is the middle of June.

In Virginia (Zone 8), **Rip Rap Hollow, Whiteoak Canyon,** and
Old Rag Mountain are three spectacular hiking areas in the Blue
Ridge Mountains that feature great mountain scenery, glimpses of old
mountaineer cabins, and 100-year-old cemeteries.

More Information

While there's a wealth of information on hiking in the Southern Appalachians, here are few publications we found particularly helpful: *The Best of the Great Smoky Mountains National Park* by Russ Manning and Sondra Jamieson (Mountain Laurel Place), *Guide to the Appalachian Trail and Side Trails in Shenandoah National Park,* and *Circuit Hikes in Shenandoah National Park* (both published by the Potomac Appalachian Trial Club, Washington, D.C.). Good maps include *Hiking Map & Guide/Great Smoky Mountains National Park* (Earthwalk Press) and the Potomac Appalachian Trail Club's northern, central, and southern section maps of Shenandoah National Park. For information on maps to the many national forests in the Southern Appalachians, see the listing of park offices that begins on page 103. You also can purchase maps at park headquarters and ranger offices, as well as hiking and fishing outfitters in towns throughout the Southern Appalachians.

Hiking With Children

Most children naturally love the outdoors, but they need their parent's help to fully enjoy a back-country outing. Parents planning on doing any extensive hiking with their children—especially babies—need to be fairly experienced outdoors persons themselves: You need to be alert, aware of potential problems, and make sure your children's needs are met.

Is it worth it? Most parents who take their children hiking say yes. It's an opportunity to instill an early and well-rooted love of the outdoors in your kids.

Clothing

Babies may be the easiest to take care of on the trail. They must be kept warm and dry, fed, and well rested. Just keep their needs in check and they'll stay healthy. Clothing: Synthetics and wool make the best outdoor clothing for infants, except during the hottest summer days. Layers of one-piece polyester sleepers work well, although special outdoor pile clothing made for babies may work better—but cost a lot more. No matter what, remember to keep their heads covered.

Dress older children in synthetic pile and polypropylene for warmth. Put several layers on your children and constantly question them on their comfort. Remember that kids who are carried or are walking and not carrying any weight will expend less energy than you—and will get colder more quickly.

Eating

Kids burn up a lot of energy on the trail, and most parents are amazed at how much they'll eat on a hike. Let them snack the whole trip; favorite foods include cheese and bread, granola bars, nuts, energy bars, and trail mix. Just make sure the snacks are nutritious and don't worry about spoiling dinner. It's much more important that youngsters maintain their energy level and stay warm.

Safety

Older children need to be watched more than babies. Use extreme caution around cliffs and waterfalls; always hold your children's hands around rock outcroppings. Carry a hiking stick; two adults can hold it horizontally, creating a hand rail that a child can hang on to over rough terrain with difficult footing. When your kids play with sticks or other sharp objects, make sure they don't poke themselves—they're a long way from a doctor. It also helps to dress youngsters in bright colors, just in case they start to wander out of sight.

Give each child a whistle, hang it around their necks on a cord, and teach them when to use it. Memorize the signs of hypothermia (see page 58) and watch for them in cold weather. And don't forget to carry an extensive first-aid kit.

Setting the Pace

Out on the trail, young children should be out in front, setting the pace. But don't let them rush ahead and get separated from you. Once they show signs of tiring, don't force them to go on; it's better to stop, eat, and take a rest break. Otherwise, they won't have fun and may never want to go on another hike.

Try choosing hiking areas that will hold your children's attention. After all, most kids live for the moment, not some goal that's a few miles down the trail. So take them on hikes that feature stream banks, ridges with views, and lots of wildflowers. The variety will keep them entertained.

How many miles should you plan on a hike with your kids? Several factors go into choosing the length of a hike, including elevation gain and loss, weather conditions, and your kids' strength and interest in hiking. A good rule of thumb is a mile for each year of age.

—— Backpacking

It's the ultimate way to beat the crowds—even in July and October. When Gatlinburg is choked by car fumes, and traffic is slowed to a crawl on Skyline Drive, strap on a backpack and disappear into the woods for a few days.

First things first: Back-country camping away from a car or vehicle requires a free permit in Great Smoky Mountains and Shenandoah national parks. Permits are available at visitor centers, park headquarters, ranger stations, and at all four entrance stations to Shenandoah. Both national parks feature back-country shelters, which also require a permit.

Note: In the national parks, camping without a permit, or camping away from designated back-country campsites (Great Smokies only), results in a fine if you're caught. A hassle-free alternative is to explore the thousands of miles of trails lacing the national forests.

The Best Backpacking Trips

The ultimate destination is a multiday hike along the Appalachian Trail, the famous footpath that stretches from Maine to Georgia. Excellent jumping-off points include **Newfound Gap** in Great Smoky Mountains National Park (Zone 1), **Deep Gap** in the Nantahala Wilderness (Zone 5), and **Roan Mountain** along the Tennessee–North Carolina border (Zone 7). In Virginia, the Appalachian Trail follows the crest of the Blue Ridge from Roanoke to Front Royal.

Another shouldn't-be-missed experience is an overnighter at **LeConte Lodge**, located on top of Mount LeConte in Great Smoky (Zone 1). While you can't drive to it—it's a four-hour hike, minimum—you can pack light: Just bring a toothbrush and a change of clothes. While there's no electricity, phones, or TV in the rustic cabins, lunch and breakfast are included in the price of a night's lodging.

Shining Rock Wilderness (Zone 6) in Pisgah National Forest features an overnighter at a quartz-topped mountain, while **Linville Gorge** and the **Wilson Creek Recreation Area** in Pisgah National Forest above Asheville (Zone 7) feature miles of trails in a rugged wilderness setting with a national reputation.

In Virginia (Zone 8), a maze of trails in the central section of **Shenandoah National Park** near Whiteoak Canyon and Big Meadows lets backpackers disappear for days in a wildly scenic area filled with waterfalls, great views, and the decaying remains of mountain communities that thrived in the days before the mountains became a park.

Check each zone description for additional information on these and other backpacking trips in the Smoky and Blue Ridge mountains. Don't forget to check with a ranger on trail conditions before you leave and to take up-to-date maps.

Rafting, Canoeing, and Kayaking

Some of the most exciting, challenging, and hauntingly beautiful streams in the United States are situated in or near the Smoky and Blue Ridge mountains. Paddling options run the entire spectrum from tranquil, scenic floats to heart-pounding whitewater adventure. According to your ability, you can paddle a canoe (open or decked), a kayak, a "ducky" (one person inflatable craft), or a raft. You can go it on your own, or choose from a veritable menu of support options ranging from personal instruction to guided commercial trips to assistance as perfunctory as hauling your boat to the river.

Respect the River

It is important to remember that a trip on a flowing river is always full of surprises. On Disney's Jungle Cruise, a robotic crocodile yawns on cue every 30 seconds, and everything from the beginning to the end of the trip is carefully programmed. Not so on a real river where rocks, current, and weather frequently combine to wreak havoc on the unprepared. Even on professionally guided trips, the unexpected sometimes happens. There is a reason that river guides are trained in advanced rescue techniques, first aid, and CPR. The river is not an amusement park: You can get hurt.

The best way to make sure that you have a pleasant experience is to choose a stream consistent with your fitness level, paddling experience, skill level, and if you have your own boat, the suitability of your equipment. There is some serious whitewater in the mountains. If you do not have experience and training in whitewater river running, either go on a guided trip or stick to scenic float streams.

For Readers with Their Own Canoe, Kayak, or Raft

If you have your own boat and know how to use it, there are literally dozens of rivers in the Smoky and Blue Ridge mountains to choose from. Difficulty runs the gamut from scenic flatwater floats to steep creeks with near lethal rapids. Describing the paddling opportunities for those with their own boat is beyond the scope of this guide. What we can do, however, is to recommend the best river guidebooks for paddling in the Smokies and Blue Ridge.

The following books are published by Menasha Ridge Press (except as noted) and can be purchased at most bookstores, camping specialty stores, or by calling (800) 247-9437.

Whitewater Home Companion, Volume I, by William Nealy, covers some of the more popular southeastern whitewater rivers with text and detailed drawings of major rapids on each stream. Includes the Chattooga, French Broad, Hiwassee, Nantahala, and Nolichucky rivers, among others. $12.95

Whitewater Home Companion, Volume II, by William Nealy, covers the Maury and Shenandoah rivers, and the Wilson Creek Gorge, among others. $9.95

Carolina Whitewater, by Bob and David Benner, is a comprehensive paddling guide to the streams of the North Carolina and South Carolina mountains and piedmont. $14.95

Northern Georgia Canoeing, by Bob Sehlinger and Don Otey, is a comprehensive paddling guide to the rivers of northern Georgia. $13.95

Classic Virginia Rivers, by Ed Grove, is a comprehensive paddling guide to the rivers of Virginia. Published by Howling Wolf Publications. $14.95

Appalachian Whitewater, Volume I: The Southern Mountains, by Bob Lantz, Bob Benner, Bob Sehlinger, William Nealy,

Don Otey, and Nicole Jones, describes the most popular whitewater runs in North Carolina, South Carolina, Tennessee, Kentucky, Georgia, and Alabama. $14.95

Appalachian Whitewater, Volume II: The Central Mountains, by Ed Grove, Bill Kirby, Charles Walbridge, Ward Eister, Paul Davidson, and Dirk Davidson, describes the most popular whitewater runs in Virginia, West Virginia, Delaware, Maryland, and Pennsylvania. $14.95

Whitewater Rafting in North America, by Lloyd Armstead, describes 200 rafting adventures in the United States, Canada, Mexico, and Costa Rica. Published by the Globe Pequot Press. $16.95

River Difficulty Ratings

When you read the river outfitter's promotional brochures, you will notice that rivers are rated on a difficulty scale of Class I to Class VI. This scale was developed many years ago to provide a more or less objective standard for rating the navigational difficulty of individual rapids.

Class I generally is understood to be moving water with perhaps a few small riffles or waves. There are few obstructions, all of which are obvious and easily missed with little training. Risk to swimmers is slight, and self-rescue is easy.

Class II describes a straightforward rapid with wide clear channels. Some maneuvering may be required, but rocks and medium sized waves are easily missed. Swimmers are seldom injured, and assistance from third parties, while helpful, is seldom needed.

Class III is defined as rapids with moderate, irregular waves, which may be difficult to avoid. Complex maneuvers in fast current and good boat control in tight passages or around ledges are often required. Large waves or strainers may be present but are easily avoided. Injuries while swimming are rare; self-rescue is usually easy but group assistance may be required.

Class IV rapids are intense and powerful, requiring precise boat handling in turbulent water. Risk of injury to swimmers is moderate to high, and water conditions may make self-rescue difficult. Group assistance for rescue is often essential and requires practiced skills.

Class V describes extremely long, obstructed, or very violent rapids, which expose a paddler to above average endangerment. Rapids may continue for long distances and require a high level of fitness. Swims are dangerous, and rescue is difficult, even for experts.

Class VI commonly is used to describe rapids and falls so violent and dangerous as to be considered unrunnable.

Although the scale relates to individual rapids, it also is used to characterize entire streams, or sections of streams. Thus, a river consisting of long stretches of pools or moving water (Class I) punctuated periodically by easy, straightforward rapids (Class II) is classified overall as Class I–II.

Sometimes, when the rapids on a river are consistent in difficulty, a single classification will serve to describe the entire run. More often, however, one or two more difficult rapids will require a sort of footnote to the overall classification. The Nantahala River in North Carolina (Zone 4), for example, is essentially a Class II stream. At the end of the run, however, there is one Class III rapid, Nantahala Falls. Thus, the Nantahala is commonly classified as Class II (III). This means that the run is primarily Class II, but that there is at least one Class III rapid which constitutes an exception. Section III of the Chattooga (Zone 5) is rated Class III (V). Most of the rapids are Class III (or below), but you can expect one Class V rapid (Bull Sluice). The Ocoee River in Tennessee (Zone 3) is rated Class III–IV, meaning that there are several rapids of each difficulty classification.

In the Smokies and Blue Ridge, outfitters rent canoes and rafts for self-guided trips on Class I and II rivers. Examples include the Shenandoah in Virginia, the Hiwassee in Tennessee, and the New River in North Carolina. On rivers a bit more difficult, both guided trips and unguided rentals are offered. The Tuckasegee and the Nantahala rivers in North Carolina are good examples. When rivers are rated Class III, the trips are always guided, though there may not be a guide in every raft. On Class IV and V rivers, as well as for Class IV and V rapids on easier rivers, a guide is assigned to every raft.

Danger Versus Difficulty

Sometimes rating a rapid or a river does not tell the whole story. Some rapids are quite powerful, even violent, but will spit you out unharmed if you end up in the water. Class III Nantahala Falls on the Nantahala River and Class IV Table Saw on the Ocoee River are good examples. Kayakers and canoeists characterize these rapids as tough but "forgiving."

In simplest terms, the difference between a forgiving rapid and an unforgiving rapid, or a forgiving river and an unforgiving river, is the possibility of entrapment—or, to put it bluntly, washing under a rock and not coming out; or getting caught in strong, recycling current known as a hydraulic or "hole"; or being snared in the branches of a tree that has fallen into the river. There are many dangerous spots on some streams, fewer on others.

Section IV of the Chattooga (GA/SC) and the Watauga Gorge (NC/TN) are the least forgiving of the southeastern commercially run rivers. Next are Wilson Creek (NC) and the upper Nolichucky (NC/TN). Though fairly forgiving on the whole, Section III of the Chattooga (GA/SC), the Ocoee (TN), the Pigeon (NC), and the French Broad (NC) each have a rapid or two that can get you in serious trouble.

Commercially rafted rivers that tend to be most forgiving include the Nantahala (NC), lower Watauga (TN), lower Nolichucky (TN), Tuckasegee (NC), and Hiwassee (TN). Don't get us wrong, you *can* get hurt on these rivers, but injury or death is significantly less likely than on rivers where a mistake puts you in real peril.

Streamflow

Some free-flowing rivers, such as the French Broad (near Asheville) and the Shenandoah in Virginia, drain large geographic areas and often can be paddled all year. Smaller streams, however, are runnable only for a few months or sometimes just for a few weeks, usually in the spring. Streamflow for still other Smoky and Blue Ridge mountain streams is dam controlled. This means that the natural flow of the stream is interrupted by a dam and an impoundment (lake). Water is released from the impoundment into the natural riverbed below the dam, usually for the purpose of generating hydroelectric power. For paddlers, this means that several streams (Ocoee, Hiwassee, Nantahala, Pigeon) can be turned on and off like the faucet on a bathtub, and can be run whenever water is being released downstream.

The practical effects of streamflow variables are these. The best water conditions on free-flowing streams usually occur in the spring and early summer. As the summer progresses, water levels drop and many streams become too low to paddle. Others, like the Chattooga, continue to be runnable, but only marginally. As the free-flowing streams dry up, paddlers converge on the dam-controlled streams and make for crowded conditions, especially in July and August. If you are interested in the free-flowing streams, try to run during April, May, or early June. If you want to do some river running in July or August, you will be relegated to the dam-controlled streams and a couple of the larger rivers that run all year. In the mid- to late summer, to avoid wall-to-wall rafts and canoes, try to do your river running on weekdays.

Temperature and Dress

The Smokies and the Blue Ridge receive a fair amount of rain. This coupled with waves, rocks, and rapids suggests a high probability of getting wet. In the early spring (March/April) renting a wetsuit or a drysuit from a friendly river outfitter is not a bad idea. At the least wear a waterproof paddling jacket, and if possible, paddling pants. Avoid cotton clothing, including socks. Cotton holds the wet and cold next to your body. Wool and polypro, on the other hand, wick moisture away from your body and provide some warmth and insulation even when wet. Shoes are a must on the river. Wear a pair that you don't mind getting wet.

May and early June can be cool in the mountains. Start off the day in quick-drying nylon shorts and a polypro T-shirt. Carry a paddling jacket to put on if you get cold. After mid-June, shorts and a T-shirt are fine. Remember that you usually do not work as hard paddling in a raft on a commercial trip as you would paddling your own canoe or kayak. On a raft trip, in other words, don't assume that your activity level will keep you warm. Keeping cool on a river trip is easy: Just take a dip whenever you get hot. On many streams there is little protection from the sun. If you are not used to being in the summer sun, apply a waterproof sunscreen and/or bring something along to cover up with. Hats with bills and sunglasses, secured with a cord or strap, also are recommended. Regardless of the temperature, leave your rings, necklaces, bracelets, and other items of jewelry at home. Watches should be water-resistant.

If you run a dam-controlled river such as the Nantahala or the Hiwassee, be aware that the water is being drawn from the bottom of a mountain lake and will be cold as hell, about 45° Fahrenheit to be specific. You can freeze your tailfeathers even in July in water this cold.

As an aside, most paddling fatalities are a result of hypothermia, also called "exposure," rather than (or in addition to) drowning. Hypothermia occurs when the body temperature falls below the point where the body can warm itself. It is both progressive and deadly, and can happen even in the summer, depending on the person, and the air and water temperatures. Erratic movement, poor coordination, slurred speech, and uncontrollable shivering are early signs of hypothermia. To prevent hypothermia, dress properly for the weather and the water temperature, and assume that you probably will get wet. If someone in your party shows signs of hypothermia, get them off the water and out of the wind. Remove wet clothing, bundle them up in something dry, and apply some external source of heat. Car heaters, hot summer sun, and hugging all work. Give warm liquids to drink, but no alcoholic beverages.

The Rivers

While canoe rentals are available on the Maury, the upper James, and the Shenandoah Rivers in the Virginia Blue Ridge (Zone 8), there are no guided raft trips. These rivers are free flowing and can be run most of the year, but are probably best in the late spring through the end of June. Though there is some mild whitewater on the sections served by canoe liveries, the trips can best be characterized as scenic Class I–II floats. The outfitter rents you equipment, transports you to the put-in (launching site), and then picks you up at the take-out when you have completed your run.

Moving southwest into the North Carolina and Tennessee Blue Ridge (Zone 7), there is the Nolichucky River, which flows out of North Carolina through a secluded mountain gorge into Tennessee. The upper section of the Nolichucky is a long Class III–IV+ run with some serious whitewater. The Class I–II (III) lower section is less demanding and is suitable for families. Commercial trips also are run on the Watauga River. The boulder clogged Class III–V Watauga Gorge is exceptionally challenging and should not be attempted unless you have had previous experience on difficult rivers. Class I–II sections of the Watauga below Wilbur Dam are OK for families and first-timers. To the south, near Lenoir, North Carolina, commercial trips are run in the spring on Wilson Creek, rated Class III–IV. Finally, both guided and unguided canoe trips are available on the tranquil New River (Class I–II) near Jefferson, North Carolina.

In the Asheville area (Zone 6), both the French Broad and the Pigeon are rafted commercially. The French Broad is a wide Class II–III (IV) river with rapids separated by relatively long sections of calm water. The Pigeon is a Class III–IV roller coaster ride of continuous waves and rapids that runs alongside I-40 west of Asheville. Both rivers are suitable for novice rafters age 12 and up. The Pigeon is often confused with a Tennessee river of the same name that flows through Gatlinburg and Pigeon Forge. The Tennessee Pigeon River supports some tubing and limited canoeing but is not rafted commercially.

To the south in Zone 5 where Georgia, North Carolina, and South Carolina come together is the Chattooga, the most pristine and beautiful of all commercially rafted streams in the mountains. Section III is a great Class II–III (V) trip for first-timers, while Section IV serves up some of the most challenging Class III–V whitewater run commercially. The Chattooga, along with the upper Nolichucky, and the Watauga Gorge offer the only true wilderness experiences of those southeastern rivers commercially rafted. Most of the other rivers, while even spectacularly scenic, run alongside major highways.

In western North Carolina near the Tennessee border (Zone 4) is the Nantahala River, a stream of exceptional beauty that offers mild yet continuous Class II (III) whitewater action. Professionally guided and self-guided trips are available. The Nantahala is hugely popular, drawing large crowds on weekends.

Across the state line in Tennessee (Zone 3) are the Ocoee and the Hiwassee. The Ocoee is a continuous Class III–IV rock and roll ride with big rapids. Along with the Nantahala in North Carolina, the Ocoee is the most heavily trafficked river in the mountain area. The Hiwassee offers whitewater so easy that it is appropriate for tubers as well as rafts. Quite beautiful, the upper Hiwassee is a favorite Class II practice river for folks learning to paddle canoes and kayaks. The lower Hiwassee offers Class I (II) swift current but few rapids. Only self-guided raft trips are available on the Hiwassee.

There are no commercially run rivers in the Great Smoky Mountains National Park (Zone 1). In Zone 2, north of the park, the Little River provides serious Class III–IV (V) whitewater for experienced canoeists and kayakers, but it is not run commercially. The Class I–II Pigeon River of Tennessee runs through Pigeon Forge and Gatlinburg, and is sometimes confused with the commercially rafted Pigeon River in North Carolina.

Commercial River Trips

The commercial river outfitting industry in the southeastern United States is more than 20 years old. You can count on the outfitters listed in this guide for professionally run trips and a strict adherence to safety standards. Always remember, however, that river running involves risks, and that some rivers are more dangerous than others. The possibility of you being injured or killed on a commercial river trip is extremely small, but it can happen.

When we discuss commercial river running, we usually are talking about guided raft trips, although trips in canoes, kayaks, and one-man inflatables also are offered by some outfitters. The outfitter provides all equipment, including rafts, life jackets, paddles, helmets (when appropriate), transportation to and from the river, and sometimes meals. Both day trips and overnighters are offered. On overnight trips the outfitter also provides camping equipment and all meals.

On easier rivers, as few as two guides may be assigned to a trip. Thus, on the Nantahala, the French Broad, and Section III of the Chattooga, you may end up in a raft without a guide. Most able bodied folks do just fine on their own after a little preliminary instruction. Being captain of your own raft is a great adventure, and for many, more fun than being chauffeured by a guide. Besides, even if there is not a guide in *your* raft, you can count on a guide being close at hand should you need help. If running the river in an unguided raft terrifies you, however, simply specify when you make your reservations that you want to be in one of the guided rafts.

On more difficult rivers like Section IV of the Chattooga and the Ocoee, you can count on having a guide in every raft. For other rivers, whether you have a guide in every raft depends on the water level. Sometimes extra guides are assigned to trips when the water level is very low and navigation is difficult, or when the water is running high and the river is pushy.

What to Expect. Your trip will run come rain or shine, unless the water level is too high or too low. You usually are requested to arrive at the outfitter's headquarters about an hour before the departure time for your trip. During this hour you will be checked in; asked to sign a liability waiver; issued a paddle, a life jacket, and sometimes a helmet; and be given a preliminary safety orientation. Most outfitters will ask if you have an existing medical condition that might affect your well-being on the river. In particular, they are interested in bad backs, heart conditions, diabetes, and hypersensitivity to insect bites and stings. Most outfitters offer changing rooms and toilets, but you must bring your own soap, shampoo, and towel. With the exception of the Ocoee and the Nantahala, you will not see another rest room until you return from the trip.

After all the administrative details are completed, you will board a bus (usually a school bus) or a van to be transported to the river. Once you arrive at the river, the equipment is unloaded, and the customers assist the guides in carrying everything to the put-in. Guides assign customers to rafts and usually follow up with a safety presentation. If your group exceeds the number of customers that can fit in one raft, try to figure out how you want to split up before you reach this point. If you are on a trip that allows children, divide up the children and adults as evenly as possible. Avoid having more than two elementary school age children in a single raft: One or two adults with a raft full of kids invariably find themselves doing all the work.

The most common scenario on southeastern rivers is for one guide to share a raft with three to eight customers. The raft is almost always propelled by canoe paddles, with both the customers and the guide pitching in. On some rivers such as the Nantahala, the Ocoee, the Chattooga, and the Pigeon, the current is so swift that nobody has to paddle strenuously to get the raft down the river. On these streams, most of the paddling activity revolves around helping the guide navigate the raft through the rapids. On the French Broad, lower Nolichucky and the Hiwassee, by contrast, there are some long flat stretches between the rapids and everybody must dig in to move the raft along.

Each expedition will have a head guide or designated trip leader. He or she will specify who runs lead (goes first), who sweeps (goes last), and the running order of the rafts in-between. Most river trips begin in a calm pool or easy current where customers can practice their strokes and get their teamwork down. On other rivers, however, like the Ocoee, you are plunged into the rapids at the very outset.

All trips on the Chattooga and upper Nolichucky, and most trips on the French Broad, include lunch. No food is served during the trip on other rivers. Most trips arrange some sort of diversion in the middle of the trip. Sometimes it's jumping off a big rock into the water or taking a short hike to see a waterfall on a tributary stream. On other trips it's lunch, a swim, a streamside discussion of plant life, or just an opportunity to stretch your legs.

When the trip is over, you help the guides carry the equipment to the vehicles and stow it away. Then it's everybody on the bus and back to the outfitter's headquarters. On your return, most outfitters offer some minimum refreshments, as well as showers and changing rooms. Many outfitters have a staff photographer who will shoot snapshots or videotape your trip. After the trip, you can purchase copies.

Water Levels

If you are running a dam-controlled river, the water level will be the same most days and the outfitter will be able to estimate accurately how long the trip will take. On free-flowing streams, the amount of water in the river largely determines how long the trip will take. If the river is running high, you will zip along and the trip will be shorter. If the water level is low, on the other hand, you may have to plug along, scraping over rocks, and taking longer to complete the run. Given a choice, never schedule a trip on a river that is running low. The Nantahala, Tuckasegee, Ocoee, Hiwassee, and Pigeon are dam controlled. As long as water is being released downstream, you normally will have an acceptable water level. For the other streams, try not to schedule a trip when the river is running below these levels:

Chattooga Section III	1.4 feet at US 76 bridge gauge
Chattooga Section IV	1.2 feet at US 76 bridge gauge
French Broad	1800 CFS on TVA gauge
Nolichucky, upper	1.6 feet on Poplar gauge
Nolichucky, lower	1.7 feet on Poplar gauge
Watauga Gorge	250 CFS on TVA Sugar Grove gauge
Wilson Creek	Minus 2 inches on the County Road 1337 paddlers' gauge

To obtain water level information, call any outfitter that runs the river. Phrase your inquiry specifically, as follows: "What's the Chattooga running at the 76 gauge?" If you act like you know what you're talking about, you are less likely to get a bullfeathers response such as "the water's fine" or "the river's at a good level."

Running a river when the water level is too low is an exhausting, frustrating experience. Definitely not fun. Since reservations for some commercial trips are made well in advance, you may have to make your go or no-go decision seven days or so before your reservation date in order to get a refund. This means keeping an eye on the weather and water levels as the date for your trip nears. If the river you plan to run is experiencing low water conditions a week before your trip, you probably are wise to cancel. Once summer comes and the foliage is full, rain runoff into streams is significantly diminished. During warm weather months, it takes a lot of rain to bring streams up to runnable levels. If the river is too low or marginal a week before your trip, the probability of rain restoring the river to an adequate level is about 25% in June, 20% in July, 13% in August, and 11% in September.

Unusually high water can make a trip more fun, more dangerous, or both. Most outfitters have specific cut-off levels for when the river becomes too high to run safely. Your main responsibility, if you learn that the water is extra high, is to quiz the outfitter concerning the suitability of the trip for children, weak swimmers, or seniors in your group.

Age Considerations

Outfitters have minimum age and sometimes minimum weight requirements for all guided trips. What you need to bear in mind is that fear of water, particularly when combined with swift current and rapids, transcends all age groups. Minimum age and weight requirements address the question of the participant's ability to meet the physical and safety requirements of the trip. The psychological dimension—the appropriateness of a given trip for a child—is left up to the parents. If you are interested in rafting as a family activity, we advise that you begin your river explorations with a guided trip on a more gentle river. Starting your children out on a tough river may result in a fear and aversion of rafting that they will never overcome. The following rivers are good for first-timer trips:

Nantahala River, North Carolina
Tuckasegee River, North Carolina
French Broad (half day), North Carolina

Lower Nolichucky, Tennessee
Watauga River below Wilbur Dam, Tennessee

These same rivers also are good choices for seniors, or for adults who are intimidated by the prospect of whitewater rafting.

Duration of Trip

Southeastern outfitters offer primarily day trips. Listed below for each river is the time you actually can expect to spend on the water as well as the duration of the entire trip. The list is arranged by duration of trip:

River	Trip Duration	Time on Water
Pigeon	3 hours	$1^1/_2$–2 hours
Ocoee	$3^1/_2$ hours	$1^1/_2$–2 hours
Tuckasegee	$3^1/_2$ hours	$1^1/_2$–$2^1/_2$ hours
French Broad (half day)	3 hours	$1^1/_2$–$2^1/_2$ hours
Nolichucky, lower	3-5 hours	2–$3^1/_2$ hours
Nantahala	$3^1/_2$ hours	$2^1/_2$ hours
Wilson Creek	$5^1/_2$+ hours	$3^1/_2$–$4^1/_2$ hours
Chattooga, Section III	6 hours	$4^1/_2$ hours
Chattooga, Section IV	7 hours	5 hours
Watauga Gorge	7 hours	5 hours
French Broad (full day)	6–7 hours	$3^1/_2$–5 hours
Nolichucky, upper	6–8 hours	$4^1/_2$–6 hours

Self-guided trips are available on the Hiwassee and Nantahala, with the outfitter transporting you and your raft to the put-in. For both rivers, it takes about 2–$3^1/_2$ hours for self-guided groups to complete the run.

Your River Hit Parade

Though all commercially run southeastern mountain rivers are beautiful, some are exceptionally so. Here is the way we rank the rivers in terms of beauty and scenery:

1. Chattooga, Section IV   A++
2. Watauga Gorge   A+
3. Nolichucky, upper   A+
4. Chattooga, Section III   A
5. Wilson Creek   B+

6. Nantahala	B+
7. Hiwassee	B+
8. French Broad	B
9. Nolichucky, lower	B–
10. Pigeon	B–
11. Ocoee	B–
12. Tuckasegee	B–

The Chattooga and the upper Nolichucky run through wilderness areas that are quite pristine. On the other rivers there are various reminders of civilization. The Nantahala, Ocoee, Pigeon, Wilson Creek, and part of the Tuckasegee are paralleled by major highways.

If you are interested in how the rivers stack up in terms of challenge, here's the ranking:

1. Watauga Gorge
2. Wilson Creek
3. Chattooga, Section IV
4. Ocoee
5. Nolichucky, upper
6. Pigeon
7. Chattooga, Section III
8. French Broad
9. Nantahala
10. Nolichucky, lower
11. Tuckasegee
12. Hiwassee

On the Watauga, Wilson Creek, and Section IV of the Chattooga, the guide needs quick response, teamwork, and an all-out effort from the guests in the raft to successfully navigate the tougher rapids. Some people discover the hard way that paddling half-heartedly or goofing off on a serious river can result in a flipped raft and a nasty swim through a Class IV rapid. On all of the other rivers, your guide can get through on his own if need be. Of course, regardless of the difficulty, your enjoyment is directly tied to the extent of your participation. Even on the Class II Hiwassee, half the fun is in the teamwork.

—— *Fishing*

The Smoky and Blue Ridge mountains are laced with rivers and streams coursing with cold, fast water full of fish. The result is some of the finest fly-fishing anywhere. Rainbow and brown trout can be hooked in the Great Smoky using artificial flies or lures; the native brook trout, called "specs" in the Smokies because of the colorful speckles on their backs, are a protected species that must be released unharmed if caught.

Not all fishing in the mountains is in natural streams. For example, Fontana Lake (Zone 4), one of the less frequented Tennessee Valley Authority impoundments that borders Great Smoky, is 29 miles long and features plenty of opportunities for anglers to hook both smallmouth and largemouth bass, as well as many other species.

Valid state fishing licenses are required to fish in national parks, as well as national forests and other public lands; they're available at sporting goods stores in nearby communities. In Shenandoah National Park (Zone 8), licenses also are available at Panorama, Big Meadows, and Loft Mountain waysides on Skyline Drive. Copies of fishing regulations are available at the visitor centers of national parks and forests.

The Best Fishing Spots

People who have never fished in the Southern Appalachians and want to test their luck—and maybe their skill—against stream-bred trout or aggressive smallmouth bass have a bewildering number of choices when it comes to destinations.

To help you narrow the search, here are some of the best streams, lakes, and rivers in the region. In the zone descriptions that follow, you'll find more details on these angling spots, as well as information on other excellent places to fish. You'll also find the names of guides who can take you to secret spots and reveal fishing techniques used by local anglers.

Deep Creek, north of Bryson City, North Carolina, in Great Smoky Mountains National Park (Zone 1), is renown for the trophy, eight-pound brown trout fished above the confluence with Indian Creek. The Horseshoe section of **Abrams Creek** out of Cades Cove in Great Smoky offers good, solid fishing that doesn't get much pressure—and is full of big fish.

Fontana Lake, a huge TVA impoundment wedged between Great Smoky and Nantahala National Forest (Zone 4), is an overlooked fishing mecca with a reputation among knowledgeable anglers for its wide range of fish species, ranging from smallmouth bass to state-record muskie.

The **Cherokee Reservation** (Zone 4), south of Great Smoky Mountains National Park, offers some of the best trout fishing in the eastern United States. No license is required—just a $5-a-day Tribal Fishing Permit—and the daily limit is an incredible ten fish. A stretch of the **Little Tennessee River** between Bryson City and Franklin (Zone 4) has a worldwide reputation for its smallmouth bass fishing.

In South Carolina's **Lake Jocassee** (Zone 5), anglers think like deep-sea fishermen when going after brown and rainbow trout lurking in the impoundment's 440-foot depths. The **Davidson River** in Pisgah National Forest near Brevard (Zone 6) is an excellent trout stream located in an area teeming with outdoor recreation opportunities.

In Virginia (Zone 8), as many as 40 trout streams are open in **Shenandoah National Park**, where fly-fishing anglers can fish one of the last completely protected strongholds of the native eastern brook trout. **Smith Mountain Lake**, east of Roanoke, is one of the state's most popular fishing lakes, while **Philpott Reservoir** to the south has a reputation for producing some of the larger rainbow trout taken each year. The state-record muskie, a 45-pounder, was taken from the **New River**, near the North Carolina state line.

More Information on Fishing

The Smoky Mountains Trout Fishing Guide, by Don Kirk (Menasha Ridge Press), offers in-depth coverage of the wheres and hows of trout fishing in the national park and nearby lakes; local anglers swear by it. *Trout Fishing in Shenandoah National Park* (Shenandoah Publishing) and *Fly-Fishing for Smallmouth Bass* (Lyons and Buford), by Harry Murray, tell you all you need to know on their respective topics.

Anglers on a visit to the Shenandoah Valley can contact Murray directly at the fly shop he operates in the Peoples Drug Store in Edinburg, Virginia. He holds clinics and offers individual instruction from April through October; call him at (703) 984-4212.

—— Bicycling

For cyclists who like to spin the cranks along a seemingly never ending ribbon of smooth asphalt, the contiguous **Blue Ridge Parkway** and **Skyline Drive** rate as one of the top biking destinations in the world. Lots of lung-busting climbing? You bet. And the scenery? Incredible.

Bikers looking for something a little less strenuous—but utterly topnotch in scenery and ambiance—also can be accommodated. **Cades Cove** in Great Smoky Mountains National Park (Zone 1) features a delightful, 11-mile loop that offers equal doses of natural beauty and history; bike rentals also are available. Near **Boone, North Carolina** (Zone 7), a 20-mile, out-and-back ride along River Road is both a scenic and flat mountain ramble.

Shenandoah Valley in Virginia (Zone 8) is one of the world's best road-riding areas; a 40-mile ride from Waynesboro and around Sherando Lake offers both great views from the Blue Ridge Parkway and a spin through the rolling Valley. We'll point out more great road rides in each zone description that follows.

A Word About Gears

If you're accustomed to riding your bike on relatively flat terrain and plan on bringing it to the mountains, get ready for a shock: Your bike's gears may be too high (too hard to push) for exploring the steep roads and trails in the Southern Appalachians.

There is a solution, however. Take your bike (road or mountain) to a reputable bike shop before your trip and ask a bike mechanic about putting lower gears on your bike.

Often, it's as simple as switching the small chainring with another that has fewer teeth, or replacing the rear freewheel or cassette (the cluster of smaller cogs on the rear axle) with one that has more teeth. A good mechanic will know if it's also necessary to lengthen your bike's chain to accommodate the new—and easier to pedal—gears.

—— Mountain Biking

Almost all new bicycles sold today are mountain bikes, also known as fat-tire or "all terrain" (ATB) bikes. They're made for riding on dirt roads and trails, and feature very low gears for climbing steep pitches, knobby tires, and beefy brakes for secure stopping.

Mountain bikes are perfect for exploring the Smoky and Blue Ridge mountains—with a few notable exceptions: There are some trails and dirt roads in Shenandoah and Great Smoky Mountains national parks, as well as some designated wilderness areas and hiking trails in national forests, in which bicycles are prohibited. Still, there's no shortage of places to ride a mountain bike.

One of the top-rated off-road destinations in the United States is the **Tsali Recreation Area** in North Carolina (Zone 4), with more than 30 miles of single-track trails along the shores of Lake Fontana. **George Washington National Forest** in Virginia (Zone 8) is another destination that's attracting mountain bikers from across the country. **The Davidson River Area** near Brevard in Pisgah National Forest (Zone 6) is building a national reputation among off-roaders. There's more than a lifetime's worth of mountain biking in the Smoky and Blue Ridge mountains. We'll show you more in the zone descriptions that follow.

Things to keep in mind on a mountain bike ramble: Wear a helmet, ride with others if the area is remote, maintain control of your speed at all times, yield to hikers and equestrians, and carry your bike over boggy and muddy spots to avoid causing erosion.

More Cycling Information

A number of books describe excellent bike routes—both road and mountain—throughout the Southern Appalachians. *Off the Beaten Track—Volumes I and II,* by Jim Parham (WMC Publishing), describe great mountain bike rides in Zones 4 and 6 (Western North Carolina). *Mountain Biking the Appalachians: Northwest North Carolina/Southwest Virginia*, by Lori Finley (John F. Blair, Publisher), covers great rides in Zones 7 and 8. In Virginia (Zone 8), *A Cyclists' Guide to the Shenandoah Valley,* by Randy Porter and Nancy Sorrells (Shenandoah Odysseys), describes rural routes on back roads in beautiful Shenandoah Valley.

—— Horseback Riding

Both Shenandoah and Great Smoky national parks, as well as most national forests in the Southern Highlands, feature designated bridal trails. It's a wonderful way to get around, and stables in the national parks (at **Skyland** in Shenandoah in Zone 8, and **Cades Cove, Smokemont, McCarter's Riding Stables,** and **Smoky Mountains Riding Stables** in Great Smoky, Zone 1) offer guided trail rides that depart throughout the day. Many equestrians say the horseback riding in Great Smoky is the best in the East.

The restrictions are minimal: Riders must be at least 4' 10" tall. Usually, pony rides are available for smaller children. At Cades Cove, carriage and hay rides also are available. Riders who own their own horses can explore bridal trails in Great Smoky and camp at five drive-in horse camps inside the park.

Private ranches also provide plenty of opportunities to explore the Smokies on horseback. One of the best is **Cataloochee Ranch** in Maggie Valley, North Carolina (Zone 6), which provides lodging in a main house and a lodge and offers half- and whole-day guided trips into the mountains. See page 376 for more information. Each zone description that follows lists more horseback riding stables that offer guided tours through the mountains.

—— *Golf*

Golf in the southeastern mountains is a quiet, understated affair. Stuck back in remote valleys and lightly promoted, golf courses throughout the mountains virtually go unnoticed by the average tourist. You can drive around in the Smokies or Blue Ridge for days and not even see a golf course. Imagine our surprise, then, when we discovered that there were almost 80 eighteen-hole golf courses in the geography covered by this guide.

The most renowned courses are **The Homestead** in Hot Springs, Virginia, and the *Golf Digest* award-winning **Hanging Rock Golf Club** in Salem, Virginia (both Zone 8); the **Maggie Valley Resort** in Maggie Valley, North Carolina, host of the Professional Golf Schools of America, and Asheville's **Grove Park Inn Resort** (both Zone 6). Farther south in Zone 5 are the **Sky Valley Resort** at Sky Valley, Georgia, ranked the tenth best course in Georgia, and the **High Hampton Inn & Country Club** in Cashiers, North Carolina. These, and other quality golf courses, are profiled under Golf in the sections describing recreational resources in each respective geographic zone.

—— *Skiing*

People from other parts of the country often are amazed that you actually can ski in the South. Because it only takes night temperatures of 28° or less and the side of the mountain to make a ski slope, the Southern Appalachians offer skiing from mid-December through February—and sometimes into March.

While the region boasts a large number of downhill ski resorts, people who have skied in the West or in New England often are disappointed by the quality of skiing in the South. Vertical drops are modest (some resorts have slopes with under 300-foot verticals), the machine-made snow is often lousy, and the hills frequently are crowded with inexperienced skiers—especially on weekends.

Because the winter days in the southern mountains are warm enough to melt the snow, and the nights are cold enough to refreeze it, icy skiing conditions are common. Ice, coupled with armies of inexperienced, out-of-control skiers, lead us to recommend avoiding southern mountain ski areas, particularly on weekends. If you are within striking distance of the **Snow Shoe** or **Canaan Valley**, West Virginia resorts, these are somewhat better. The best bet of all is to save your money and go to Colorado or Utah, where the skiing conditions are excellent, the mountains larger, and the crowds more dispersed. Skiing is about snow, not ice. You can learn more, and progress faster, in one week of skiing in the West, where conditions are good, than in seasons of crashing down the icy mountains of the South.

The Better of the Downhill Resorts in the South

If you can't get out West, but are dying to ski, there are two southeastern ski resorts that offer more vertical, longer runs, and better snow conditions than average. In North Carolina, try **Sugar Mountain** and **Ski Beech** (both in Zone 7).

Sugar Mountain offers the biggest vertical drop around (1,200 feet), while Ski Beech claims the highest elevation. Both resorts, the locals say, are consistently colder than other ski venues in the South and get more snow, both natural and man-made. The downside: Both resorts draw big crowds.

Another well-regarded ski area is **Cataloochee**, located in Maggie Valley, North Carolina (Zone 6). It's a ski resort with a 60s feel: The ski lodge is huge with a cafeteria in the basement—and no condominiums are on site. The altitude is an impressive 5,500 feet and the resort borders Great Smoky Mountains National Park, which gives a big, wide-open ambiance to the slopes. For a really unique experience, stay in the adjacent dude ranch. Cataloochee also boasts an excellent ski school and day-care facilities.

The best time to ski any of the southeastern resorts is after a big snowstorm, which can happen at least once a winter and sometimes more. After a significant dump of natural snow, Cataloochee opens The Meadows, a big bowl which, locals say, offers powder that rivals the white stuff out West.

In Virginia. The best ski resort in the Southern Appalachians, however, is probably **Wintergreen Resort** (Zone 8), near Waynesboro and the Blue Ridge Parkway. Wintergreen's claim to fame is The Highlands, an experts-only slope that boasts 1,000 feet of *continuous* vertical—no flat sections break up the drop. The resort's ski school and day-care facilities also are highly rated. Wintergreen is an upscale resort that draws big crowds from Washington, D.C. and Richmond.

Massanutten, on the other hand, is on a par with Sugar Mountain and Ski Beech: good, but not great. The resort, located ten miles east of Harrisonburg off US 33, is on Massanutten Mountain in the Shenandoah Valley. The trails are adequate—not outstanding—with lots of flat connecting trails between the drops.

The Others. What about the rest of the ski resorts that dot the landscape of North Carolina and Georgia? They're fine for beginners—and cheap and easy to get to for folks on escapes from nearby cities, such as Atlanta and Charlotte. It also means they're crowded on weekends.

Learning to Ski

If you're a beginner skier on vacation in the Southern Appalachians, our local experts recommend heading to either Cataloochee or Wintergreen for topnotch instruction at their ski schools. If your destination is one of the other resorts, call the ski school in advance and ask about their programs.

A good sign: The person answering the phone gives you straight responses without looking anything up or asking someone else for the answers. If the lines of communications are good over the phone, they'll probably be good on the snow.

Crowds

It's safe to say all the resorts are packed on weekends, although Sundays aren't quite as bad as Saturdays. Avoid **Appalachian Ski Mountain** (Zone 7) on big holiday weekends: The resort specializes in attracting large bus groups, and the slopes get flooded with skiers. Night skiing is another way to beat the crowds at ski resorts in the Southern Appalachians. Just make sure you wear goggles: If the temperature is cold enough, the snowmaking equipment will be blasting out the white stuff. For more information on these ski resorts and others, check the write-ups in Zones 2, 5, 6, 7, and 8.

Cross-Country Skiing

What about cross-country skiing? Without being able to depend on snowmaking capability, cross-country skiers must trust Mother Nature to look out for them. When she does dump a heavy load of the white stuff on the Southern mountains, many cross-country skiers head for **Skyline Drive** or the **Blue Ridge Parkway.** They'll be closed to traffic and are perfect places for slapping around on skinny boards. **Roan Mountain** in Pisgah National Forest (Zone 7) is another popular place after it snows.

—— Waterfalls

Most people love waterfalls—and the Smoky and Blue Ridge mountains harbor an incredible number of places where streams tumble in a free-fall or cascade down a rock slide. Waterfalls offer a magnetic draw, enticing drivers to pull over on a wayside and explore, especially on hot summer days. The attraction of viewing a waterfall deep in the forest is also a great excuse to take a hike.

Getting to the Falls

Trails leading to waterfalls are especially popular, so stay on marked trails, walk and talk quietly, travel in small groups, and don't litter. Unfortunately, many people walking the trails don't follow these simple rules, and as a result, many trails are showing serious signs of erosion and overcrowding.

Safety. Accidents around waterfalls are a serious problem. To avoid becoming a statistic, don't lean out over high ledges, watch your footing (even dry rocks can be slippery), watch children carefully, and be especially cautious when taking photographs.

The Best Waterfalls

The most spectacular falls in North Carolina include **Looking Glass Falls** (85 feet) in Zone 6. In Zone 5, **Rainbow Falls** (200 feet) and **Whitewater Falls,** the highest waterfall in the eastern United States (441 feet) are breathtaking.

In Virginia (Zone 8), **Whiteoak Falls** is the highest waterfall in the state's Blue Ridge Mountains, with six cascades ranging from 86 feet to 35 feet. **Lewis Spring Falls** (81 feet) and **Dark Hollow Falls** (70 feet) are favorites in Shenandoah National Park. In George Washington National Forest, **Crabtree Falls** features five major cascades that fall for a total of 1,200 feet.

More Information

More than 100 waterfalls in the Blue Ridge Mountains of Virginia and North Carolina are described—and some illustrated with color photos—in *Waterfalls of the Blue Ridge,* by Nicole Blouin, Steve Bordonaro, and Marylou Wier Bordonaro (Menasha Ridge Press).

—— Gems

North Carolina sits on some of the more unusual geological deposits in the United States. (Tiffany's, the famous jewelry emporium in New York, once owned an emerald mine near Franklin, located south of Great Smoky Mountains National Park.) As a result, mineral museums are located throughout the Southern Highlands. But you also can try your own hand at prospecting at roadside mines for emeralds, garnets, rubies, sapphires, and amethysts.

"Prospectors" buy a bucket of mud, priced anywhere from $5 to $100, that they wash in sluices at the mines. (The buckets, by the way, usually are enriched, so everyone is guaranteed a find. If your goal is to take home a valuable gemstone, our advice is to stop at a rock shop and buy one.)

Sifting through the bucketful of mud can be exciting, especially for children. Lucky finders can have their stones cut and set into jewelry. In the zone descriptions that follow, we'll point out some of the more popular gem mines in North Carolina—including a spot where prospectors can pan for rubies in a roadside stream near Franklin (Zone 4). And it's free!

—— *Scenic Drives*

Motor touring is the number one outdoor activity in the United States. So where are the best places to take a scenic drive in the Blue Ridge and Great Smoky mountains?

In the Southern Appalachians, the Big Enchilada of scenic drives is **Skyline Drive,** which starts near Front Royal, Virginia (less than a two-hour drive from Washington, D.C.), and meets the **Blue Ridge Parkway,** 105 miles to the south. The Parkway then continues another 469 miles to Cherokee, near the eastern entrance to Great Smoky Mountains National Park. The 45 mph speed limit (35 mph on Skyline Drive), a profusion of scenic overlooks, and the absence of commercialism (no billboards) make this a relaxing, world-class drive.

But that's just the tip of the iceberg. In Tennessee, the **Foothills Parkway** parallels Great Smoky through Cherokee National Forest, while in North Carolina, **US 64** (south of Great Smoky) provides mile after mile of breathtaking mountain scenery. The drive along the highway as it approaches Highlands from Franklin reminds many people of mountain passes in Europe.

In Georgia, **US 76** between Hiawassee and Clayton passes over the crest of the Blue Ridge Mountains. And **US 74/19** between Asheville and Bryson City offers views of the Smokies to the north and Pisgah and Nantahala national forests to the south.

For those who like to explore deep in the woods on unpaved roads, the national forests offer unsurpassed opportunities. Example: A drive to **Wayah Bald**, in Pisgah National Forest north of Franklin, North Carolina (Zone 4), takes you on a winding, climbing, four-mile trek to a mountaintop with a stone observation tower and an impressive, 360-degree view of the surrounding mountains. It's one heck of a picnic spot.

Each zone description that follows supplies specific information on all of these drives, as well as other scenic journeys on low-traffic back roads.

—— *Shopping*

The retail spirit is alive and well throughout the Smoky and Blue Ridge mountains, and ways to spend your money vary from the silly to the sublime.

For shoppers looking to give their credit cards a workout, opportunities range from a nearly endless procession of T-shirt shops, cheap souvenir stands, and tacky gift shops in Gatlinburg, to intricately decorated pottery, colorful jewelry, and crafts made by Native American artists in Cherokee and displayed at the Qualla Arts and Crafts Mutual Co-Op.

Genuine Mountain Crafts

The Southern Appalachians are also where you'll find the traditional crafts of mountain folk: weaving, woodcarving, enameling, pottery, jewelry making, blacksmithing, rag rug weaving, and quilting.

While craft shops abound throughout the region, one of the best places to explore—and to purchase high-quality crafts—is the **John C. Campbell Folk School,** the nation's oldest school of traditional crafts, located outside of Murphy, North Carolina (Zone 4).

The school offers 344 courses to 3,000 students a year on a 365-acre campus listed on the National Register of Historic Places. Visitors can observe students at work, visit the Folk Museum, and make a purchase at the Craft Shop, where more than 300 artists market their wares.

Another place for crafts is outside Gatlinburg: the **Great Smoky Arts and Crafts Community,** located three miles east of town on US 321 (Zone 2). More than 100 artisans in more than 70 shops and studios display and sell their crafts.

More Shopping

Other not-to-be-missed shopping venues in North Carolina are Asheville (crafts and antiques), Blowing Rock (crafts), Bryson City (at **Nantahala Outdoor Center**, one of the best outdoor-equipment dealers in the United States), and Franklin (gems). Highlands features a wide array of sophisticated, pricey boutiques.

In Virginia, unique shopping opportunities include wine (Virginia is one of the top ten wine-producing states in the country, with more than two dozen wineries close to the Blue Ridge Parkway and Skyline Drive), crafts and antiques (Charlottesville, Roanoke, and Lexington), and Virginia's oldest farmer's market in downtown Roanoke.

Factory Outlet Malls

You'll also find plenty of factory outlet malls, where smart consumers save up to 70% off retail on brand names such as Bugle Boy, Bass Shoes, Van Heusen, Corning, Revereware, Levi's, and many more. Pigeon Forge, Tennessee (Zone 2), boasts nearly 200 outlet stores located in malls a block north of US 441 (the main drag).

In Virginia's Shenandoah Valley (Zone 8), Waynesboro is only minutes from Interstates 81 and 64, Skyline Drive, and the Blue Ridge Parkway. The town features more than 30 factory outlet stores, with brand names such as Liz Claiborne, London Fog, Royal Doulton, Capezio, and Virginia Metalcrafters (a factory showroom featuring garden and patio products handcrafted in solid, sandcast brass, cast iron, mahogany, and white bronze).

Getting More Information

In addition to this guide, you may wish to obtain some of the free information available from local chambers of commerce or tourism offices. Most of the oganizations listed below will send you a whole packet of information on hotels, restaurants, attractions, and recreational opportunities in their area.

Be specific about your plans when you contact the offices and you can receive additional information on the place or places you plan to visit. National forest offices will send you general information and an order form for highly detailed maps of their various districts (typical prices range from $4–7 each).

Georgia

Georgia Department of Industry, Trade, and Tourism
Tourist Division
P.O. Box 17766
Atlanta, GA 30301
(404) 656-3590

Rabun County (Northeastern Georgia) Chamber of Commerce
(706) 782-5113

North Carolina

North Carolina Travel and Tourism Division
Department of Commerce
430 North Salisbury Street
Raleigh, NC 27611
(800) VISIT NC; (919) 733-4171

Asheville Convention and Visitors Center
(800) 257-5583

Banner Elk Chamber of Commerce
(800) 972-2183

Boone Convention and Visitors Bureau
(800) 852-9506

Brevard-Transylvania Visitor Information
(800) 648-4523

Cashiers Chamber of Commerce
(704) 743-5941

Cherokee County (Southwestern North Carolina) Chamber of
    Commerce
(704) 837-2242

Franklin Chamber of Commerce
(800) 336-7829

Hendersonville Chamber of Commerce
(800) 828-4244

Highlands Chamber of Commerce
(704) 526-2112

Swain County (Northwestern North Carolina) Chamber of
    Commerce
(704) 488-3681

South Carolina

South Carolina Division of Tourism
P.O. Box 71
Columbia, SC 29202
(803) 734-0122

South Carolina Mountains: Discover Upcountry
(800) 849-4766

Tennessee

Tennessee Tourist Development
P.O. Box 23170
Nashville, TN 37202
(615) 741-2158

Gatlinburg Chamber of Commerce
(800) 568-4748

Pigeon Forge Visitors Center
(615) 453-8574

Smoky Mountain Visitors Bureau
(800) 525-6834

Virginia

Division of Tourism
Department of Economic Development
1021 East Cary Street
Richmond, VA 23219
(804) 786-2051

Charlottesville/Albemarle Convention and Visitors Bureau
(804) 977-1783

Front Royal–Warren County Chamber of Commerce
(703) 635-3185

Harrisonburg-Rockingham Convention and Visitors Bureau
(703) 434-2319

Lexington Visitors Center
(703) 463-3777

Roanoke Valley Convention and Visitors Bureau
(800) 635-5535

Staunton Department of Economic Development
(703) 885-8504

Other Information

Great Smoky Mountains National Park
107 Park Headquarters Road
Gatlinburg, TN 37738
(615) 436-1200

Shenandoah National Park
Route 4, Box 348
Luray, VA 22835
(703) 999-2266
(800) 828-1120 (voice/TDD)

Nantahala and Pisgah national forests
Supervisor's Office
National Forests in North Carolina
100 Otis Street
Asheville, NC 28802
(704) 257-4200

Cherokee National Forest
Forest Supervisor
USDA Forest Service
2800 North Ocoee Street
Cleveland, TN 37312
(615) 476-9700

Chattahoochee National Forest
USDA Forest Service
508 Oak Street, NW
Gainesville, GA 30501
(404) 536-0541

George Washington National Forest
Superintendent
P.O. Box 233
Harrisonburg, VA 22801
(703) 564-8300

Jefferson National Forest
Forest Supervisor
5162 Valleypointe Parkway
Roanoke, VA 24019

Blue Ridge Parkway Association
P.O. Box 453
Asheville, NC 28802

The Zones

A Big Chunk of Geography

The geographical area that encompasses the Great Smoky and Blue Ridge mountains is huge. Consider: Skyline Drive and the Blue Ridge Parkway meander for almost 600 miles from Shenandoah to Great Smoky Mountains national parks. And while the Appalachians are only 80 miles wide at their northernmost reaches, the range broadens to a considerable 350 miles in the south.

Moreover, the mountains that encircle Great Smoky in all directions are a vacation and outdoor recreation mecca for millions of people each year. The region also includes small sections of the Blue Ridge Mountains located in Georgia and South Carolina.

To help you get a handle on this immense chunk of Southern Appalachia, we've divided it into eight geographic zones:

- Zone 1: Great Smoky Mountains National Park
- Zone 2: The Northern Foothills of Tennessee
- Zone 3: The Southwest Foothills of Tennessee
- Zone 4: The Southern Foothills of North Carolina
- Zone 5: The Tri-State Mountains of North Carolina, Georgia, and South Carolina
- Zone 6: Asheville and Brevard
- Zone 7: The Blue Ridge Mountains of North Carolina
- Zone 8: The Blue Ridge Mountains of Virginia

The centerpiece of our zone layout is Great Smoky Mountains National Park (Zone 1)—with 10 million visitors annually, it's the Number One tourist attraction in the Southern Appalachians. Going in a counter-clockwise direction, the park is surrounded by Zones 2 and 3 (in Tennessee), and Zones 4 and 6 (in North Carolina). Zone 5, the Tri-State Mountains, is southeast of the park, while Zone 7 and

Zone 8 encompass the Blue Ridge Mountains of North Carolina and Virginia to the northeast of Great Smoky.

Self-Contained Zones . . . and Jumping-Off Points

Each zone description that follows is a self-contained chapter that includes information on outdoor recreation, restaurant listings, and tourist attractions. We also provide an overview of the zone that puts it in perspective with its neighboring zones.

Here's why: Some zones are fairly self-contained destinations. People who visit, say, the Tri-State Mountains (Zone 5) find that the region fulfills virtually all their vacation needs—from lodging to enjoying the outdoors, shopping, eating out, or taking in cultural events.

Highlands (Zone 5), for example, is a charming town full of shops, restaurants, and things to do. It's also surrounded by gorgeous mountains featuring spectacular waterfalls and a wide array of outdoor recreation options. Many people who visit Highlands return year after year—and they aren't jumping in their cars every day and trekking to Great Smokies.

Other zones, however, serve as jumping-off points for destinations in nearby regions. Unless you're camping, backpacking, or have made reservations for LeConte Lodge a year or more in advance, your visit to Great Smokies will mean you're spending the evenings at lodgings located outside the park—in, say, Gatlinburg (Zone 2).

Hard-core whitewater enthusiasts, on the other hand, congregate around Tennessee's Ocoee River (Zone 3) and North Carolina's Nantahala Gorge (Zone 4)—and most of them don't venture far from the sound of rushing water. Other areas that are fairly self-contained are North Carolina's Blue Ridge (Zone 7) and Virginia's Blue Ridge (Zone 8).

Note: Although most visitors to the self-contained regions may not often day trip to tourist spots in other zones, that doesn't mean that *you* shouldn't. There's much to see and do in the mountains—and while it's a big region, you'll find many world-class destinations outside the zone where you're headquartered which, in fact, are within in easy striking distance from where you're staying. We'll point out great places that make easy day trips in each zone description that follows.

Who Goes Where

Before we divided the Smoky and Blue Ridge regions into zones, we also looked at where people from outside the area tend to stay when vacationing in these southern mountains.

For example, on the Tennessee side of Great Smokies (Zones 2 and 3), you'll see many license tags from the Midwest, the Deep South, and Ohio; on the North Carolina side of the national park (Zones 4, 5, and 6), New England and mid-Atlantic states predominate. In the Tri-State Mountains (Zone 5), look for a proliferation of Florida tags.

Organization

In order to give you fast access to information about the *best* in the Smoky and Blue Ridge mountains, we've also organized our chapter on hotels around zones.

Since most people visiting the mountains stay in one hotel, motel, inn, or lodge for the duration of their trip, we have summarized our coverage of hotels in charts, maps, ratings, and rankings that allow you to quickly focus your decision-making process. We do not go on for pages describing lobbies and rooms, which, in the final analysis, sound much the same. Instead, we concentrate on the specific variables that differentiate one hotel from another: location, size, room quality, services, amenities, and cost.

All discussion of hotels, restaurants, and attractions include zone numbers. If you are planning to stay in Pigeon Forge and looking for a room, scanning the hotel listings in Zone 2 (the Northern Foothills of Tennessee) will provide you with the best choices.

A Calendar of Events

March

Great Smoky Arts & Crafts Community Spring Show, Gatlinburg, TN (Zone 2). A welcome to spring featuring all handmade crafts and art by Craft Community members. (615) 436-4448.

April

Annual Spring Wildflower Pilgrimage, Gatlinburg, TN (Zone 2). A three-day program of conducted wildflower walks, motorcades, and photographic tours in Great Smoky Mountains National Park. Free. (615) 436-1262.

Festival of Flowers, Biltmore Estate, Asheville, NC (Zone 6). A profusion of flowers inside Biltmore House and in gardens; special activities. Admission fee required. (704) 255-1700.

Shenandoah Apple Blossom Festival, Winchester, VA (Zone 8). A spring celebration of apples with crafts, arts, a parade, the Queen's coronation, and a circus. (800) 662-1360.

Annual Vinton Dogwood Festival, Vinton, VA (outside Roanoke in Zone 8). Celebrate spring with a parade, band competition, bike race, antique car show, children's activities, and pageant. (703) 983-0613.

May

Gatlinburg Scottish Festival and Games, Gatlinburg, TN (Zone 2). Traditional athletic and dance competitions, colorful parades, and social events in a "highland" weekend. (615) 442-5297.

Liberty Fest, Liberty, SC (Zone 5). Entertainment, arts and crafts sales, a children's tent, and more as the event focuses on Liberty's culture and history. (803) 843-3021.

Concourse Botanique, Clemson, SC (Zone 5). A spring cultural conservation festival featuring music, storytelling, dance, arts and crafts displays, and demonstrations from around the world. (803) 656-4289.

Annual Virginia Mushroom Festival, Front Royal, VA (Zone 8). Featuring shiitake mushrooms, arts and crafts, children's activities, demonstrations, wine tastings, exhibits, and live entertainment. (800) 338-2576.

Roanoke Festival in the Park, Roanoke, VA (Zone 8). A multifaceted regional event highlighting the performing and visual arts, children's activities and a parade, and live music. (703) 342-2640.

June

Unto These Hills Outdoor Drama, Cherokee, NC (Zone 4). An outdoor drama about the history of the Cherokee Indians. Admission fee required. Nightly except Sundays. (704) 497-2111.

Horn In the West Outdoor Drama, Boone, NC (Zone 7). Outdoor drama about Daniel Boone and early Appalachian settlers. Nightly except Mondays. Admission fee required. (704) 264-2120.

Theater at Lime Kiln, Lexington, VA (Zone 8). Outdoor drama, musicals, and concerts throughout the summer with stone ruins as a stage. Plays presented Tuesday through Saturdays, rain or shine. (703) 463-3074.

Ash Lawn—Highland Summer Festival of the Arts, Charlottesville, VA (Zone 8). Performances, music, lectures, and picnics in Boxwood Gardens on the restored estate of President James Monroe. Admission fee required. (804) 979-0122.

July

Annual Gatlinburg's Summer Craftsmen's Fair, Gatlinburg, TN (Zone 2). More than 125 of the nation's finest craftspeople display, demonstrate, and sell their crafts; country and bluegrass shows. (615) 436-7479.

Unto These Hills Outdoor Drama, Cherokee, NC (Zone 4).   An outdoor drama about the history of the Cherokee Indians. Admission fee required. Nightly except Sundays. (704) 497-2111.

Horn In the West Outdoor Drama, Boone, NC (Zone 7).   Outdoor drama about Daniel Boone and early Appalachian settlers. Nightly except Mondays. Admission fee required. (704) 264-2120.

Grandfather Mountain Highland Games and Gathering of the Scottish Clans, Linville, NC (Zone 7).   Scottish dance, music, and athletic events. (704) 733-1333.

Annual Southern Folk Expressions Folk Art Show, Clayton, GA (Zone 5).   Features work by more than 60 artists. (706) 782-2440.

Bele Chere Festival, Asheville, NC (Zone 6).   North Carolina's largest street festival as downtown Asheville closes its avenues to motor traffic for three days of live music, crafts, street entertainers, and food. (704) 251-9973.

Brevard Music Festival, Brevard, NC (Zone 6).   A month-long series of classical music concerts with a world-class reputation. (704) 884-2011.

August

Unto These Hills Outdoor Drama, Cherokee, NC (Zone 4).   An outdoor drama about the history of the Cherokee Indians. Admission fee required. Nightly except Sundays. (704) 497-2111.

Horn In the West Outdoor Drama, Boone, NC (Zone 7).   Outdoor drama about Daniel Boone and early Appalachian settlers. Nightly except Mondays. Admission fee required. (704) 264-2120.

Georgia Mountain Fair, Hiawassee, GA (Zone 5).   Arts and crafts; regional food; parade; country, bluegrass, and gospel music by nationally known performers. (706) 896-4191.

Arts on the Square Invitational Show, Hiawassee, GA (Zone 5). A juried show of 85 artisans from throughout the Southeast. (704) 896-4550.

Mountain Dance and Folk Festival, Asheville, NC (Zone 6).   Clogging, a traditional mountain dance, is the main event at this festival that attracts visitors from 30 states and nine foreign countries. (704) 258-6111.

Annual Vinton Old-Time Bluegrass Festival and Competition, Vinton, VA (near Roanoke in Zone 8). Concerts by nationally known musicians (band and individual competitions), craft show, and carnival. (703) 983-0613.

North Carolina International Folk Festival: Folkmoot, USA, Waynesville, NC (Zone 6). A festival of international dancing and music held at venues throughout the area. (704) 452-2997.

September

Annual NC Apple Festival, Hendersonville, NC (Zone 6). Crafts, food, entertainment, parade. (800) 828-4244.

Annual Virginia Blues Festival, Charlottesville, VA (Zone 8). A Labor Day tradition with live performances, film presentations, workshops, and special children's activities. (804) 296-8548.

Annual Traditional Frontier Festival, Staunton, VA (Zone 8). Traditional crafts, food, and entertainment from Germany, England, Ireland, and America at the Museum of American Frontier Culture. (703) 332-7850.

Annual Vinton Folklife Festival, Vinton, VA (outside Roanoke in Zone 8). Traditional music, crafts, food, living history, children's area, exhibits, and storytelling. (703) 983-0613.

VA/NC Craftsmen's Fall Classic, Roanoke, VA (Zone 8). More than 220 exhibits of arts and crafts. Admission fee required. (919) 275-0188.

October

Dollywood National Crafts Festival, Pigeon Forge, TN (Zone 2). Craftspeople from across the nation demonstrate old-time skills; music and fun at an authentic harvest festival held in the theme park. (800) DOLLYWOOD, (615) 428-9488.

Annual Gatlinburg Fall Craftsmen's Fair, Gatlinburg, TN (Zone 2). More than 150 of the nation's finest craftspeople display, demonstrate, and sell their crafts; country and bluegrass music shows daily. (615) 436-7479.

Virginia Fall Foliage Festival, Waynesboro, VA (Zone 8). Crafts, apple butter making, gem and mineral show, chili cookoff, car show, and special art exhibits. (703) 949-8203.

Black Mountain Folk Festival, Black Mountain, NC (Zone 6). Some of the nation's best traditional and contemporary musicians converge on this hamlet 15 miles east of Asheville each year for this festival. (704) 669-0780.

Oktoberfest, Walhalla, SC (Zone 5). German and American food, carnival rides, hot air balloon rides, German music and dancers, sky divers, clowns, and magicians in this heritage festival. (803) 638-2727.

Roanoke Railway Festival, Roanoke, VA (Zone 8). Steam-engine excursions, entertainment, children's trains, railfair, car show, and more. (703) 342-2028.

Page County Heritage Festival, Luray, VA (Zone 8). Shenandoah Valley heritage celebrated by soapmaking, basket weaving, mule riding, and demonstrations of early American farming techniques. Admission fee required. (703) 743-3915.

November

Gatlinburg's Smoky Mountain Lights, Gatlinburg, TN (Zone 2). More than $600,000 worth of lighting displays turn the town into a winter wonderland; driving and walking tours. Free. (800) 568-4748.

Smoky Mountain Winterfest, Pigeon Forge, Gatlinburg, and Sevierville, TN (Zone 2). The three resort towns turn winter into a wonderland of lights. Driving and walking tours, special events, outlet sales, and more. (800) 251-9100.

Great Smoky Arts and Crafts Community Thanksgiving Craft Show, Gatlinburg, TN (Zone 2). More than 50 local artists and craftspeople featured in a Christmas marketplace setting. (615) 436-9214.

Toccoa Harvest Festival, Toccoa, GA (Zone 5). Features steam excursion train, antique car and gasoline engine shows, Civil War reenactments, arts, crafts, entertainment, food, and children's activities. (706) 886-2132.

December

Christmas at Biltmore Estate, Asheville, NC (Zone 6).   A 225-room French Renaissance chateau decorated for a Victorian Christmas; reservations required for candlelight tours offered Tuesday through Sunday during the holiday season. Admission fee required. (704) 255-1770.

PART TWO: Arriving and Getting Oriented

Coming into the Mountains

—— The Smokies

By Car

Just about everyone on a Smoky Mountain vacation arrives by car. The *crème de la crème* route to reach the Great Smoky Mountains National Park and the western mountains of North Carolina is the Blue Ridge Parkway, which runs from Shenandoah National Park in Virginia to the southern entrance of Great Smoky.

Practical, it's not: The scenic, two-lane road twists for 469 miles along the crest of the Blue Ridge Mountains. The speed limit is 45 mph, but with long stretches where you can't pass slow-moving RVs, most people go much slower. Relax—you're on vacation. The idea is to enjoy the scenery, not rush down this beautiful stretch of highway.

From the North and West.　　Drivers coming from Ohio and the Midwest can take I-75, which goes south through Detroit, Toledo, Cincinnati, and Lexington, Kentucky, to Knoxville, Tennessee. Then go east on I-40 for about 25 miles to US 66; take it south to US 441. This is the way to the northern entrance of Great Smoky and the resort towns of Gatlinburg, Pigeon Forge, and Sevierville.

From the West, motorists arrive via I-40, which enters Tennessee from Arkansas at Memphis, and crosses the center of the state through Nashville and Knoxville.

From the South.　　From New Orleans and the Deep South, take I-59 northeast through Birmingham, Alabama, to Chattanooga, Tennessee. Then pick up I-75 north to Oak Ridge, where it merges with I-40; go east and take US 66 to the northern entrance of Great Smoky. If you're heading for the southern entrance of the park or Asheville on I-59, take US 64 east in Cleveland, Tennessee. In Murphy, North Carolina, go north on US 19/74 to Cherokee.

Drivers from Atlanta, the southeast coast, or Florida can take US 441 from I-85 out of Atlanta and head north to Cherokee and the southern entrance to the national park. From Charleston, South Carolina, take I-26 north through Columbia, South Carolina, and Hendersonville, North Carolina, to I-40 and go west.

From the East and Northeast. Vacationers driving south from the mid-Atlantic states, New York, and New England have two choices: I-95 or I-81, both of which link up with I-40, the highway that passes just to the north of Great Smoky.

From Richmond, Virginia, and points north along the Atlantic Seaboard, take I-95 south to I-85 south in Petersburg, Virginia (a few miles below Richmond), which links up with I-40 near Durham, North Carolina; from there, drive west on I-40 to Asheville. If your destination is the southern entrance to Great Smoky at Cherokee, take US 74/23 south in Asheville; continue west on I-40 into Tennessee to reach the Gatlinburg entrance to the park.

The other option, usually better for people who live away from the coast, is I-81, which starts in upstate New York and goes south through Harrisburg, Pennsylvania. It passes through Maryland near Hagerstown and heads along the western side of the Blue Ridge Mountains in Virginia's Shenandoah Valley.

Then the highway enters Tennessee at Bristol and ends at I-40, about 40 miles east of Knoxville. If your destination is Asheville or the southern entrance to Great Smoky, go east on I-40; if you're heading to Gatlinburg and the northern entrance, head west to US 66.

By Plane

McGhee Tyson Airport. The nearest major airport to Great Smoky, McGhee Tyson is located 45 miles west of Gatlinburg between Knoxville and Alcoa, Tennessee. It's the most convenient airport if your destination is east Tennessee or the northern entrance to Great Smoky at Gatlinburg. Airlines serving the airport include Delta, United, and Comair.

Shuttle service between Gatlinburg and McGhee Tyson is available through **Smoky Mountain Tours.** One-way service is $50 for the first person and $5 for each additional person (up to 47 total). The service is available by reservation only; call (800) 962-0448 a week in advance.

Asheville Regional Airport. Located about 60 miles east of Great Smoky, this airport serves the small cities of Asheville and Hendersonville. It's a small, modern airport that gets visitors to their rental car ten minutes after getting off the plane.

The airport is served by USAir and Delta air lines; travelers on American Airlines can connect through American Eagle. Two regional carriers, Atlantic Southeast Airlines and Comair, also fly into Asheville.

—— The Blue Ridge Mountains

By Car

Like the Smokies, the Blue Ridge Mountains are mainly a driving destination. Here's a south-to-north description of major routes leading to the mountains.

Drivers from the South can take I-40 to Asheville from the east or the west to pick up the Blue Ridge Parkway, which follows the crest of the mountain chain. Vacationers coming from eastern Ohio and West Virginia should get on I-77, which passes through Charleston, West Virginia, and crosses I-81 and the Blue Ridge Mountains below Roanoke, Virginia, in the Shenandoah Valley. Drivers from Pittsburgh and points west can pick up I-68 in Morgantown, West Virginia, go east, and then get on I-81 south near Hagerstown, Maryland.

Travelers from Richmond, Virginia, can head west on I-64 to reach the mountains at Waynesboro; day-trippers from Washington, D.C., and its suburbs should go west on I-66 and enter Shenandoah National Park in Front Royal, Virginia.

From the North. Visitors coming from Baltimore and other points up the Atlantic Seaboard can circumvent Washington's notoriously congested traffic by taking I-70 west from I-695, Baltimore's Beltway. Get on I-695 north of Baltimore (before the Baltimore Harbor Tunnel) and go west toward Towson to reach I-70.

While I-70 links up with I-81 in Hagerstown, drivers headed for Skyline Drive and points south can save a few miles by taking this scenic shortcut that knocks about 25 miles off the trip to Winchester, Virginia, where I-81 enters the Shenandoah Valley.

On I-70 in Frederick, take the US 15 south exit toward Harpers Ferry and Charles Town, West Virginia. When US 15 goes left toward Leesburg, Virginia, continue straight on US 340. Cross the Potomac River into Virginia, go through Harpers Ferry, and then turn right onto the US 340 bypass around Charles Town.

Continue south on US 340 toward Berryville, Virginia. Just before reaching Berryville, go west on VA 7 toward Winchester. I-81 is another 10 miles on this four-lane, dual highway. If you're heading for Front Royal and Skyline Drive, continue straight on US 340 through Berryville.

By Plane

Charlottesville-Albemarle Airport. Located eight miles south of Charlottesville, this facility is served by several major airlines: American Eagle, Comair, The Delta Connection, United Express, and USAir Express. More than 30 departures a day connect travelers with six major hub airports: Raleigh/Durham, Charlotte, Pittsburgh, Greater Northern Kentucky/Cincinnati, Baltimore/Washington International, and National and Dulles airports outside Washington, D.C. USAir Express also provides daily nonstop service to New York's LaGuardia Airport.

The 60,000-square-foot terminal has six gates, a 500-space daily parking area, and a 61-space hourly parking area. Car rental agencies include Avis, Budget, and Hertz.

Roanoke Regional Airport. Located three miles north of the city, just off I-81, this new, $25 million terminal is served by USAir, USAir Express, United Express/Air Wisconsin, Comair, The Delta Connection, The Delta Connection/Atlantic Southeast Airlines, and Nashville Eagle. More than 50 departures a day connect Roanoke with 12 major hub cities with direct or nonstop service to 27 cities.

Car rental agencies include Avis, Dollar, Hertz, and National. A number of local hotels provide free courtesy shuttles to and from their properties.

Dulles International Airport. This major international airport is about 40 miles from the mountains in the rolling Virginia countryside outside Washington, D.C. and is a good jumping-off point for people heading to Front Royal, Shenandoah National Park, and Skyline Drive.

By Train

Amtrak provides daily service to Charlottesville, Virginia, from Washington, D.C.'s Union Station. In addition, service three times a week is available to Clifton Forge, Virginia, with connecting bus service to Roanoke.

Getting Around

—— *Great Smoky Mountains National Park*

US 441

The main road in Great Smoky is US 441, known inside the park as Newfound Gap Road. It's a high mountain highway closed to commercial traffic that cuts across the ridge near the center of the park and provides travelers with outstanding views—and slow-moving, bumper-to-bumper traffic in the summer and fall. The presence of the two-lane federal highway that bisects Great Smoky also explains why there's no admission charge to the park.

Both tourists and other folks traveling between Gatlinburg, Tennessee (the northern entrance to Great Smoky), and Cherokee, North Carolina (the southern entrance), use the road; it's a 33-mile drive across the park that crests midway at Newfound Gap, where there's a huge overlook. On weekends and during the summer and fall, go early in the morning to avoid the worst of the traffic.

The Gatlinburg Bypass lets travelers in a hurry get around congested US 441 in downtown Gatlinburg. This scenic drive starts near the park's northern border and bypasses the town to the west, rejoining US 441 between Gatlinburg and Pigeon Forge. More of a parkway than bypass, the road has several scenic overlooks with terrific vistas of the mountains.

Other Routes Through—and Around—Great Smoky

Interstate 40 is the major highway connecting east Tennessee and the mountains of North Carolina as it loops over the northern boundary of Great Smoky. While this part of I-40 is a scenic stretch of highway, vacationers can explore roads much more interesting that will get them through—and around—the park.

At the Sugarlands Visitor Center (just inside the northern entrance of Great Smoky near Gatlinburg), Little River Road connects Newfound Gap Road (US 441) and Cades Cove, a popular tourist destination inside the park about 20 miles away.

Another alternative for reaching Cades Cove is US 321 out of Pigeon Forge. This pleasant road heads to Townsend and the western entrance to the park that leads to Cades Cove, which features a visitor center (open from mid-April through October), camping, horseback riding, bike riding, and other outdoor activities.

Between Townsend and Maryville, the Foothills Parkway is a scenic road that swings south around the western edge of the park toward North Carolina. At Chilhowee, the parkway connects with US 129 (which leads to Robbinsville, North Carolina, and the Joyce Kilmer Memorial Forest) and Route 28 (the road to Fontana Dam, Fontana Village, and Bryson City, North Carolina). All the routes are spectacularly scenic—and lightly traveled.

From Cherokee, North Carolina, near the southern entrance to Great Smoky, US 19 goes east to Maggie Valley (just after the highway crosses the Blue Ridge Parkway). In Dellwood, US 276 goes north to I-40, where you can take the interstate west to another small section of the Foothills Parkway. Then take US 321 at Cosby, which follows the northern boundary of Great Smoky to Gatlinburg.

—— *East Tennessee*

The major route paralleling Great Smoky and Cherokee National Forest is US 411, which intersects US 441 in Sevierville (one of three resort towns outside the northern entrance to the national park). The road goes southwest through Maryville, Madisonville, Etowah, and Ocoee, and provides a number of jumping-off points into the national forest to the east.

This is the route to take for whitewater boaters and rafters, hikers, mountain bikers, and other outdoor enthusiasts heading to Tellico Plains, the Hiwassee River, the Ocoee River, and other destinations in Cherokee National Forest. For a more scenic drive, pick up Route 68 in Madisonville and follow it south through the national forest to Ducktown and US 64.

—— Northeast Georgia and Northwest South Carolina

In Copperhill, Route 60 goes south into Georgia, where drivers in search of more great scenery can take US 76 east to Blairsville. The road continues north and east through Hiawassee, then drops south over the crest of the Blue Ridge Mountains to Clayton through Chattahoochee National Forest. US 76 continues east into Westminster, South Carolina.

Take US 23 north in Clayton to Franklin, North Carolina. If your destination is Highlands or Cashiers, however, turn right off US 23 onto GA 246, which turns into NC 106, a scenic, windy road through Nantahala National Forest.

—— Southwest North Carolina

US 64 is the major road connecting southeast Tennessee to the southwest corner of North Carolina as it follows the Ocoee River east. It's a spectacularly scenic drive along a road that's crowded with river outfitters—and not much else.

The highway continues east to Murphy, North Carolina, where you can pick up US 74/19 and go north toward Andrews, Bryson City, Cherokee, Maggie Valley, and Asheville. Or continue straight on US 64 for more high mountain scenery as the highway passes through Nantahala National Forest, and past Chatuge Lake and the Southern Nantahala Wilderness on its way to Franklin.

Past Franklin, US 64 swings southeast to Highlands; the scenery just doesn't let up on this spectacular highway. In Highlands, NC 28 goes south and nips Georgia, then passes into South Carolina. US 64 swings east to Cashiers, Brevard, and Hendersonville, where it intersects with I-26.

—— Asheville

The main road linking Asheville and the southwestern corner of North Carolina below Great Smoky is US 74, a four-lane highway that merges with US 19 near Bryson City. It's a fast, modern road that's not only scenic, but a timesaver for travelers heading to the outdoor recreation mecca of Nantahala National Forest.

A slower route that's lined with cheesy souvenir stands and roadside amusements is US 19 between Asheville and Cherokee; it's a nostalgia trip for folks 40 and older that's reminiscent of motor touring in the 50s. The road passes through Maggie Valley, the location of several ski resorts and Ghost Town in the Sky, an amusement park on top of a mountain.

I-40 is the main transportation artery for Asheville. In addition, the Blue Ridge Parkway winds its way south of town before passing to the northeast between Asheville and Black Mountain to the east. US 74 heads southeast toward Chimney Rock and Lake Lure; from there, US 64 goes west toward Hendersonville and Brevard.

—— *The Blue Ridge Mountains of North Carolina*

US 19 heads north out of Asheville, then swings northeast through Burnsville, Spruce Pine, Banner Elk, and Boone; it's a pretty drive that parallels the Blue Ridge Parkway. On the other side of the ridge, US 221 connects Little Switzerland, Linville Falls, and Linville before reaching the college town of Boone.

North of Boone, NC 194 goes to Jefferson and West Jefferson through rolling—and gorgeous—countryside. US 221 meets US 21 at Twin Oaks, where drivers can head south to pick up the Blue Ridge Parkway and, a little farther on, I-77.

—— *Virginia*

The Blue Ridge Parkway

Heading north out of North Carolina into Virginia on the Blue Ridge Parkway, drivers cross I-77, which connects Charleston, West Virginia, and Charlotte, North Carolina; I-81, which runs up the center of Virginia's Shenandoah Valley, is about 10 miles north on I-77.

The Parkway continues northeast to Roanoke, paralleling I-81 on the valley below. This is a quiet, less-visited stretch of the Blue Ridge Parkway that features views of farms as well as mountains.

The Parkway crosses many small state roads that can be used to create loops for scenic drives—or to simply get off the ridge. North of Roanoke, VA 130 goes to Natural Bridge, one of the Seven Natural Wonders of the World. Near Lexington, VA 56 is a steep road that drops to Steeles Tavern, site of the Cyrus McCormick Farm, and close to I-81. VA 664 descends to Lake Sherando, a national forest recreation area with swimming, fishing, and camping.

On its way to Waynesboro, the Parkway intersects US 220, US 460, and US 60. It ends at Waynesboro, where I-64, US 250, and Skyline Drive converge. Charlottesville is about 20 miles east on I-64; Staunton (pronounced "Stanton") and I-81 are about 15 miles to the west.

Skyline Drive

Continuing north on the crest of the Blue Ridge is Skyline Drive, which differs from the Blue Ridge Parkway in several ways: It's a toll road ($5 per car, good for five days) that bisects long, but narrow, Shenandoah National Park. Furthermore, access is limited to four entrance stations: Rockfish Gap (I-64 and Waynesboro), Swift Run Gap (US 33), Thornton Gap (US 211), and Front Royal (I-66, the highway that links I-81 with I-495, Washington's Capital Beltway).

The 105-mile-long Skyline Drive provides easy access to most park sights and services. Mile markers on the west side of the road help locate park facilities, services, and points of interest. During the winter, the road may be closed temporarily in bad weather.

I-81

Travelers interested in getting from one end of the Blue Ridge Mountains to the other in a hurry should get off the Blue Ridge Parkway or Skyline Drive and drive a few miles west to the Shenandoah Valley and get on I-81.

Other roads in the Shenandoah Valley that parallel the Blue Ridge are US 340 (between Front Royal and Staunton) and US 11 (which follows the interstate along its entire route through the valley). To the east of the mountains, US 29 parallels the Blue Ridge from Warrenton to Lynchburg.

Tips for Disabled Travelers

Visitors to Great Smoky and Shenandoah national parks with disabilities will find activities and facilities that are fully accessible. Printed scripts of slide presentations are available for hearing-impaired visitors, and park-orientation audio cassettes for visually impaired visitors are available at most visitor centers. Disabled parking permits can be picked up at visitor centers and ranger stations.

—— Great Smoky

At Great Smoky (Zone 1), the Oconaluftee Visitor Center and Sugarlands Visitor Center are wheelchair accessible. The rest rooms at Cades Cove, Oconaluftee, and Sugarlands visitor centers are wheelchair accessible with assistance. Additional accessible rest rooms are at the Chimney Tops, Cosby, and Mingus Mill picnic areas.

Wheelchair-accessible picnic sites are available at Chimney Tops (two sites) and Cosby Picnic Area (one site). Visitors in wheelchairs who want to explore trails should head for walks near Oconaluftee, Cades Cove, and Sugarlands, which feature walks that are relatively flat and paved.

—— Shenandoah

At Shenandoah (Zone 8), most park rest rooms and buildings are wheelchair accessible, or accessible with help. Skyland and Big Meadow lodges, the three campgrounds, and the seven picnic grounds are wheelchair accessible, as are the concession-operated hot showers at Big Meadows Campground.

Interpretive guide booklets and signs make the five self-guided nature trails in Shenandoah accessible for hearing-impaired visitors.

A voice/TDD phone is available at Byrd Visitor Center (milepost 51 along Skyline Drive).

Sight-impaired visitors can pick up taped narrations of the *Park Folder,* information on the park, a history handout, two nature trail booklets, and a bird identification guide; all are available for loan with a tape recorder at visitor centers. The handout and booklets also are available in Braille.

—— National Forests

Like the national parks, national forests offer facilities to aid disabled visitors. In many cases, the Forest Service is attempting to provide universal access that allows all people to use the same walkways, entrances, fountains, phones, and rest rooms.

George Washington National Forest in Virginia (Zone 8), for example, provides guide ropes and Braille interpretive signs on its Lion's Tail Trail near the forest's Massanutten Visitors Center on US 211, three miles east of New Market. Anglers can take a level, paved trail to a wooden fishing pier at Bealer's Pond, off VA 684, nine miles north of Luray. Elkhorn Lake near Bridgewater boasts three barrier-free piers for handicapped visitors who enjoy fishing.

Visitors interested in access for the handicapped should contact the appropriate District Ranger Office in each national forest for details about specific areas they want to visit; see pages 103–104 for a list of addresses and phone numbers of the national forest headquarters in the Smoky and Blue Ridge mountains.

Medical Emergencies

—— Great Smoky

First aid facilities are available at park headquarters and visitor centers. Medical emergency services are available at the following hospitals: **Sevier County Hospital** (Zone 2), located on Middle Creek Road in Sevierville, Tennessee (15 miles north of Gatlinburg), phone (615) 453-7111; **Blount Memorial Hospital** (Zone 3) on US 321 in Maryville, Tennessee (25 miles north of Cades Cove), phone (615) 983-7211; and **Swain County Hospital** (Zone 4) in Bryson City, North Carolina (10 miles southeast of Oconaluftee Visitor Center), phone (704) 488-2155.

—— Shenandoah and Virginia's Blue Ridge

The nearest hospital to Shenandoah National Park's northern section is in Front Royal at **Warren Memorial Hospital**, three miles north of the north entrance station, phone (703) 636-0300. The closest medical assistance to the central section is in Luray, 10 miles west of the Thornton Gap Entrance Station on US 211. The closest medical help to the southern section is in Waynesboro, at the **Augusta Medical Center** (between Staunton and Waynesboro in Fishersville), phone (703) 942-2273; and in Charlottesville, at the **University of Virginia Medical Center,** phone (804) 924-0211. Emergency first-aid help is available at all visitor centers and ranger stations throughout the park.

Below Shenandoah National Park and close to the Blue Ridge Parkway are the following hospitals: **Stonewall Jackson Hospital** in Lexington, (703) 463-9141; and the **Roanoke Memorial Hospital,** (703) 981-7000. Both feature 24-hour emergency service.

Publications for Visitors

No major metropolitan newspapers are published in the Smoky and Blue Ridge mountains. But a wide range of free weekly and monthly newspapers and magazines feature information on motels, restaurants, attractions, and outdoor recreation opportunities.

The Parkway Milepost is a tabloid newspaper offering information on the cultural and natural history of the Blue Ridge Parkway and the surrounding region. The paper is distributed free to Parkway visitors. An annual subscription is available by contributing $15 or more to the Friends of the Blue Ridge Parkway, Inc., P.O. Box 341, Hendersonville Road, Arden, North Carolina 28704; phone (800) 228-PARK.

The Blue Ridge Digest is a tabloid newspaper published quarterly and covers the entire Smoky and Blue Ridge mountains area. Maps, tourist information agencies, toll-free numbers, seasonal calendars of events, and feature articles on the area are included in each issue. The paper is distributed free and is available by subscription from The Blue Ridge Digest Publishing Co., P.O. Box 40, Clyde, North Carolina 28721; phone (704) 627-1344. Annual rates are $8 U.S., $10 Canadian, and $12 foreign for four issues.

Touring East Tennessee is a quarterly tabloid newspaper featuring information on parks, attractions, motels, stores, resorts, and restaurants in the mountains bordering Great Smoky. One-year subscriptions are $8. Call or write: Greeneville Publishing Co., P.O. Box 1630, Greeneville, Tennessee 37744; phone (615) 638-4181.

The Mountain Review is a magazine covering the Georgia mountains that features a calendar of events, a centerfold map, points of interest, information on retirement life, and a business and service directory. The magazine is published eight times a year; an annual subscription is $12. Send a check to: Mountain Review, P.O. Box E, Mountain City, Georgia 30562.

The Lantern is a weekly tabloid newspaper published in Copperhill, Tennessee, and serves communities in northern Georgia, southwestern North Carolina, and southeastern Tennessee. Subscriptions are $5 (12 issues), $10 (24 issues), and $18 (48 issues). Send a check to: The Lantern, P.O. Box 873, Copperhill, Tennessee 37317-0873.

Adventure in the Smokies is a monthly tabloid guide for visitors to the Great Smoky Mountains of North Carolina published during the summer and winter travel seasons. The paper concentrates on outdoor recreation, including fishing, horseback riding, crafts, and hiking, and is distributed free throughout western North Carolina. To get a copy, call or write: The Mountaineer, P.O. Box 129, Waynesville, North Carolina 28786; phone (704) 452-0661.

V Magazine covers the art, club, and restaurant scene in Roanoke, Virginia, and throughout the Shenandoah Valley and central Virginia. Each issue includes a restaurant listing, events calendar, and book reviews. Distributed throughout Virginia; free.

Smokies Guide is a free newspaper for visitors to Great Smoky Mountains National Park. It features seasonal information on National Park Service naturalist walks, programs, and other activities. The paper is available at park entrance stations, visitor centers, and campgrounds.

Shenandoah Overlook provides visitors to Shenandoah National Park with seasonal information about various activities. Free copies of the newspaper are available at all ranger stations and visitor centers in the park.

How to Avoid Crime and Keep Safe in Public Places

—— Crime in the Mountains

Some people heave a sigh of relief when entering the Smoky and Blue Ridge mountains—and it's not just because of stunning alpine vistas and fresh mountain air. Deep forests and endless views give the reassurance they've entered a part of the world where crime isn't an overbearing concern.

And they're right. By and large, you *do* leave behind a world of senseless crime upon entering the mountains—at least, personal crimes of violence. Getting mugged, shot, kidnapped, raped, or murdered is highly unlikely for visitors to the Southern Appalachians. In Gatlinburg, for example, where the annual visitor count runs into the millions, there has not been a homicide for more than nine years.

Great Smoky

Yet crime happens everywhere—even here. Drunk drivers, for example, are a constant threat on the highways. But the biggest danger that visitors face while vacationing in Great Smoky Mountains National Park is car theft: This is a drive-through park and much of the flotsam cruising US 441 is looking for cars to steal or rob.

"Most crimes committed in Great Smoky Mountains National Park are property crimes—the breaking and entering of vehicles and auto theft," reports Bill Acree, a criminal investigator at Great Smoky Mountains National Park.

How to Protect Your Car from Getting Stolen. "To avoid having your car stolen, don't park it in peripheral areas of the park, such as highways along the borders, like Highway 32 [near the northern-most end of the park near I-40]," Acree says. "Go to designated parking areas inside the park. Otherwise, you're leaving your car where it's ripe for the picking."

No matter where you leave your car, Acree says, the steps to avoid having your car ripped off in Great Smoky are no different than those in large cities. "Don't leave anything of value in the car, and if possible, you'll have an alarm—though it may not help if no one can hear it," Acree notes. "Also, a disconnect switch that kills the ignition helps. If you can't afford an alarm system, at least put one of those stickers on the window of your car that says you've got an alarm. It's cheap."

Preventing Car Break-Ins.   To avoid having your car broken into, Acree says, follow this simple rule: Don't leave anything of value in your car when you leave it at an overlook or trail head.

"Or at the very least take your wallet or billfold," Acree adds. "If a woman doesn't want to carry her purse on a hike—most don't—then take out the wallet and any jewelry and carry it in a fanny pack. When you have to replace all your personal ID, it's a pain."

Hide anything of value that you can't take with you in the trunk. "But put it there before you get to the area where you're leaving the car," Acree adds. "Thieves sit in their cars and watch people in parking lots throwing stuff into the trunk. So put it in before you get to where you're going."

More advice: Don't leave your car keys on top of the rear tire or under the bumper. "That's naive," Acree says. "Take your keys and anything of value with you. Pros go for cash, credit cards, bank-teller cards, expensive cameras, and loaded guns—which, by the way, are illegal inside the park."

Finally, remember that the most sophisticated alarm system won't work if a crook is really determined to get inside your car. "It only takes a big rock to break a window—and we have a lot of big rocks," the investigator notes wryly.

Report Any Problems.   In 1993, Great Smoky Mountains National Park reported 152 car break-ins and six auto thefts. But about half the break-ins go unreported, Acree estimates. "If your vehicle is broken into, report it as soon as possible," Investigator Acree advises. "Quite often we can get at least part of your stuff back. We make a number of arrests for break-ins and often find some of the stuff on the side of the road."

Shenandoah

Criminal Investigator Glen Knight at Shenandoah National Park reports that the number one problem is theft from vehicles—and that some people inadvertently ask for trouble.

"A lot of times folks out on overnight trips in the park will leave notes on their cars saying that they'll be back in a few days," Knight says. "It's not a good idea. It's an open invitation that the vehicle isn't occupied. Instead, get a back-country camping permit and we'll know where to find you if you're not back on schedule."

More advice to hikers and backpackers who park on the periphery of Shenandoah: "Use common sense when deciding where to put your car," Knight advises. "Don't trespass on private property. Some of the locals can get pretty testy. It may be your first visit to the park, but some of the landowners over the years have put up with hundreds of people who trespass—and they get sick and tired of it."

Outside the Parks

Outside the park, motel and car break-ins lead the crime list. "It happens, but it's not a big problem," reports Captain Randy Bracken of the Gatlinburg police. But it's still a good idea to leave valuables in the motel safe or take them with you when you go out, he adds.

"And don't leave valuables in mountain chalets and cabins, which usually are isolated," Bracken advises. "We've had reports of valuables, such as expensive jewelry, stolen from them. When that happens, I think to myself, 'Why did they even bring it?'"

The moral: Don't. Leave expensive items such as jewelry at home (preferably in a bank's safe deposit box), and you won't have to worry about theft from your motel room or car while you're vacationing in the mountains.

—— Having a Plan to Avoid Street Crime

Acree says muggings are rare in the park. "Use common sense, but it's not like in an inner city here—we don't have any alleys," the investigator notes. But, he adds, random violence and street crime are facts of life everywhere.

You've got to be cautious and alert, and plan ahead. Police are rarely able to actually foil a crime in progress. When you are out and about, use caution because you are on your own; if you run into trouble, it's unlikely that police or anyone else will be able to come to your rescue. You must give some advance thought to the ugly scenarios that might occur, and consider both preventive measures that will keep you out of harm's way, and an escape plan just in case.

Not being a victim of street crime is sort of a survival of the fittest thing. Just as a lion stalks the weakest member of the antelope herd, muggers and thieves target the easiest victims. Simply put, no matter where you are or what you are doing, you want potential felons to think of you as a bad risk.

On the Street. For starters, you always present less of an appealing target if you're with other people. Secondly, if you must be out alone, act alert and always have at least one of your arms and hands free. Felons gravitate toward preoccupied folks, the kind found plodding along staring at the sidewalk, with both arms encumbered by briefcases or packages. Visible jewelry (on either men or women) attracts the wrong kind of attention. Men, keep your billfolds in your *front* trouser or coat pocket, or in a fanny pack. Women, keep your purses tucked tightly under your arm; if you're wearing a jacket, put it on *over* your shoulder bag strap.

If You're Approached. Police will tell you that a felon has the least amount of control over his intended victim during the first few moments of his initial approach. A good strategy, therefore, is to short circuit the crime as quickly as possible. If a felon starts by demanding your money, for instance, quickly take out your billfold and hurl it in one direction while you run shouting for help in the opposite direction. The odds are greatly in your favor that the felon will prefer to collect your billfold rather than pursue you. If you hand over your wallet and just stand there, the felon likely will ask for your watch and jewelry next. If you're a woman, the longer you hang around, the greater your vulnerability to personal injury or rape.

Secondary Crime Scenes. Under no circumstances, police warn, should you ever allow yourself to be taken to another location—a "secondary crime scene" in police jargon. This move, they explain, provides the felon more privacy and, consequently, more control. A felon can rob you on the street quickly and efficiently. If he tries to remove you to another location, whether by car or on foot, it is a certain indication that he has more in mind than robbery. Even if the felon has a gun or knife, your chances are infinitely better running away. If the felon grabs your purse, let him have it. If he grabs your jacket, shed it. Hanging onto your money or jacket is not worth getting mugged, raped, or murdered.

Another maxim: Never believe anything a felon tells you, even if he's telling you something you desperately want to believe, for example, "I won't hurt you if you come with me." No matter how logical or benign he sounds, assume the worst. Always, always, break off contact as quickly as possible, even if that means running.

—— Personal Attitude

While some places are more dangerous than others, never assume that any area is completely safe. Never let down your guard. You can be the victim of a crime, and it can happen to you anywhere.

Never let your pride or sense of righteousness and indignation imperil your survival. This is especially difficult for many men, particularly for men in the presence of women. It makes no difference whether you are approached by an aggressive drunk or an actual felon, the rule is the same: Forget your pride and break off contact as quickly as possible. Who cares whether the drunk insulted you, if everyone ends up back at the hotel safe and sound? When you wake up in the hospital with a concussion and your jaw wired shut, it's too late to decide that the drunk's filthy remark wasn't really all that important.

Felons, druggies, and even some drunks play for keeps. They can attack with a bloodthirsty hostility and hellish abandon that is beyond the imagination of most people. Believe me, you are not in their league—nor do you want to be.

—— Self-Defense

In a situation where it is impossible to run, you'll need to be prepared to defend yourself. Most policemen insist that a gun or knife is not much use to the average person. More often than not, they say, the weapon will be turned against the victim. Also, concealed firearms and knives are illegal in most jurisdictions. The best self-defense device for the average person is Mace. Not only is it legal in most states, it is nonlethal and easy to use.

When you shop for Mace, look for two things: It should be able to fire about eight feet, and it should have a protector cap so it won't go off by mistake in your purse or pocket. Carefully read the directions that come with your device, paying particular attention to how it should be carried and stored and how long the active ingredients will remain potent. Wearing a rubber glove, test-fire your Mace, making sure that you fire downwind.

When you are out, make sure your Mace is someplace easily accessible, for example, attached to your keychain. If you are a woman and you keep your Mace on a keychain, avoid the habit of dropping your keys (and your Mace) into the bowels of your purse when you leave your hotel room or your car. *The Mace will not do you any good if you have to dig around in your purse for it.* Keep your keys and your Mace in your hand until you have reached your destination safely.

PART THREE: Hotels

Narrowing Your Choices

Lodging in the Smoky and Blue Ridge mountains runs the gamut from mammoth, full-service resorts, like the Grove Park Inn in Asheville (Zone 6), to small, rustic bed-and-breakfasts. There are dormitory accommodations for river runners, condos for families, and Alpinesque chalets for lovers. LeConte Lodge (Zone 1), a sort of motel for hikers, characterizes in many ways the quirkiness of accommodations in the mountains. Situated atop Mount LeConte, the only way to reach the hotel is by ascending the mountain on foot. Once you arrive, there are no showers or electricity, and worst of all, no bar. There are, however, magnificent sunsets, hearty meals, and all of the beauty and solitude a person could ever want. And, if this is not your gig, there is a perfectly good Holiday Inn at the foot of the mountain in Gatlinburg. That's the way it is in the mountains, a little something for everyone.

In the years before interstate highways, millions of midwesterners crossed the mountains on US 441, US 19, US 23, and US 25, among others, on their way to Florida. To accommodate these Yankee pilgrims, hundreds of mom-and-pop hotels blossomed along the primary routes south. By the time that most Florida traffic was circumventing the Smokies and Blue Ridge on the interstates, the mountains had become a vacation destination unto themselves. In every other part of the country, the major hotel chains edged privately owned hotels and motels into the annals of tourism history. In the southern mountains, however, the mom-and-pops hung on and survived, and continue to this day to be the area's largest supplier of hotel rooms. Guest houses, likewise, have endured and continue to thrive. Now restyled as bed-and-breakfasts, these most intimate of accommodations deliver southern hospitality at its best, allowing guests to slip back into a more relaxed, personal, and less standardized era of travel.

Finally, there are the mountain homes, cabins, and so-called chalets. These represent the answer to a growing tourist demand to retreat away from the busy highways to the solitude of the mountains.

This fastest growing segment of the lodging industry evolved from the practice of mountain property owners offering their homes for rent when they were not in residence. Today, the market has been usurped largely by developers who have dotted the peaks and valleys with cabins and houses built specifically for rental.

—— *Seasons*

Demand for accommodations in the Smoky and Blue Ridge mountains is predictable. Summer and the October fall color season are the busiest, most crowded times of year. Christmas, Easter, Thanksgiving, and other major holiday periods also are brisk. January and February are pretty dead except around ski areas, and some highways occasionally are closed due to snow or ice. The best months for small crowds, good weather, and bargain accommodations are September, mid-November, December before Christmas, and late March through May. Both the Smokies and the Blue Ridge are popular for weekend getaways; so regardless of the time of year, weekends are busier than weekdays.

When visiting the mountains, most visitors either drive their own cars or book a motorcoach tour. For those who enjoy group travel, motorcoach tours often offer both value and convenience. The downside of group touring, always, is the regimentation. If you are considering a motorcoach tour, first make sure the tour itinerary is consistent with your vacation agenda. Second, check the hotel the tour uses against the hotel ratings in this chapter. A tour packager's choice of hotels speaks volumes about the overall quality of the tour.

—— *Cabins, Chalets, and Condominiums*

Many motels and hotels in the mountains offer not-so-beautiful views of highways, parking lots, and goofy golf courses. While, of course, there are exceptions, we nevertheless recommend renting a cabin or chalet as the best way to enjoy the mountains. Many private cabins and chalets can be had for less than the price of a motel room, and include such amenities as full kitchens, decks, fireplaces, and even hot tubs. Most important, in our estimation, however, is that the cabins and chalets provide exactly the kind of quiet, solitude, and remote beauty that most people come to the mountains to experience.

During our research for this guide, we asked a Gatlinburg real estate agent to explain the different types of rental properties. "Well," he said, "you got your log cabins and you got your chalets. Do you know what a log cabin is? Good. If it ain't a log cabin, then it's a chalet." That pretty well sums it up. A log cabin is a log cabin, but a chalet could be anything. We saw everything from small, A-frame structures to huge, four-bedroom luxury homes: all chalets.

There are also, of course, condominiums. Where cabins and chalets are free-standing structures, condominiums usually are part of a large development and almost always share a common wall with adjoining units on either side. Many condos, however, offer the same features as the chalets and cabins. While cabins and chalets usually do not offer swimming pools, condominium complexes frequently do.

The way to go about renting a cabin, chalet, or condo is to make a list of features that are important to you. How many beds, bedrooms, and baths do you require? Do you need a full kitchen? When you get your list together, call a rental agency and order your cabin or chalet like you would order a pizza. We phoned a Gatlinburg agency and said, "We want a two-bedroom, two-bath cabin for four adults. We prefer to be high on the mountain, with a good view, in a remote quiet area. We don't care about a hot tub, but we do want a fireplace and a nice big deck."

Whether you get what you want depends on how far in advance you make your reservation, the time of year you want to visit, what you are willing to spend, and what area of the mountains you want to visit. The largest selection of cabins and chalets by far is in the Gatlinburg, Pigeon Forge, Townsend (Zone 2) area, just north of the Great Smoky Mountains National Park. In this area, with advance planning, you can find almost any combination of features. In other areas of the Smokies and Blue Ridge the selection is much more limited. For condominiums, Zones 2, 5 (Highlands and Cashiers, North Carolina), and Zone 6 (Asheville, North Carolina) offer the best selection.

When you have figured out what type of accommodation you need, where in the Smokies or Blue Ridge you want to be, and when you want to go, then you can start shopping. Except in Zone 2 (the Gatlinburg area), initiate your search by calling the local chamber of commerce or tourist information office at your chosen destination (numbers listed on pages 101–103). Information operators will provide you with the names and phone numbers of local area agencies and real estate agents that rent the kind of accommodation you are looking for. If you are interested in the Gatlinburg area, obtain a copy of the *Vacation Rental Guide of the Smokies* by writing:

Rental Guide Magazine
Attention: Sales Office
P.O. Box 5018
Tallahassee, FL 32314-9959

The guide contains 80 pages of rental listings including photographs of many of the cabins, condos, and chalets, as well as descriptions of amenities.

When you talk with a rental agent about a particular cabin, chalet, or condo, ask how old the property is. If its older than five or six years, ask if it has been renovated recently. If the property sounds appealing, request that you be mailed photos of both the exterior and interior. Color is better than black and white, but either will do. Some agents have only one set of color photos. If this is the case, suggest that the agent send black and white or color photocopies. Write off any agent that will not supply some sort of photograph. Never reserve a property strictly on the basis of a rendering, sketch, or line drawing. Insist on a photograph. As an aside, be aware that many mountain chalets, cabins, and condos, while beautiful outside, offer interiors that range from truly tasteless to absolutely bewildering. Country Bordello, Elvis Museum, and Honeymoon Hearts and Ruffles are but three of the major decorating styles alive and well in mountain rental properties.

Once you have found a suitable property, you usually will have to prepay two nights with a credit card or check. Some agencies will mail you a rental contract to sign and return, while others will process the whole deal over the phone. Cancellation policies vary, so be sure to inquire.

During the summer, October, and holidays, because demand is greater than supply, you usually will have to pay the agency's asking price for your cabin, chalet, or condo. Other times of year (except for rentals located near ski resorts in January and February), there is usually room for some negotiation. We have seen rates for small chalets as low as $45 a night, but this is unusual. Couples should expect to pay $85–150 a night in season. For comparison purposes, the average rate for a hotel room in the Gatlinburg area (Zone 2) is $69 a night.

Some agencies charge a set price for the rental property, while others charge on a per-head basis for the number of persons accommodated. The real savings on chalets, cabins, and condos occur when two or more couples share a property. Likewise, families that require more than one motel room also can save financially by renting a house or condo. Additional savings can be realized by using your rental house kitchen facilities to eat in rather than going to restaurants.

Particularly during the busier times of year, agencies require a seven-day minimum rental. We were able to work around the minimum, however, by finding properties with two, three, and four days gaps between renters. We found a two-bedroom cabin, for example, that was reserved from June 10 through June 16, and from June 20 to June 26. The agency was more than happy to rent us the cabin for the short intervening period (June 17–19). Reservation gaps, as well as cancellations, are common, but unpredictable. You have to call around and ask the right questions to uncover the deals.

The better cabins, chalets, and condos are reserved well in advance. Some renters sign up for next year during this year's stay. The farther ahead you plan, therefore, the better your chances of getting what you want.

Once the reservation is made, most agents will provide written confirmation. If written confirmation is not routinely provided, ask for it. Along with your confirmation, the agent also will provide directions to the rental office. Most rental offices operate seven days a week during the warm weather months. Here, you will register, pick up your keys, and be given directions to your rental unit. Once in your cabin, chalet, or condo, check to make sure that everything is in order. If there is a problem, most agencies offer 24-hour maintenance service.

The majority of area cabins, chalets, and condos that rent to visitors also work with travel agents. In many cases, the condo owners pay an enhanced commission to agents who rent the units for reduced consumer rates. It's worth a call to your travel agent.

Another good source of information is the book *Condo & Villa Vacations Rated,* by Clinton and Ellen Burr, published by Prentice Hall Travel. Recently updated, the $17 guide describes and rates the better condos and time-shares in the mountains of Georgia, North Carolina, and Tennessee.

—— *Bed-and-Breakfasts and Country Inns*

Many travelers think of B&Bs as a low cost lodging option. In New York or San Francisco that may be true, but in the Smokies and Blue Ridge, bed-and-breakfasts are often the *crème de la crème*. Each guest room is individually and lovingly decorated. Often furnished with antiques, B&B guest rooms are among the most tasteful and luxurious in the mountains. Private baths are the rule, rather than the exception. Most B&Bs are off the beaten path, situated on lush mountain hillsides or in quiet river valleys. Romantic and peaceful, B&Bs in the Smoky and Blue Ridge mountains offer a lodging alternative based on personal service and southern hospitality that transcends the sterile, predictable product of chain hotels.

Bed-and-breakfasts are quirky. Most, but not all, B&Bs are open year-round. Some only accept cash or personal checks, while others take all major credit cards. Not all rooms come with private baths. Some rooms with private baths may have a tub, but not a shower, or vice versa. Some allow children, but not pets; at others, pets but not children. Many B&Bs provide only the most basic breakfast, while some provide a sumptuous morning feast. Still others offer three meals a day. Most B&Bs are not wheelchair accessible, but it never hurts to ask.

Because staying at a B&B is like visiting someone in their home, reservations are recommended, though B&Bs with more than ten rooms usually welcome walk-ins.

To help you sort out your B&B options, we recommend the following guides. Updated regularly, these books describe B&Bs in more detail than is possible in the *Unofficial Guide.*

Inspected, Rated, and Approved, Bed & Breakfasts and Country Inns, by Sarah W. Sonke, published by the American Bed & Breakfast Association. Covers the entire United States. To order, phone (804) 379-2222.

Bed & Breakfasts-Country Inns, The Official Guide to American Historic Inns, by Tim and Deborah Sakach, published by American Historic Inns, Inc. Covers the entire United States. To order, phone (714) 496-6953.

Recommended Country Inns, The South, by Sara Pitzer, published by the Globe Pequot Press. Covers Alabama,

Kentucky, North Carolina, Florida, Arkansas, Louisiana, South Carolina, Georgia, Mississippi, and Tennessee. To order, phone (800) 243-0495.

Recommended Country Inns, Mid-Atlantic and Chesapeake Region, by Brenda Boelts Chapin, published by the Globe Pequot Press. Covers Virginia, Delaware, Maryland, Pennsylvania, New Jersey, New York, and West Virginia. To order, phone (800) 243-0495.

Listed below are some of the better B&Bs and country inns in the Smoky and Blue Ridge mountains. Because space limitations preclude describing each one, we suggest you call the number provided and request a copy of the B&B's promotional brochure. Many of the B&Bs listed also are described in the books referenced above.

Zone 1: Great Smoky Mountains National Park

LeConte Lodge, atop Mount LeConte: (615) 429-5704

Zone 2: The Northern Foothills of Tennessee

Gatlinburg, Tennessee

Buckhorn Inn: (615) 436-4468
Butcher House: (615) 436-9457

Pigeon Forge, Tennessee

Day Dreams Country Inn: (615) 428-0370

Sevierville, Tennessee

Blue Mountain Mist Country Inn: (615) 428-2335
Von-Bryan Inn: (615) 453-9832

Townsend, Tennessee

Richmont Inn: (615) 448-6751

Zone 3: The Southwest Foothills of Tennessee

Loudon, Tennessee

River Road Inn: (615) 458-4861

Zone 4: The Southern Foothills of North Carolina

Bryson City, North Carolina

Fisher House: (704) 497-5921
Peggy's Mountain Laurel B&B: (704) 488-2055
Randolf House: (704) 488-3472

Dillsboro, North Carolina

Jarrett House: (704) 586-9964

Franklin, North Carolina

Franklin Terrace B&B: (704) 524-7907
Heritage Inn B&B: (704) 524-4150

Wesser (Nantahala Gorge), North Carolina

Euchella Sport Lodge: (704) 488-8835

Zone 5: The Tri-State Mountains

Highlands, North Carolina

The Lodge: (704) 526-9644
Long House: (704) 526-4349
Olde Stone House: (704) 526-5911

Lake Toxaway, North Carolina

Greystone Inn: (704) 966-4700

Long Creek, South Carolina

River House: (803) 647-5336

Zone 6: Asheville and Brevard

Asheville, North Carolina

Aberdeen Inn: (704) 254-9336
Albemarle Inn: (704) 255-0027
Applewood Manor: (704) 254-2244

Cedar Crest: (704) 252-1389
Cornerstone Inn: (704) 253-5644
Flint Street Inns: (704) 253-6723
Reynolds Mansion: (704) 254-0496
Richmond Hill Inn: (704) 252-7313
Wright Inn: (704) 251-0789

Balsam, North Carolina

Balsam Mountain Inn: (704) 456-9298

Brevard, North Carolina

Inn at Brevard: (704) 884-2105
Folkestone Inn: (704) 488-2730

Clyde, North Carolina

Windsong Mountain Inn: (704) 627-6111

Flat Rock, North Carolina

Woodfield Inn: (704) 693-6016

Hendersonville, North Carolina

Claddagh Inn: (704) 697-7778
Waverly Inn: (704) 692-1090

Lake Junaluska, North Carolina

Providence Lodge: (704) 452-9588

Lake Lure, North Carolina

Lodge on Lake Lure: (704) 625-2789

Sylva, North Carolina

Mountain Brook: (704) 586-4329

Waynesville, North Carolina

Grandview Lodge: (704) 456-5212
Hallcrest Inn: (704) 456-6457
The Swag: (704) 926-0430

Zone 7: The Blue Ridge Mountains of North Carolina

Banner Elk, North Carolina

Archers Inn: (704) 898-9004

Boone, North Carolina

Mast Farm Inn at Valle Crucis: (704) 963-5857

Blowing Rock, North Carolina

Ragged Garden B&B: (704) 295-9703

Spruce Pine, North Carolina

The Fairway Inn: (704) 765-4917
Richmond Inn B&B: (704) 765-6993

Zone 8: The Blue Ridge Mountains of Virginia

Abingdon, Virginia

Victoria and Albert Inn: (703) 676-2797

Charlottesville, Virginia

Clifton Country Inn: (804) 971-1800
Prospect Hill Plantation: (800) 277-0844
Silver Thatch Inn: (804) 978-4686
Woodstock Hall: (804) 293-8977

Christiansburg, Virginia

The Oaks: (703) 381-1500

Flint Hill/Washington, Virginia

Caledonia Farm: (703) 675-3693

Harrisonburg, Virginia

Joshua Wilton House Inn: (703) 434-4464

Lexington, Virginia

Maple Hall: (703) 463-2044

Oak Spring Farm: (703) 377-2398

Millboro, Virginia

Fort Lewis Lodge: (703) 925-2314

Orange, Virginia

The Hidden Inn: (703) 672-3625
The Shadows B&B: (703) 672-5057
Willow Grove Inn: (703) 672-5982

Paris, Virginia

Ashby Inn: (703) 592-3900

Smith Mountain Lake, Virginia

The Manor at Taylor's Store: (703) 721-3951

Sperryville, Virginia

Conyers House: (703) 987-8025

Stanley, Virginia

Jordan Hollow Farm Inn: (703) 778-2285

Staunton, Virginia

Ashton Country House: (703) 885-7819
Belle Grae Inn: (703) 886-5151
Frederick House: (703) 885-4220
Sampson Eagon Inn: (703) 886-8200

Upperville, Virginia

1763 Inn: (703) 592-3848

Vesuvius, Virginia

Irish Gap Inn: (804) 922-7701

Warm Springs, Virginia

The Inn at Gristmill Square: (703) 839-2231
Meadow Lane Lodge: (703) 839-5959

Washington, Virginia

Blue Rock Inn: (703) 987-3190
The Inn at Little Washington: (703) 675-3800
Sycamore Hill: (703) 675-3046

Winchester/White Post, Virginia

L'Auberge Provencale: (703) 837-1375

Wintergreen, Virginia

Trillium House: (804) 325-9126

Woodstock, Virginia

The Inn at Narrow Passage: (703) 459-8000

Hotels and Motels: Getting a Good Deal on a Room

The first thing you need to know is that more than half of the hotels and motels in the mountains will not be found in Mobil, AAA, or bookstore-distributed travel guides. This is because, as mentioned earlier, many of the properties are small mom-and-pop operations. Most of these are older hotels and motels, and though clean and well maintained, offer smaller, less luxurious rooms. Even among newer properties, both proprietary and chain, the standard of quality in Smokies and Blue Ridge accommodations is generally below what you would find in major cities or other resort areas. This is because the mountains target primarily families and leisure travelers as opposed to convention and business travelers. It is no coincidence that the nicest hotels in the southern mountains, such as the Grove Park Inn in Asheville (Zone 6), also are important conference and meeting venues.

—— Beating Rack Rates

The benchmark for making cost comparisons is always the hotel's standard rate, or rack rate. This is what you would pay if, space available, you just walked in off the street and rented a room. In a way, the rack rate is analogous to an airline's standard coach fare. It represents a straight, nondiscounted room rate. In the mountains, you assume the rack rate is the most you should have to pay, and that with a little effort you ought to be able to do better.

To learn the standard room rate, call room reservations at the hotel(s) of your choice. Do not be surprised if there are several standard rates, one for each type of room in the hotel. Have the reservation clerk explain the difference in the types of rooms available in each price bracket. Also ask the hotel which of the described class of rooms you would get if you came on a wholesaler, tour operator, or motorcoach package. This information will allow you to make meaningful comparisons among various packages and rates.

—— *Helping Your Travel Agent Help You*

In general, travel agents cannot make much money selling trips to the Smokies or Blue Ridge. There are few air fare sales because most people travel to the mountains in their own car. For the same reason, there is not much business in car rentals. Unless the agent sells a motorcoach tour, a golf package, or the like, the agent essentially will be relegated to booking your lodging. Since the average stay in the mountains is short, this adds up to a lot of work for the agent with little potential for a worthwhile commission. Because an agent derives only a small return for booking travel to the Smokies and Blue Ridge, there isn't much incentive for the travel agent to become product knowledgeable.

Except for a handful of agents who sell southeastern mountain travel in volume (usually in the area's primary markets), there are comparatively few travel agents who know much about the Smokies and Blue Ridge. This lack of information translates into travelers not getting reservations at the more interesting hotels, paying more than is necessary, or being placed in out-of-the-way, or otherwise undesirable, lodging.

When you call your travel agent, ask if he or she has been to the Smokies or Blue Ridge. Firsthand experience is valuable. If the answer is no, be prepared to give your travel agent considerable direction. Do not accept any recommendations at face value. Check out the location and rates of any suggested hotel and make certain that the hotel is suited to your itinerary.

Because travel agents tend to be unfamiliar with the southeastern mountains, your agent may try to plug you into a motorcoach tour or some other preset package. This essentially allows the travel agent to set up your whole trip with a single phone call and still collect an 8–10% commission. The problem with this scenario is that most agents will place 90% of their mountain business with only one or two packagers or tour operators. In other words, it is the path of least resistance for them, and not much choice for you.

To help your travel agent get you the best possible deal, do the following:

1. Determine where you want to stay (what towns, areas), and if possible choose specific hotels. This can be accomplished by reviewing the hotel information provided in this guide, and by writing or calling hotels which interest you.

2. Check out the Smoky and Blue Ridge mountains travel ads in the Sunday travel section of your local newspaper and compare them to ads running in the newspapers of one of mountains' key markets. Key Markets for the Blue Ridge are Baltimore; Washington, D.C.; Richmond, Virginia; Raleigh and Charlotte, North Carolina; and Atlanta. Primary markets for the Smokies include Atlanta, Cincinnati, and Nashville. The southern Smokies (where Georgia, North Carolina, and South Carolina come together) target Atlanta and the larger cities of Florida. See if you can find some hotel discounts or packages that fit your plans and that include a hotel you like.

3. Call the packagers, hotels, or tour operators whose ads you have collected. Ask any questions you might have, but do not book your trip with them directly.

4. Tell your travel agent about what you found and ask if he or she can get you something better. The packages in the paper will serve as a benchmark against which to compare alternatives proposed by your travel agent.

5. Choose from among the options uncovered by you and your travel agent. No matter which option you elect, have your travel agent book it. Even if you go with one of the packages in the newspaper, it probably will be commissionable (at no additional cost to you) and will provide the agent with some return on the time invested on your behalf. Also, as a travel professional, your agent should be able to verify the quality and integrity of the package.

—— *No Room at the Inn*

If you are having trouble getting a reservation at the hotel of your choice, let your travel agent assist you. As discussed, the agent might be able to find a package with a tour operator that bypasses the hotel reservations department. If this does not work, he or she can call the sales and marketing department of the hotel and ask them, as a favor, to find you a room. Most hotel sales reps will make a special effort to accommodate travel agents, particularly travel agents who do a lot of Smokies or Blue Ridge business.

Do not be shy or reluctant about asking your travel agent to make a special call on your behalf. This is common practice in the travel industry and affords the agent an opportunity to renew contacts in the hotel's sales department. If your travel agent cannot get you a room through a personal appeal to the sales department and does not know which tour operators package the hotel you want, have the agent call hotel room reservations and:

1. Identify himself or herself as a travel agent.

2. Inquire about room availability for your required dates; something might have opened up since his (or your) last call.

3. If the reservation clerk reports that there are still no rooms available, have your travel agent ask for the reservations manager.

4. When the reservations manager comes on the line, have your agent identify himself and ask whether the hotel is holding any space for tour operators or wholesalers. If the answer is yes, have your agent request the wholesalers' or tour operators' names and phone numbers. This is information the reservations manager ordinarily will not divulge to an individual but will release to your travel agent. Armed with the names and numbers of wholesalers and tour operators holding space, your agent can start calling to find you a room.

To protect yourself, always guarantee your first night with a major credit card (even if you do not plan to arrive late), send a deposit if required, and insist on a written confirmation of your reservation. When you arrive and check in, have your written confirmation handy.

—— *Where the Deals Are*

Hotel room marketing and sales is confusing even to travel professionals. Sellers, particularly the middle-men, or wholesalers, are known by a numbing array of different, and frequently ill defined, terms. Furthermore, roles overlap, making it difficult to know who specifically is providing a given service. We try below to sort all of this out for you, and encourage you to slog through it. Understanding the system will make you a savvy consumer and will enable you to get the best deals on hotels regardless of your destination.

Tour Operators and Wholesalers

Southeastern mountain hotels always have had a difficult time filling their rooms from Sunday through Thursday. On the weekends, when thousands of weekenders arrive from Louisville, Nashville, Charlotte, and Atlanta, the mountains come alive. But on Sunday evening, as the last of the low-landers retreat, the mountains lapse into the doldrums. On many weekdays, even during summer high season, there remain many empty hotel rooms.

Recognizing that an empty hotel room is a liability, various travel entrepreneurs have stepped into the breach, volunteering to sell rooms for the hotels. These entrepreneurs, who call themselves tour operators, inbound travel brokers, travel wholesalers, travel packagers, or receptive operators, require as a quid pro quo that the hotels provide them a certain number of rooms, at a significantly reduced nightly rate, which they in turn resell at a profit. As this arrangement extends the sales outreach of the hotels, and since the rooms are going unoccupied, the hotels are only too happy to cooperate with this group of independent sales agents. Though a variety of programs have been developed to sell the rooms, most are marketed as part of motorcoach tours or group and individual travel packages.

This development has been beneficial both to the tourist and to the hotel. Predicated on volume, some of the room discount generally is passed along to consumers as an incentive to come to the mountains during the week or, alternatively, to stay longer than a weekend.

By purchasing your room through a tour operator or wholesaler, you may be able to obtain a room at the hotel of your choice for considerably less than if you went through the hotel's reservations department. The hotel commits rooms to the wholesaler or tour operator at a specific deep discount, usually 18–30% or more off the standard quoted rate, but makes no effort to control the price the wholesaler offers to his customers.

Wholesalers and tour operators holding space at a hotel for a specific block of time must surrender that space back to the hotel if the rooms are not sold by a certain date, usually 10–30 days in advance. Since the wholesaler's or tour operator's performance and credibility are determined by the number of rooms filled in a given hotel, they always are reluctant to give rooms back. The situation is similar to when the biology department at a university approaches the end of the year without having spent all of its allocated budget. The department head reasons that if the remaining funds are not spent (and the surplus is returned to the university), the university might reduce the biology department's budget for the forthcoming year. Tour operators and wholesalers depend on the hotels for their inventory. The more rooms the hotels allocate, the more inventory they have to sell. If a wholesaler or tour operator keeps returning rooms unsold, it is logical to predict that the hotel will respond by making fewer rooms available in the future. Therefore, the wholesaler would rather sell rooms at a bargain price than give them back to the hotel unsold.

Taking Advantage of Tour Operator and Travel Wholesaler Deals. There are several ways for you to tap into the tour operator and wholesaler market. First, check the travel sections of your Sunday paper for travel packages or tours to your preferred Smoky or Blue Ridge mountains destination. If you cannot find any worthwhile tours or packages advertised in your local paper, go to a good newsstand and buy a Sunday paper, preferably from Atlanta, Cincinnati, or Washington D.C., but alternatively from Nashville, Chattanooga, or Knoxville, Tennessee; Birmingham, Alabama; Raleigh or Charlotte, North Carolina; Richmond, Virginia; Indianapolis; Columbus, Ohio; or Louisville or Lexington, Kentucky. These cities are hot markets for the mountains, and their newspapers will almost always have a nice selection of packages and tours advertised. Because the competition among tour operators and wholesalers in these cities is so great, you often will find deals that beat the socks off anything offered in other parts of the country.

Tours and travel packages generally consist of room and bus transportation, and often other features such as meals, golf, and attraction admissions. Sometimes you can buy a package or tour for any dates desired; other times the operator or wholesaler will specify the dates. In either event, if a particular package fits your needs, you (or your travel agent) can book it directly by calling the phone number listed in the newspaper ad.

Find a package that you like and call for information. Do not be surprised, however, if the advertised package is not wholly available to you. If you live, say, in Pittsburgh, a tour operator or wholesaler in Atlanta may not be able to package your round-trip bus to the Great Smokies. This is because tour operators and wholesalers usually limit the transportation they sell to round trips originating from their primary market areas. In other words, they can take care of your transportation if you are coming from Nashville or Louisville, but most likely will not have a tour that originates in Pittsburgh. What they sometimes do, however, and what they will be delighted to do if they are sitting on some unsold rooms, is sell you the "land only" part of the package. This means you buy the room and on-site amenities (golf, admissions, etc.), if any, but will take care of your own travel arrangements.

Buying the "land only" part of a package can save big bucks since the tour operator always has more flexibility in discounting the "land" part of the package rather than in discounting the round-trip transportation component. One of the sweetest deals in travel is to find a motorcoach tour that is not sold out and buy primo hotel rooms from the operator at his deeply discounted rate.

Reservation Services

When wholesalers and consolidators deal directly with the public, they frequently represent themselves as "reservation services." When you call, you can ask for a rate quote for a particular hotel, or alternatively ask for their best available deal in the area where you prefer to stay. If there is a maximum amount you are willing to pay, say so. Chances are the service will find something that will work for you, even if it has to shave off a dollar or two of its own profit. Sometimes you must pay for your room when you make your reservation using your credit card. Other times you will pay as usual, when you check out. Listed below are three services that sell rooms in the Smokies and Blue Ridge:

> *Smoky Mountain Tour Connect:* A full-service operator that books accommodations and packages tours for both consumers and travel agents. Call (800) 782-1061 or (615) 436-2108.

> *Smoky Mountain Accommodations:* This service, for consumers only, obtains reservations for hotels, motels, condos,

and chalets in Gatlinburg and Pigeon Forge, Tennessee. Bookings are not commissionable for travel agents. Call (800) 231-2230. The local phone is (615) 436-9700. By and large, room rates are not discounted.

The Room Exchange: A New York–based room consolidator that books hotel rooms throughout the country. Though large cities are its specialty, the Room Exchange can book hotels throughout the Smokies and Blue Ridge. In big cities, the Room Exchange usually can get you a good discount. In the mountains, however, owing to the geographical dispersion of hotels and the seasonality of demand, discounts on rooms are less certain. Call (800) 846-7000.

Our experience in the Smokies and Blue Ridge has been that reservation services are more useful in finding rooms when availability is scarce than in obtaining deep discounts. Calling the hotels ourselves, we usually were able to equal or beat the reservation services' rates when rooms were available. On summer weekends, however, when demand was at its highest, and we could not find a room by calling the hotels ourselves, the reservations services could almost always get us a room at a fair price.

Hotel-Sponsored Packages

In addition to selling rooms through tour operators, consolidators, and wholesalers, most hotels periodically offer exceptional deals of their own. Sometimes the packages are specialized, as with golf or ski packages, or the packages are only offered at certain times of the year, for instance November and December.

Promotion of hotel specials tends to be limited to the hotel's primary markets, which for most properties is Indiana, Ohio, Kentucky, Tennessee, Virginia, Maryland, North Carolina, South Carolina, Georgia, Alabama, and Florida. If you live in other parts of the country, you can take advantage of the packages, but probably will not see them advertised in your local newspaper.

An important point regarding hotel specials is that the hotel reservation department usually does not inform you of existing specials or offer them to you. In other words, *you have to ask.* Finally, if you are doing your own legwork and are considering a hotel that is part of a national chain, always call the hotel instead of using the chain's national 800 number. Quite frequently, the national reservations service is unaware of local specials.

Exit Information Guide

A company called EIG (Exit Information Guide) publishes books of discount coupons for bargain rates at hotels at mountain destinations in Tennessee, Virginia, North Carolina, South Carolina, and Georgia. These books are available free of charge in many restaurants and motels along the main interstate highways. Since most people make reservations prior to leaving home, picking up the coupon book en route does not help much. If you call and use a credit card, EIG will send the guides first class for $3 for the first guide purchased and $1 for each additional guide. Write or call:

Exit Information Guide
4205 NW 6th Street
Gainesville, FL 32609
(904) 371-3948

AAA and AARP

Members of the American Automobile Association and the American Association of Retired Persons are eligible for discounts at many of the hotels in the Smoky and Blue Ridge mountains area. Call your local AAA office or check the AARP monthly magazine for additional information.

Special Weekend Rates in Big Cities

Hotels in Asheville, North Carolina, in the mountains, as well as those in Chattanooga and Knoxville, Tennessee, near the mountains, are good prospects for weekend lodging deals. Most downtown hotels that cater to business, government, and convention travelers offer special weekend discount rates, which range from 15–40% below normal weekday rates. You can find out about weekend specials by calling the hotel or by consulting your travel agent. Knoxville and Chattanooga are about a 60–90 minute commute from popular mountain recreation and tourism areas.

Getting Corporate Rates

Many hotels offer discounted corporate rates (5–20% off rack). Usually you do not need to work for a large company or have a special relationship with the hotel to obtain these rates. Simply call the hotel of your choice and ask for their corporate rates. Many hotels will guarantee you the discounted rate on the phone when you make your reservation. Others may make the rate conditional on your providing some sort of *bona fides,* for instance a fax on your company's letterhead requesting the rate, or a company credit card or business card on check in. Generally, the screening is not rigorous.

Half-Price Programs

Some discounts (35–60%) on rooms in the mountains are available through half-price hotel programs, often called travel clubs. Program operators contract with an individual hotel to provide rooms at a deep discount, usually 50% off the rack rate, on a "space available" basis. Space available in practice generally means that you can reserve a room at the discounted rate whenever the hotel expects to be at less than 80% occupancy. A little calendar sleuthing to help you avoid local festivals, meetings, and special events will increase the chances of your choosing a time for a visit when the discounts are available.

Most half-price programs charge an annual membership fee or directory subscription charge of $25–125. Once enrolled, you are mailed a membership card and a directory listing of all the hotels participating in the program. Examining the directory, you will notice immediately that there are many restrictions and exceptions. Some hotels, for instance, "black out" certain dates or times of year. Others may only offer the discount on certain days of the week, or require you to stay a certain number of nights. Still others may offer a much smaller discount than 50% off the rack rate.

Some programs specialize in domestic travel, some in international travel, and some specialize in both. The more established operators offer members between one and 4,000 hotels to choose from in the United States. All of the programs have a heavy concentration of hotels in California and Florida, and most have a limited selection of participating properties in New York City or Boston. Offerings in other cities and regions of the United States vary considerably. The program with the largest selection of hotels in the southeastern mountains is Encore, which lists about 35 hotels in the overall area. Call (800) 638-0930.

One problem with half-price programs is that not all hotels offer a full 50% discount. Another slippery problem is the base rate against which the discount is applied. Some hotels figure the discount on an exaggerated rack rate that nobody would ever have to pay. A few participating hotels may deduct the discount from a supposed "superior" or "upgraded" room rate, even though the room you get is the hotel's standard accommodation. Though hard to pin down, the majority of participating properties base discounts on the published rate in the *Hotel & Travel Index* (a quarterly reference work used by travel agents) and work within the spirit of their agreement with the program operator. As a rule, if you travel several times a year, you will more than pay for your program membership in room rate savings.

A noteworthy addendum to this discussion is that deeply discounted rooms through half-price programs are not commissionable to travel agents. In practical terms, this means that you must ordinarily make your own inquiry calls and reservations. If you travel frequently, however, and run a lot of business through your travel agent, he or she probably will do your legwork, lack of commission notwithstanding.

Preferred Rates

If you cannot book the hotel of your choice through a half-price program, you and your travel agent may have to search for a lesser discount, often called a preferred rate. A preferred rate could be a discount made available to travel agents to stimulate their booking activity, or a discount initiated to attract a certain class of traveler. Most preferred rates are promoted through travel industry publications and are often accessible only through an agent.

We recommend sounding out your travel agent about possible deals. Be aware, however, that the rates shown on travel agents' computerized reservations systems are not always the lowest rates obtainable. Zero in on a couple of hotels that fill your needs in terms of location and quality of accommodations, and then have your travel agent call for the latest rates and specials. Hotel reps are almost always more responsive to travel agents because travel agents represent a source of additional business. As discussed earlier, there are certain specials that hotel reps will disclose *only* to travel agents.

Travel agents also come in handy when the hotel you want is supposedly booked. A personal appeal from your agent to the hotel's director of sales and marketing will get you a room more than 50% of the time.

If you want to do your own research, Travelgraphics, in Norcross, Georgia (phone (800) 633-7918), will sell you a directory of preferred rates just like travel agents use. With the directory in hand you can make your own arrangements or have your agent make them for you.

—— Hotel/Motel Toll-Free 800 Numbers

For your convenience, we've listed the toll-free numbers for the following hotel and motel chains' reservation lines:

Best Western	(800) 528-1234 U.S. & Canada
	(800) 528-2222 TDD (Telecommunication Device for the Deaf)
Comfort Inn	(800) 228-5150 U.S.
Courtyard by Marriott	(800) 321-2211 U.S.
Days Inn	(800) 325-2525 U.S.
Doubletree	(800) 528-0444 U.S.
Econo Lodge	(800) 424-4777 U.S.
Embassy Suites	(800) 362-2779 U.S. & Canada
Fairfield Inn by Marriott	(800) 228-2800 U.S.
Guest Quarters	(800) 424-2900 U.S. & Canada
Hampton Inn	(800) 426-7866 U.S. & Canada
Hilton	(800) 445-8667 U.S.
	(800) 368-1133 TDD
Holiday Inn	(800) 465-4329 U.S. & Canada
Howard Johnson	(800) 654-2000 U.S. & Canada
	(800) 654-8442 TDD
Hyatt	(800) 233-1234 U.S. & Canada
Loew's	(800) 223-0888 U.S. & Canada
Marriott	(800) 228-9290 U.S. & Canada
	(800) 228-2489 TDD
Quality Inn	(800) 228-5151 U.S. & Canada
Radisson	(800) 333-3333 U.S. & Canada
Ramada Inn	(800) 228-3838 U.S.
	(800) 228-3232 TDD

Residence Inn by Marriott	(800) 331-3131 U.S.
Ritz-Carlton	(800) 241-3333 U.S.
Sheraton	(800) 325-3535 U.S. & Canada
Stouffer	(800) 468-3571 U.S. & Canada
Wyndham	(800) 822-4200 U.S.

Hotels and Motels: Rated and Ranked

—— What's in a Room?

Except for cleanliness, state of repair, and decor, most travelers do not pay much attention to hotel rooms. There is, of course, a discernible standard of quality and luxury which differentiates Motel 6 from Holiday Inn, Holiday Inn from Marriott, and so on. In general, however, hotel guests fail to appreciate that some rooms are better engineered than others.

Contrary to what you might suppose, designing a hotel room is (or should be) much more complex than picking a bedspread to match the carpet and drapes. Making the room usable to its occupants is an art, a planning discipline which combines both form and function.

Decor and taste are important, certainly. No one wants to spend several days in a room where the decor is dated, garish, or even ugly. But beyond the decor, there are variables which determine how "livable" a hotel room is. In Las Vegas, for example, we have seen some beautifully appointed rooms that are simply not well designed for human habitation. The next time you stay in a hotel, pay attention to the details and design elements of your room. Even more than decor, these are the things that will make you feel comfortable and at home.

It takes the *Unofficial Guide* researchers about 40 minutes to inspect a hotel room. Here are a few of the things we check that you may want to start paying attention to:

Room Size.   While some smaller rooms are cozy and well designed, a large and uncluttered room generally is preferable, especially for a stay of more than three days.

Temperature Control, Ventilation, and Odor.   The guest should be able to control the temperature of the room. The best system, because it's so quiet, is central heating and air conditioning, controlled by the room's own thermostat. The next best system is a room module heater and air conditioner, preferably controlled by an automatic thermostat, but usually by manually operated button controls. The worst system is central heating and air without any sort of room thermostat or guest control.

The vast majority of hotel rooms have windows or balcony doors that have been permanently secured shut. Though there are some legitimate safety and liability issues involved, we prefer windows and balcony doors that can be opened to admit fresh air. Hotel rooms should be odor-free, smoke-free, and not feel stuffy or damp.

Room Security. Better rooms have locks that require a plastic card instead of the traditional lock and key. Card and slot systems allow the hotel, essentially, to change the combination or entry code of the lock with each new guest who uses the room. A burglar who has somehow acquired a room key to a conventional lock can afford to wait until the situation is right before using the key to gain access. Not so with a card and slot system. Though larger hotels and hotel chains with lock and key systems usually rotate their locks once each year, they remain vulnerable to hotel thieves much of the time. Many smaller or independent properties rarely rotate their locks.

In addition to the entry lock system, the door should have a deadbolt, and preferably a chain that can be locked from the inside. A chain by itself is not sufficient. Doors also should have a peephole. Windows and balcony doors, if any, should have secure locks.

Safety. Every room should have a fire or smoke alarm, clear fire instructions, and preferably a sprinkler system. Bathtubs should have a nonskid surface, and shower stalls should have doors which either open outward or slide side-to-side. Bathroom electrical outlets should be high on the wall and not too close to the sink. Balconies should have sturdy, high rails.

Noise. Most travelers have been kept awake by the television, partying, or amorous activities of people in the next room, or by traffic on the street outside. Better hotels are designed with noise control in mind. Wall and ceiling construction are substantial, effectively screening routine noise. Carpets and drapes, in addition to being decorative, also absorb and muffle sounds. Mattresses mounted on stable platforms or sturdy bed frames do not squeak even when challenged by the most passionate and acrobatic lovers. Televisions enclosed in cabinets, and with volume governors, rarely disturb guests in adjacent rooms.

In better hotels, the air conditioning and heating system is well maintained and operates without noise or vibration. Likewise, plumbing is quiet and positioned away from the sleeping area. Doors to the hall, and to adjoining rooms, are thick and well fitted to better keep out noise.

Darkness Control.   Ever been in a hotel room where the curtains would not quite come together in the middle? In Las Vegas, where many visitors stay up way into the wee hours, it's important to have a dark, quiet room where you can sleep late without the morning sun blasting you out of bed. Thick, lined curtains, which close completely in the center and extend beyond the dimensions of the window or door frame, are required. In a well-planned room, the curtains, shades, or blinds should almost totally block light at any time of day.

Lighting.   Poor lighting is an extremely common problem in American hotel rooms. The lighting usually is adequate for dressing, relaxing, or watching television, but not for reading or working. Lighting needs to be bright over tables and desks, and alongside couches or easy chairs. Since so many people read in bed, there should be a separate light for each person. A room with two queen beds should have an individual light for four people. Better bedside reading lights illuminate a small area, so if you want to sleep and someone else prefers to stay up and read, you will not be bothered by the light. The worst situation by far is a single lamp on a table between beds. In each bed, only the person next to the lamp will have sufficient light to read. This deficiency is often compounded by light bulbs of insufficient wattage.

In addition, closet areas should be well lit, and there should be a switch near the door that turns on lights in the room when you enter. A seldom seen, but desirable, feature is a bedside console that allows a guest to control all or most lights in the room from bed.

Furnishings.   At bare minimum, the bed(s) must be firm. Pillows should be made with nonallergenic fillers and, in addition to the sheets and spread, a blanket should be provided. Bedclothes should be laundered with a fabric softener and changed daily. Better hotels usually provide extra blankets and pillows in the room or will on request, and sometimes use a second topsheet between the blanket and the spread.

There should be a dresser large enough to hold clothes for two people during a five-day stay. A small table with two chairs, or a desk with a chair, should be provided. The room should be equipped with a luggage rack and a three-quarter- to full-length mirror.

The television should be color, cable-connected, and ideally have a volume governor and remote control. It should be mounted on a swivel base, and preferably enclosed in a cabinet. Local channels should be posted on the set, and a local TV program guide should be supplied.

The telephone should be touchtone, conveniently situated for bedside use; there should be easily understood dialing instructions and a rate card on or near the phone. Local white and yellow pages should be provided. Better hotels have phones in the bath and equip room phones with long cords.

Well-designed hotel rooms usually have a plush armchair or a sleeper sofa for lounging and reading. Better headboards are padded for comfortable reading in bed, and there should be a nightstand or table on each side of the bed(s). Nice extras in any hotel room include a small refrigerator, a digital alarm clock, and a coffeemaker.

Bathroom. Two sinks are better than one, and you cannot have too much counter space. A sink outside the bath is a great convenience when two people are bathing and dressing at the same time. Sinks should have drains with stoppers.

Better bathrooms have both tub and shower with a nonslip bottom. Tub and shower controls should be easy to operate. Adjustable shower heads are preferred. The bath needs to be well lit and should have an exhaust fan and a guest-controlled bathroom heater. Towels should be large, soft, fluffy, and provided in generous quantities, as should hand towels and washcloths. There should be an electrical outlet for each sink, conveniently and safely placed.

Complimentary shampoo, conditioner, and lotion are a plus, as are robes and bathmats. Better hotels supply their bathrooms with tissues and extra toilet paper. Luxurious baths feature a phone, a hair dryer, sometimes a small television, or even a jacuzzi.

Vending. There should be complimentary ice and a drink machine on each floor. Welcome additions include a snack machine and a sundries (combs, toothpaste) machine. The latter are seldom found in large hotels that have 24-hour restaurants and shops.

—— *Room Ratings*

To separate properties according to the relative quality, tasteful-ness, state of repair, cleanliness, and size of their *standard rooms,* we have grouped the hotels and motels into classifications denoted by stars. Star ratings in this guide apply to Smoky and Blue Ridge mountain prop-erties only and do not necessarily correspond to ratings awarded by Mobil, AAA, or other travel critics. Because stars have little relevance when awarded in the absence of commonly recognized standards of comparison, we have tied our ratings to expected levels of quality estab-lished by specific American hotel corporations.

★★★★★	*Superior Rooms*	Tasteful and luxurious by any standard
★★★★	*Extremely Nice Rooms*	What you would expect at a Hyatt Regency or Marriott
★★★	*Nice Rooms*	Holiday Inn or comparable quality
★★	*Adequate Rooms*	Clean, comfortable, and functional without frills—like a Motel 6
★	*Super Budget*	

Star ratings apply to *room quality only* and describe the property's standard accommodations. For most hotels and motels, a "standard accommodation" is a hotel room with either one king bed or two queen beds. In an all-suite property, the standard accommodation is either a one- or two-room suite. In addition to standard accommoda-tions, many hotels offer luxury rooms and special suites, which are not rated in this guide. Star ratings for rooms are assigned without regard to whether a property has a restaurant, recreational facilities, entertainment, or other extras.

In addition to stars (which delineate broad categories), we also employ a numerical rating system. Our rating scale is 0–100, with 100 as the best possible rating, and zero (0) as the worst. Numerical ratings are presented to show the difference we perceive between one property and another. Rooms in Gatlinburg (Zone 2) at the River Terrace Resort, the Best Western Crossroads, and the Edgewater

Hotel, for instance, are all rated as ★★★. In the supplemental numerical ratings, River Terrace Resort and the Best Western are rated 73 and 72, respectively, while the Edgewater Hotel is rated 68. This means that within the three-star category, River Terrace and the Best Western Crossroads are comparable, and both have somewhat nicer rooms than the Edgewater.

—— How the Hotels Compare

Here is a comparison of the hotel rooms in the Smokies and Blue Ridge, organized by zone and by cities within zones. We've focused strictly on room quality, and excluded any consideration of location, services, recreation, or amenities. In some instances, a one- or two-room suite can be had for the same price or less than that of a hotel room.

If you use a subsequent edition of this guide, you will notice that many of the ratings and rankings change. These changes are occasioned by such positive developments as guest-room renovation, improved maintenance, and improved housekeeping. Failure to properly maintain guest rooms and poor housekeeping negatively affect the ratings. Finally, some ratings change as a result of enlarging our sample size. Because we cannot check every room in a hotel, we inspect a number of randomly chosen rooms. The more rooms we inspect in a particular hotel, the more representative our sample is of the property as a whole. Some of the ratings in this edition will change as a result of extended sampling.

Cost estimates are based on the hotel's published rack rates for standard rooms, averaged between weekday and weekend prices. Each "$" represents $30. Thus a cost symbol of "$$$" means a room (or suite) at that hotel will average about $90 a night. (It may be less for weekdays or more on weekends.)

Finally, before you begin to shop for a hotel take a hard look at this letter we received from a couple in Hot Springs, Arkansas:

"We canceled our room reservations to follow the advice in your book [and reserved a hotel highly ranked by the *Unofficial Guide*]. We wanted inexpensive, but clean and cheerful. We got inexpensive, but [also] dirty, grim, and depressing. I really felt disappointed in your advice and the room. It was the pits. That was the one real piece of information I needed from your book! The room spoiled the holiday for me aside from our touring."

Needless to say, this letter was as unsettling to us as the bad room was to our reader. Our integrity as travel journalists, after all, is based on the quality of the information we provide our readers. Even with the best of intentions and the most conscientious research, however, we cannot inspect every room in every hotel. What we do, in statistical terms, is take a sample: We check out several rooms selected at random in each hotel and base our ratings and rankings on those rooms. The inspections are conducted anonymously and without the knowledge of the property's management. Although unusual, it is certainly possible that the rooms we randomly inspect are not representative of the majority of rooms at a particular hotel. Another possibility is that the rooms we inspect in a given hotel *are* representative, but that by bad luck a reader is assigned a room that is inferior. When rechecking the hotel our reader disliked so intensely, we discovered our rating was correctly representative, but that the reader and his wife unfortunately had been assigned to one of a small number of threadbare rooms scheduled for renovation.

The key to avoiding disappointment is to do some advance snooping around. We recommend that you ask to be sent a photo of a hotel's standard guest room before you book, or at least get a copy of the hotel's promotional brochure. Be forewarned, however, that some hotel chains use the same guest room photo in their promotional literature for *all* hotels in the chain, and that the guest room in a specific property may not resemble the photo in the brochure. When you or your travel agent call, ask how old the property is and when the guest room you are being assigned was last renovated. If you arrive and are assigned a room inferior to that which you had been led to expect, demand to be moved to another room.

How the Hotels Compare in Zone 2

Gatlinburg

Hotel	Room Star Rating	Room Quality Rating	Room Value Rating	Cost ($=$30)	Phone (A/C 615)
Oak Square Motel	★★★½	81	59	$$+	436-7582
Gazebo Inn	★★★½	79	51	$$$–	436-2222
Park Vista Hotel	★★★½	78	43	$$$+	436-9211
Riverhouse at the Park	★★★½	77	49	$$$–	436-2070
Best Western Fabulous Chalet	★★★½	76	45	$$$	436-5151
Riverhouse Motor Lodge	★★★½	76	48	$$$–	436-7821
Travelodge	★★★½	76	76	$$–	436-7851
Best Western Zoder's	★★★	73	43	$$$–	436-5681
Homestead House	★★★	73	56	$$+	436-6166
River Terrace Resort	★★★	73	45	$$$–	436-5161
Best Western Crossroads	★★★	72	52	$$+	436-5661
Rocky Waters Motor Inn	★★★	70	45	$$+	436-7861
The Edgewater Hotel	★★★	68	34	$$$+	436-4151
Best Western Twin Islands	★★★	67	42	$$+	436-5121
Comfort Inn Downtown	★★★	67	44	$$+	436-5043
Holiday Inn Resort Complex	★★★	67	34	$$$+	436-9201
Master Hosts Inns Rivermont	★★★	67	46	$$+	436-5047
Colony Inn	★★★	65	61	$$–	436-5811
Days Inn	★★★	65	38	$$$–	436-9361
Hampton Inn	★★★	65	41	$$+	436-4878
Family Inns of America	★★½	64	33	$$+	436-3300
Mountain Heritage Inn	★★½	63	35	$$+	436-3474

Gatlinburg (continued)

Hotel	Room Star Rating	Room Quality Rating	Room Value Rating	Cost ($=$30)	Phone (A/C 615)
Quality Inn Smokyland	★★½	62	27	$$$	436-5191
Stony Brook Motel	★★½	62	41	$$	436-5652
Gillette Motel	★★½	62	37	$$+	436-5601
Howard Johnson	★★½	61	32	$$+	436-5621
Quality Inn Convention Center	★★½	60	33	$$+	436-5607
River Edge Motor Lodge	★★½	59	36	$$+	436-9292
Terrace Motel	★★½	59	33	$$+	436-4965
Microtel	★★½	58	34	$$+	436-0107
Creekstone Motel	★★½	58	51	$+	436-4628
Highland Motor Inn	★★½	58	36	$$+	436-4110
LeConte Creek Inn	★★½	57	33	$$+	436-4865
Midtown Lodge	★★½	57	32	$$+	436-5691
Spruce Flats Motel	★★½	57	38	$$	436-4387
Ramada Inn	★★½	56	26	$$$–	436-7881
McKay's Motor Lodge	★★	55	26	$$+	436-5102
Brookside Resort	★★	54	26	$$+	436-5611
Econo Lodge	★★	54	32	$$–	436-5836
Le Conte View Motor Lodge	★★	54	24	$$+	436-5032
Carver's Motel	★★	54	32	$$–	436-9750
Comfort Inn South	★★	53	28	$$	436-7813
Rainbow Motel	★★	52	36	$+	436-5887
Royal Town House Motor Inn	★★	50	20	$$$–	436-5818
Riverside Motor Lodge	★★	49	19	$$$–	436-4194

Pigeon Forge

Hotel	Room Star Rating	Room Quality Rating	Room Value Rating	Cost ($=$30)	Phone (A/C 615)
River Place Condominiuns	★★★★	89	51	$$$$–	428-4440
Riverside Motor Lodge	★★★★	85	51	$$$+	453-5555
Willow Brook Lodge (new rooms)	★★★½	81	68	$$+	453-5334
Heartland Country Resort	★★★½	79	49	$$$	453-4106
Capri Motel	★★★½	75	75	$$–	453-7147
Rivergate Motel	★★★	73	46	$$+	428-0872
Creekstone Inn	★★★	72	57	$$	453-3557
River Lodge	★★★	71	63	$$–	453-0783
Super 8	★★★	70	48	$$+	429-2047
Best Western Plaza	★★★	70	44	$$+	453-5538
Budgetel Inn	★★★	68	49	$$+	428-7305
Willow Brook Lodge (old rooms)	★★★	68	49	$$+	453-5334
Holiday Inn Resort	★★★	68	36	$$$	428-2700
Old Forge Inn	★★★	67	45	$$+	428-3200
Grand Resort Hotel	★★★	67	46	$$+	453-1000
Hampton Inn	★★★	66	35	$$$	428-5500
Mountain Trace Inn	★★★	65	37	$$$–	453-6785
River Place Inn	★★★	65	68	$+	453-0801
Shular Inn	★★★	65	34	$$$	453-2700
Grand Inns of America	★★½	64	36	$$+	453-0056
Park Tower Inn	★★½	64	39	$$+	453-8605
Norma Dan Motel	★★½	64	36	$$+	453-2403
Colonial House	★★½	64	46	$$–	453-0717
Ramada Inn	★★½	64	42	$$	453-9081
Smokey Meadows Lodge	★★½	63	47	$$–	453-4625
Conner Hill Motor Lodge	★★½	63	49	$$–	428-0287
Best Western Toni	★★½	63	36	$$+	453-9058

Pigeon Forge (continued)

Hotel	Room Star Rating	Room Quality Rating	Room Value Rating	Cost ($=$30)	Phone (A/C 615)
Family Inns of America West	★★½	63	33	$$+	453-4905
Red Carpet Inn	★★½	63	29	$$$–	453-5568
Bilmar Motor Inn	★★½	62	31	$$$–	453-5593
Mountain Valley Lodge	★★½	62	44	$$–	453-1823
Timbers Log Motel	★★½	62	44	$$–	428-5216
Pigeon Forge Motor Lodge	★★½	61	32	$$+	453-1715
River Breeze Motel	★★½	61	34	$$+	453-3906
Days Inn	★★½	61	33	$$+	453-4707
McAfee Motor Inn	★★½	61	36	$$+	453-3490
Howard Johnson	★★½	60	30	$$$–	453-9151
Econo Lodge	★★½	59	39	$$	428-1231
Vacation Lodge Motel	★★½	58	33	$$+	453-2640
Family Inns of America Twin Malls	★★½	56	37	$$	429-2244
Valley Forge Inn	★★½	56	29	$$+	453-7770
Family Inns of America East	★★½	56	37	$$	453-5573
Family Inns of America North	★★	55	27	$$+	453-7151
Family Inns of America South	★★	54	24	$$+	453-5549
Parkview Motel	★★	53	30	$$–	453-5051
Smoky Shadows Motel	★★	52	33	$$–	453-7155

Sevierville

Hotel	Room Star Rating	Room Quality Rating	Room Value Rating	Cost ($=$30)	Phone (A/C 615)
Comfort Inn Mountain View Suites	★★★★	85	82	$$+	428-5519
The Wonderland Hotel	★★★	72	54	$$+	428-0779
Oak Tree Lodge	★★★	70	47	$$+	428-7500
Greenbrier Motel	★★★	66	57	$$−	453-4018
Days Inn	★★★	65	53	$$	428-3353
River View Inn	★★¹/₂	63	32	$$$−	428-6191
Fairfield Inn	★★¹/₂	63	41	$$	429-8300
Landmark Inn	★★¹/₂	61	41	$$	453-0318
Travel Inn Motel	★★¹/₂	60	43	$$−	453-7165
Mize Motel	★★	55	33	$$−	453-4684

—— Good Deals and Bad Deals

Having compared the guest room quality of hotels in Zone 2, let's reorder the list to rank the best combinations of quality and value in a room. As before, the rankings are made without consideration of location or the availability of restaurant(s), recreational facilities, entertainment, and/or amenities. Once again, each lodging property is awarded a value rating on a 0–100 scale. The higher the rating, the better the value.

We recently had a reader complain to us that he had booked one of our top-ranked rooms in terms of value and had been disappointed in the room. We noticed that the room the reader occupied had a quality rating of ★★¹/₂. We would remind you that the value ratings are intended to give you some sense of value received for dollars spent. A ★★¹/₂ room at $30 may have the same value rating as a ★★★★ room at $85, but that does not mean the rooms will be of comparable quality. Regardless of whether it's a good deal or not, a ★★¹/₂ room is still a ★★¹/₂ room.

Listed below are the best room buys for the money, regardless of location or star classification, based on averaged rack rates. Note that sometimes a suite can cost less than a hotel room. We present this reordered list only for Zone 2 where there are such a large number of hotels in Gatlinburg, Pigeon Forge, and Sevierville. For other zones and other destinations, the number of hotels is more manageable, and you can make value comparisons by using the quality rating charts.

The Best Deals in Gatlinburg

Hotel	Room Value Rating	Room Star Rating	Cost ($=$30)
Travelodge	76	★★★½	$$–
Colony Inn	61	★★★	$$–
Oak Square Motel	59	★★★½	$$+
Homestead House	56	★★★½	$$+
Best Western Crossroads	52	★★★	$$+
Gazebo Inn	51	★★★½	$$$–
Creekstone Motel	51	★★½	$+
Riverhouse at the Park	49	★★★½	$$$–
Riverhouse Motor Lodge	48	★★★½	$$$–
Master Hosts Inns Rivermont	46	★★★	$$+
Best Western Fabulous Chalet	45	★★★½	$$$
River Terrace Resort	45	★★★	$$$–
Rocky Waters Motor Inn	45	★★★	$$+
Comfort Inn Downtown	44	★★★	$$+
Park Vista Hotel	43	★★★½	$$$+
Best Western Zoder's	43	★★★	$$$–
Best Western Twin Islands	42	★★★	$$+
Hampton Inn	41	★★★	$$+
Stony Brook Motel	41	★★½	$$
Days Inn	38	★★★	$$$–
Spruce Flats Motel	38	★★½	$$
Gillette Motel	37	★★½	$$+
Highland Motor Inn	36	★★½	$$+
River Edge Motor Lodge	36	★★½	$$+
Rainbow Motel	36	★★	$+
Mountain Heritage Inn	35	★★½	$$+
Holiday Inn Resort Complex	34	★★★	$$$+

The Best Deals in Gatlinburg (continued)

Hotel	Room Value Rating	Room Star Rating	Cost ($=$30)
The Edgewater Hotel	34	★★★	$$$+
Microtel	34	★★¹/₂	$$+
Family Inns of America	33	★★¹/₂	$$+
LeConte Creek Inn	33	★★¹/₂	$$+
Quality Inn Convention Center	33	★★¹/₂	$$+
Terrace Motel	33	★★¹/₂	$$+
Howard Johnson	32	★★¹/₂	$$+
Midtown Lodge	32	★★¹/₂	$$+
Carver's Motel	32	★★	$$−
Econo Lodge	32	★★	$$−
Comfort Inn South	28	★★	$$
Quality Inn Smokyland	27	★★¹/₂	$$$
Ramada Inn	26	★★¹/₂	$$$−
Brookside Resort	26	★★	$$+
McKay's Motor Lodge	26	★★	$$+
Le Conte View Motor Lodge	24	★★	$$+
Royal Town House Motor Inn	20	★★	$$$−
Riverside Motor Lodge	19	★★	$$$−

The Best Deals in Pigeon Forge

Hotel	Room Value Rating	Room Star Rating	Cost ($=$30)
Capri Motel	75	★★★¹/₂	$$−
Willow Brook Lodge (new rooms)	68	★★★¹/₂	$$+
River Place Inn	68	★★★	$+
River Lodge	63	★★★	$$−
Creekstone Inn	57	★★★	$$
River Place Condominiuns	51	★★★★	$$$$−
Riverside Motor Lodge	51	★★★★	$$$+
Heartland Country Resort	49	★★★¹/₂	$$$
Budgetel Inn	49	★★★	$$+

The Best Deals in Pigeon Forge (continued)

Hotel	Room Value Rating	Room Star Rating	Cost ($=$30)
Willow Brook Lodge (old rooms)	49	★★★	$$+
Conner Hill Motor Lodge	49	★★½	$$–
Super 8	48	★★★	$$+
Smokey Meadows Lodge	47	★★½	$$–
Rivergate Motel	46	★★★	$$+
Grand Resort Hotel	46	★★★	$$+
Colonial House	46	★★½	$$–
Old Forge Inn	45	★★★	$$+
Best Western Plaza	44	★★★	$$+
Mountain Valley Lodge	44	★★½	$$–
Timbers Log Motel	44	★★½	$$–
Ramada Inn	42	★★½	$$
Park Tower Inn	39	★★½	$$+
Econo Lodge	39	★★½	$$
Mountain Trace Inn	37	★★★	$$$–
Family Inns of America Twin Malls	37	★★½	$$
Family Inns of America East	37	★★½	$$
Holiday Inn Resort	36	★★★	$$$
Grand Inns of America	36	★★½	$$+
Norma Dan Motel	36	★★½	$$+
Best Western Toni	36	★★½	$$+
McAfee Motor Inn	36	★★½	$$+
Hampton Inn	35	★★★	$$$
Shular Inn	34	★★★	$$$
River Breeze Motel	34	★★½	$$+
Family Inns of America West	33	★★½	$$+
Days Inn	33	★★½	$$+
Vacation Lodge Motel	33	★★½	$$+
Smoky Shadows Motel	33	★★	$$–
Pigeon Forge Motor Lodge	32	★★½	$$+
Bilmar Motor Inn	31	★★½	$$$–
Howard Johnson	30	★★½	$$$–
Parkview Motel	30	★★	$$–
Red Carpet Inn	29	★★½	$$$–

The Best Deals in Pigeon Forge (continued)

Hotel	Room Value Rating	Room Star Rating	Cost ($=$30)
Valley Forge Inn	29	★★½	$$+
Family Inns of America North	27	★★	$$+
Family Inns of America South	24	★★	$$+

The Best Deals in Sevierville

Hotel	Room Value Rating	Room Star Rating	Cost ($=$30)
Comfort Inn Mountain View Suites	82	★★★★	$$+
Greenbrier Motel	57	★★★	$$–
The Wonderland Hotel	54	★★★	$$+
Days Inn	53	★★★	$$
Oak Tree Lodge	47	★★★	$$+
Travel Inn Motel	43	★★½	$$–
Fairfield Inn	41	★★½	$$
Landmark Inn	41	★★½	$$
Mize Motel	33	★★	$$–
River View Inn	32	★★½	$$$–

How the Hotels Compare in Zone 3

Cleveland

Hotel	Room Star Rating	Room Quality Rating	Room Value Rating	Cost ($=$30)	Phone (A/C 615)
Budgetel Inn	★★½	63	50	$$–	339-1000
Days Inn	★★½	62	49	$$–	476-2112
Holiday Inn	★★½	62	47	$$–	472-1504
Quality Inn Chalet	★★½	61	46	$$–	476-8511
Ramada Inn	★★½	60	46	$$–	479-4531
Econo Lodge	★★½	58	52	$+	472-3281

Ducktown/Ocoee

Hotel	Room Star Rating	Room Quality Rating	Room Value Rating	Cost ($=$30)	Phone (A/C 615)
Best Western Copper Inn	★★½	59	35	$$+	496-5541
Ocoee Inn (cabins)	★★	55	29	$$	338-2064
Ocoee Inn (rooms)	★★	51	37	$+	338-2064

Townsend

Hotel	Room Star Rating	Room Quality Rating	Room Value Rating	Cost ($=$30)	Phone (A/C 615)
Days Inn (suites)	★★★½	81	56	$$$–	448-9111
Best Western (suites)	★★★½	81	74	$$	448-2237
Hampton Inn	★★★	74	46	$$+	448-9000
Days Inn (rooms)	★★★	74	44	$$$–	448-9111
Talley-Ho Inn	★★★	70	63	$$–	448-2465
Wear's Motel	★★½	60	59	$+	448-2296
Best Western (rooms)	★★½	56	37	$$	448-2237
Scenic Motel	★★	54	43	$+	448-2294

How the Hotels Compare in Zone 4

Almond/Fontana Dam

Hotel	Room Star Rating	Room Quality Rating	Room Value Rating	Cost ($=$30)	Phone (A/C 704)
Euchella Sport Lodge	★★★½	76	61	$$+	488-8835
Fontana Village Inn	★★★	73	45	$$$–	498-2211

Bryson City

Hotel	Room Star Rating	Room Quality Rating	Room Value Rating	Cost ($=$30)	Phone (A/C 704)
Nantahala Village	★★★	73	49	$$+	488-2826
Hemlock Inn*	★★½	63	21	$$$$	488-2885

Cherokee

Hotel	Room Star Rating	Room Quality Rating	Room Value Rating	Cost ($=$30)	Phone (A/C 704)
Comfort Inn	★★½	64	36	$$+	497-2411
Holiday Inn	★★½	64	36	$$+	497-9181
Tee Pee Village Inn Econo Lodge	★★½	64	37	$$+	497-2226
Hampton Inn	★★½	63	38	$$+	497-3115
Best Western Great Smokies Inn	★★½	62	34	$$+	497-2020
Days Inn	★★½	61	40	$$	497-9171
Newfound Lodge (river)	★★½	60	47	$$–	497-2746
Pioneer Motel	★★½	59	40	$$	497-2435
ELA Motor Court	★★½	58	47	$$–	488-2284
Cherokee Plaza Motel	★★½	56	44	$$–	497-2301
Pageant Hills Motel	★★	55	38	$+	497-5371

* Price includes meals

Cherokee *(continued)*

Hotel	Room Star Rating	Room Quality Rating	Room Value Rating	Cost ($=$30)	Phone (A/C 704)
Drama Motel	★★	52	22	$$+	497-3271
Newfound Lodge (mountain)	★★	48	30	$$–	497-2746

Franklin

Hotel	Room Star Rating	Room Quality Rating	Room Value Rating	Cost ($=$30)	Phone (A/C 704)
Franklin Motel	★★½	59	46	$$–	524-4431
Country Inn	★★½	56	59	$+	524-4451

Murphy

Hotel	Room Star Rating	Room Quality Rating	Room Value Rating	Cost ($=$30)	Phone (A/C 704)
Comfort Inn	★★½	64	42	$$	837-8030
Best Western	★★½	61	45	$$–	837-3060
River Core Cabins	★★½	61	37	$$+	644-5979

How the Hotels Compare in Zone 5

Clayton/Dillard

Hotel	Room Star Rating	Room Quality Rating	Room Value Rating	Cost ($=$30)	Phone (A/C 706)
The Dillard House	★★★½	76	70	$$	746-5348
Best Western Dillard	★★★	73	55	$$+	746-5321
Quality Inn Dillard	★★½	63	41	$$	746-5373
Stonebrook Inn	★★½	59	37	$$+	782-2214
Regal Inn	★★	54	31	$$–	782-4269

Hiawassee

Hotel	Room Star Rating	Room Quality Rating	Room Value Rating	Cost ($=$30)	Phone (A/C 706)
Fieldstone Inn	★★★★	84	67	$$$–	896-2262

Highlands/Cashiers

Hotel	Room Star Rating	Room Quality Rating	Room Value Rating	Cost ($=$30)	Phone (A/C 704)
The Highlands Inn	★★★★½	93	83	$$$–	526-9380
The Chandler Inn	★★★★½	91	95	$$+	526-5992
Old Edwards Inn	★★★★½	90	80	$$$–	526-5036
Highlands Suite Hotel	★★★★	87	50	$$$$–	526-4502
Mountain High Motel	★★★★	84	68	$$$–	526-2790
Skyline Lodge	★★★½	76	42	$$$+	526-2121
High Hampton Inn	★★★	66	40	$$$–	743-2411
Oakmont Lodge	★★½	58	41	$$–	743-2298
Laurelwood Mountain Inn	★★½	57	37	$$	743-9939

Lake Toxaway/Sapphire

Hotel	Room Star Rating	Room Quality Rating	Room Value Rating	Cost ($=$30)	Phone (A/C 704)
The Greystone Inn	★★★★★	98	30	$$$$$ $$$$–	966-4700
Woodlands Inn of Sapphire	★★★½	81	74	$$	966-4709

How the Hotels Compare in Zone 6

Asheville

Hotel	Room Star Rating	Room Quality Rating	Room Value Rating	Cost ($=$30)	Phone (A/C 704)
Haywood Park Hotel	★★★★½	91	54	$$$$	252-2522
Grove Park Inn	★★★★	85	34	$$$$$+	252-2711
Radisson	★★★½	81	37	$$$$	252-8211
Quality Inn Biltmore	★★★	74	41	$$$−	274-1800
Holiday Inn Sunspree Resort	★★★	73	35	$$$+	254-3211
Holiday Inn East	★★★	66	41	$$+	298-5611
Best Western	★★★	65	51	$$	298-5562
Holiday Inn Tunnel Road	★★½	63	46	$$−	252-4000
Sleep Inn	★★½	63	33	$$+	277-1800
Ramada Inn West	★★½	62	35	$$+	665-2161
Best Inns of America	★★½	62	44	$$−	298-4000
Days Inn	★★½	61	34	$$+	298-5140
Howard Johnson	★★½	61	39	$$+	274-2300
Cricket Inn	★★½	59	50	$$−	298-7952
Ramada Inn Central	★★½	58	33	$$+	254-7451
Days Inn East	★★½	56	37	$$	298-5140
Forest Manor Motel	★★½	56	28	$$$−	274-3531
Plaza Motel	★★	52	33	$$−	274-2050

Balsam/Sylva/Waynesville

Hotel	Room Star Rating	Room Quality Rating	Room Value Rating	Cost ($=$30)	Phone (A/C 704)
Balsam Mountain Inn	★★★★½	93	77	$$$−	456-9498
Days Inn Waynesville	★★★	67	46	$$+	926-0201
Best Western Smoky Mountain Inn	★★★	65	41	$$+	456-4402
Waynesville Country Club Inn*	★★★	65	22	$$$$$−	456-3551

* Price includes meals

Balsam/Sylva/Waynesville (continued)

Hotel	Room Star Rating	Room Quality Rating	Room Value Rating	Cost ($=$30)	Phone (A/C 704)
Comfort Inn Sylva	★★½	63	28	$$$	586-3315
Econo Lodge Waynesville	★★½	63	45	$$–	452-0353
Scottish Inns Waynesville	★★	55	38	$+	926-9137

Black Mountain

Hotel	Room Star Rating	Room Quality Rating	Room Value Rating	Cost ($=$30)	Phone (A/C 704)
Red Rocker Inn	★★★★½	92	99	$$–	669-5991
Monte Vista Hotel	★★★½	76	76	$$–	669-2119
Apple Blossom Motel	★★	54	29	$$	669-7922

Brevard/Penrose

Hotel	Room Star Rating	Room Quality Rating	Room Value Rating	Cost ($=$30)	Phone (A/C 704)
Penrose Motel	★★½	56	49	$+	884-2691
Sunset Motel	★★	54	28	$$	884-9106
Brevard Motor Lodge	★★	54	24	$$+	884-3456
Imperial Motor Lodge	★★	52	27	$$	884-2887

Chimney Rock/Lake Lure

Hotel	Room Star Rating	Room Quality Rating	Room Value Rating	Cost ($=$30)	Phone (A/C 704)
Esmerelda Inn	★★★	70	63	$$–	625-9105
Mountain Village Chalets	★★★	67	63	$$–	625-9783
Lake Lure Inn	★★★	66	35	$$$	625-2525
Chimney View Motel	★★	54	31	$$–	625-1429

Flat Rock/Hendersonville/Saluda/Tryon

Hotel	Room Star Rating	Room Quality Rating	Room Value Rating	Cost ($=$30)	Phone (A/C 704)
Pine Crest Inn	★★★★¹/₂	95	54	$$$$+	859-9135
The Orchard Inn	★★★★¹/₂	92	62	$$$+	749-5471
The Woodfield Inn	★★★★	84	56	$$$+	693-6016
Echo Mountain Inn	★★★	73	53	$$+	693-9626
Highland Lake Inn	★★★	71	42	$$$–	693-6812
Comfort Inn Hendersonville	★★★	66	52	$$	693-8800
Days Inn Hendersonville	★★★	66	39	$$$–	697-5999
Hampton Inn Hendersonville	★★¹/₂	64	39	$$+	697-2333
Holiday Inn Hendersonville	★★¹/₂	63	31	$$$–	692-7231
Ramada Inn Hendersonville	★★¹/₂	60	34	$$+	692-0521

Maggie Valley

Hotel	Room Star Rating	Room Quality Rating	Room Value Rating	Cost ($=$30)	Phone (A/C 704)
Mountain Joy Cabins	★★★½	81	56	$$$–	926-1257
Maggie Valley Resort	★★★½	76	40	$$$+	926-1616
Four Seasons Inn	★★★½	75	64	$$+	926-8505
Stony Creek Motel	★★★	68	49	$$+	926-1996
Jonathan Creek Inn	★★★	67	42	$$+	926-1232
Comfort Inn	★★½	64	32	$$$–	926-9106
Mountainbrook Inn	★★½	64	39	$$+	926-3962
Abbey Inn	★★½	56	34	$$+	926-1188

How the Hotels Compare in Zone 7

Banner Elk/Beech Mountain/Blowing Rock/Boone

Hotel	Room Star Rating	Room Quality Rating	Room Value Rating	Cost ($=$30)	Phone (A/C 704)
Chetola Lodge	★★★★¹⁄₂	93	60	$$$$–	295-5500
Meadowbrook Inn	★★★★	88	56	$$$+	295-4300
Azalea Garden	★★★★	83	76	$$+	295-3272
Archers Inn	★★★¹⁄₂	82	69	$$+	898-9004
Boxwood Lodge	★★★¹⁄₂	82	75	$$	295-9984
Brookside Inn	★★★¹⁄₂	82	54	$$$–	295-3380
Cliff Dwellers Inn	★★★¹⁄₂	81	56	$$$–	295-3121
Green Park Inn	★★★¹⁄₂	78	41	$$$+	295-3141
The Beech Alpen Inn	★★★¹⁄₂	77	45	$$$+	387-2252
Hemlock Inn	★★★¹⁄₂	77	65	$$+	295-7987
Blowing Rock Inn	★★★	69	47	$$+	295-7921
Homestead Inn	★★★	68	64	$$–	295-4300
Quality Inn Boone	★★★	68	43	$$+	262-0020
Days Inn Blowing Rock	★★¹⁄₂	64	39	$$+	295-4422
Hampton Inn Boone	★★¹⁄₂	64	34	$$+	264-0077
Holiday Inn Express Boone	★★¹⁄₂	64	36	$$+	264-2451
Holiday Inn Banner Elk	★★¹⁄₂	63	41	$$	898-4571
High Country Inn	★★¹⁄₂	63	41	$$	264-1000
Greystone Lodge	★★¹⁄₂	62	46	$$–	264-4133

Burnsville/Linville/Little Switzerland/Spruce Pine

Hotel	Room Star Rating	Room Quality Rating	Room Value Rating	Cost ($=$30)	Phone (A/C 704)
Nu Wray Inn	★★★★¹/₂	95	89	$$+	682-2329
Eseeola Lodge*	★★★¹/₂	80	18	$$$$ $$$+	733-4311
Pinebridge Inn	★★★¹/₂	77	71	$$	765-5543
Switzerland Inn	★★★	67	39	$$$–	765-2153
Big Lynn Lodge*	★★¹/₂	60	28	$$$–	765-4257
Alpine Inn	★★¹/₂	56	55	$+	765-5380

* Price includes meals

How the Hotels Compare in Zone 8

Charlottesville

Hotel	Room Star Rating	Room Quality Rating	Room Value Rating	Cost ($=$30)	Phone (A/C 804)
Boars Head Inn & Sports Club	★★★★¹/₂	94	50	$$$$+	296-2181
Courtyard	★★★¹/₂	81	66	$$+	973-7100
English Inn	★★★¹/₂	75	61	$$+	971-9900
Sheraton	★★★	68	36	$$$	973-2121
Days Hotel	★★★	66	44	$$+	977-7700
Hampton Inn	★★¹/₂	64	41	$$+	978-7888
Comfort Inn	★★¹/₂	63	35	$$+	293-6188
Best Western Mount Vernon	★★¹/₂	61	43	$$–	296-5501
Holiday Inn Monticello	★★¹/₂	61	27	$$$	977-5100
Econo Lodge North	★★¹/₂	59	47	$$–	295-3185
Knights Inn	★★¹/₂	58	47	$$–	973-8133
Budget Inn	★★	55	41	$+	293-5141
Econo Lodge South	★★	54	34	$$–	296-2104

Front Royal/Middletown/Strasburg/Winchester

Hotel	Room Star Rating	Room Quality Rating	Room Value Rating	Cost ($=$30)	Phone (A/C 703)
Wayside Inn	★★★★¹/₂	94	60	$$$$–	869-1797
Hotel Strasburg	★★★★¹/₂	90	71	$$$	465-9191
Best Western Winchester	★★★	66	62	$$–	662-4154
Budgetel Inn Winchester	★★¹/₂	64	51	$$–	678-0800
Hampton Inn Winchester	★★¹/₂	63	48	$$–	667-8011
Comfort Inn Winchester	★★¹/₂	63	50	$$–	667-5000

Front Royal/Middletown/Strasburg/Winchester (continued)

Hotel	Room Star Rating	Room Quality Rating	Room Value Rating	Cost ($=$30)	Phone (A/C 703)
Holiday Inn Winchester	★★½	62	37	$$+	667-3300
Bluemont Inn	★★½	60	51	$$–	635-9447
Twin Rivers Motel	★★½	58	54	$+	635-4101
Apple Blossom Motor Lodge	★★½	56	48	$$–	667-1200
Travelodge Winchester	★★½	56	46	$$–	665-0685
Twi-Lite Motel	★★½	56	44	$$–	635-4148
Super 8 Front Royal	★★	54	36	$$–	636-4888
Super 8 Winchester	★★	54	36	$$–	665-4450
Bonds Motel	★★	53	49	$+	667-8881
Midtown Motel	★★	52	47	$+	635-2196
Scottish Inn	★★	51	36	$+	636-6168

Harrisonburg

Hotel	Room Star Rating	Room Quality Rating	Room Value Rating	Cost ($=$30)	Phone (A/C 703)
Sheraton	★★★	68	43	$$+	433-2521
Ramada Inn	★★★	65	55	$$–	434-9981
Hampton Inn	★★½	63	45	$$–	432-1111
Comfort Inn	★★½	63	41	$$	433-6066
Days Inn	★★½	63	47	$$–	433-9353
Shoney's Inn	★★½	62	47	$$–	433-6089
HoJo	★★½	62	54	$+	434-6771
Econo Lodge	★★½	60	51	$$–	433-2576
Motel 6	★★	53	46	$+	433-6939

Lexington/Buena Vista

Hotel	Room Star Rating	Room Quality Rating	Room Value Rating	Cost ($=$30)	Phone (A/C 703)
Maple Hall Country Inn	★★★¹/₂	78	45	$$$+	463-2044
Holiday Inn Lexington	★★★	65	44	$$+	463-7351
Lexington Inn	★★¹/₂	63	45	$$−	463-9131
Comfort Inn Lexington	★★¹/₂	63	36	$$+	463-7311
Ramada Inn Lexington	★★¹/₂	62	39	$$+	463-6666
Howard Johnson Lexington	★★¹/₂	62	36	$$+	463-9181
Buena Vista Motel	★★¹/₂	56	44	$$−	261-2138
Super 8 Lexington	★★	54	34	$$−	463-7858
Econo Lodge Lexington	★★	54	34	$$−	463-7371

Luray/Mount Jackson/New Market/Woodstock

Hotel	Room Star Rating	Room Quality Rating	Room Value Rating	Cost ($=$30)	Phone (A/C 703)
The Mimslyn	★★★	70	48	$$+	743-5105
Best Western Mount Jackson	★★★	66	63	$$−	477-2911
Luray Caverns West	★★★	65	57	$$−	743-4536
Quality Inn New Market	★★★	65	51	$$	740-3141
Ramada Inn Woodstock	★★★	65	49	$$+	459-5000
Days Inn New Market	★★¹/₂	64	44	$$−	740-4100
Ramada Inn Luray	★★¹/₂	64	42	$$	743-4521
Intown Motel	★★¹/₂	60	34	$$+	743-6511
Luray Caverns East	★★¹/₂	58	38	$$	743-4531

Natural Bridge

Hotel	Room Star Rating	Room Quality Rating	Room Value Rating	Cost ($=$30)	Phone (A/C 703)
Natural Bridge Resort	★★¹/₂	61	39	$$+	291-2121

Roanoke/Rocky Mount/Hillsville/Salem

Hotel	Room Star Rating	Room Quality Rating	Room Value Rating	Cost ($=$30)	Phone (A/C 703)
Radisson Patrick Henry	★★★★¹/₂	91	72	$$$	345-8811
Sheraton Inn Roanoke	★★★¹/₂	80	52	$$$–	362-4500
Ramada Inn Roanoke	★★★	67	57	$$–	343-0121
Days Inn Civic Center	★★★	66	65	$$–	342-4551
Holiday Inn Civic Center	★★★	65	44	$$+	342-8961
Holiday Inn Roanoke	★★★	65	43	$$+	366-8861
Comfort Inn Rocky Mount	★★¹/₂	64	42	$$	489-4000
Hampton Inn Franklin Road/ Roanoke	★★¹/₂	64	39	$$+	989-4000
Hampton Inn Roanoke	★★¹/₂	64	37	$$+	563-0853
Econo Lodge Roanoke	★★¹/₂	63	55	$+	343-2413
Comfort Inn Roanoke	★★¹/₂	63	50	$$–	563-0229
Holiday Inn Salem	★★¹/₂	63	39	$$+	389-7061
Colony House Motor Lodge	★★¹/₂	62	42	$$	345-0411

Roanoke/Rocky Mount/Hillsville/Salem (continued)

Hotel	Room Star Rating	Room Quality Rating	Room Value Rating	Cost ($=$30)	Phone (A/C 703)
Comfort Inn Hillsville	★★½	62	41	$$	728-4125
Quality Inn Salem	★★½	62	45	$$–	562-1912
Econo Lodge Hillsville	★★½	61	44	$$–	728-9118
Franklin Motel	★★½	57	77	$	483-9962
Jefferson Lodge	★★	55	38	$$–	342-2951
Super 8	★★	54	34	$$–	563-8888
Friendship Inn	★★	50	37	$+	981-9341

Staunton/Waynesboro

Hotel	Room Star Rating	Room Quality Rating	Room Value Rating	Cost ($=$30)	Phone (A/C 703)
Holiday Inn Staunton	★★★	68	42	$$$–	248-6020
Comfort Inn Staunton	★★★	67	49	$$+	886-5000
Best Western Staunton	★★★	66	37	$$$–	885-1112
Days Inn Waynesboro	★★★	66	48	$$+	943-1101
Hampton Inn Staunton	★★★	66	57	$$–	886-7000
Holiday Inn Waynesboro	★★½	64	43	$$	942-5201
Comfort Inn Waynesboro	★★½	63	46	$$–	942-1171
Shoney's Inn Staunton	★★½	63	50	$$–	885-3117
Innkeeper	★★½	61	50	$$–	248-5111
Super 8 Staunton	★★½	57	45	$$–	886-2888
Econo Lodge Staunton	★★	55	40	$+	885-5158
Deluxe Budget Motel	★★	53	33	$$–	949-8253
Super 8 Waynesboro	★★	53	33	$$–	943-3888

PART FOUR:
Great Smoky Mountains
National Park—Zone 1

A Brief History and Orientation

The Cherokee called these ancient mountains the "Land of a Thousand Smokes." Today, 800-square-mile Great Smoky Mountains National Park is the most visited national park in the United States. Roughly oval-shaped and straddling the Tennessee–North Carolina border (which bisects the park and is traced by the Appalachian Trail), Great Smoky contains more than 700 miles of rivers and streams, 800 miles of trails, and 200,000 acres of virgin forest. The Smokies are the highest mountains east of the Rockies; vistas from the many scenic overlooks evoke images of ocean waves receding into the distance.

With its wide diversity of plant and animal life, the park is more than a playground for vacationers. It's also a refuge for many endangered plants and animals, such as the red wolf and the eastern river otter. Great Smoky has become one of the world's most important ecological research sites.

—— Pollution and "Exotics"

While it's easy to think of Great Smoky as an island of pristine nature in a sea of civilization, air pollution is an increasing problem: Over the last 30 years visibility has decreased by 30%. Sulfates and nitrogen oxide emissions from factories and cities are carried into the park and settle across its ridges.

The pollution is doing more than obscuring the view: It's having a visible effect on park vegetation and streams. Acid rain damages sensitive plant foliage and affects the chemical balance of streams and soils. As a result, many plants and animals fail to reproduce or may die.

Pollution isn't the only problem affecting Great Smoky. Nonnative species (sometimes called "exotic" species) threaten native plants and animals with extinction. Lacking natural checks on their growth, nonnative species sometimes dominate the system.

An example is a tiny insect called the balsam woolly adelgid, a European native that drinks the sap of the native Fraser fir. Up to 50,000 adelgids can infest a single tree, killing it within six to eight years. As a result, more than 90% of the mature Fraser firs in the park are dead.

Today Great Smoky is no longer isolated from the rest of the world, and park officials and scientists are facing the challenges of preserving a unique region with problems as diverse as the wilderness itself.

History

Great Smoky Mountains National Park was established on June 15, 1934. But the idea for a national park in the populous East originated years earlier, after a librarian from St. Louis named Horace Kephart came to the Smokies for a cure. At the time, large-scale logging was devastating the land and forests, and the lives of the mountain folk were being disrupted.

Over the years, Kephart promoted preserving the Smokies as a national park. In the 1920s, many prominent Knoxville citizens formed a citizens' organization and joined his efforts. Since about this time, the National Park Service was hoping to generate support for more national parks by establishing a park in the East, the NPS joined with the private efforts to promote a national park in the Smokies.

Getting the Funds

Money, however, was a problem. While Tennessee and North Carolina, along with many private citizens, donated millions of dollars to purchase land for the park, the federal government balked. Because national parks in the West were established on land already owned by the government, the idea of spending money to buy additional land was difficult to accept.

Eventually, however, the federal government chipped in $2 million. Coupled with $5 million donated by philanthropist John D. Rockefeller, Jr., the goal was attained. The 507,869 acres now included in the park were held in more than 6,600 private tracts. With the funds, lumber companies were bought out. Individuals living in the proposed park who didn't want to sell were allowed to live out their lives on the land. Great Smoky is unique for being the first national park given to the government by the people.

President Franklin D. Roosevelt dedicated the park in September 1940, at a ceremony held at the Rockefeller Monument at Newfound Gap, where US 441 crosses the state boundary and the Appalachian Trail.

—— *Most Folks Come for the Day*

Great Smoky is located at the southernmost—and widest—part of the great Appalachian Mountain chain. From the Smokies in the west, the mountains stretch east to the Blue Ridge Mountains across western North Carolina.

As a tourist destination, however, the park isn't self-contained—unless you're camping in one of its campgrounds, setting off on a multiday hike with a loaded pack on your back, or you've made reservations a year in advance to stay at LeConte Lodge (a rustic mountaintop destination that requires a minimum five-mile hike to reach).

The park doesn't offer visitors the option of staying in motor lodges, hotels, or motels inside its boundaries: There aren't any. Nor will you find restaurants, fast-food joints, or grocery stores. The emphasis in Great Smoky is on the rustic and natural.

As a result, the overwhelming majority of visitors to the park come by car during the day, then return to their rooms or to developed campgrounds outside the park in one of the "gateway" towns: Gatlinburg, Pigeon Forge, Sevierville (all in Zone 2, the Northern Foothills of Tennessee); Cherokee, Bryson City, Fontana (in Zone 4, the Southern Foothills of North Carolina); or Maggie Valley (in Zone 6, Asheville and Brevard).

People who like to contrast the natural beauty of the park with the hustle and bustle of carnival rides, theme parks, and night life should head for Gatlinburg or Pigeon Forge (Zone 2). Those seeking to combine the quiet of Great Smoky with low-key commercial entertainment should find accommodations in Cherokee, Bryson City, Fontana (Zone 4), or Maggie Valley (Zone 6) in North Carolina. One drawback, however, is that it's a somewhat longer drive to major attractions in the park, such as Cades Cove.

Townsend, in Zone 3 (the Southwest Foothills of Tennessee), is an off-the-beaten-track option, with a few motels, restaurants, fast-food joints, some low-key tourist attractions, and outdoor activities located outside the western entrance to the park leading to Cades Cove. The tourist hype along the side of the road is significantly lower compared to that in the towns on US 441: horseback riding, yes; twenty-foot-tall plastic dinosaurs in water slide parks, no.

—— Entrances

The two main entrances to Great Smoky are on US 441, the scenic, two-lane highway called Newfound Gap Road inside the park; the road crosses Great Smoky from north to south. The northern entrance is just south of Gatlinburg, Tennessee, while the southern entrance is 33 miles away at Cherokee, North Carolina. Both entrances feature visitor centers, where you can pick up maps and other free information on activities in the park.

People staying in the gateway resorts of Gatlinburg, Pigeon Forge, and Sevierville will use the northern entrance, which puts them closer to the major attractions in Great Smoky. Then in the evenings they'll return to an area with an abundance of restaurants and things to do—especially for children. The towns near the southern entrance are relatively low-key—although there's plenty of tourist schlock along the roadside—compared to their counterparts in Tennessee. Bryson City and Fontana are the least developed tourist towns and are popular with hard-core outdoor enthusiasts.

A western entrance to the park is located at Townsend, Tennessee. From there, it's a seven-mile drive to Cades Cove and another five miles to the visitor center on the Cades Cove Loop Road. Cades Cove and the northern entrance also are connected via Little River Road.

Which entrances get the most use? Of the 10 million or so people who visit the park each year, about 40% enter Great Smoky through Gatlinburg, 23% by way of Cherokee, and about 15% through Townsend.

Campers also can enter the park at seven campgrounds on the periphery of the park: Cosby, Look Rock, and Abrams Creek (in Tennessee); and Deep Creek, Cataloochee, Balsam Mountain, and Big Creek (in North Carolina). But the roads leading to the campgrounds don't go far into the park or connect with other roads. The most popular—and largest—campgrounds are Elkmont, Cades Cove, and Smokemont, which are accessed via US 441 or the western entrance at Cades Cove.

The only major roads that connect with other routes are Newfound Gap Road (US 441), Little River Road (linking Sugarlands Visitor Center and Newfound Gap Road to the western entrance near Townsend), and the Blue Ridge Parkway. The Parkway terminates near the Oconaluftee Visitor Center (at the southern entrance to the park) and crosses US 19 at Soco Gap, between Cherokee and Maggie Valley, on its 469 miles to Shenandoah National Park in Virginia.

—— *Visitor Centers*

Great Smoky offers three visitor centers that help orient visitors, provide free information, and feature interesting exhibits—even a film. *Sugarlands* (on the Tennessee side) and *Oconaluftee* (in North Carolina) are open year round; *Cades Cove* (near the western entrance to the park in Tennessee) is open from mid-April through October. Hours are 8 A.M. to 4:30 P.M. daily; hours are extended in the spring and summer. (During the winter, Oconaluftee is open 8:30 A.M. to 4:30 P.M.) You can call any of the visitor centers through the park's main number: (615) 436-1200.

In addition, the park operates two welcome centers, in Gatlinburg (8 A.M. to 6 P.M. daily) and Townsend (9 A.M. to 6 P.M.). The centers are staffed by volunteers who offer advice and free information on Great Smoky. Visitors also can make lodging reservations and pick up touring information on attractions outside the park. The *Gatlinburg Welcome Center* is located on US 441 at the northern entrance to the town. The *Townsend Visitor Center* is on US 321 in the Chamber of Commerce building in Townsend.

Sugarlands Visitor Center/Park Headquarters. This large, modern building, two miles south of Gatlinburg on Newfound Gap Road (US 441), includes natural history exhibits (the stuffed black bear, oddly enough, looks rather small, while the wild boar is huge); a ten-minute film that highlights the natural beauty of the Smokies; and a desk staffed by volunteers that answer questions and give out advice on things to do inside the park.

The parking lot is large, and often it's shoulder to shoulder inside the center; try to arrive in the morning if you don't want to battle crowds or if you're in a hurry. You also can get information on camping, pick up free back-country camping permits, and get first-aid assistance. Brief ranger talks and slide shows also are scheduled each day from spring through fall.

While the center is informative and a worthwhile stop for first-time visitors, there's not much to do in the immediate area, with these exceptions: the Gatlinburg Trail, an easy, scenic foot and bicycle trail that goes to Gatlinburg (two miles away); and a one-mile, self-guided nature trail.

Oconaluftee Visitor Center. Smaller than the visitor center 30 miles to the north, Oconaluftee has a few exhibits and is staffed by volunteers who will answer questions and offer advice. Nearby is the *Pioneer Homestead*, one of 70 restored farms in the park that show how the mountain people lived in the years before the park was developed. Just up the road is *Mingus Mill*, a large water-powered mill for grinding corn that operates from mid-April through October.

Cades Cove Visitor Center. Located about 12 miles southwest of Townsend, Tennessee, the Cades Cove Visitor Center is located in a group of preserved, 19th-century farms, historic buildings, and an old mill. It's the least convenient of the visitor centers in the park, but it's located in an incredibly beautiful and tranquil setting. While you can pick up information on park activities at Cades Cove, back-country camping permits aren't issued here.

—— Parking Your Car

Vacationing in Great Smoky is a car trip for almost everyone. When the crowds are biggest—July and October—finding a place to park can be a problem.

Newfound Gap Road features scenic overlooks, pullouts, and walks along its entire length between Cherokee and Gatlinburg. Some of the parking lots are huge, especially at Newfound Gap Overlook and Clingmans Dome (located on a spur off of the road that leads to the highest point in the park). If the lots are full, it's just a question of waiting a few minutes until another driver leaves.

Casual walkers can stop at "Quiet Walkways," quarter-mile strolls located along the roads inside the park. The parking lots, however, are intentionally small to restrict the number of people on the trails at any one time—and to keep areas quiet. If a lot is full, just keep going until you find a space at another Quiet Walkway down the road.

Major trail heads and trails leading to waterfalls offer larger parking facilities, but they fill up fast. Try to arrive early in the day during busy periods to get a spot. And don't sleep in your car overnight. That's called "camping" by park officials, and you can't legally camp except in designated areas (called "campgrounds"). If you're caught, you'll get a ticket.

When you park your car, don't leave anything of value inside. For more information on avoiding crime, see "Crime in the Mountains," pages 132–37.

Lodging in and near the Park

—— LeConte Lodge

Guests stay in rough-hewn, private cabins or private rooms in cabins with shared living rooms near the top of Mount LeConte, a few miles north of Newfound Gap. Breakfast and dinner are served family-style, and there's no electricity, indoor plumbing, television, or telephones. Sound rustic? You haven't heard it all: The only way to reach this mountaintop aery is by foot—and it's a minimum four-hour hike up a steep trail.

Getting a Reservation

That's not all: The place is so popular you need to make reservations up to a year in advance. The phone number to call for reservations is (615) 429-5704. The lodge begins accepting bookings on October 1 (unless it's a Sunday) for the following year.

Weekends book up in a few hours, and the popular months of June and October are booked in a couple of business days. By October 10 or so, LeConte Lodge is booked for the entire season, which runs April through October.

Other Strategies

Don't give up hope if you're not able to book a reservation in October. As full payments become due in early November and again in early December, cabins and rooms become available when the checks don't arrive. In early March, cancellations begin to come in for April. (There's a 30-day notice required to get a refund.) On the average, LeConte gets one or two cancellations a day throughout the season, so it's always a good idea to call.

The basic rate for a one-room cabin that sleeps four is $58.50 per night for each adult, which includes dinner the night you arrive and breakfast the next morning. (If you stay more than one night, lunch also is included.) The rate for children age 4–11 is $50.50 per night. Each cabin is equipped with a kerosene heater and lantern.

Two-bedroom lodges that sleep up to eight people rent for $256 per night; meals are $26.50 for adults and $18.50 for children. Three-bedroom cabins are $384 per night.

—— *Accommodations Outside the Park*

For people who didn't get a reservation at LeConte Lodge—or don't relish the thought of a four-hour hike to reach their room—the gateway towns outside the park offer thousands of motel rooms, mountain cabins, campsites, and chalets for rent. See Part Three (Hotels) for detailed, zone-by-zone reviews of places to stay around Great Smoky. Here's an overview of the different "gateway" towns outside the park.

Gatlinburg, Tennessee (Zone 2). Located two miles north of the Sugarlands Visitor Center, Gatlinburg is what most people think of when they think of the Smoky Mountains. It's a crowded little town full of craft shops, aerial tramways, fast-food restaurants, cheesy souvenir shops, wedding chapels, and lots to do (especially for families with kids). The town's traffic jams in high tourist season (mid-summer and October) are legendary.

Gatlinburg is close to the northern entrance to the park, although you'll still have to drive to get to virtually all of its attractions. The town also offers an astounding array of accommodations, shopping, tourist attractions, and restaurants; for more information, call (800) 568-4748 or (615) 430-4148.

Pigeon Forge, Tennessee (Zone 2). Located five miles farther north on US 441, Pigeon Forge is like a spread-out version of Gatlinburg. The main highway is lined with motels, miniature golf courses, kiddy rides, go-cart tracks, helicopter tours, and at least one representative (usually more) of every fast-food chain in the industry. It's even got its own theme park—Dollywood.

It's a much more family-oriented town than Gatlinburg (no booze served in Pigeon Forge restaurants) and not as convenient to the national park. Luckily, there is a bypass around Gatlinburg that goes directly into Great Smoky, so folks staying in Pigeon Forge don't have to fight Gatlinburg's horrendous traffic. Call (800) 251-9100 for more information.

Sevierville, Tennessee (Zone 2).   Located on US 441 north of Pigeon Forge, this town is nine miles from I-40 to the north and 13 miles from Great Smoky to the south. While Sevierville is not convenient to the national park, its room rates are generally less expensive. The tourism hype and congestion, however, is formidable. For more information, call (615) 453-6411.

Cherokee, North Carolina (Zone 4).   Next to Great Smoky on US 441 in North Carolina is the only Indian reservation in the mid-Atlantic states. Tourism is the economic foundation of the Cherokee tribe, which now numbers about 10,000 people. The reservation boasts 56 motels, 28 campgrounds, shops, a few cultural attractions, and excellent fishing.

The town of Cherokee, which is in the center of the reservation, is just south of the southern entrance to Great Smoky. While you'll see plenty of roadside amusements and souvenir stands selling Korean-made junk there, the tourism hype is more subdued than in the gateway towns in Tennessee. For those old enough to remember car touring in the 50s, it's actually quaint.

Folks interested in learning more about Cherokee culture will enjoy staying here, too. (You'll just have to get off of US 441 to discover it. See our write-up in Zone 4 for more information.) Call (800) 438-1601 or (704) 488-3681 to get additional information.

Townsend, Tennessee (Zone 3).   This town outside Great Smoky's western entrance is another place where the tourist hype is less intense. In addition to a modest selection of motels, log cabins for rent, and campgrounds, Townsend offers golf, tennis, swimming, tubing in the river, and horseback riding.

While the town provides the easiest access to popular Cades Cove inside the national park, it's a much longer haul to visit places such as Newfound Gap and Clingmans Dome. For more information, call (800) 525-6834.

Bryson City, North Carolina (Zone 4).   Located off US 74 a few miles south of the park's southern entrance, Bryson City is another place that's off the main tourist track. It's also a popular destination for whitewater rafters and canoeists, anglers, and hard-core outdoor types in general.

You'll also find easy access to many little-used trails and streams in Great Smoky, although you must drive north to Cherokee and the southern entrance on US 441 to reach the more popular spots. Call (704) 488-3681 for more information.

Fontana Dam, North Carolina (Zone 4). Located across Lake Fontana on the park's southern border, Fontana Dam and Village Resort is located on NC 28 that features a marina, sightseeing cruises on the lake, horseback riding, and organized activities for children. Accommodations include cottages with kitchens, an inn, houseboats, and camping sites.

Originally designed to house the workers who built huge Fontana Dam during World War II, the site later was converted to a resort. This is *way* off the beaten track, and there isn't a souvenir stand in sight. In fact, Fontana is quite isolated. But for anglers and folks looking for peace and quiet—and maybe the adventure of exploring the southern border of Great Smoky by canoe or sea kayak—this is the place. For more information, call (800) 849-2258.

—— *Camping*

All ten campgrounds in Great Smoky provide cold running water, fire grills, picnic tables, and flush toilets. What you won't find are electrical hookups, water hookups, or showers. Extensive hiking and horse trails are located close to all the campgrounds. Opening and closing dates for the campgrounds that aren't open all year vary from year to year, so be sure to call before making any plans.

Reservations for campsites can be made during the warm weather months at the park's three major campgrounds: Cades Cove, Elkmont, and Smokemont. If you're planning a trip in July or October, make your reservations at least four weeks ahead of time. (Reservations aren't accepted more than eight weeks in advance.) Call (800) 365-CAMP.

The campgrounds fill up quickly on weekends in the spring and early summer; during the summer and in October, they're almost always full on weekdays and weekends. For more information on camping in the park, call park headquarters at (615) 436-1200.

Cades Cove

Formerly an isolated valley first settled in 1818, today this beautiful area is one of the most popular destinations in Great Smoky. The Cades Cove Campground is large and, unlike most of the other campgrounds in the park, features open campsites with few trees or shrubbery between sites. Located on fairly flat terrain, the sprawling campground is a popular destination for RVs.

Cades Cove, at an elevation of 1,807 feet, features 161 sites and is open all year, although only a limited number of sites are available from November through mid-May (when no reservations are accepted). The daily fee is $11; the fee is $8 in the off-season. There's a 7-day camping limit from mid-May through October, and a 14-day limit the rest of the year.

Facilities include a camp store, bike rentals (for riding the 11-mile loop road through the valley), a disposal station, and wood for sale. Naturalist programs are held in the small amphitheater and riding stables are nearby.

Elkmont

Located off Little River Road about five miles from the Sugarlands Visitor Center, Elkmont is the closest campground to Gatlinburg and the northern entrance to the park. Many campsites are located along fast-moving mountain streams, and most are well spaced with many trees and shrubbery between them. It's a comfortable campground.

Elkmont, which is open year-round, offers 220 sites during the main season and 29 in the off-season. Camping is $11 a night during the busy season and $8 a night from November through mid-May (when no reservations are accepted). Elevation is 2,150 feet, and services include a disposal station, firewood for sale, a phone, and a couple of vending machines. The stay limit is 7 days from mid-May through October and 14 days from November through mid-May.

Smokemont

Located on the North Carolina side of the park, Smokemont is on Newfound Gap Road six miles north of Cherokee. The campground provides 140 sites during the main season and is open all year.

It's a beautiful campground with lots of foliage between sites; many are located alongside or close to streams. The elevation is 2,198 feet.

The nightly fee is $11 from mid-May through October and $8 the rest of the year. Facilities include a disposal station and firewood for sale; fishing, naturalist programs, and horseback riding are all nearby.

Additional Campgrounds

Seven smaller campgrounds are located throughout Great Smoky along its boundary. All are closed in the off-season, and no reservations are accepted. The daily fee is $8 per night, except where noted.

Balsam Mountain. Open from late May through mid-October, this campground is located eight miles north of the Blue Ridge Parkway between mile markers 458 and 459, east of the Oconaluftee Visitor Center on the North Carolina side of the park. It features 46 sites; the elevation is 5,310 feet. The stay limit is seven days, and firewood is available.

Cosby. Located off TN 32 at the northeastern end of the park, Cosby has 175 campsites and is open from late May through October. Elevation is 2,459 feet, and facilities include a disposal station. Activities nearby include fishing, naturalist programs, and horseback riding.

Deep Creek. Open from mid-May through October, Deep Creek is three miles north of Bryson City, North Carolina. It offers 108 sites, a disposal station, and firewood for sale. Nearby activities include fishing and naturalist programs.

Look Rock. Located on Tennessee's Foothills Parkway between Walland and Chilhowee, this campground is open from Memorial Day through Labor Day. It offers 92 sites, hiking, and many scenic overlooks. The elevation is 2,600 feet.

Abrams Creek. Located west of Cades Cove, Abrams Creek offers 16 sites restricted to tents and trailers up to 12 feet in length. The campground is open mid-May through October; the daily fee is $6. The elevation is 1,125 feet.

Big Creek. Open from mid-May through October, Big Creek is located off Exit 451 on I-40, eight miles east of Newport, Tennessee. The campground has 12 tent sites; the daily fee is $6. The elevation is 1,700 feet.

Cataloochee. Located off US 276 near I-40 in North Carolina, this campground has 27 sites and is open from mid-May through October. The daily fee is $6; the elevation is 2,610 feet.

Outdoor Recreation and Activities

—— **Nature Trails**

Great Smoky offers visitors a number of self-guided nature trails—easy walks through the forest that contain numbered stakes keyed to pamphlets that describe the various points of interest along the trail. Pick up brochures at a visitor center or from stands at the beginning of the trail.

Sugarlands. This one-mile trail begins behind the Sugarlands Visitor Center. It meanders through part of a lowland called "Sugarlands" because of the sugar maples that once grew in the area. The loop walk also takes you by the restored John Ownby cabin.

Noah "Bud" Ogle Nature Trail. This three-quarter-mile trail begins on Cherokee Orchard Road, three miles south of Gatlinburg, and takes visitors through an abandoned farmstead. In Gatlinburg, take Airport Road (traffic light 8), which becomes Cherokee Orchard Road, to the parking area.

Cosby Nature Trail. This one-mile trail introduces visitors to the stream environment of Cosby Creek as the path passes over the stream and its tributaries on footbridges. It starts in the Cosby Campground, located east of Gatlinburg, off TN 32.

Laurel Falls Trail. Located three miles west of the Sugarlands Visitor Center, this popular, paved, two-and-a-half-mile path leading to the falls is also a nature trail.

Elkmont Nature Trail. This beautiful, three-quarter-mile footpath starts in the parking area opposite Elkmont Campgroud, five miles west of the Sugarlands Visitor Center. It takes visitors to an area where a railroad once hauled logs out of the mountains.

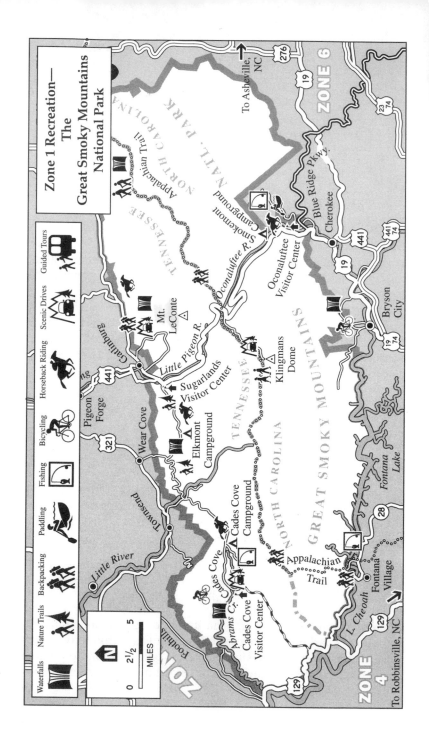

Zone 1 Recreation—
The Great Smoky Mountains National Park

Waterfalls | Nature Trails | Backpacking | Paddling | Fishing | Bicycling | Horseback Riding | Scenic Drives | Guided Tours

Cades Cove Nature Trail.   Located a little more than six miles along the Cades Cove Loop Road, the half-mile trail explains how settlers used native plants.

Cove Hardwood Nature Trail.   Beginning at Chimney Tops picnic area on Newfound Gap Road, this trail guides visitors three-quarters of a mile through second-growth woods to a mature cove hardwood forest.

Alum Cave Bluffs Nature Trail.   This five-mile trail, which climbs 1,000 feet, is the longest and most difficult nature trail in the park. It passes through a bald (an open, unforested field on a mountain ridge) and through Arch Rock to Alum Cave. It starts at Alum Cave Bluffs trail head on Newfound Gap Road.

Spruce-Fir Nature Trail.   It's a half-mile walk that begins on Clingmans Dome Road and takes visitors through a forest of red spruce and Fraser fir. The trail is a great alternative to the observation tower atop Clingmans Dome when a cloud envelops the mountain and obscures the view.

Smokemont Nature Trail.   Starting in the Smokemont Campground, this three-quarter mile walk shows how humans affected the land through logging and farming.

Balsam Mountain Nature Trail.   Starting at Balsam Mountain Campground in the southeastern corner of the park, this trail takes walkers three-quarters of a mile through a once-logged northern hardwood forest.

—— *Hiking*

At Great Smoky, the choice of trails runs the gamut from challenging, all-day scrambles up steep mountainsides to easy, roadside paths called "Quiet Walkways." But unless you're an experienced hiker, limit the length of a day hike to eight or ten miles. If you're a novice hiker or haven't strapped on your boots in a while, try to limit hikes to about five miles or so until your stamina increases. And don't forget: Leave word with someone about where you're hiking and when you plan to return.

The Appalachian Trail

The most famous—and by far the most heavily used—trail in the park is the Appalachian Trail, a 2,100-mile footpath that goes from Georgia to Maine. The 68-mile segment that passes through Great Smoky follows the Smokies' ridge line west to east on its way to Mount Katahdin in Maine.

The Appalachian Trail can be accessed at Newfound Gap, Clingmans Dome, the end of TN 32 just north of Big Creek Campground (at the northeastern end of the park), and at Fontana Dam (which the trail crosses before entering Great Smoky at the southwestern end of the park). One of the most popular segments of the trail with day hikers starts at Newfound Gap; see below.

With the profusion of choices, we've selected a few of the most popular—and scenic—trails to help you find a hike that matches your abilities and interests. And except for self-guided nature trails, be sure to take a good trail map along on your hike.

Easy Hikes

Laurel Falls Trail.   This is the most popular waterfall trail in the park. Two and a half miles round trip on a paved and relatively flat path, this trail passes through a pine and oak forest before reaching the falls. Total elevation gain is about 200 feet.

Intrepid hikers can continue on another half mile past the falls to a stand of virgin timber—just make sure you're wearing appropriate footwear. The trail head is located on Little River Road, a few miles from the Sugarlands Visitor Center.

Indian Creek Falls Trail.   Located on the southern edge of the park near Bryson City, North Carolina, this easy, two-mile round-trip trail leads to Indian Creek Falls, which cascade 60 feet down a series of ledges into a wide pool. The trail head is at the end of Deep Creek Road just past Deep Creek Campground. The total elevation gain is 100 feet. To get there, follow the signs to Deep Creek Campground out of Bryson City to the parking lot at the trail head and walk upstream through the gate.

Abrams Falls Trail.   Located on the Cades Cove Loop Road, this easy, five-mile hike is relatively flat and leads to 20-foot-high Abrams

Falls. Total elevation gain is about 340 feet. The trail begins at the Abrams Falls parking lot at the west end of the loop road.

Moderate Hikes

Newfound Gap to Charles Bunion on the Appalachian Trail. This eight-mile round-trip, out-and-back hike is one of the most popular stretches on the Appalachian Trail. The trail passes through a spruce and fir forest and provides spectacular vistas. Total elevation gain is 980 feet. Park in the Newfound Gap Overlook parking lot on Newfound Gap Road (US 441).

Alum Cave Bluffs Trail. This is a trail that starts off easy but gets more difficult as you go. The first one and a half miles leads to Arch Rock, where erosion has created a tunnel through the rock. The next eight-tenths mile is steeper and goes to a 100-foot-high cliff, Alum Cave Bluffs. The last three-plus miles take you to Mount LeConte and one of the best views in the park.

Total length is 11 miles, round trip; total elevation gain is an impressive 2,800 feet. Park in the Alum Cave Bluffs parking area, nine miles south of Sugarlands Visitor Center on Newfound Gap Road.

Hen Wallow Falls Trail. This trail, which starts near the picnic area near Cosby Campground in the northeastern corner of the park, makes for a worthwhile, but relatively short, day hike. The main trail leads to the top of the falls; a narrow side trail leads to the base. The total length, out and back, is four miles; total elevation gain is 520 feet.

Strenuous Hikes

Ramsay Cascades. This is a strenuous, eight-mile round-trip hike that leads to the park's highest waterfall. It passes through an old-growth, deciduous forest before reaching the 100-foot-high Ramsay Cascades. From Gatlinburg, take US 321 to Greenbrier Cove and follow the signs to the trail head. Total elevation gain, by the way, is a whopping 2,375 feet.

Boulevard Trail to Mount LeConte. While some hikers would call this hike moderate, its length—16 miles—puts it in the strenuous category for most folks. But it's the easiest and most popular trail to

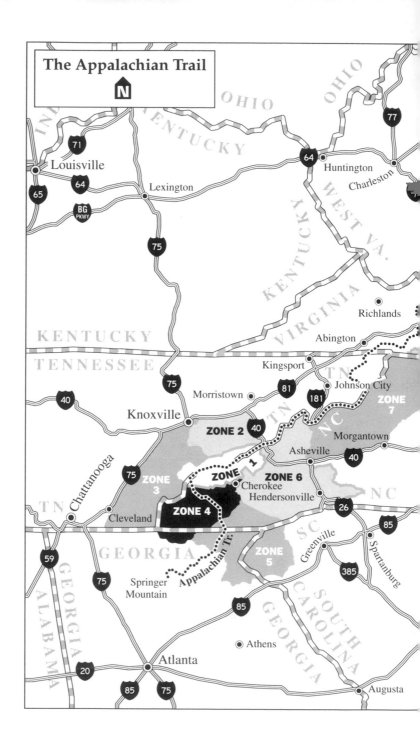

The Appalachian Trail

N

OHIO
KENTUCKY
OHIO

INDIANA

Louisville
71

64

BG PKWY

65

Lexington

75

64

Huntington
77
Charleston

WEST VA.

KENTUCKY

VIRGINIA

Richlands

Abington

KENTUCKY

TENNESSEE

75

40

Kingsport

Morristown

TN

81

181

Johnson City

ZONE 7

Knoxville

ZONE 2

40

Asheville

Morgantown

40

Chattanooga

75

ZONE 3

ZONE 1

Cherokee

ZONE 6

NC

Hendersonville

Cleveland

ZONE 4

TN

26

SC

85

GEORGIA

Springer
Mountain

Appalachian Tr.

ZONE 5

Greenville

Spartanburg

385

59

75

85

SOUTH

ALABAMA

GEORGIA

CAROLINA

Athens

GEORGIA

20

Atlanta

85

75

Augusta

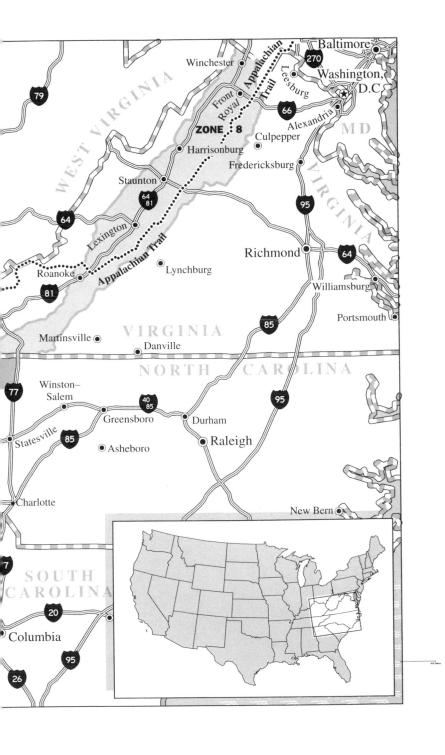

the top of Mount LeConte. Start at Newfound Gap on the Appalachian Trail and hang a left onto the Boulevard Trail. Total elevation gain is 1,545 feet.

—— Backpacking

Overnight hikers in Great Smoky can experience the ultimate in wilderness solitude and scenic vistas on trails that thread the whole fabric of the Smokies' back country. But before embarking on a multiday trip, hikers must first obtain a back-country permit.

Back-Country Permits

Camping in the back country is free, but a permit system protects the park, its natural environment, and the quality of each hiker's experience. The goal, in a nutshell, is to spread out the impact of backpacking and prevent hikers from loving the park to death.

How? By limiting the number of hikers allowed to stay each night in about 15 popular back-country campsites (out of the 98 camping areas scattered across the park). Note: You must camp in designated back-country campsites; setting up your tent just anywhere isn't allowed and results in a fine if you're caught.

To use one of the rationed campsites, you must call the park's Back Country Reservation Service to get permission. It's best to work up your itinerary at least one month in advance, determine if your trip requires the use of a rationed campsite, and, if it does, call for a reservation. The office is open daily from 8 A.M. to 6 P.M.; phone (615) 436-1231.

If your trip doesn't include rationed sites, you can self-register at any ranger station or visitor center (except Cades Cove) when you arrive at the park. Call the park's main number to get information on trails and a list of back-country campsites at (615) 436-1200.

More rules for back-country camping: You may stay up to three consecutive nights at a campsite; the maximum size of a hiking group is eight; all trash must be carried out. And don't forget to take trail maps along.

Shelters

In addition to back-country campsites, the park has a system of 18 shelters. The shelters confine the impact caused by heavy overnight use at popular areas. Reservations are required for their use; stays are limited to one night. The shelters are three-sided structures with a fourth side made of chain link fence to bear-proof the buildings.

Tents are prohibited at shelter areas, and wood fires are discouraged. Most of the shelters are located along the Appalachian Trail about eight to ten miles apart. Designed primarily for through-hikers, the shelters usually don't provide the degree of solitude you'll find at back-country campsites.

With more than 800 miles of hiking trails in the park, most backpackers would take a lifetime to explore it. Here are a couple of trips to get you started.

LeConte Lodge.   Some purists may argue that a hike to the summit of Mount LeConte and an overnight stay at rustic LeConte Lodge isn't really backpacking. But who can argue with the romance of hiking at least five miles and spending the night in a mountaintop cabin that's heated and lighted by kerosene? And don't worry about food: Dinner and breakfast are included in the deal. One thing's for sure— you don't have to pack much for the hike.

Five trails lead to the summit of Mount LeConte, and it's possible to make a circuit hike out of the trip. Here's how: Find an amenable group of hikers who also are spending the night at the top and trade car keys. Then you can hike back to their car on a different trail. It also makes it possible for you to take the easiest trail up to the lodge (the Boulevard Trail) and a more difficult trail down. Pretty smart. For more information on obtaining reservations at this *extremely* popular destination, see page 208.

Spence Field Shelter.   This overnight hike leads from Cades Cove to Spence Field on the Appalachian Trail via the Russell Field, Bote Mountain, and Anthony Creek trails. The reward is terrific views from 5,000 feet. Though not a long trip, the hike is strenuous due to the elevation gain and loss: Cades Cove is at 2,000 feet, Russell Field Shelter is at 4,360 feet, and Spence Field Shelter is at 4,900 feet.

Start the hike at the Cades Cove Campground entrance on Anthony Creek Trail. Follow the trail past the horse camp about one and a half miles to the junction with Russell Field Trail. Turn right onto the Russell Field Trail and go three and a half miles to the shelter at the juncture with the Appalachian Trail. Camp here or continue north another two and a half miles to the Spence Field Shelter.

On a clear day, a rewarding extension is to hike north on the Appalachian Trail to take in the view from Thunderhead Mountain (a five-mile round trip). For a loop return to Cades Cove, from Spence Field Shelter, take a left on the Bote Mountain Trail. Go to the junction with Anthony Creek Trail and turn left; go past the junction with Russell Field Trail and return to your car.

Eagle Creek Canoe Camp.   This is an overnight trip that's different: A canoe or sea kayak voyage across Fontana Lake into Great Smoky to camp at a beautiful, isolated campsite, explore trails, and fish in Eagle Creek. If you don't have any water transportation, you can rent some at marinas on the lake.

Put in on Fontana Lake at Fontana Dam on NC 28. There's a large parking lot near the dam, and it's a short carry to the water. Cross the main body of the lake to the north shore; Eagle Creek Cove is the first long cove (look for a small island marking its entrance). It's about three miles to the head of the cove and campsite 90, where Twentymile and Eagle Creek trails intersect.

Where to Get a Hot Shower

For a lot of backpackers, a return to civilization after experiencing the joys of the back country doesn't really begin until they've had a hot shower.

If your first stop isn't a motel in one of the gateway towns, then **The Happy Hiker,** an outfitter in Gatlinburg, is the place to go: Next door is **Camp Suds,** a coin-operated laundry and hot shower emporium run by the hiking shop.

Showers are open every day (except Christmas) from 8 A.M. to 7 P.M.; the laundry is open from 8 A.M. to midnight. Showers are $2, and towel rental is fifty cents. The shop is open from 8 A.M. to 9 P.M. daily. Both are located in the Burning Bush Plaza, a block from traffic light 10 in Gatlinburg; phone (615) 436-6000.

—— *Canoeing, Kayaking, and Rafting*

There are no commercial river trips available within the Great Smoky Mountains National Park. For advanced whitewater canoeists and kayakers, however, the Class III–IV (V) Little River on the north side of the park can be run from Elkmont to Townsend in periods of high water. On the south side of the park, the Class II–III Oconaluftee River is a good run for intermediate paddlers. The last seven miles of the Smokemont Campground to Birdtown run pass through the Cherokee Indian Reservation. From April to October, this section can only be run on Tuesdays. For detailed information on these and other area rivers, check our list of recommended reading for canoeing, kayaking, and rafting on pages 76–77. If you are camping in the park, the closest commercially run rivers are the Nantahala and the Tuckasegee below Dillsboro in Zone 4.

—— *Trout Fishing*

In Great Smoky, fishing means angling for trout: With more than 300 fishable streams, the park is one of the last wild trout habitats in the eastern United States. Among the ten million or so visitors who come to the park each year, thousands are anglers eager to test their luck against the stream-bred trout in Great Smoky's famed waters. Should you join them? Here's a brief introduction to trout fishing in the Smokies.

Three Species

Brook trout, known locally as "spec" due to the speckled design on their back, are true natives to the Smokies. While once abundant, wholesale logging devastated their habitat and depleted their numbers. Today, the brook trout are protected inside the park and cannot be taken by anglers. If you hook a brookie, release it.

Rainbow trout are renown for their superb fighting ability, arching leaps—and good eating. Rainbows are recognizable by their silvery flanks slashed with scarlet and their greenish back. They are beautiful fish. Most average 7 inches in length, but an occasional 12- to 16-incher is taken.

Brown trout are distinguished by their generally brownish-yellow color with orange spots on the sides. They prefer slower water than rainbow do. The largest brown trout taken in the park weighed 16 pounds.

When to Fish

Spring is a season of brisk activity in the streams of Great Smoky. As the season gets milder, the water gets warmer and insects become more common—along with the surface feeding of the trout. The activity peaks in late spring—mid-May through mid-June. That's when the fish can afford to be selective, and fly selection becomes important.

Summer action, on the other hand, is usually slow. The remaining insect hatches are less frequent, streams suffer from occasional dry weather, and water temperatures rise, which causes trout to seek deep, cool havens during the day and feed at night. The action picks up again in the **fall.** Sensing the coming winter, trout feed with abandon. During the **winter**, cold weather slows the fish's metabolism, reducing the amount of food needed to survive. But on mild days—and there are many afternoons during the winter months when temperatures creep into the 70s—trout will move to sunny areas and do a mild amount of feeding.

How to Catch Trout

The usual question is, "What's the best way to fish the park's streams—fly-fishing or spinners?" Alas, there's no single answer to the question. But the simplest—and cheapest—method for people who aren't experienced anglers and would like to try their hand at fishing for trout in the park is to use a simple cane pole.

Fly rods, which start at eight feet in length, usually are made of graphite and start around $150. Spinning rod kits start around $30. Individual flies—live bait is not allowed in Great Smoky—start around $1.60.

Casting. On the stream, keep in mind that most trout face upstream into the current. Most experienced Smoky Mountain anglers prefer to fish walking upstream, coming up behind their quarry. A quiet approach and an accurate presentation of the lure can't be overemphasized. If you cast to the right spot with the right offering often enough, you will catch fish.

Spinners. Most experienced anglers concentrate on large- to medium-sized streams. On long, slow-moving pools of water, stand below the pool and cast upstream. Retrieve the lure at a pace slightly faster than the speed of the current. Work upstream, reeling in your lure at different speeds and depths.

Where to Find the Trout

There are 13 major watersheds in Great Smoky, as well as a number of smaller ones—which means there is plenty of good fishing in streams close to the major entrances to the park, as well as deep in the interior. Here's a brief rundown on some convenient spots:

Gatlinburg. The West Prong of the Little Pigeon River flows through the middle of town, offering excellent rainbow and brown trout fishing.

Cherokee. The Raven Fork and Oconaluftee River flow together upstream of town; both offer fine fishing. Newfound Gap Road on the North Carolina side of the park follows the Oconaluftee, which provides plenty of access. It's noted for its large brown trout, some exceeding 12 pounds. As with many streams in the Smokies, brook trout can be found in the higher elevation tributaries of the stream.

Bryson City. Deep Creek, which exits the park near Bryson City, also offers plenty of good fishing opportunities. Anglers can avoid the throngs of tubers by fishing above the confluence of Indian Creek, about a mile upstream of the campground. Trophy brown trout of over eight pounds have been caught in this stream. Brook trout can be found near the headwaters above 3,600 feet.

Abrams Creek. This stream flowing out of Cades Cove is known for its large rainbow trout, which flourish in the limestone-enriched water. Two sections are of particular note: Little Bottoms, accessible from Abrams Creek Campground, is relatively remote and offers solitude. The second section, the Horseshoe section between Abrams Creek Falls and Cades Cove, is accessible from Cades Cove via the Abrams Falls Trail, which starts near the Cades Cove Visitor Center.

Fontana. Streams that enter Fontana Lake include Eagle, Hazel, Forney, and Chambers creeks. Anglers can rent boats at Fontana Resort's marina to cross the lake. It's definitely the way to beat the crowds and fish some remote streams.

Regulations

Anglers must possess a valid Tennessee or North Carolina fishing license and can fish anywhere inside the national park, regardless of which state they are in. Trout stamps, however, aren't required. Tennessee requires that residents and nonresidents age 13 and older have a license, except for residents who were 65 prior to March 1, 1990. North Carolina requires everyone age 16 and older to obtain a license. While licenses aren't sold in the park, they're available in towns outside the park.

Fishing is permitted year-round in open waters from sunrise to sunset. Some streams are posted to protect the native brook trout. The daily possession limit is five rainbow or brown trout, smallmouth bass, or any combination. Fishing regulations vary throughout the park, so be sure to pick up a copy of the rules at a visitors center or ranger station.

More Information

The ins and outs of this subtle sport can take a lifetime to explore. But there is a shortcut: Hook up with a guide.

"Even people who know how to fly-fish but have never visited the Smokies before can benefit from going with an experienced guide," reports one of the pros at **Old Smoky Outfitters,** a fly-fishing outfitter and shop in the Riverbend Mall in Gatlinburg. Half-day trips for novices and experienced anglers begin at $50 per person; phone (615) 430-1936.

You also can stop by the shop and park visitor centers for specific recommendations for places where the fish are biting.

—— Bicycling

Riding a *road bike* in Great Smoky is one of those good news/bad news scenarios: The good news is—there are plenty of places to ride a skinny-tire bike. The bad news? All the routes are on extremely steep, narrow mountain roads that are often clogged with traffic. Unless you're a Greg LeMond looking for strenuous training rides, leave your road bike at home when vacationing in the park.

The situation is only slightly better for *mountain biking:* As in all national parks, forest trails and dirt roads are off-limits to bicycles. All is not lost, however: There are a couple of excellent destinations for both fat- and skinny-tire bikers.

Cades Cove Loop. The 11-mile loop traverses beautiful Cades Cove and provides two-wheel visitors with lovely views, wildlife sightings, and a history lesson on the old community that once thrived in this magnificent setting.

Experienced cyclists will find the ride a bit hilly, but not very challenging. (They'll also smile when they see the warning signs for "steep" grades.) Folks who don't often ride a bike may have to walk some of the short, but steep, hills along the way. Rental bikes are available at the Cades Cove Campground store. Note: On Saturday mornings June through Labor Day, the loop road is closed to cars from dawn to 10 A.M.

Townsend/Cades Cove Loop. For a longer (40 miles) ride than the simple tour of Cades Cove, try this mostly paved road ride with a 10-mile stretch of gravel road. It's a ride for ambitious intermediate riders who don't mind getting whipped and for strong riders. It's a death march for inexperienced cyclists.

Start in Townsend, outside the western entrance to Great Smoky. Ride into the park and turn right onto the Laurel Creek Road. Continue on it approximately 12 hilly miles to Cades Cove.

Take the Cades Cove Loop Road to the gravel Rich Mountain Road and turn right. At the summit of the ridge, the road turns to pavement as you exit the park. A steep, switchback-filled descent leads down into Tuckaleechee Cove. At the end of Tuckaleechee Cove Road, turn right onto US 321 for the ride back into Townsend. Local riders say this loop is perfect for hybrid bikes with mildly knobby tires.

Deep Creek/Indian Creek. This is the only not-open-to-normal-traffic road in Great Smoky where you legally can get your tires dirty. It is a series of hard-surface gravel roads driven by rangers where the riding is easy. As a result, the muddy spots are hard-bottomed if you stay in the tire ruts. The route is Y-shaped, with two long out-and-backs along Deep Creek and Indian Creek.

The trail head is next to the Deep Creek Picnic Area just outside Bryson City; follow the signs from downtown. From the trail head, pedal through the gate upstream (watch for tubers in the river). After a half mile, take the right turn up Indian Creek past Indian Creek Falls. Turn around where the gravel roads and trail begin after about four miles. Return to Deep Creek and turn right at the intersection.

Ride up Deep Creek about five miles to the turnaround at the end of the gravel road and return. The total distance is about 18 miles. Note: Although single-track trails split off in every direction from the roads, fight the urge and stay off them. It's illegal to ride trails in national parks.

—— Horseback Riding

Many equestrians say Great Smoky offers some of the best horseback riding in the East. Folks who own their own horse should contact the park for information and regulations on riding the park's trails and camping with horses; call (615) 436-1200.

Horses are restricted to trails specifically designated for horse use; off-trail and cross-country riding is prohibited. Reservations at five drive-in horse camps provide easy access to back-country horse trails: Anthony Creek (capacity 12 campers/12 horses), Big Creek (capacity 20), Cataloochee (capacity 28), Round Bottom (capacity 20), and Towstring (capacity 20). Call the Back Country Reservations Office to make reservations no more than a month in advance: (615) 436-1231.

People who don't have their own horse can rent horses by the hour and half day from four private stables inside the park: **Cades Cove,** phone (615) 448-6286; **Smokemont,** (704) 497-2373; **McCarter's Riding Stables,** near Park Headquarters on Newfound Gap Road, (615) 436-5354; and **Smoky Mountains Riding Stables,** two miles east of Gatlinburg on US 321, (615) 436-5634. All horse rentals in the park are guided tours; prices start at $12 an hour.

—— Waterfalls

The sight, sound, and feel of cool water cascading down a mountain slope entice visitors to get out of their cars and explore the Smokies away from paved roads. It's a great excuse to enjoy the back country.

It's no surprise that so many rushing streams and waterfalls are here to reward hikers for their efforts: Annual precipitation averages about 50 inches at lower elevations inside the park and up to 83 inches at Clingmans Dome, the park's highest point. The rain comes from warm, moist air masses that move inland from the Gulf of Mexico and the Atlantic Ocean. These air masses cool as they rise over the mountains and release excess moisture in the form of precipitation.

From Your Car

Three waterfalls can be seen from the road without leaving your car. Twelve miles west of Sugarlands Visitor Center on Little River Road is **The Sinks**. A mile farther west look for Meigs Creek dramatically joining Little River as it plunges down **Meigs Falls.**

Near the end of the Roaring Fork Motor Nature Trail is **The Place of a Thousand Drips**—a "sometimes" waterfall on a tall, rocky cliff where water seeps out of every crevice during dry spells and gushes forth to form a series of waterfalls during wet periods.

Waterfalls Along Trails

Rainbow Falls Trail is reached by driving south on Airport Road in Gatlinburg (traffic light 8) to Cherokee Orchard. The trail passes through a cool, shady cove hardwood forest before reaching the falls, which drop straight down for 80 feet. It's a moderate, five-and-a-half-mile round-trip hike with 1,750 feet of altitude gain.

Grotto Falls Trail begins at stop five on the Roaring Fork Motor Nature Trail. It's an easy, three-mile hike through a hemlock forest; the elevation gain is 560 feet. The cool, moist environment around the falls makes it a favorite spot on hot summer days.

Ramsay Cascades, the highest waterfall in the park, plunges 100 feet over rocks. Many big trees line the trail on the eight-mile, strenuous hike to the falls. Note: Don't attempt climbing to the top of the falls; many have died trying it.

The trail to **Hen Wallow Falls** is a pleasant walk through a hemlock, poplar, and rhododendron forest. It's a moderate, four-mile round-trip hike that starts in the Cosby Campground, on TN 32 at the northeastern corner of the park.

Indian Creek Falls is reached on a trail that follows an old road paralleling Deep Creek that provides an easy grade and good walking surface. The falls drop 60 feet over rocky ledges to form a big pool at the base. The easy, two-mile hike starts in the Deep Creek Campground amphitheater, a couple miles north of Bryson City.

—— Scenic Drives

Vistas

Drives through Great Smoky reward visitors with panoramic views of tumbling mountain streams, weathered pioneer dwellings, and uninterrupted forest stretching from ridge to ridge. More than 270 miles of roads are located in the half-million-acre park—and they're here for visitors to explore and enjoy.

To get the most from a scenic driving tour of the park, drive slowly and stop often. Each road, valley, and mountain peak has a character of its own—but you'll have to get out of the car occasionally to really discover it.

Other things to keep in mind on a scenic drive: Picnic areas and rest room facilities are located throughout the park. Also, allow more time than usual to complete a drive—the roads are steep and winding. You'll also enjoy a more leisurely pace during the early morning and during late afternoon and early evening hours—there's less traffic. In addition, you'll see more wildlife.

Finally, don't get too absorbed with the scenery if you're behind the wheel. Watch the road while driving and pull over frequently at scenic overlooks and pullouts—don't stop in the roadway. When the traffic gets too heavy, pull over and explore a quiet trail along the side of the road (look for the "Quiet Walkways" signs).

Escaping the Crowds

An odd fact about Great Smoky is that while it's our most visited national park, the back country is barely used. Except for the

Appalachian Trail along the Tennessee–North Carolina state line, most hiking trails in the park offer outstanding opportunities for solitude in a wilderness setting. As one frequent visitor to the park told us, "Get out of your car and onto a trail and you're more likely to see a bear than another person." Before embarking on a back-country trek, however, check with a ranger about trail conditions and make sure to take a map.

Newfound Gap Road (US 441).   This road, the only one that crosses the park, starts at 2,000 feet of elevation and climbs to 5,048 feet at Newfound Gap Overlook, which straddles the Tennessee–North Carolina state line. As you drive along the road, look for distinct changes in vegetation and temperature along the way.

The forests range from southern cove hardwood and pine-oak at the lower elevations and change to northern hardwood, heath bald, and spruce-fir forests as you climb. In fact, you can compress a trip from Georgia to Canada in this relatively short drive up the mountain—at least, in the types of vegetation you'll see along the way.

While breathtaking views are the norm on this drive, one of its more unusual features is The Loop, where, about seven miles from Gatlinburg, the highway literally crosses over itself! The loop design was necessary because of the steep slope.

Clingmans Dome Road.   This spectacular, seven-mile-long road follows the crest of the Smokies along the state line. Most of the drive is through spruce-fir forests. From the parking lot at the end of the road, you can get out of the car and hike a half mile to the observation tower and see a panoramic view of the park and the surrounding mountains. You'll also wade through crowds of crying babies and puffing tourists on the way.

Keep in mind, however, that bad weather or low clouds can obscure the vista; the road is closed from December to April. Clingmans Dome, at 6,642 feet, is the highest point in the park and in Tennessee. For an unusual and rewarding way to enjoy the hike, go on a clear night during a full moon after the leaves have dropped off the trees. It's easy to follow the path in the moonlight, and the view from the observation tower is terrific.

Roaring Fork Motor Nature Trail.   Most nature trails are easy paths through the woods where you hike and read information about the forest and wildlife. On this trail, however, you *drive* five miles through a vigorous young forest. A self-guiding booklet is available at the trail head. Sights along the way include aging pioneer structures and water cascading down the side of a mountain. There are plenty of places to park the car and get out to explore.

The trail is a one-way loop along a narrow, and sometimes steep, paved road that can be rough in a few spots. Drive slowly, though, and the family car is okay. Figure on an hour to drive the loop, longer if you make a few stops. The nature trail is closed in the winter.

The trail starts in Gatlinburg, Tennessee. From US 441 in town, turn at traffic light 8 (Airport Road) and follow the signs to the loop. The trail brings you out on US 321 when you're done; turn left to return to Gatlinburg.

Cades Cove Loop Road.   This 11-mile loop is a favorite with both motorists and bicyclists. The one-lane, one-way road takes visitors on a trip through the history of the people who once lived here, and provides glimpses of wildlife that thrive in the 6,853-acre valley: deer, bears, red wolves, foxes, wild turkeys, river otters, as well as domesticated cattle that graze to keep the grass down.

At the beginning of the loop, pick up a tour guide at the pull-off. Founded in 1818, Cades Cove established schools before 1830 and was a virtually self-supporting community until the 1930s. On the tour, visitors see log homes, churches, graveyards, cabins, barns, and the beautiful valley surrounded by mountains. It's a unique spot in the Smokies and shouldn't be missed.

At Cable Mill, about halfway through the trip, visitors can explore a mill, millrace, barn, corncrib, blacksmith shop, and sorghum mill. The Cades Cove Visitor Center is located here, and you can pick up information and see exhibits. Pioneer demonstrations are given during the summer.

The best time to drive the loop is the early morning and late afternoon, when the light is at its best. (You're also sure to see herds of deer grazing in the fields.) On Saturday mornings from June through Labor Day, the loop is only open to bicycles from sunrise until 10 A.M. In July and October, the traffic is usually bumper to bumper.

Cades Cove/Parsons Branch/Foothills Parkway Loop.   Figure half a day for this spectacularly scenic outing. The drive connects the Cades Cove Loop Road with US 129 when you exit the park on the dirt Forge Creek and Parsons Branch roads. Several water crossings on Parsons Branch Road add to the novelty of the drive. On a clear day, don't miss the view from Look Rock Tower on the Foothills Parkway.

Start the drive in Townsend, near the western entrance to Great Smoky (in Zone 3). Drive into the park, turn right on Laurel Creek Road, and drive to Cades Cove. Follow the loop road to the visitor center and inquire about road conditions. Unless there's been a lot of rain and the creeks are high, this drive is fine for passenger cars.

Just past the visitor center, go right onto the gravel Forge Creek Road (two-way traffic). Stay on the road until it merges with Parsons Branch Road, which is one-way. Follow this road for about 10 miles through several creek crossings until it ends at US 129, which is paved.

Turn right and go about 12 miles past Chilhowee Lake and turn right onto the Foothills Parkway. The scenic highway climbs and then descends Chilhowee Mountain, passing Look Rock along the way. It takes you back to US 321, where you turn right and return to Townsend.

Little River Road. Use this road, which runs inside the park between the Sugarlands Visitor Center and the western entrance near Cades Cove, to create a loop drive from Gatlinburg, to the visitor center, past Cades Cove, to Townsend, and, via US 321, to Pigeon Forge. Return to Gatlinburg on US 441.

The road crosses Sugarlands Mountain at Fighting Creek Gap and then descends into Little River Gorge, paralleling the course of the river to Townsend. East of Fighting Creek Gap, at Maloney Point, is an excellent view of Mount LeConte and the Sugarlands Valley.

The Road to Nowhere. This road starts near Bryson City (Zone 4) and ends at a gate in front of a tunnel. This elaborately constructed road goes three miles into the park before abruptly stopping; work on it ceased in 1943. Weird . . . but scenic.

To get to it, follow the signs off old US 19 in downtown Bryson City for the Great Smokies Railroad. Cross the railroad tracks and continue straight. (Look for Swain County High School, located just before the park boundary.) Ride through the gate and go three miles before reaching the tunnel. Turn around and drive back. You've been "nowhere."

—— *Guided Tours*

Folks who would rather leave the driving to someone else can take a guided tour of the park. **Smoky Mountain Tours** in Gatlinburg offers half-day and full-day guided bus tours of Great Smoky. The *Cherokee Tour* crosses the park on Newfound Gap Road and makes frequent stops for spectacular views. Then the bus continues south out of the park to the Cherokee Indian reservation; there you have 30–40 minutes to see the sights, shop, and have lunch. The half-day tours leave at 7:45 A.M. and 12:45 P.M. daily; the cost is $18 for adults and $12 for children ages 5–11. Meals aren't included.

The *Smoky Mountain Deluxe Tour* includes stops at the Indian reservation, the Oconaluftee Indian Village in Cherokee, the Qualla Arts & Crafts Co-Op, Clingmans Dome, and other sights inside the park. The seven-and-a-half-hour tour departs at 8:30 A.M. Monday through Friday; the cost is $36 for adults and $24 for children ages 3–12. Lunch is included.

The half-day *Cades Cove Tour* takes visitors to an early pioneer homestead in a beautiful mountain valley in Great Smoky. Tours leave Monday, Wednesday, and Friday at 7:45 A.M. The cost is $18 for adults and $12 for children.

The bus will pick you up at your motel or campground in Gatlinburg, Pigeon Forge, or Sevierville. For reservations, call (615) 453-0864.

PART FIVE:
The Northern Foothills
of Tennessee—Zone 2

A Brief History and Orientation

Rising up from the Tennessee Valley in the west to the Great Smoky Mountains to the east, the Northern Foothills of Tennessee are the primary gateway to Great Smoky Mountains National Park. Millions of visitors each year get off I-40 at TN 66 south (which soon merges with US 441) and stream south through the towns of Sevierville, Pigeon Forge, and Gatlinburg toward Great Smoky.

Some of them never make it.

Taking commercialization to often breathtaking extremes, the towns are tourist destinations unto themselves—especially for families with kids.

Dollywood, for example, is a Dolly Parton–inspired theme park near Pigeon Forge that attracts two million visitors a year. The country-and-western singer and movie star (who actually doesn't own the theme park, but has an agreement with the owners about the use of her name) was born and raised in Sevier County; see her statue in downtown Sevierville.

Looking like Coney Island minus the sea, US 441 is a seemingly endless procession of water parks, go-cart speedways, factory outlet stores, carnivals, family-style eateries, fast-food restaurants, and amusement parks. There's even an Elvis museum. If it weren't for the mountain peaks to the south, it would be easy to forget you're only a few miles from the largest wilderness area in the East.

On clear days, helicopters roar overhead as they lift tourists on sightseeing flights over the nearby mountains. Traffic on warm weekends throughout the summer and in October is bumper-to-bumper on the traffic-light laden highway. Everybody looks as if they're having fun (children, especially, appear ecstatic). For millions of Americans, Gatlinburg and the other gateway towns *are* the Smoky Mountains.

—— *Both a Jumping-Off Point and a Destination*

Without the creation of Great Smoky Mountains National Park in the 1930s, the towns of Sevierville, Pigeon Forge, and Gatlinburg would have remained the sleepy little East Tennessee towns they were—instead of becoming today's tourist meccas.

But with a wide variety of things to do—not to mention thousands of motel rooms in close proximity to amenity-less Great Smoky— the towns on US 441 entice many visitors to focus their vacations outside the park.

Sure, they'll jump in the car for a drive to Clingmans Dome or Cades Cove at least once. But for many people, the wholesome temptations of the carnival atmosphere in the towns are often more tantalizing than the lush mountain scenery inside the park.

Except for campers who don't mind sites without electricity and no showers, backpackers, and folks staying at rustic (and not very accessible) LeConte Lodge, people looking for a place to stay have no choice but to go outside the park. The three gateway towns along US 441 are the closest places to the major sights in Great Smoky where you can stay in a room with electricity.

Mountain Stereotypes

Some people detest Gatlinburg because of its commercialism and tendency to play on the worst stereotypes about mountain people ("Hillbilly Golf"). While the tackiness can be aggravating to folks just back from a day watching raptors float on thermals, others appreciate the contrast between the solitude of the mountains and the bustle of the towns. After all, you can descend into Gatlinburg for a good meal without changing out of your hiking clothes or worrying about your appearance.

And while Gatlinburg takes a lot of heat for its gaudiness, even people from places with more refined reputations will confess to a certain, uh, *affection* for the Tennessee gateway town. "A lot of people from Asheville go slumming in Gatlinburg on day trips," confessed one tourist bureau employee from North Carolina who would rather not see her name in print.

—— *Major Roads*

The main route into the Northern Foothills is I-40; most people exit the interstate 20 miles east of Knoxville onto TN 66 south, which runs into US 441 in Sevierville. US 441 continues south through the other gateway towns and through Great Smoky to Cherokee, North Carolina. The highway is a four-lane road loaded with traffic lights—and it's the only convenient way for visitors to reach the park from the north.

In Pigeon Forge, US 321 swings southwest to Townsend (Zone 3), location of the western entrance to Great Smoky (Zone 1). In Gatlinburg, US 321 heads northeast as it traces the boundary of Great Smoky to Cosby, where it joins TN 32. From Cosby the road swings north to Newport; a seven-mile segment of the incomplete Foothills Parkway connects the road to I-40. Under construction since 1960, the Foothills Parkway eventually will parallel the northwest boundary of the park for 72 miles.

US 411 connects I-40 to the east to Sevierville, where it joins US 441 for an eastern swing toward Knoxville; US 411 splits off and goes southwest to Alcoa and Maryville.

—— *Eating Out*

The gateway towns along US 441 probably qualify as the Fast-Food Capital of the World. But you'll find more than hamburgers and fried chicken: There's a seemingly endless procession of family eateries, all-you-can-eat buffets, ice cream and candy shops, and barbecue joints along the highway.

In the Northern Foothills, it's quantity over quality when it comes to eating out. People trying to control their cholesterol levels or watch their waistlines are advised to burn as many calories as they can on the trails in Great Smoky before dinnertime. And vegetarians? Forget it: This is meat and potatoes country.

Dixie Stampede

Bus loads of vacationers troop each night to the Dixie Stampede, a Dollywood-operated dinner theater in Pigeon Forge. The show features a live rodeo with 30 horses and trick riders in the cast, and dinner is a "more-than-you-can-eat" feast. Popular? The place packs in two to three seatings of 1,200 folks a night. That's a lot of chicken and ribs.

Reservations are suggested; call (800) 356-1676 or (615) 453-4400. Tickets are $23.95 for adults and $13.95 for children ages 4–11. Dixie Stampede is closed January through March. In the summer and in October, call at least one week in advance.

Alcohol

One consideration when planning a night on the town is whether you'd like to enjoy a beer, a glass of wine, or a cocktail with dinner: Pigeon Forge is "dry" (no alcohol is served in restaurants, but beer and wine are available in grocery stores). Gatlinburg, on the other hand, is "wet"—adults can order a drink with a meal in restaurants that serve alcohol, and the town has a few package liquor stores. However, Gatlinburg has no bars: The family atmosphere prevails all along US 441.

—— Entertainment

Fans of country-and-western music and Elvis will find plenty to keep their feet stomping and hearts throbbing in Pigeon Forge, which is positioning itself to become a second Nashville. An entire section of the town called Music Road has been zoned to accommodate new theaters. The first, **Music Mansion Theater** (615) 656-7469, opened in 1994, and more are on the way.

Memories Theater features Elvis impersonator Eddie Miles in concert along with a 50s and 60s music review and live comedy. Call (615) 428-7852 for show times. **The Music Mountain Amphitheater** is a 3,500-seat outdoor theater featuring national rock and roll, country, and family attractions. Call (615) 428-3539.

Dollywood features top country-and-western acts throughout the season in the Celebrity Theatre; show times are at 2 P.M. and 7 P.M. During the Sunset Musicfest, 20 stages throughout the theme park feature live entertainment each night for three weeks in July. Call (800) DOLLYWOOD for a schedule and ticket information.

The Smoky Mountain Jubilee features country-and-western, bluegrass, gospel, clogging, and comedy. Call (615) 428-1836 for more information.

—— *Getting Around*

To avoid the traffic gridlock of downtown Gatlinburg during spring weekends, anytime during the summer, and in October, tourists can ride motorized, open-air trolleys that run about every 20 minutes along four routes. Our advice: Park your car and use the trolleys as a stress-free way to get around this congested town.

The cost is a quarter a ride, and the trolleys make regular stops throughout town. Be sure and note the color of the line of the trolley you board. That way you'll be sure to grab the correct one to get back to your car or motel.

The Orange Route leaves Gatlinburg Convention Center on US 441, turns up Airport Road, goes down Cherokee Orchard Road, and then out US 321 to Proffit's Grocery Store and returns. Hours are 8 A.M. to midnight during the busy season and 9 A.M. to 7 P.M. off-season.

The Green Route leaves the Gatlinburg "park and ride" lot north of town and goes to Ski Mountain Road in town via the Parkway, River Road, and Ski Mountain Road and then returns. Note: This is the bus for day-trippers. Hours are 8 A.M. to midnight during the busy season and 9 A.M. to 7 P.M. off-season.

The Yellow Route is the "arts and crafts" route leaving the City Hall "park and ride" on US 321. The trolley goes out US 321 to Buckhorn Road, then to Glades Road and back. Hours are 9 A.M. to 5 P.M. from April through October only; the daily fare is $1 with unlimited reboarding.

The Red Route is the Dollywood trolley that leaves the Gatlinburg "park and ride" north of town 30 minutes prior to the theme park's opening. The bus also stops at the Dollywood Welcome Center in Pigeon Forge. The last trolley leaves 30 minutes after the park closes; the fare is fifty cents.

Handicapped Services

Until all the trolleys are retrofitted with wheelchair lifts (some already are), a special van for physically disabled visitors is available upon request from the Gatlinburg Mass Transit Department.

The cost is fifty cents per person per ride in town, and $1 per person to Dollywood. Call (615) 436-3897 from 8 A.M. to 4:30 P.M. daily to arrange for a pickup or for more information. The van usually arrives within about a half hour of the time you call, but customers

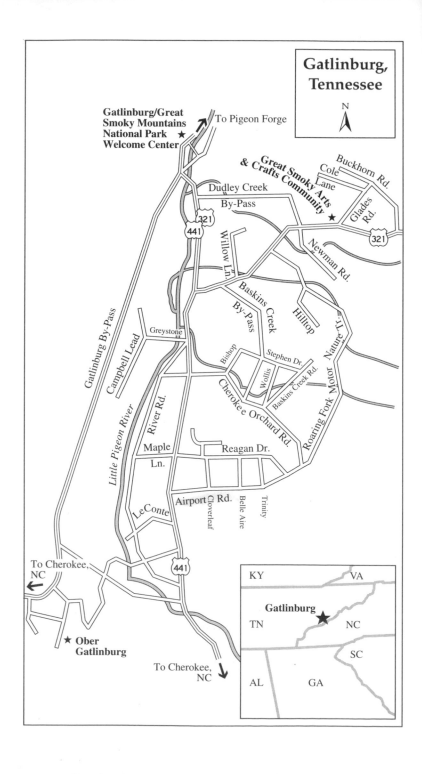

are at the mercy of the availability of a driver. Rides can be arranged for after 4:30 P.M. until the trolleys stop running (see above) if you call before 4:30 P.M.

—— *Parking in Gatlinburg*

Hemmed in by mountains and a national park, Gatlinburg is a town where real estate is at a premium. The result is tight quarters downtown as buildings have no place to go but up, creating a claustrophobic feel that only gets worse when traffic is bumper-to-bumper and the sidewalks are jammed with visitors.

Gridlock

How bad is the traffic? A sales clerk at the Happy Hiker, an outdoor equipment store in town, looked quietly amused when asked about the "heavy" traffic on a warm Sunday during the spring. That's nothing, he said: One summer afternoon it took four hours to drive from Gatlinburg to Sevierville, about 10 miles. The average person can walk faster than that.

"You can predict the heavy traffic," our friend added. "Friday afternoons, everyone's trying to get into town. At one or two on Sunday afternoons, everyone leaves. The road to I-40 will be jammed, and Gatlinburg is empty."

Park Outside of Town and Take the Trolley

If you care to navigate the traffic jams, you *will* find parking in Gatlinburg—once you get there. Our recommendation: If you're coming into the town for the day, leave your car at the park and ride located behind the Welcome Center north of town on US 441. Then take the trolley into town (see above). Otherwise, try to arrive early on a weekday if your destination is a Gatlinburg motel.

If you ignore our advice and drive into town, parking lots are located at the Welcome Center/Chamber of Commerce building (in town on the left, where US 321 intersects US 441), and along US 441 (called the Parkway in town). Two small lots also are located on River Road, which parallels the Parkway along the Little Pigeon River.

If you'd rather not deal with the congestion and just want to get to Great Smoky, take the Gatlinburg Bypass, a scenic road that skirts the town and ends on US 441 at the park boundary, a short drive from the Sugarlands Visitor Center.

The northern entrance to the bypass is just south of the Welcome Center located north of town on US 441. Keep in mind the bypass is often closed during the winter.

—— *Getting Hitched*

Approximately 10,000 couples a year are married in Gatlinburg, making it the Honeymoon Capital of the South. If the urge strikes, go to the **Sevier County Courthouse** in Sevierville to pick up a license—there's no residency requirement.

Office hours are 8 A.M. to 4:30 P.M. Monday through Friday. Bring along either a birth certificate or driver's license to prove your age—and $33.50. Then it's a 20-minute drive to Gatlinburg and one of its many wedding chapels along the parkway.

Outdoor Recreation and Activities

—— Walks

On your first drive down US 441 toward Great Smoky Mountains National Park it becomes obvious that this part of Tennessee is a car-oriented place—and, as a result, not friendly to walkers and pedestrians. Going for a stroll usually means dodging traffic and inhaling huge quantities of automotive exhaust. For a quality walk, your best bet is to jump in the car and head to one of the many **"Quiet Walkways"** along Newfound Gap Road (US 441) inside Great Smoky Mountains National Park (Zone 1).

Another alternative is a stroll along **River Road** in Gatlinburg. It follows the Little Pigeon River—an honest-to-God trout stream—and the road isn't nearly as traffic choked as the parallel Parkway (US 441) up the hill. In Pigeon Forge, there's a one-mile paved path in **Patriot Park,** located east of US 441 on Middle Creek Road (traffic light 7). You'll also find an outdoor track at Gatlinburg High School on US 321 north.

—— Hiking

Those looking to stretch their legs on a mountain trail should jump into their cars and drive south on US 441 to Great Smoky Mountains National Park (Zone 1). While there are a number of unmaintained (read: unmarked) trails that lead into the park along US 321 as it skirts the park border east of town, they should be left to experienced hikers familiar with the terrain.

With one exception: **The Gatlinburg Trail,** a pleasant, easy footpath that leads from town to the Sugarlands Visitor Center two miles inside the park. The trail starts on the west side of traffic light 10, the last traffic signal in town as you head south toward the park.

247

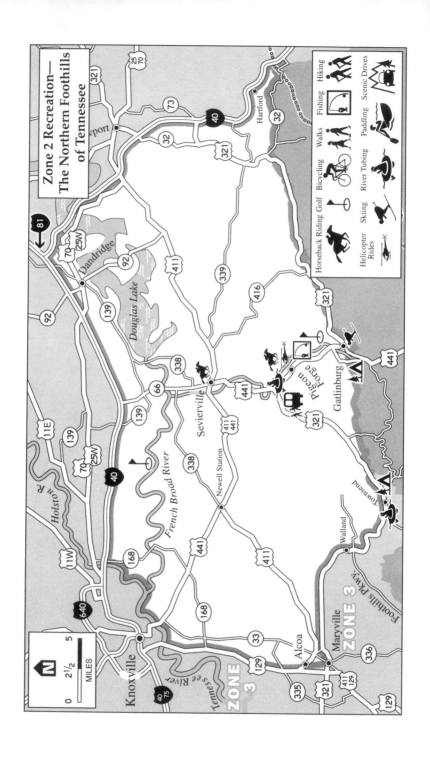

Zone 2 Recreation—
The Northern Foothills
of Tennessee

Horseback Riding Golf   Bicycling Walks Fishing Hiking

Helicopter   Skiing   River Tubing Paddling Scenic Drives
Rides

MILES
0   2½   5

Knoxville

Newport

Dandridge

Douglas Lake

French Broad River

Sevierville

Newell Station

Pigeon
Forge

Gatlinburg

Townsend

Walland

Maryville

Alcoa

Hartford

Holston R.

Tennessee River

Foothills Pkwy.

ZONE 3

ZONE 3

From the visitor center you can hike a one-mile nature trail that starts at the visitor center. By the way, the Gatlinburg Trail is the only trail in the park where it's legal to ride your bicycle.

—— *Canoeing, Kayaking, and Rafting*

There are no commercial river trips available in Zone 2, north of the Great Smoky Mountains National Park. In Pigeon Forge, however, you can rent inner tubes for a self-guided float on the Class I (II) Little Pigeon River (see below). Farther upstream, the Little Pigeon runs right through Gatlinburg. Intermediate canoeists and kayakers can run this Class II (III) section when water levels allow. The Little Pigeon, incidentally, should not be confused with the Class III–IV Pigeon River in North Carolina, where guided commercial raft trips are offered. For canoeists and kayakers, the Little Pigeon River below Townsend, Tennessee, is a scenic Class I (II) float. For detailed information on these and other area rivers, check our list of recommended reading for canoeing, kayaking, and rafting on pages 76–77. The closest commercially run rivers are the Pigeon in Zone 6 and the Nantahala and Tuckasegee in Zone 4.

—— *River Tubing*

Cool off during the summer while (inner) tubing down the Middle Prong of the Little Pigeon River, about six miles behind Dollywood. **Smoky Mountain River Run** in Pigeon Forge transports customers by van for the three-mile float trip, which lasts about two hours.

River Run opens at 10 A.M. daily from mid-May through Labor Day and closes when it runs out of inner tubes; it's best to arrive before noon. Rates are $13.26 for adults and $8.84 for children under 12. Call (615) 428-4403 for more information.

—— *Trout Fishing*

From April through November, rainbow trout are stocked into eight miles of freshwater streams and the Little Pigeon River in Gatlinburg. Streams are open year-round during daylight hours to anglers, who must have a valid Tennessee fishing license, trout stamp, and daily fishing permit to fish in the city. The streams inside the city limits are closed each Thursday for restocking.

Popular trout streams include the West Prong of the Little Pigeon River (paralleled by US 441 and River Road), Dudley Creek, Roaring Fork Creek (both near US 321 east of downtown), and LeConte Creek (near Airport Road).

Permits, information, and the latest word on hot fishing spots are available at the Gatlinburg Chamber of Commerce Welcome Center (downtown), City Hall, Trenthams Hardware, and Wynn's Sporting Goods.

Those looking for some professional help in exploring the streams around Gatlinburg and in Great Smoky can call **Smoky Mountain Anglers** at (615) 436-8746. Full-day trips with a professional guide are $120 per person (lunch included) and $200 for two people. Catch and release is practiced, but owner Bobby Shults reports that an occasional trout lands in the frying pan for a streamside lunch.

—— Bicycling

The car reigns supreme in Gatlinburg, Pigeon Forge, and Sevierville—and that's bad news for cyclists looking to go for a spin while staying in the resort towns along US 441. Our advice: Load your bike on the car and head for **Cades Cove** in Great Smoky Mountains National Park (Zone 1) or any of the other nearby zones for a place to turn the cranks.

—— Horseback Riding

Several private stables operate in the gateway towns. In Sevierville, **Five Oaks Stables** offers half-hour- ($10) and hour-long ($15) rides through the scenic foothills of the Smokies year-round. The guided rides leave approximately every 20 minutes; call (615) 428-9764 for more information.

Smoky Mountain Stables in Gatlinburg offers guided rides into Great Smoky. One-hour, three-and-a-half-mile rides cost $12 per horse, and two-hour, seven-mile rides are $22. The stables are open from mid-March through Thanksgiving. Call (615) 436-5634 for more information.

Willowbridge Farms outside Sevierville specializes in unguided tours on a three-and-a-half-mile trail leading to a 1,900-foot overlook. Grooms match a horse to a rider's ability (including novices) and give customers two-way radios—just in case. The ride lasts about an hour and costs $20 per person; the stables are open 8 A.M. to 6 P.M. year-round. Call (615) 453-2257 for more information.

—— Golf

The most outstanding course in the Gatlinburg/Pigeon Forge area is Bent Creek near Gatlinburg. River Islands Golf Course is also highly rated. These and other quality golf courses in the area are profiled below.

Baneberry Golf and Resort

Established: 1972
Address: 704 Harrison Ferry Road, I-81 at I-40, Baneberry TN 37890
Phone: (615) 674-2500 or (800) 951-4653
Status: Resort course
Tees:
    Championship: 6,694 yards, par 71, USGA 72.6, slope 125.
    Men's: 6,127 yards, par 72, USGA 69.1, slope 120.
    Ladies': 4,829 yards, par 72, USGA 68.5, slope 117.

Fees: Green fees: $11 weekdays, $14 weekends and holidays. Carts: $10 per person per 18 holes, not mandatory. Golf package: $39.50 per person, double, weeknights; $43 weekends and holiday. Package includes all green fees and accommodations. Tee times required.

Facilities: Pro shop, driving range, putting greens, restaurant, lounge, snack bar, lighted tennis courts, large pool, boat ramp into Douglas Lake, golf villas, and motel.

Bent Creek Golf Resort

Established: 1973
Address: 3919 East Parkway, Gatlinburg TN 37738
Phone: (800) 251-9336
Status: Resort course

Tees:

Championship: 6,182 yards, par 72, USGA 70.3, slope 127.
Men's: 5,802 yards, par 72, USGA 67.9, slope 123.
Ladies': 5,111 yards, par 73, USGA 69.2, slope 117.

Fees: Green fees: $28 nonguest, $23 lodge guest. Higher for holidays and weekends. Cart fee: $26 for 2 persons. Golf carts required prior to 2 P.M. Sunday through Thursday and before 4 P.M. on Friday and Saturday. The 90° rule is in effect, weather permitting. Tee times required.

Facilities: 108-room lodge with banquet and meeting space for 250+, condo and chalet rental available, restaurant, snack shop, lighted tennis courts, swimming pool, driving range, putting green, practice chipping, and sand green.

Dandridge Golf and Country Club

Established: 1980
Address: 1247 Stonewall Jackson Drive, Dandridge TN 37725
Phone: (615) 397-2655
Status: Public course
Tees:

Championship: 6,061 yards, par 72, slope 127.
Men's: 5,778 yards, par 72, slope 124.
Ladies': 4,729 yards, par 72, slope 118.

Fees: Green fees: $13 weekdays, $15 weekends. Cart fee, $18.
Facilities: Clubhouse, snack bar, pro shop, bent grass greens, and Bermuda grass tees and fairways.

Egwani Farms Golf Course

Established: 1991
Address: 3920 Singleton Station Road, Rockford TN 37853
Phone: (615) 970-7132
Status: Daily fee
Tees:

Championship: 6,708 yards, par 72, USGA 71.9, slope 126.
Men's: 6,150 yards, par 72, USGA 69.3, slope 120.
Ladies': 4,680 yards, par 72, USGA 66.1, slope 113.

Fees: Monday through noon Friday, $40; noon Friday through weekend and holidays, $50. Price includes greens fee, cart, range balls, and tax. Club rentals including tax, $15.

Facilities: Pro shop, deli, driving range, practice bunker and chipping green, and practice putting green.

River Islands Golf Course

Established: 1990

Address: 9610 Kodak Road, Kodak TN 37764

Phone: (615) 933-0100 or (800) 34-RIVER

Status: Public course

Tees:

Championship: 7,001 yards, par 72, USGA 75.4, slope 133.
Men's: 6,300 yards, par 72, USGA 72, slope 129.
Ladies': 5,790 yards, par 72, USGA 68.1, slope 117.

Fees: In season, $34–45 including cart fee and tax. Carts required. The 90° rule is in effect, weather permitting. Twilight rates available.

Facilities: Clubhouse, conference room, turnshack, and grill.

—— *Skiing*

Ober Gatlinburg offers downhillers eight slopes with a 550-foot vertical drop serviced by two quad and one double chairlift. The slopes are open from mid-December to early March. A snowmaking system provides 100% coverage of the slopes. Two thousand pairs of rental skis and certified ski instruction are available.

During the ski season, morning sessions are 8:30 A.M. to 4:30 P.M., and afternoon sessions are 3 P.M. to 10 P.M. Lift tickets are $25 per session during the week and $30 a session on weekends and holidays. Midweek evening sessions (6 P.M. to 10 P.M.) are $12. For a report on ski conditions, call (800) 251-9202.

—— *Helicopter Rides*

For the ultimate in scenic touring, take a helicopter tour of the foothills and the Great Smokies. As the constant roar of choppers overhead attests, it's a popular way to see the park.

Rainbow Jet Helicopter Mountain Flights, located between Pigeon Forge and Townsend on US 321 south, offers seven tours lasting from five minutes to an hour; prices range from $18 to $180 per person. Hours are 9 A.M. to sunset, but the best flying times are early in the morning and late afternoon.

Don't assume rain means the flights are canceled; the pilots usually can find a location where the scenery is good, regardless of the weather in Pigeon Forge. For more information, call (615) 429-2929.

—— *Scenic Drives*

After battling the heavy traffic on US 441 (called the Parkway in the three gateway towns), most people head to Great Smoky (Zone 1) to explore roads leading to Clingmans Dome, Newfound Gap Overlook, and Cades Cove. While the traffic is often heavy, the absence of commercialism in the park is a welcome relief.

An alternative route to Cades Cove is US 321 out of Pigeon Forge. It's a pleasant, two-lane road leading to Townsend and Great Smoky's western entrance. You can create a loop ride by returning via Little River Road inside the park, which ends at Newfound Gap Road (US 441) and the Sugarlands Visitor Center. Turn left to reach Gatlinburg and points north.

The Gatlinburg Bypass, while short, offers spectacular views of the town and the mountains from several overlooks, where you can pull over and enjoy the vista. US 321, which heads east out of Gatlinburg to Cosby, is another scenic drive that skirts the boundary of the park.

Attractions

By far, the greatest tourist attraction for visitors staying along the US 441 corridor is next door in Zone 1—Great Smoky Mountains National Park. Yet after a morning, afternoon, or an entire day spent exploring the overlooks, waterfalls, and trails in the park, folks staying in the Northern Foothills have some leisure-time options that have nothing to do with woods, streams, and viewing wild animals.

But don't expect high culture. Tourist attractions in the gateway towns range from the truly wholesome (Dollywood) to the truly tacky (the Elvis Presley Museum, home to the King's last pickup truck). All the attractions, however, are places families can enjoy together.

Devoted fans of Elvis (you know who you are) won't want to miss the **Elvis Presley Museum**, a monument to the rock and roll great who died in 1977. But just about everyone else should.

It's a one-room museum filled with ho-hum items such as swim suits, furniture, a leather and fur coat, jewelry, and guns—but nothing really bizarre like, say, a shot-up TV set.

During the summer, the museum (located on the Parkway in Pigeon Forge) is open from 9 A.M. to 9 P.M. Off-season hours are 9 A.M. to 6 P.M. Admission is $6.50 for adults and $2.99 for children. Call (615) 453-6499 for more information.

Almost as bad is **Carbo's Police Museum,** a tribute to cop mania. Talk about tasteless: The museum's big attraction is Buford Pusser's "Death Car," a cremated Corvette in which the sheriff who inspired the *Walking Tall* movies died in a crash. Didn't see the *Walking Tall* movies? Then skip this one.

Located on the Parkway in Pigeon Forge, the Police Museum is open 10 A.M. to 5 P.M. daily April through October. Admission is $5.50 for adults and $3 for children. For more information, call (615) 453-1358.

The Smoky Mountain Car Museum, also in Pigeon Forge, will appeal to auto aficionados. Cars on exhibit range from a 1953

Allstate (sold by Sears) to Billy Carter's pickup truck (cans of Billy Beer on the dash). Other memorable exhibits include Hank Williams' "Silver Dollar Car" (a Bonneville decked out with 547 silver dollars, three rifles, ten small pistols, and 12 large pistols) and the Astin Martin driven by Sean Connery in *Goldfinger*. Unless you're a certified car freak, this is a rainy day kind of place.

Hours are 9 A.M. to 8 P.M. Memorial Day through Labor Day and 10 A.M. to 5 P.M. in April and May. The museum is only open on weekends in November and is closed December through March. Admission is $5 for adults and $2 for children ages 3–10.

Note: Two well-known attractions were closed during our research trips to Gatlinburg. **The Ripley's Believe or Not Museum** had burned down and the about-to-be-opened **Guinness Museum** was damaged by heavy floods in the spring of 1994. Both museums should be open in 1995.

American Historical Wax Museum

Type of Attraction: A wax museum featuring 45 scenes from United States history. A self-guided tour.

Location: On the parkway in Gatlinburg, Tennessee.

Admission: $5 for adults, $2.50 for children, under 6 free.

Hours: 9 A.M. to 10 P.M. daily.

Phone: (615) 436-4462

When to Go: Any time.

Special Comments: If you only have time for one wax museum in Gatlinburg, don't make it this one: Christus Gardens is much better.

Overall Appeal by Age Group:

Pre-school	Grade School	Teens	Young Adults	Over 30	Senior Citizens
★★	★★½	★★	★★	★★	★★

Author's Rating: Shades of an elementary school field trip. Cheesy. ★½

How Much Time to Allow: One hour.

DESCRIPTION AND COMMENTS   A figure of President Clinton—well, the sign *says* it's him—greets you as you enter this small roadside attraction in the heart of Gatlinburg. Life-size figures ranging from

Columbus to some still-living ex-presidents, including a barely recognizable effigy of Carter.

TOURING TIPS   The most dynamic displays recreate the battles of
Yorktown (where Washington defeated Cornwallis) and the Alamo.

OTHER THINGS TO DO NEARBY   Everything from ski lifts to fudge making can be found along the streets of Gatlinburg. Rumor has it there's
a big national park south of traffic light 10.

Christus Gardens

Type of Attraction: A series of dioramas depicting the life of Christ. A
   tour automatically guided by lighting and a soundtrack.

Location: 510 River Road, Gatlinburg, Tennessee

Admission: $7.50 for adults, $3.50 for children ages 7–11.

Hours: 8 A.M. to 9 P.M. daily (April through October); 9 A.M. to 5 P.M.
   daily (November through March).

Phone: (615) 436-5155

When to Go: Any time.

Special Comments: There's no seating on the leisurely paced, 45-
   minute tour.

Overall Appeal by Age Group:

Pre-school	Grade School	Teens	Young Adults	Over 30	Senior Citizens
★★	★★	★★½	★★	★★★	★★★

Author's Rating: The 80 life-like and life-sized figures are of high
   quality. But in today's world of virtual reality and talking robots,
   the place is a snooze. ★★

How Much Time to Allow: One hour.

DESCRIPTION AND COMMENTS   This single-story contemporary building is located across the fast-moving Little Pigeon River in Gatlinburg. Inside is a series of detailed dioramas presenting the life of
Christ, from the Nativity to the crucifixion and ascension. The figures
(created by the same English firm that created the figures for Madame
Tussaud's Wax Museum in London) are convincing, the costumes
look authentic (they were created by the firm that created the costumes
for Hollywood's *Ben Hur* and *Quo Vadis*), and the lighting is dramatic.

Other attractions on site include a collection of bibles and biblical coins, a six-ton sculpture of Christ's face, a collection of oil paintings interpreting Jesus' 39 parables, and a gift shop. While the tone of the museum is nondenominational, its religious message is about what you'd expect in the heart of the Bible Belt—and the atmosphere is churchlike, quiet, and a bit dull.

TOURING TIPS   The gardens outside the museum feature seasonal floral displays.

OTHER THINGS TO DO NEARBY   Gatlinburg offers a wide range of things to do, including shopping, amusements, and places to eat. A block up the hill toward the Parkway is **Skylift,** a ski lift that whisks you on a 20-minute sightseeing trip up a mountain; $6 for adults, $3 for children 11 and under.

Dollywood

Type of Attraction: A Dolly Parton–based theme park featuring rides, crafts, music, entertainment, and food. A self-guided tour.

Location: In the foothills of the Smokies about a mile outside Pigeon Forge, Tennessee.

Admission: $22.99 for adults, $19.99 for seniors 60 and older, $15.99 for children ages 4–11 (all plus tax). Parking is an additional $3. People who arrive after 3 P.M. can return the next operating day without buying another ticket.

Hours: Dollywood's season begins in late April and runs through October. In the spring and fall, hours are 10 A.M. to 6 P.M. (except some Wednesdays and Thursdays; see below). During the summer, the park opens at 9 A.M. and closes between 7 P.M. and 10 P.M. daily; call for a current schedule.

In May, Dollywood is closed Thursdays. In September, the park is closed Wednesdays and Thursdays; in October, the park is closed Thursdays only. In November and December, the park is open on a limited schedule; call for details.

Phone: (800) DOLLYWOOD, (615) 656-9488

When to Go: As early as possible during the summer and on spring and fall weekends to beat long lines at the most popular rides and attractions.

Special Comments: Wear comfortable shoes; the park covers 90 acres. While plenty of food is sold inside the park, it's on the expensive side: At Mountain Dan's Burger House, quarter-pound burgers are $3, a regular fry is $1.29, and a Philly cheese steak sub is $5. To save a few bucks, bring something to eat or eat a big meal just before you come—and walk it off.

Overall Appeal by Age Group:

Pre-school	Grade School	Teens	Young Adults	Over 30	Senior Citizens
★★★★★	★★★★★	★★★★★	★★★★	★★★★	★★★★

Author's Rating: "Homespun fun" and ersatz mountain heritage meet celebrity glitz. ★★★

How Much Time to Allow: Four hours for a light once-over; all day if your feet can take it.

DESCRIPTION AND COMMENTS   Born in 1946 and one of 12 children in a poor mountain family, Dolly Parton left for Nashville on her last day at Sevier County High School. Now a star (*9 to 5, The Best Little Whorehouse in Texas*), hometown girl Parton lends her name to this theme park (called Silver Dollar City prior to 1985).

If you're hoping to see the fabled country-and-western star, make it a point to come to the park's opening weekend, usually in late April. Otherwise, you'll have to soak up her persona at Dolly's Dressing Room (a women's clothing shop), at the Dolly Parton Museum (which chronicles her "rags to riches" career), or the butterfly gardens (butterflies are Parton's trademark).

Located in a lush mountain setting, the park emphasizes local culture and crafts, including demonstrations by lye soap makers, carriage makers, blacksmiths, potters, leather workers, basket weavers, and glass blowers. You'll find plenty of locally made crafts for sale.

But it's the amusement rides and constantly ongoing music shows and entertainment that really pack in the crowds. With the exception of celebrity music shows, all the attractions and entertainment are included in the price of admission.

The Showstreet Palace Theater, the Back Porch Theatre, Dollywood's Celebrity Theatre (tickets range from $8 to $16), Heartsong Theatre, and the Valley Theatre offer country, pop, gospel, patriotic, and traditional mountain music in nearly 40 live shows a day.

Other attractions include the Eagle Mountain Sanctuary (a million-cubic-foot outdoor aviary), the Dollywood Grist Mill (the only functioning hand-built grist mill constructed in Tennessee in more than 100 years), a ride on a train pulled by a steam locomotive, and a replica of the mountain home where Dolly and her 11 siblings grew up.

Rides include the Smoky Mountain Rampage (a splashy water ride), the Log Flume (a watery roller coaster), the Flooded Mine (a combination tunnel of love and fright show), Blazing Fury (an indoor roller coaster), the Thunder Express (a fast outdoor roller coaster), and the Mountain Slidewinder (a mountainside waterslide). There's also an assortment of carnival rides for the kiddies.

TOURING TIPS Popular attractions such as rides are strategically spread throughout the park, making it difficult to create an efficient touring plan that won't exhaust nonmarathoners.

But for a whirlwind tour of the park's major rides, try this: From the park entrance, head straight to Rivertown Junction and the Country Fair for two water rides. Then backtrack, turn right up the hill toward Craftsmen's Valley for two roller coaster rides and a cave ride. Then backtrack to Daydream Ridge for a water slide down the side of a mountain.

Here are the specifics on the park's big rides:

The Smoky Mountain Rampage is a splashy, but fairly gentle, water ride through "rapids," under "waterfalls," and through a "fog." Rafts of three boats holding 12 to 18 people leave about every two minutes; it's about a 20-minute wait for every 100 people ahead of you in line. The ride lasts about four minutes. And like the sign says, "You will get wet." Rampage is located near Rivertown Junction (behind the Back Porch Theatre and before the railroad tracks).

Log Flume is a waterborne roller coaster that's faster and bumpier than Rampage. It has lots of twists and turns, but only one heart-stopping (and splashy) descent. The ride lasts three minutes and loads continuously; figure on about a 12-minute wait for every 100 people ahead of you in line. The ride is located in the Country Fair area (below Heartsong in the Village).

The Flooded Mine is near Craftmen's Valley; it's part tunnel of love, part fright show, but not a "thrill" ride. Customers get in boats that hold about 12 people and load continuously; figure on a 10-minute wait for every 100 people in front of you in line. The ride lasts about six minutes.

Blazing Fury is an indoor roller coaster near the back end of the park that's dark, loud, and scary, with three drops that leave your stomach about two cars back. It's a jolting, high-speed ride that lasts about three minutes. About 18 people file through the starting gates to the cars every two minutes.

Next door is **Thunder Express**, an aptly named outdoor roller coaster that features plenty of steep drops and sharp corners: It features both safety bars *and* seat belts. Lots of jolts and terrifying descents make this a ride one to avoid for the faint of heart. The ride leaves every two to three minutes with about 30 passengers.

Slidewinder is located at Daydream Ridge. After a long walk up the side of the mountain, you board a boat that launches down a waterway. It's steep, fast, and scary—and lasts about a minute. About 12 folks make the plunge every two minutes.

OTHER THINGS TO DO NEARBY   Pigeon Forge offers visitors just about every kind of fast-food imaginable and many more roadside amusements to keep the children happy. But if you've done Dollywood justice, you'll only want to get back to your room or campsite and collapse.

Ober Gatlinburg

Type of Attraction: An amusement park and ski area overlooking Gatlinburg that's reached by aerial tram car. A self-guided tour.

Location: 1001 Parkway, Gatlinburg, Tennessee.

Admission: $6 for adults, $3 for children ages 3–11.

Hours: Ski season (December–March): 8:30 A.M. to midnight Monday through Thursday, 10 A.M. to 1 A.M. Friday through Sunday. Non-ski season: 10 A.M. to midnight Monday through Saturday, 10 A.M. to 3:20 P.M. Sundays. See "Skiing" (above) for more information on winter activities in the park.

Phone: (615) 436-5423

When to Go: Any time. The two trams depart every 20 minutes for the top of the mountain from downtown Gatlinburg. During peak periods (weekends during the ski season, July, and October), the trams run almost continuously.

Special Comments: The view of Gatlinburg from the tram at night is spectacular. For folks who would rather skip the tram ride, you can reach Ober Gatlinburg by car via Ski Mountain Road (traffic light 10 in downtown Gatlinburg).

Overall Appeal by Age Group:

Pre-school	Grade School	Teens	Young Adults	Over 30	Senior Citizens
★★★	★★★★	★★★★	★★★½	★★★	★★★

Author's Rating: Great views on the ride up, but essentially it's a mountaintop carnival and penny arcade. ★★½

How Much Time to Allow: The tram ride takes 10 minutes. After that, it all depends on your appetite for amusement park rides. Kids will want to spend the day.

DESCRIPTION AND COMMENTS The Swiss-built tram whisks visitors two miles and 1,500 vertical feet up the side of Mt. Harris. After arrival, you can explore a live bear habitat ($1 for adults, $.50 for children), go ice skating, explore an arcade, or try bungee jumping ($25 a plunge, three for $50). For more mountain views, take the chairlift to the summit of Mt. Harris, a 20-minute round trip ($3 for adults, $1.50 for children ages 6–11). Half way up you can ride the alpine slide, a kind of controlled toboggan; $2.50 for adults, $1.50 for children ages 6–11.

The ski area, with 100% snowmaking facilities, features eight slopes serviced by two quad and one double chairlift. Facilities include a ski school, rentals, restaurant, and lounge. For ski conditions from November 1 through March 1, call (800) 251-9202.

TOURING TIPS Most visitors must stand during the ten-minute tram ride—seating is limited. The cars are restricted to 120 passengers, which is a big crowd for the small cars. Stand on the left-hand side going up and you'll get a brief aerial glimpse of the bear habitat.

OTHER THINGS TO DO NEARBY Downtown Gatlinburg is jammed with shops, restaurants, and amusements.

PART SIX:

The Southwest Foothills

of Tennessee—Zone 3

A Brief History and Orientation

The local tourist industry calls this "The Peaceful Side of the Smokies." And that's an accurate description of the mountains, lakes, and valleys to the west and southwest of Great Smoky Mountains National Park (Zone 1).

Stretching down from Townsend and the western entrance to Great Smoky along Cherokee National Forest to the Georgia border, the Southwest Foothills offer visitors tranquillity, beautiful scenery, and lots of things to do outdoors. There's hardly an echo of the rampant, go-go commercialism of Gatlinburg, Pigeon Forge, and Sevierville to the north (Zone 2).

While Townsend is a convenient jumping-off point to visit Cades Cove in Great Smoky, the rest of the Southwest Foothills is a self-contained region attracting serious outdoor recreation enthusiasts—who find plenty to do in the area. The biggest user group is whitewater rafters running rapids on the exciting Ocoee River and the tamer Hiwassee River. Both rivers have commercial rafting operations leading raft trips. Neither river, however, is convenient to Great Smoky Mountains National Park.

Other visitors who come to the Southwest Foothills include hikers and backpackers exploring 650 miles of trails in Cherokee National Forest. In addition, 11% of the land lies in designated wilderness areas, including the Gee Creek, Little Frog, and Big Frog.

The Southwest Foothills are bordered by Great Smoky Mountains National Park, the Northern Foothills of Tennessee (Zone 2), and the Southern Foothills of North Carolina (Zone 4). The largest cities close to the area are Knoxville (to the north) and Chattanooga (to the southwest).

—— History

This part of East Tennessee originally was settled by colonists in the early 1700s on land that was home to the Cherokee Indians for hundreds of years. Attracted by the lush mountain scenery, international tourists first started coming to this corner of the Smokies in the early 1800s by stagecoach and, later, by train.

Many stayed at Montvale Springs, a famous resort that burned in 1933. The large hotel attracted the famous and nonfamous, including poet Sidney Lanier and the Swiss geologist Arnold Guyot, who surveyed much of what was to become the national park and who named Clingmans Dome (the highest point in Great Smoky). Today it's a YMCA camp.

By around 1900, the lumbering industry had cut most of the forests in the area and tourism declined. Then industry started to move in.

Cheap Electricity

Attracted by an area abundant in rivers and the promise of cheap hydroelectric power, the Aluminum Company of America (ALCOA) moved into the area around 1910, constructed dams, and built the world's largest aluminum smelting plant. It's located in a town named after the company, Alcoa. Much of the aluminum sheet used to build bomber wings in World War II aircraft was produced here.

The Tennessee Valley Authority (TVA) continues to leave a strong imprint on the Southwest Foothills. In the 1930s, it changed the local economy by building huge dams to produce inexpensive electricity for industry. TVA's Tellico Dam (remember the snail darter?) on the Little Tennessee River and the Fort Loudoun Dam on the Tennessee River created huge lakes that cross the northern end of the Southern Foothills. Farther south, Lake Ocoee and the Ocoee River Recreation Area provide recreational opportunities for power boaters, anglers, hikers, and whitewater boating enthusiasts.

A Tourism Revival

Following the establishment of Great Smoky (dedicated in 1940) and the end of World War II, tourism rebounded as vacationers, especially from Georgia and Florida, rediscovered the area around Townsend, at the northern end of the Southwest Foothills.

Each year thousands of people center their vacations around Cherokee National Forest, 625,000 acres of forest and mountains on Tennessee's eastern border (the southern districts extend south from Great Smoky to Georgia).

Established in 1911, the national forest offers visitors beautiful scenery, campgrounds, world-class whitewater rafting and canoeing, hiking, backpacking, fishing, and picnic areas. Another plus: It's a destination that doesn't attract the bumper-to-bumper traffic of the national park to the north.

—— *Major Roads*

Forming the Southwest Foothills' western border are Interstates 75 and 40. I-75 heads north out of Atlanta to Chattanooga, then turns northeast on its way to Oak Ridge, where it joins I-40. I-75 then continues north to Lexington, Kentucky; Cincinnati and Toledo, Ohio; and Detroit.

The major noninterstate is US 411, which parallels I-75 from Cleveland (just east of Chattanooga) northeast to Maryville. US 64, a scenic highway that goes through Cherokee National Forest, takes an east-west route between Cleveland and Ducktown before entering North Carolina.

US 321 meanders between Townsend and Maryville; it's a major route for folks coming and going from the tourist meccas of Gatlinburg and Pigeon Forge. US 129 links US 411 to North Carolina as it slips between Great Smoky and Cherokee National Forest along the Tennessee River. It's a convenient—but little used—route to the North Carolina towns of Bryson City, Cherokee, and Asheville. As you might suspect, it's also fabulously scenic.

The incomplete Foothills Parkway parallels Great Smoky between US 321 and US 129; the 17-mile stretch of scenic highway is the longest section extant in what will be a 72-mile road that follows the boundary of the park through Tennessee. TN 68 is a scenic road that snakes through Cherokee National Forest from Madisonville to Ducktown.

—— A Self-Contained Region and a Jumping-Off Point

Travelers staying in Townsend, at the western entrance to Great Smoky Mountains National Park, use the town to explore the half-million-acre wilderness on their doorstep. But other people who come to the Southwest Foothills—to fish the streams, hike the trails, and, especially, run the rapids of the Ocoee and Hiwassee rivers—use the Southwest Foothills as a primary destination that fulfills all their recreational needs. And while day trips to Gatlinburg, Cades Cove, and Bryson City are possible, they're not particularly convenient—unless you're staying in Townsend.

—— Night Life

Most people who were "born to boogie" feel a little out of place in the evening serenity of the southern mountains, unless, of course, they happen to be in Benton, Tennessee, near the Ocoee River. In addition to being close to the site for the 1996 Olympic whitewater slalom competition, this rural crossroads is also the home of Grumpy's, the wildest, most rockin' honky tonk in the Smokies. Big name and soon-to-be-big-name rock bands play oldies, frat rock, alternative, and C&W in a building more reminiscent of a barn than a concert hall. Drawing party animals from as far away as Asheville, Knoxville, and Atlanta, Grumpy's has one of the most diverse clienteles you'll ever encounter. On Friday and Saturday nights, raft guides mix with schoolteachers, farmers, hikers, business execs, and college students in a deafening celebration of good music and good beer. Security is tight, the management friendly, and the crowd enthusiastic, but generally well behaved. There's plenty of room for dancing (including table tops), and if you do not want to dance, there is a set of bleachers for watching the band and the more extroverted customers.

Grumpy's is open Friday and Saturday nights from late March to late October, 8 P.M. to midnight. Legal drinking age in Tennessee is 21 and the Polk County Police are not to be trifled with. Grumpy's is located on US 64 about 20 miles east of Cleveland, Tennessee. Grumpy's also has a deli that's open year round. For more information and to find out what band is scheduled, call (615) 338-8060.

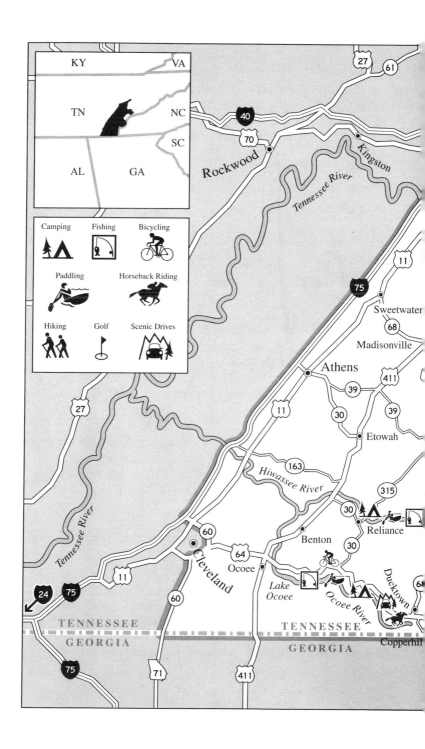

Outdoor Recreation and Activities

—— Camping

Cherokee National Forest

While undistinguished roadside campgrounds and RV parks abound in the Southwest Foothills, Cherokee National Forest provides some exceptional camping sites located in beautiful, wooded settings. Most of the 16 campgrounds in the southern districts of the national forest (the sections south of Great Smoky) are open from May through October, and campers can stay for up to 14 days.

Each site includes a parking spot, a tent pad (which also will accommodate trailers up to 22 feet long), a fireplace or fire ring, and a picnic table. Water, toilets, and showers are close by, but no electrical hookups are provided. Each site is limited to groups of five or less.

Chilhowee.   Located a few miles east of Benton (on US 411), Chilhowee offers 88 campsites located on a mountaintop next to seven-acre McKamy Lake. It's also close to whitewater activities on the Ocoee River.

Nearby activities include swimming, hiking, mountain biking, fishing, a "watchable" wildlife trail, and summer weekend campfire programs. Facilities include a trailer dump station, flush toilets, cold-water showers, a bathhouse, and picnic tables and grills. The campground is open from early April to early November.

Campsites on two loops can be reserved; call (800) 280-CAMP at least ten days in advance. (Reservations can't be made through the ranger's office.) Overnight camping is $8 a night. To reach the campground, take US 64 east to Forest Service Road 77. Turn left and go up the mountain for seven miles.

Parksville Lake.   Just off US 64 about 16 miles east of Cleveland, this campground offers superb access to whitewater sports along the

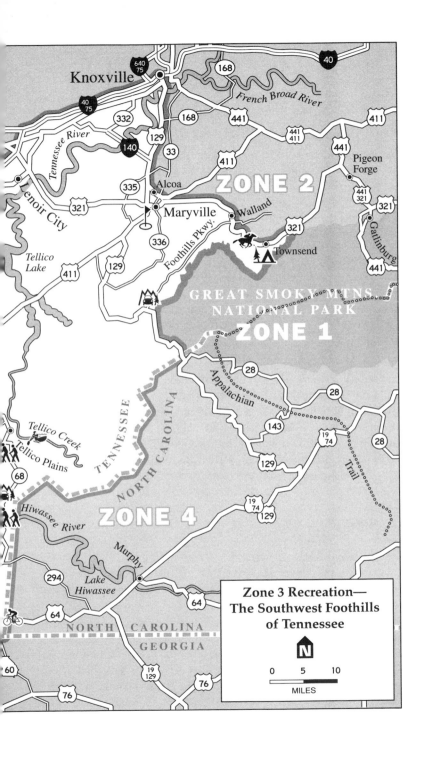

Knoxville

French Broad River

Tennessee River

Lenoir City

Tellico Lake

Alcoa

Maryville

Walland

Foothills Pkwy.

Townsend

Pigeon Forge

Gatlinburg

ZONE 2

**GREAT SMOKY MTNS.
NATIONAL PARK**

ZONE 1

Appalachian

Tellico Creek

Tellico Plains

TENNESSEE

NORTH CAROLINA

ZONE 4

Trail

Hiwassee River

Murphy

Lake Hiwassee

NORTH CAROLINA

GEORGIA

Zone 3 Recreation—
The Southwest Foothills
of Tennessee

N

0   5   10

MILES

Ocoee River. Facilities include 41 campsites, water, hot showers, and flush toilets; the campground is open from late March to mid-November. The camping fee is $6. The Clemmer Trail, a four-mile trail for mountain bikers, starts near the campground on US 64.

Thunder Rock. Close to whitewater activities on the Ocoee River, Thunder Rock features 29 sites, vault toilets, and picnic tables; some sites have grills. The campground is open year-round and is located 25 miles east of Cleveland. Turn right at the Ocoee No. 3 Powerhouse, cross the concrete bridge, follow the road around the powerhouse, and take the first right. Camping is $4 a night.

Gee Creek. Located a mile east of US 411 north of the Hiwassee River bridge, this campground has 42 sites, each with a table and fire ring. Facilities include a bathhouse with flush toilets and hot showers.

More Places to Camp for River Runners

In addition to the national forest campgrounds, many river outfitters along the Ocoee offer camping facilities to their rafting customers *only*. Be sure to ask when calling an outfitter for information or making reservations for a river trip.

River runners looking for a central place to camp that puts them in striking distance of rapids on the Ocoee, the Tellico, and the Nantahala rivers should consider **Hanging Dog Campground** in North Carolina's Nantahala National Forest. It's located five miles northwest of Murphy in Zone 4 (see page 301).

—— Hiking

An Easy Hike

Chilhowee Watchable Wildlife Trail. This three-quarter-mile loop takes visitors through a dense hardwood forest, a grassy opening, an area of white pine seedlings, and an area of thinned and regenerating hardwood trees—all human-created habitats that provide diversity for survival of forest animals. Be quiet and patient, visit in the early morning or late afternoon, and you'll have an excellent chance to see some wildlife. The trail starts near loops E and F in the Chilhowee Campground, a few miles east of Benton.

A Moderate Hike and an Easy Backpacking Trip

The Bald River Trail. This easy, five-and-a-half-mile trail (one way) is off the beaten track but offers superb trout fishing, excellent camping for overnight trips, and a great day hike. From Tellico Plains, take Tellico River Road to Forest Service Road 210 and park; the trail head starts here. Hike upstream to some gorgeous spots along the river for great fishing for rainbow trout. Walk as far as you like and retrace your steps to the car.

John Muir Trail. A beautiful section of this 20-mile trail in Cherokee National Forest starts at the base of the bridge across the Hiwassee River from the powerhouse. It's a short walk from the parking area to the bridge and the trail head just across the bridge.

The trail winds up and down for about five miles on its way east to Farner. It crosses creeks, narrowly winds along the top of the mountainside, and offers panoramic views of the famous Hiwassee narrows—a spot where the river is less than 20 feet wide and almost dry.

—— Canoeing, Kayaking, and Rafting

Ocoee River

The Southern Tennessee Foothills (Zone 3) offer some of the best paddling in the southern Appalachian Mountains. The Class III–IV Ocoee River, west of Cleveland, Tennessee, on US 64, is one of the most popular of all commercially rafted streams. Nonstop action from start to finish, the five-mile run serves up huge waves, big rapids, and a roller coaster ride. The scenery is beautiful, though the traffic on US 64 (which parallels the river) dispels any illusion of a real wilderness experience. Guided commercial raft trips on the Ocoee last about four hours with about two to two and a half hours on the water, making for a nice half-day excursion. For most outfitters, 12 years is the minimum age requirement. No lunch is served. On summer weekends, the Ocoee is incredibly congested. It is said that on these days a person could walk from the put-in to the take-out by stepping from raft to raft. If possible, schedule your Ocoee trip on a weekday. Because the Ocoee is a dam-controlled stream, you can almost always be assured of ideal water levels.

Outfitters offering guided raft trips on the Ocoee include:

High Country Outfitters	(615) 338-8634
Nantahala Outdoor Center	(800) 232-7238
Ocoee Inn Rafting	(615) 338-2064
Ocoee Outdoors	(615) 338-2438
Southeastern Expeditions	(800) 868-7238
Sunburst Expeditions	(800) 247-8388
USA Raft	(800) 872-7238
Wildwater Ltd.	(800) 451-9972

East of the section of the Ocoee where commercial raft trips operate is a nearly dry, boulder-strewn riverbed paralleling US 64. The river is dry because TVA diverts the water in a flume to generate hydroelectric power downstream. In 1996, however, the water will be released into the dry Ocoee riverbed to create the whitewater venue for the Olympics. In the summer of 1996, you will be able to see the world's best paddlers compete in whitewater slalom and downriver events. Tickets can be applied for one year in advance. Call the Atlanta Committee for the Olympic Games (ACOG) in Atlanta for an application, (404) 224-1996.

Hiwassee River

Just north of the Ocoee near Etowah and Reliance, Tennessee, is the Class II Hiwassee River. This stream, like the Ocoee, is dam controlled, but unlike the Ocoee, the Hiwassee draws its water from the bottom of a mountain lake. When the water is released into the Hiwassee streambed, it is a frigid 45° Fahrenheit. The Hiwassee is one of the widest whitewater streams you are ever likely to encounter and, consequently, is almost totally exposed to the sun. Rapids run the gamut from river-wide ledges to narrow sluices. Because of its beautiful scenery, mild rapids, and forgiving nature, the Hiwassee is a great favorite of novice whitewater canoeists and kayakers, and of tubers. Rental rafts are available on the Hiwassee for self-guided tours, but truth to tell, the long pools between rapids make powering a raft down the river a lot of work. On the Hiwassee, unless you have a lot of time, canoes and kayaks are definitely the preferred craft. The upper Hiwassee, from the powerhouse to Reliance, is where most of the whitewater action is. Including the shuttle, most trips on this five-and-a-half-mile section take about four to five hours. From Reliance down to the US 411 bridge, the current is swift, but there are few rapids. The lower section takes most paddlers about two hours plus shuttle time.

Outfitters on the Hiwassee include:

Webb's Float Service:	(615) 338 2373
Hiwassee Outfitters:	(615) 338-8142
John's Float Service:	(615) 338-5936

Tellico River

North of the Hiwassee near Tellico Plains is the Tellico River, offering Class III+ whitewater for experienced canoeists and kayakers. A free-flowing stream, the Tellico is runnable from January through April most years. For detailed information on this and other area rivers, check our list of recommended reading for canoeing, kayaking, and rafting on pages 76–77.

—— *Fishing*

Trout Fishing for Trophies on the Hiwassee

If you'd like a monster brown trout on the rec room wall (or in a streamside frying pan), consider this: A part of the Hiwassee River has been designated as a trophy-trout section north and east of Reliance from the Big Bend area to the railroad crossing; only artificial lures can be used.

The Hiwassee is heavily stocked with hatchery-raised brown trout—some of them dropped in by helicopter because the area is so remote. A Tennessee fishing license plus a trout stamp are required. The limit? Two fish and a 14-inch minimum.

Other fish found in the Hiwassee include rainbow trout, bass, bream, catfish, and yellow perch. The TVA regulates the flow of water, and it's essential to know the water level of the river and adjust your fishing technique accordingly. To find out what the water level will be during a particular period, call (800) 362-9250.

When the river is down, it's best to fish the large pools and holes with light spinning tackle or fly-fishing gear. The most popular method is to use a small hook and corn as bait. When the river level is high, either use a boat to float the river or fish from the bank.

Bass Fishing on the Hiwassee

Above the Appalachia Powerhouse, the TVA doesn't regulate the water level. As a result, the river on this stretch abounds with deep holes, rocky crevices, and woody thickets. While you'll find bluegill and largemouth bass here, the smallmouth bass fishing is reputed to be the best in East Tennessee.

Use top-water baits, spring lizards (salamanders), or float minnows when working near the weed beds, brush, and banks. Small imitation crayfish seem to work well, too.

Parksville Lake

Located on US 64 about four miles east of Ocoee, Parksville Lake offers excellent fishing for bluegill, catfish, largemouth and smallmouth bass, crappie, and trout. Bass can be taken with crank baits, spinners, grubs, and plastic worms. Creek mouths, sloughs, and underwater structures are productive April through July.

Conasauga River

An excellent but underused area is this river located just north of the Tennessee-Georgia state line off US 411. Bluegill and sauger are popular catches, as well as the Coosa bass and rock bass. Local anglers suggest using minnows or grubs for sauger in the fast current and shoals. To catch bluegill and bass, try crickets, grubs, and yellow rooster tails in the shallow, slow water.

—— Bicycling

Road Riding

A popular loop with river guides working out the kinks after a few days running rapids is a strenuous 85-mile loop out of Murphy, North Carolina (Zone 4), to NC 294 that goes past Fields of the Wood and Lake Hiwassee and into Tennessee. In Turtletown, take TN 68 south to Ducktown and take the wide-shouldered US 64 east into North Carolina to Murphy. The ride offers plenty of beautiful scenery and light traffic on the backroads.

The trip also makes a great credit card road tour. Leave the saddle-bags at home; pack some clothes, a toothbrush, and rain gear into a large fanny pack or handlebar bag; and spend the night at a bed-and-breakfast in Murphy and a motel in Ducktown.

Mountain Biking

An easy fat-tire ramble is the **Indian Boundary Lake Loop**, a three-and-a-half-mile ride around a scenic lake that affords beautiful views of the surrounding mountains. And it's flat. To get there, drive to the Indian Boundary Campground, east of Tellico Plains.

Chilhowee Campground, a few miles east of Benton on Forest Service Road 77, has a number of loops that are open to fat-tire bikes and are easy to explore. More advanced riders will want to try the challenging **Clemmer Trail,** located east of Ocoee on US 64. This single track designed specifically for intermediate and advanced mountain bikers runs for four and three-tenths miles one way.

The trail leads to Benton Falls, where you can explore a spectacular waterfall deep in Cherokee National Forest. The trail starts on US 64 near its intersection with TN 30 (look for the sign to Parkville Lake Campground).

Off-roaders looking for single-track excitement should cross over the state line into Georgia and head for the **Cuhutta Mountains**, about ten miles over the line. From Ducktown, take TN 68 south, which becomes GA 5; follow it through McCaysville. Soon after, it becomes Forest Service Road 68. At the top of Potato Patch Mountain, turn left, follow the road for five miles, and take a left into Bear Creek Campground and park.

The Bear Creek Loop is a fantastic loop for strong beginners and intermediate riders that's well marked. It follows a stream with a reputation for excellent trout fishing. But it's the single-track trails that are the main attraction on this ten-mile loop.

—— Horseback Riding

Davy Crockett Riding Stables in Townsend offers guided, three-and-a-half-mile horseback tours on private property bordering Great Smoky. The cost is $12 an hour per person. Summer hours are

9 A.M. to 8 P.M., and the stables are open year-round. For more information, call (615) 448-6411.

Action Eagle Adventures, three miles east of Ducktown on US 64, offers two-hour trail rides on the Action Eagle ranch, which straddles the Tennessee–North Carolina border. The guided rides leave at 9 A.M., noon, and 3 P.M. daily from May through October. The cost is $30 per person, plus tax.

Action Eagle also offers a two-day, one-night package with horseback riding one day and rafting on the Ocoee the next. Guests stay in a bunkhouse on the ranch or camp; the deal includes a Cajun cookout. The cost is $99 per person. Call (800) 288-3245 or (615) 496-1843 to make reservations, which are required.

—— *Golf*

While not exactly a golfer's paradise, there are a number of challenging courses in Zone 3. The best of these is at the Royal Oaks Country Club, Maryville, Tennessee. This and other quality golf courses in the area are profiled below.

Etowah Valley Country Club and Golf Lodges

Established: 1967

Address: 450 Brickyard Road, Etowah NC 28729

Phone: (704) 891-7022

Status: Private course

Tees: (South course)

   Championship: 3,507 yards, par 36, USGA 36, slope 125.
   Men's: 3,392 yards, par 36, USGA 36, slope 123.
   Ladies': 3,114 yards, par 36, USGA 36, slope 118.

Fees: Green fees: $25 for 18 holes, $15 for 9 holes. Cart fees: $14 per person for 18 holes, $8 per person for 9 holes.

Facilities: Pro shop, lodging, golf packages, restaurant, pool, three putting greens, driving range, and croquet.

Lambert Acres Golf Club

Established: 1964

Address: 3402 Tuckaleechee Park, Maryville TN 37803

Phone: (615) 982-9838

Status: Public course

Tees:

Championship: 6,480 yards, par 72, USGA 70.8, slope 118.
Men's: 6,152 yards, par 72, USGA 69.3, slope 116.
Ladies': 4,911 yards, par 72, USGA 66.2, slope 102.

Fees: Green fees: $15 per player all day. Cart fees: $4 per player per nine holes.

Facilities: Pro shop, snack bar, two putting greens, 27-hole golf course, bent grass greens, and Bermuda fairways.

Riverview Golf Course

Established: 1981

Address: 101 Club Drive, Loudon TN 37774

Phone: (615) 986-6972

Status: Public course

Tees:

Championship: 6,349 yards, par 72, USGA 66.9, slope 117.
Men's: 6,020 yards, par 72, USGA 66.1, slope 111.
Ladies': 5,400 yards, par 72, USGA 66.1, slope 109.

Fees: Green fees (include cart): $18 weekdays, $23 weekends and holidays.

Facilities: Pro shop, deli-style restaurant, and new clubhouse.

Royal Oaks Country Club

Established: 1992

Address: 4411 Legends Way, Maryville TN 37801

Phone: (615) 984-4260

Status: Semiprivate course

Tees:

> Championship: 6,441 yards, par 71, USGA 70.1, slope 121.
> Men's: 5,553 yards, par 71, USGA 68, slope 117.
> Ladies': 4,283 yards, par 72, USGA 67, slope 112.

Fees: Green fees (cart included and required): Monday through 2 P.M. Friday, $22 per guest; after 2 P.M. Friday, $19 per guest; before 2 P.M. Saturday, Sunday, and holidays, $27 per guest; after 2 P.M. Saturday, Sunday, and holidays, $24 per guest. All rates subject to tax and change.

Facilities: 18-hole course, driving range, chipping and putting green, clubhouse with full service golf shop, sports bar and grill, swimming pool, and tennis courts.

White Oaks Golf Course

Established: 1992

Address: 705 County Road 105, Athens TN 37303

Phone: (615) 745-3349

Status: Public course

Tees:

> Championship: 6,608 yards, par 36, USGA 36, slope 119.
> Men's: 5,936 yards, par 36, USGA 36, slope 116.
> Ladies': 4,970 yards, par 36, USGA 36.

Fees: Green fees: $6.50 for 9 holes, $9.50 all day. Cart fees: $4.50 per person for 9 holes, $9 per person for 18 holes. Carts required on weekends and holidays.

Facilities: Pro shop, driving range, and snack bar. Second nine holes to open August 1995.

—— Scenic Drives

The Foothills Parkway. This 17-mile stretch of scenic roadway follows the ridge of Chilhowee Mountain from US 321 to US 129 along the northwest boundary of Great Smoky. The parkway offers excellent views of the higher elevations inside the national park and (to the west) of the Tennessee Valley and the Cumberland Mountains in the distance. On a clear day, you can see the smokestacks of TVA's

Bull Run Steam Plant near Oak Ridge. There's also a lookout tower at Look Rock, which provides even better views.

US 129. Squeezing between Great Smoky Mountains National Park to the north and Cherokee and Nantahala national forests to the south, this beautiful, low-traffic road provides glimpses of spectacular mountains, rivers, and lakes as it heads east from Tennessee to Robbinsville, North Carolina. For more incredible views, take NC 28 at Tapoco for a drive past huge Fontana Dam and along Fontana Lake in Zone 4 (the Southern Foothills of North Carolina).

US 64. This highway follows the Ocoee River, one of the most popular whitewater rafting rivers in the United States. The river will be the site for canoeing and kayaking events in the 1996 Olympic Games in Atlanta.

Heading east from the town of Ocoee, sights include Ocoee Powerhouse No. 2, which receives its flow of water from a flume 11 feet deep and 14 feet wide. About three miles past the powerhouse you can look up and see what appears to be a railroad bridge. It's the flume supplying water to the generators.

Several scenic pulloffs offer views of Lake Ocoee with Cherokee National Forest in the background. Parksville Beach is popular in the summer for swimming. Stop at the Ocoee Ranger District Office, which serves as a welcome center with information, brochures, and maps. Farther west, mountain views include the Big Frog and Little Frog wilderness areas and the bluffs of the Ocoee River Gorge. It's a heck of a drive.

Tennessee 68. This scenic, windy, and narrow state road passes through Cherokee National Forest between Ducktown and Madisonville. Along the way are Tellico Plains (the location of a major Cherokee town before settlers moved in), Coker Creek (the second area in the United States where gold was discovered), the Hiwassee River, and Turtletown.

Attractions

In addition to great outdoor recreation, the Southwest Foothills offer visitors a chance to explore the region's long and interesting history. From Cherokee towns collectively known as the Tennessee Overhill (the towns rested on the western slopes of the Appalachian Mountains, "overhill" from the Lower Cherokee settlements) and colonial-era British forts to a museum dedicated to a Cherokee genius, there's much to do or see. And if it's a rainy day, consider visiting one of the commercial caverns listed below.

Ducktown Basin Museum

Type of Attraction: A small museum and historic industrial site dedicated to the heritage of copper mining in the region. A self-guided tour.

Location: Ducktown, Tennessee.

Admission: $3 for adults, $.50 for children.

Hours: 10 A.M. to 4:30 P.M. Monday through Saturday; closed Sundays.

Phone: (615) 496-5778

When to Go: Any time.

Special Comments: The best time to photograph the moonscape of the adjacent Burra Burra Mine pit is in the morning. Locals say the devastation caused by decades of mining in the area is the only man-made feature visible to the naked eye of astronauts circling the earth.

Overall Appeal by Age Group:

Pre-school	Grade School	Teens	Young Adults	Over 30	Senior Citizens
★	★★	★★	★★	★★	★★★

Author's Rating: The old mine resembles a moonscape, while the small, old-fashioned museum is a bit gloomy. ★★

How Much Time to Allow: One hour.

DESCRIPTION AND COMMENTS   The museum, which also includes old buildings and equipment used in the early days of copper mining, overlooks the barren hills of the Ducktown Basin. While you can see into Georgia and North Carolina, the view is desolate from years of pollution. Displays in the museum focus on minerals, mining, and Cherokee Indians.

TOURING TIPS   The 15-minute slide show that precedes the self-guided tour is repetitious and boring—and on the day we visited, the soundtrack was often difficult to understand and out of sync with the photos. Unless you've got a keen interest in copper mining and local history, skip it.

OTHER THINGS TO DO NEARBY   Rafting on the Ocoee River.

Fort Loudoun State Historic Area

Type of Attraction: A replica of a British fort built during the French and Indian War, the ruins of a late-18th-century U.S. fort, a visitor center, and a nature trail. A self-guided tour.

Location: Vonore, Tennessee.

Admission: Free.

Hours: Visitor center: 8 A.M. to 4:30 P.M. daily. Forts, blockhouse, and nature trail: 8 A.M. to sunset daily.

Phone: (615) 884-6217

When to Go: Any time.

Special Comments: Don't miss the small but classy exhibit area in the visitor center.

Overall Appeal by Age Group:

Pre-school	Grade School	Teens	Young Adults	Over 30	Senior Citizens
★★★	★★★¹/₂	★★★	★★★	★★★	★★★¹/₂

Author's Rating: A fascinating glimpse into America's colonial past. ★★★¹/₂

How Much Time to Allow: An hour to explore the small fort; half a day for the visitor center, blockhouse, and nature trail.

DESCRIPTION AND COMMENTS   The original Fort Loudoun was constructed in the wilderness during the winter of 1756-57 to help ally the powerful Cherokee Nation to the English cause and to block French penetration of the area from the west.

But, as usual, relations between the English and Cherokee broke down; in 1760, the Indians laid siege to the fort. A garrison of 180 men and 60 women and children left the fort on August 9; the next morning the Cherokee attacked the garrison's camp, killing 20–30 people, including all the officers except one. The rest were taken as slaves.

The recreation of the fort, located on the same site as the original, looks like a set from a 30s movie starring a buckskin-clad Spencer Tracy. Twelve-foot-high walls made of pointed logs surround a grass field, officers' quarters, a blacksmith shop, and a munitions building; cannons are mounted on platforms in the corners. The view of the surrounding lake and countryside is impressive.

Across Tellico Lake is the Tellico Blockhouse, an archaeological ruin of a fort constructed in 1794 by the young U.S. government to protect the Cherokee from continued white advances into the Little Tennessee Valley. The site, a short drive from Fort Loudoun, is reached from Old Highway 72, just north of Vonore on US 411.

TOURING TIPS   The small, modern visitor center features excellent exhibits on period uniforms and clothing, colonial living, and archaeology. There's also a 15-minute film on the fort's history.

OTHER THINGS TO DO NEARBY   Sequoyah Birthplace Museum is about one mile away.

The Lost Sea

Type of Attraction: A cavern featuring a four-and-a-half-acre underground lake. A guided tour.

Location: Sweetwater, Tennessee.

Admission: $7.50 for adults and $3.75 for children ages 6–12.

Hours: 9 A.M. to dusk daily. Closed Christmas Day.

Phone: (615) 337-6616

When to Go: Any time.

Special Comments: No steps to negotiate on this cavern tour—all passageways in the cave are connected by ramps.

Overall Appeal by Age Group:

Pre-school	Grade School	Teens	Young Adults	Over 30	Senior Citizens
★★	★★★	★★★	★★★	★★★	★★½

Author's Rating: The lake is unusual, but 75% of the cavern's natural features have been destroyed. ★★

How Much Time to Allow: One hour.

DESCRIPTION AND COMMENTS   At the Lost Sea, visitors cruise on a glass-bottom, electric-powered boat on an underground lake that's still not completely explored. Yet don't expect to be overwhelmed by lots of natural features such as stalactites—the cave saw heavy use from the Civil War until the 1930s and most were destroyed.

TOURING TIPS   Wear comfortable shoes: The tour requires about three-quarters of a mile of walking. Groups of ten or more can reserve overnight tours that use the cave's natural entrance and do some exploration of areas the public doesn't see.

OTHER THINGS TO DO NEARBY   Fort Loudoun and Sequoyah Birthplace Museum are located northeast of Sweetwater off US 411.

Sequoyah Birthplace Museum

Type of Attraction: A Cherokee-owned museum dedicated to the inventor of the Cherokee writing system that features exhibits on Indian artifacts, crafts, myths, and legends. A self-guided tour.

Location: Vonore, Tennessee

Admission: $2.50 for adults, $1.50 for children ages 6–12.

Hours: 9 A.M. to 5 P.M. Monday through Saturday; noon to 5 P.M. Sundays. Closed Thanksgiving, Christmas, and New Year's days.

Phone: (615) 884-6246

When to Go: Any time.

Special Comments: The small, modern museum is located on a dramatic lakefront setting.

Overall Appeal by Age Group:

Pre-school	Grade School	Teens	Young Adults	Over 30	Senior Citizens
★	★★½	★★½	★★½	★★½	★★★

Author's Rating: Tasteful, interesting, informative. ★★★
How Much Time to Allow: One hour.

DESCRIPTION AND COMMENTS   Sequoyah, who lived from 1776 to 1843, developed a Cherokee syllabary in 1821 that preserved the Cherokee language in written form. In addition to exhibits about this intellectual achievement, the museum features displays of Cherokee myths and legends, artifacts from 2,000 years of continuous human habitation in the Little Tennessee Valley, and exhibits on more recent Cherokee history, including the Trail of Tears.

TOURING TIPS   Outside the museum, the Cherokee Memorial marks a common grave holding the remains of 18th-century Cherokees excavated from burial sites in the Little Tennessee Valley prior to completion of the Tellico Reservoir.

OTHER THINGS TO DO NEARBY   Fort Loudoun State Historic Area is about one mile away.

Tuckaleechee Caverns

Type of Attraction: A natural cavern on the edge of the Great Smoky Mountains National Park featuring stalagmites, an underground stream, and the largest subterranean room in the East. A guided tour.

Location: Townsend, Tennessee.

Admission: $7 for adults, $4 for children ages 6–12.

Hours: 9 A.M. to 6 P.M. daily from March 15 through November 15.

Phone: (615) 448-2274

When to Go: Any time.

Special Comments: Wear comfortable shoes with non-skid soles: There's lots of walking on the hour-and-fifteen-minute, three-quarter-mile tour, plenty of steep stairs, and a few tight passages. But most of the underground rooms are large and filled with interesting natural features.

Overall Appeal by Age Group:

Pre-school	Grade School	Teens	Young Adults	Over 30	Senior Citizens
★★	★★★	★★★	★★★	★★★	★★¹/₂

Author's Rating: A family-run attraction that's friendly and not
overly commercial. Plus, many of the formations are large and
unusual. ★★★

How Much Time to Allow: One hour and fifteen minutes once your
tour begins.

DESCRIPTION AND COMMENTS   The Big Room, reputed to be the largest
underground room in the East, is about 400 feet long and 200 feet
wide. Ironically, even though it's the deepest room in the cavern, you
walk *up* to reach it. (Why? The mountain overhead is higher directly
over the room.) All the walkways are paved and have handrails. Look
up and you may spot a pygmy bat, about the size of your thumb.

TOURING TIPS   A great destination on a rainy day.

OTHER THINGS TO DO NEARBY   Cades Cove in Great Smoky National
Park is about a 30-minute drive; Townsend features shops, restaurants, camping, motels, horseback riding, and river activities such as
tubing, canoeing, and fishing.

PART SEVEN:
The Southern Foothills of
North Carolina—Zone 4

A Brief History and Orientation

Southwestern North Carolina, tucked directly below Great Smoky Mountains National Park, always has been the most isolated part of North Carolina. Mostly, it's a factor of distance and big mountains: Murphy, the seat of Cherokee County, is closer to the state capitals of Tennessee, Georgia, Alabama, and Kentucky than to its own capital, Raleigh.

High mountain ranges running east to west through the Southern Foothills connect the Smoky and Blue Ridge mountains, the major ranges running southwest to northeast up the interior of the East Coast. The Cowee, the Nantahalas, the Pisgah Ledge, the Balsams, the Great Craggies, and the Black Mountains are like rungs on a ladder connecting the two larger mountain chains.

The Southern Foothills' isolation, however, may be coming to an end. Its abundance of natural beauty is attracting growing numbers of outdoor enthusiasts, especially whitewater rafters and kayakers, anglers, and mountain bikers. But they're not the first to discover these ridges and valleys: Outsiders have been coming to these mountains for almost half a millennium.

—— History

The original inhabitants of these richly forested hills were the Cherokee Indians, who may have moved here around 1000 A.D. The first outsider to visit was Spanish explorer Hernando De Soto, who came in 1540 along with 600 soldiers. He was looking for a city of gold and didn't stay.

In the 1700s, settlers pushed into the mountains of western North Carolina and encroached on the Cherokees' land. After decades of skirmishes, broken treaties, and unresolved conflict, the low point of relations between the Native Americans and the settlers came in the 1830s.

President Andrew Jackson signed the Removal Act and the majority of Indians were transferred by force to Indian Territory in Oklahoma on the infamous Trail of Tears; thousands died along the way. Many of the Cherokee were assembled for the forced march at Murphy, North Carolina, close to where Tennessee, Georgia, and North Carolina meet.

Not all the Cherokee Indians made the tragic march on the Trail of Tears. Today about 10,000 of their descendants, called the Eastern Band of the Cherokee, live on the Qualla Reservation, centered around the town of Cherokee. The larger Western Band of the Cherokee is based in Oklahoma, where the descendants of the survivors of the Trail of Tears live.

Early Tourists

After the settlers, there came another invasion, of sorts: Wealthy planters from South Carolina and Georgia migrated to the mountains to escape the summer heat of their coastal plantations. By the mid-19th century, many towns and villages were experiencing seasonal fluctuations in population as the rich folk came and went from second homes. It still happens today.

In the late 18th century, clay for Wedgwood porcelain was exported to Great Britain from the Cowee Valley, just north of Franklin. Today, the Cowee gem region remains one of the richest areas on earth for rubies and other gems.

After the Civil War, the railroads came, bringing with them another wave of outsiders. This time it was lumber companies and other exploiters of the area's rich natural resources. Naturalists and tourists followed, and inns and hotels were built to accommodate them. The region prospered in the late 19th century.

Lakes and Forests

In the 20th century the Tennessee Valley Authority constructed dams on the rivers that generate electricity and created beautiful lakes for recreation. The establishment of Nantahala and Pisgah national forests assured that much of the natural beauty would remain protected—and a constant draw to those who enjoy wilderness and the outdoors.

Tourism Today

The major recreational attraction in the Southern Foothills is 516,000-acre Nantahala National Forest, which offers access to world-class whitewater rafting through the Nantahala Gorge on the Nantahala River, mountain biking in nationally renowned Tsali Recreation Area, and fishing and boating on huge TVA impoundments: Fontana Lake, Chatuge Lake, Santeetlah Lake, Nantahala Lake, and Lake Hiwassee.

Many hikers and backpackers head for the Joyce Kilmer Memorial Forest and the Joyce Kilmer/Slickrock Wilderness, while both young and old enjoy a ride on the Great Smoky Mountains Railway. The gateway communities of Cherokee, Bryson City, and Fontana provide access to less visited parts of half-million-acre Great Smoky Mountains National Park, which borders the Southern Foothills to the north.

Attractions in nearby zones that are within striking distance of the region include Asheville, the economic and cultural center of Western North Carolina (Zone 6); the upscale resort town of Highlands (Zone 5); and Tennessee's Ocoee River (Zone 3), whitewater venue for the 1996 Olympics.

If you're staying in the northern part of the region, don't rule out a day trip to Gatlinburg or Pigeon Forge (Zone 2) across the national park in Tennessee. If you've got kids, they'll love you for it.

Northern Georgia. Across the border in Northern Georgia, Nantahala National Forest becomes Chattahoochee National Forest. Major recreation attractions include Blue Ridge Lake, Lake Nottely, and Lake Chatuge. At 4,784 feet, Brasstown Bald is the highest point in the state—and you can drive to the top.

Chattahoochee National Forest offers hikers more than 430 miles of trails and many beautiful waterfalls to explore. Fishermen can try their luck in more than 1,000 miles of primary trout streams, as well as ten lakes containing trout, bass, and catfish.

—— A Self-Contained Destination and a Jumping-Off Point

Vacationers in the Southern Foothills of North Carolina get the best of both worlds. For many, especially whitewater enthusiasts, hikers, and anglers, the vast expanses of pristine mountains found in Nantahala National Forest offer enough potential for outdoor recreation to last a lifetime. For them, there's no compelling reason to trek to the national park to the north—at least, not during the busy tourist season.

Many visitors staying in Bryson City and Cherokee, however, use these towns as departure points for exploring amenity-less Great Smoky. The towns are less fancy or overtly commercial than the Tennessee towns near the northern entrance. They also offer easy access to some infrequently visited trails and trophy trout streams along the southern boundary of the national park. They're just not as close to some of the national park's more popular attractions.

Another off-the-beaten-track option is Fontana Village, a resort on the shores of Lake Fontana, the huge TVA impoundment that hugs the southern boundary of the national park. It's in a beautiful setting, and offers fishing, a marina, lodging, horseback riding, and organized children's activities. The resort, located on NC 28, also makes a great jumping-off point for exploring the southern part of Great Smoky by canoe or sea kayak.

If they have the time, though, people staying near the park's southern border should look to the south for more things to do outdoors. The mountains may not be quite as high as those in the national park, but the roads are a lot less crowded. The reverse is also true, at least during the off-seasons: Folks staying in the Southern Foothills aren't far from Great Smoky, and should make the effort to visit this remarkable—and beautiful—park.

—— *The Cherokees*

The only Indian reservation in the mid-Atlantic region is the 56,000-acre Qualla Boundary, adjacent to Great Smoky Mountains National Park. Today, the 10,000 descendants of the Cherokee who hid in the mountains to escape the forced march along the Trail of Tears depend primarily on tourism for their livelihood.

Visitors to Cherokee, the tourist center in the heart of the reservation, can learn much about the tribe—but you've got to do more than shop in the seemingly endless number of tawdry souvenir shops that line the roadsides in town.

History

Dig a little deeper and you'll discover that this isn't tipi and feathered headdress country: Before the European settlers arrived, the 25,000 Cherokee who lived in these mountains and foothills were part of a powerful, unified, peaceful nation. They lived in log cabins (not tents) in small villages and farmed the land stretching to the Ohio River in the north and into Georgia and Alabama in the south.

Later, the Cherokee were one of the first tribes to develop a written language. Invented by Sequoyah in the 1820s, the Cherokee syllabary (pictures that represent words) became part of the daily life of many Cherokee; by the early 1840s, a Cherokee newspaper, *The Phoenix,* circulated throughout the territory.

The syllabary may have saved the Cherokee language. While for a time Cherokee students weren't permitted to speak their native language and it was nearly lost, today it's a popular course in area schools and spoken by many Cherokee.

While few Cherokee who live and work in the tourist areas speak the language, in traditional communities such as Snowbird (near Robbinsville) up to 90% of the Cherokee speak and write their language.

Learning More

Visitors wanting to learn more about the rich Cherokee culture should make at least two stops on a visit to the reservation: the Museum of the Cherokee Indian and the Oconaluftee Indian Village (see "Attractions"). Both are high quality visitor attractions that will fascinate anyone interested in U.S.—and Native American—culture and history.

—— Location

The Southern Foothills (Zone 4) are bordered by Great Smoky Mountains National Park (Zone 1) to the north, the Southwest Foothills of Tennessee (Zone 3) to the west, the Tri-State Mountains of North Carolina, Georgia, and South Carolina (Zone 5) to the east, and Asheville and Brevard (Zone 6) to the northeast. The closest large cities are Chattanooga, Tennessee (to the west), Asheville, North Carolina (to the northeast), and Greenville, South Carolina (to the east).

—— *Major Roads*

Two major highways bisect the Southern Foothills. Coming in from Tennessee, US 64 goes east to Murphy, where it meets the other major road, US 74/19. From Murphy, US 64 continues east past Chatuge Lake and through Nantahala National Forest, and then swings northeast into Franklin.

From Murphy, US 74/19 goes northeast through Andrews on its way to Bryson City and Cherokee (and the southern entrance to Great Smoky). From Bryson City and points east, the highway is a high-speed, limited-access freeway that whisks travelers to Asheville and I-40.

NC 28 starts at the Tennessee–North Carolina state line at the western edge of Great Smoky at Deals Gap and heads east along Fontana Lake toward its juncture with US 74/19 below Bryson City. NC 28 then continues south to Franklin.

US 129 enters North Carolina at the same point as NC 28 but takes a more southerly route through Robbinsville before hitting US 74/19. Both are good alternative routes to US 64 and I-40 for getting to and from Tennessee.

US 441, the only road to cross Great Smoky, goes south from Cherokee (the southern entrance to the national park) to Dillsboro and Franklin.

In Georgia, US 76 parallels US 64 through Chattahoochee National Forest and the towns of Blairsville (where it crosses US 19) and Young Harris.

Outdoor Recreation and Activities

—— Nantahala National Forest

In Cherokee, "nantahala" means "land of the noonday sun"—an apt description of the steep valleys and gorges located in the deep recesses of the Appalachian Mountains of southwestern North Carolina: In many places the sun only penetrates to the valley floor at midday.

Many people say this is the most unspoiled section of the Southern Appalachians. It's also a place to escape the hordes of tourists who clog the roads of Great Smoky and to enjoy mountain vistas unchanged since the days when the Cherokees roamed these hills. And the tourism hype along the roads is minimal.

Encompassing more than a half million acres, the national forest includes habitats in secluded areas for endangered species and unique plant communities. Elevations in the national forest range from a high of 5,800 feet to a low of 1,200 feet. For recreation, visitors can enjoy fishing and boating on picturesque reservoirs, camping, hiking, backpacking, whitewater rafting and kayaking, and horseback riding.

Cheoah Ranger District

Located west of US 74/19 between Bryson City and Murphy, this 120,000-acre slice of the national forest adjoins four large mountain reservoirs, contains a section of the Appalachian Trail, and features a network of hiking trails totaling 225 miles.

Special attractions of the Cheoah Ranger District include Joyce Kilmer Memorial Forest (one of the most impressive remnants of old-growth forest in the United States) and the Tsali Recreation Area near Fontana Lake (one of the best mountain biking destinations in the East).

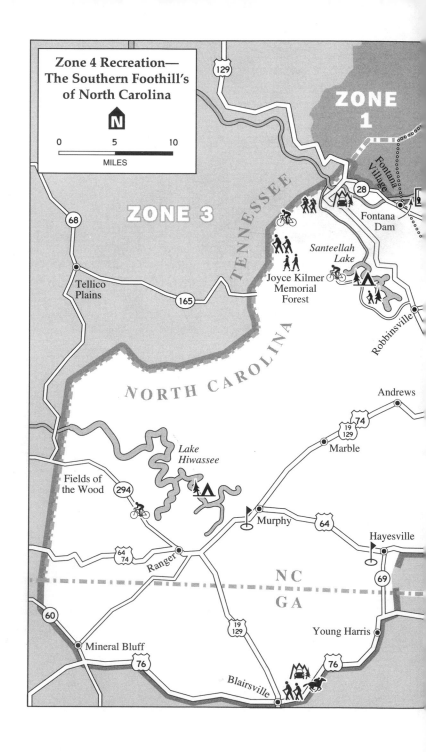

Zone 4 Recreation—
The Southern Foothill's
of North Carolina

N

0   5   10
MILES

ZONE 1

ZONE 3

129

TENNESSEE

68

Tellico
Plains

165

Fontana
Village

28

Fontana
Dam

Santeellah
Lake

Joyce Kilmer
Memorial
Forest

Robbinsville

NORTH CAROLINA

Andrews

19
129   74

Marble

Lake
Hiwassee

Fields of
the Wood   294

Murphy   64

Hayesville

64
74   Ranger

69

NC
GA

60

19
129

Young Harris

Mineral Bluff

76

76

Blairsville

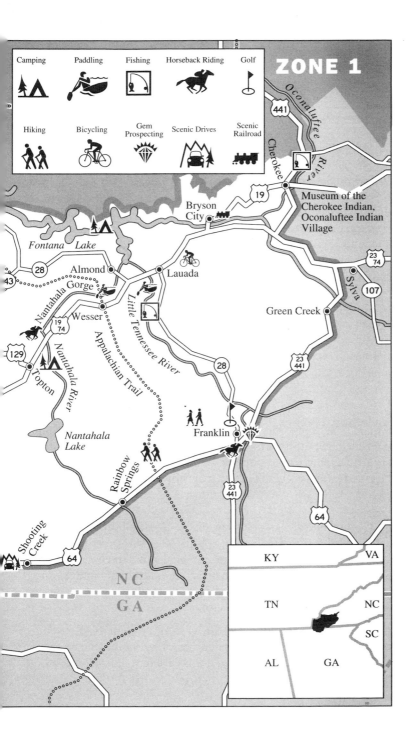

ZONE 1

Camping Paddling Fishing Horseback Riding Golf

Hiking Bicycling Gem Prospecting Scenic Drives Scenic Railroad

Oconaluftee River

Cherokee

441

19

Museum of the Cherokee Indian, Oconaluftee Indian Village

Bryson City

Fontana Lake

28

Almond

43

Nantahala Gorge

Lauada

23 74

Sylva

107

Green Creek

19 74

Wesser

Little Tennessee River

129

Nantahala River

Topton

Appalachian Trail

28

23 441

Nantahala Lake

Franklin

23 441

64

Rainbow Springs

Shooting Creek

64

NC
GA

KY VA

TN NC

SC

AL GA

Wayah Ranger District

Named after the Cherokee word meaning "wolf," this 134,000-acre section is located in the central portion of the national forest along US 64 between Murphy and Franklin. Outstanding attractions in the Wayah Ranger District include Wayah Bald, which rewards visitors with a 5,200-foot vantage point with views stretching from the Great Smoky Mountains in Tennessee to the rolling hills of Georgia.

Nantahala River Gorge is a nine-mile stretch of the Nantahala River between Beechertown and Fontana Lake with a worldwide reputation for excellent whitewater. Continuous rapids and moderately high water levels during the summer months provide challenging rapids for rafters and kayakers.

Periodic releases of water by the Nantahala Power and Light Company produce the racing water needed for whitewater slalom races held in the winter and spring. US 74/19 is lined with commercial river outfitters, which provide guides, equipment rentals, instruction and clinics, restaurants, and lodging.

—— *Camping*

The U.S. Forest Service maintains many well-developed campgrounds in the Southwest Foothills' Nantahala National Forest. Here are four located close to popular—and scenic—Lake Fontana. For more information, call (704) 479-6431; however, no reservations are accepted.

Tsali Campground.   Located on the southern shores of Fontana Lake along NC 28, Tsali offers 41 wooded sites with centrally located bathrooms equipped with flush toilets and hot showers. Facilities include a boat launch, 18 miles of hiking, horse and mountain biking trails, and, nearby, whitewater rafting. Camping is $10 a site per night; open mid-April through October.

Little Cove Campground.   Farther west on Fontana Lake's southern shore, Little Cove has 26 wooded sites, bathrooms (but no showers), and a boat launch. It's located a mile and a half off NC 28 on Forest Service Road 3618. It's open mid-April through October; camping is $5 per night.

Cheoah Point Campground.   Located near Santeetlah Lake off US 129 about five miles north of Robbinsville, this campground offers 26 wooded sites, fishing, and a boat launch; it's open April 15 through October 31. Facilities include flush toilets but no hot showers. The nearby Wauchecha Bald Trail provides access to the Appalachian Trail.

Horse Cove Campground.   Located across from the Joyce Kilmer Memorial Forest, this campground has 17 wooded sites and flush toilets, but no showers. It's open from mid-April through October; six sites are open year-round, but there's no water. For more information, call (704) 479-6431.

Near Murphy

Hanging Dog Campground.   Located five miles from Murphy on Hiwassee Lake, this Forest Service campground is popular with whitewater boaters and rafters due to its central location. Although rapids aren't found in the immediate area, popular nearby rivers include the Tellico to the south, the Ocoee to the west, and the Nantahala to the east.

Hanging Dog is a primitive campground (vault toilets, no hot showers) with 69 sites available on a first come, first served basis; the daily fee is $4 and check-out time is 2 P.M. To get there from Murphy, take NC 1326 (Joe Brown Highway) northwest for five miles. Elevation at the campground is 1,580 feet.

A Private Campground

Lost Mine Campground.   This 100-acre, wooded campground in Nantahala Gorge is convenient for folks rafting its world-famous rapids. Most of the 60 sites are located along a creek and half offer water and electrical hookups. Facilities include fireplaces, picnic tables, hot showers, and washers and dryers.

Campsites are restricted to one vehicle (no RVs); the cost is $5 per person with a $12 minimum per night. Families are charged $4 per person with the same minimum, but children six and under are free. A site with an electrical hookup is $1 extra per night; no credit cards are accepted but personal checks are okay. Lost Mine is located twelve and seven-tenths miles west of Bryson City, one mile off US

19; turn right onto Silver Mine Creek Road at the Nantahala Outdoor Center. The campground is open from mid-March through the first week in November. For reservations, call (704) 488-6445.

—— *Hiking*

The two best known trails in the Southern Foothills are the 2,000-mile, Maine-to-Georgia **Appalachian Trail** and the **Bartram Trail,** the route used by Quaker naturalist William Bartram more than 200 years ago.

The Appalachian Trail crosses US 64 midway between Franklin and Lake Chatuge on its way north. Then it crosses Wayah Bald and Wesser Bald before swinging west above Nantahala Gorge on its way to Fontana Dam (which the trail crosses) and Great Smoky Mountains National Park.

The section of the incomplete Bartram Trail in North Carolina goes west from Franklin, where it meets the Appalachian Trail at Wayah Bald, to Nantahala Lake. Another eight-mile section stretches from Topton to Tatham Gap; while it's frequently overgrown, local hikers say it's a gorgeous hike.

Easy Hikes and Walks

The Cheoah Trail.   Located two miles north of Robbinsville off US 129 (turn on NC 1116; the trail starts behind the U.S. Forest Service ranger station), this self-guided interpretive trail is an easy, two-and-three-tenths-mile ramble with 400 feet of elevation gain.

Wayah Bald.   This three-tenths-mile paved trail is suitable for physically disabled folks and leads to a lookout tower on 5,200-foot Wayah Bald. The tower is a National Historic Landmark providing panoramic views from Tennessee to Georgia.

To get there, go three miles west on US 64 out of Franklin and turn right at the sign for Wayah Bald. Next, take the first left onto Wayah Road (NC 1310). After about seven miles, turn right onto Forest Service Road 69; it's another four and a half miles of smooth gravel road to the parking area.

Big Tree Cove/Joyce Kilmer Trail.   An easy, but not flat, two-mile hike through Joyce Kilmer Memorial Forest on a figure-eight-shaped footpath through a rare stand of virgin timber. Early spring may be the most interesting time to walk the trail because of the carpets of delicate wildflowers set amidst tree trunks the size of minivans. See "Attractions," page 323, for more information.

Moderate Hikes

High Country Day Hike.   Located in the Joyce Kilmer/Slickrock Wilderness, this out-and-back hike leads from Wolf Laurel Basin trail head to a scenic spot called "the Hangover" and spectacular views.

Although the route is over 4,500 feet in elevation, most of the high ground is gained on the steep drive to the trail head. On this high-country, Y-shaped excursion, it's possible to cross the summit of three bald mountains: Bob's Bald, Stratton Bald, and Haoe Bald.

To get there: From Robbinsville, follow signs for Joyce Kilmer Forest off US 129 north. At Santeetlah Gap, turn left onto what looks like a closed, paved road, then immediately turn downhill onto dirt Forest Service Road 81. Follow FS 81 along Santeetlah Creek approximately five miles to a right turn onto FS 81-F. Follow this steep road to its dead end at the trail head.

On the trail, hike uphill to the left to its junction with Stratton Bald Trail (Trail 54). Turn left on Trail 54 and continue to the next trail junction, about half a mile. Turn right and descend to Naked Ground Trail (Trail 53). From Naked Ground Trail, follow the ridgeline over Haoe Bald to the Hangover. The view from this narrow ridge point is breathtaking.

Then turn around and retrace your steps back to the junction with Stratton Bald Trail. Hike out Trail 54 (keeping to the right) over Stratton Bald to an open meadow on top of Bob's Bald (look for a rock inscribed "A. L. Swann" in the field). Return over Stratton Bald to Trail 54 to a right turn on a spur trail back to your car. While this hike is only eight miles, give yourself plenty of time to complete it.

Strenuous Hikes/Backpacking

Big Tree Cove to Naked Ground Overnight Loop.   This strenuous, 12-mile backpacking trip in the Joyce Kilmer/Slickrock Wilderness climbs from 2,000 feet at the picnic-area trail head to 5,000 feet at Naked Ground in five miles; the steepest climbing is in the last half mile. There is a reasonably dependable spring at Naked Ground, but no water at Bob's Bald.

From the parking area at Big Tree Cove picnic area, take Naked Ground Trail (Trail 55) uphill for five miles to the ridgeline at Naked Ground. Camp here or turn left and hike over Stratton Bald to the meadow atop Bob's Bald. Return to the picnic area on Stratton Bald Trail (Trail 54), which comes out on a road half a mile from the road to Big Tree Cove. Turn left and hike back to the left to the picnic area.

Slaughter Creek/Blood Mountain Loop. This is a strenuous, 12-mile day hike or a moderate overnight backpacking trip to some of the best scenery in northern Georgia. It's a fairly easy hike up to the Appalachian Trail, followed by a nice ridge walk, fantastic views from Blood Mountain, and an easy ramble down to your car. Overnighters can camp at Slaughter Gap and day hike to the top of the mountain the next morning.

The hike starts at Lake Winfield Scott Recreation Area, about ten miles south of Blairsville, Georgia. From town, take US 129 south for ten miles to Vogel State Park and turn right onto GA 180 for the five-mile drive to the recreation area.

Park near the dam and hike the blue-blazed trail three miles to Jarrard Gap. Turn left onto the Appalachian Trail northbound; it's four fairly easy miles to Slaughter Gap, the site of a big Indian battle.

Take the side trail for two miles to the summit of Blood Mountain, the highest point on the Appalachian Trail in Georgia. The views northward from the well-situated outhouse just below the summit are so good, there's no door!

Complete the loop by taking the Slaughter Creek Trail downhill along the creek for four miles to Lake Winfield Scott. You also can car camp in the recreation area.

—— *Canoeing, Kayaking, and Rafting*

Nantahala River

The Southwestern Foothills of North Carolina (Zone 4) is home to the Nantahala River, the most beloved of all Smoky and Blue Ridge mountain streams. The Nantahala is located south of Bryson City, North Carolina, and runs next to US 19. Dam controlled, with frigid

45° Fahrenheit water, the Nantahala serves up eight miles of continuous Class II (III) action. The current is swift and most of the rapids are straightforward with many small standing waves. Running through a steep, forested gorge, the stream is intimate, canopied by hardwoods, and exceptionally scenic. Though US 19 parallels the Nantahala for most of the run, the vehicle traffic is usually not intrusive. Because the Nantahala is challenging without being particularly threatening, it is immensely popular with all sorts of paddlers. If you sit by the river on a Saturday afternoon, you can witness a veritable parade of canoes, kayaks, rafts, tubes, and duckies.

The run begins just below the Nantahala Power Plant and ends just downstream of Nantahala Falls, the largest rapid (Class III) on the river. As you approach Nantahala Falls on the river, a sign warns you that a big rapid is just ahead. With little effort, you can beach your boat and walk up to the falls and check it out. If the falls appear too challenging, you easily can portage around.

As an aside, if you don't have time to run the river, stop for a while on a weekend afternoon and watch the endless procession of boaters coming through the falls. In one hour you will witness more strange events than on a whole season of "America's Funniest Home Videos."

Area outfitters rent rafts, canoes, kayaks, tubes, and duckies for self-guided trips; they also offer guided trips. Shuttle service is almost always provided. Guided trips last about three and a half hours with about two and a half hours on the water. Rates for guided raft trips range from around $18–27. If you elect to take a guided raft trip, be aware that there probably will not be a guide in every raft. If you are adamant about having a guide in your raft, make your requirement known when you secure your reservation. Because of the river's swift current and forgiving nature, however, most able bodied folks will get along fine without a guide. There is no way to get lost on the Nantahala, though several midstream islands present route options. If you are inexperienced and do not have a guide, just ask one of the hundred of canoeists or kayakers to point out the preferred passage.

Like the Ocoee River in Tennessee, the Nantahala is amazingly congested on summer weekends. If at all possible, therefore, try to run on a weekday. Minimum age for most guided trips is ten years; minimum weight is 60 pounds. The weight requirement ensures that a young paddler can be fitted securely with a life jacket. Rest room facilities are provided at the put-in and midway in the run at a small park just after the river crosses under US 19. No food is served on guided raft trips.

If you've been itching to try a duckie (one- or two- person inflatable paddled like a kayak but not decked (enclosed)), the Nantahala is a perfect river. Duckies are forgiving (that word again), extremely stable, and relatively easy to guide. Do not, however, attempt the Nantahala in a canoe or kayak unless you have been trained in paddling whitewater. Trust us, it's not anything like paddling a canoe on the lake at camp.

Nantahala outfitters include:

Great Smokies Rafting Company	(800) 238-6302
Nantahala Outdoor Center	(800) 232-7238
Rolling Thunder River Company	(800) 344-5838
USA Raft	(800) 344-5838
Wildwater Ltd.	(800) 451-9972

In addition to guided trips and rentals, the Nantahala Outdoor Center (NOC) operates one of the nation's oldest and most respected whitewater canoe and kayak instruction programs. From weekend introductions to week-long clinics, the NOC training courses are exceptional in every respect. Students without boats can rent equipment from the center. Lodging and meals are available on some programs. For a catalog of courses offered, call (800) 232-7238.

Tuskasegee River

Just east of the Nantahala, at Dillsboro, North Carolina, is the Tuckasegee River. One of several rivers in the state that have recovered from a polluted past, the Tuckasegee runs through a five-mile gorge downstream of Dillsboro. The five- to seven-mile Class II run is a relaxed alternative to the more crowded Nantahala, and the water is warmer, too. The river usually can be run year-round with a dependable natural flow augmented by power plant releases on the stream's upper tributaries. The Tuckasegee is quite scenic, though not as pretty as the Nantahala. Winding through a valley gorge, there are frequently houses, roads, and other signs of civilization visible from the river. Rapids consist primarily of small rock gardens and ledges. On the whole, the Tuckasegee is less intense and less challenging than the Nantahala.

Both guided and self-guided trips are offered on the Tuckasegee, though most rafters opt for the self-guided alternative. Rafts, duckies, and tubes are available for rent. Depending on water level and how hard you paddle, the run takes one and a half to two and a half hours in a raft or duckie. Minimum weight for children is 40 pounds. Shuttle is provided. The primary commercial outfitter on the river is Tuckasegee Outfitters, (704) 586-5050.

Little Tennessee River

In addition to the Nantahala and the Tuckasegee, canoeists and kayakers can enjoy the Little Tennessee River from Lost Bridge, off NC 28 to Fontana Lake. Depending on the pool level of the lake and the water level of the river, this run can serve up some good Class II (III) whitewater. For detailed information on this and other area rivers, check our list of recommended reading for canoeing, kayaking, and rafting on pages 76–77.

—— *Fishing*

Cherokee Reservation

Some of the best trout fishing in the eastern United States happens along the 30 miles of streams (all tributaries of the Oconaluftee River) on the Cherokee Indian reservation, bordering Great Smoky Mountains National Park to the south. Anglers need a $5 Tribal Fishing Permit, available at nearly two dozen businesses in Cherokee and good for a day; no state fishing license is required.

How good is the fishing? A regular stocking program of the streams and three ponds on the reservation adds nearly a million rainbow, brook, and brown trout each year. The waters are stocked twice a week; the daily creel limit is a generous ten trout per permit holder. It's quite a bargain.

No bait restrictions apply; perennial favorites include canned, whole-kernel sweet corn; miniature marshmallows; cheese balls; chunks of hot dogs; as well as more traditional baits such as red wigglers, millworms, wasp larvae, minnows, grubs, crickets, and night crawlers.

Some fishing tips: Taking trout with bait usually is easier than opting for flies, especially for beginners. Bait, by the way, is most effective when fished with current; fly-fishing is best in fast-moving waters.

The ponds are good bets for children or folks unable to scramble around stream-side rocks and boulders. The three ponds are located about five miles north of Cherokee beside Big Cove Road. They're often crowded, though, and fly-fishing isn't permitted.

The season opens the last Saturday in March and continues through the last day of February the following year. For more information, call (704) 497-5201.

Fontana Lake

Stunning Fontana Lake, at nearly 2,000 feet of elevation and wedged between Great Smoky Mountains National Park and Nantahala National Forest, is a 10,530-surface-acre TVA impoundment of the Little Tennessee River. Development is limited along its shoreline; and the surrounding mountains, forests, and cloud-dotted skies often make it appear natural.

The angling is superb, making the sport the number one drawing card to Fontana Lake. The fishing is almost always good here—and fishless days are made bearable by the outstanding scenery.

The lake sports a surprisingly diverse number of game fish species, including smallmouth bass, walleye, white bass, rainbow and steelhead trout, muskie, and bream. Catfish are plentiful, as are largemouth bass, brown trout, redbreast bream, and crappie.

But the lake's reputation with knowledgeable anglers is based on the **smallmouth bass,** a top battler that when hooked puts on energetic displays of acrobatics. With its steep, rocky shoreline and year-round cool waters, Fontana is a perfect habitat for smallmouths. Ten- to 14-inchers are the usual size range, but fish up to seven pounds have been reeled in.

The best smallmouth fishing occurs between mid-April and late June; bait fishing with three-inch minnows works in the early season. Hot weather sends the smallmouth deep from July through September during daylight hours; fishing usually is frustrating for inexperienced anglers.

The lake also has a reputation for outstanding **walleye** fishing. This large-growing perch is best caught by working the riverbanks while casting green or yellow quarter-ounce leadhead jigs or live minnows along the rocky bottoms.

Fishing for **trout** often is overlooked at Fontana. But recent introductions of steelhead and rainbow trout may change that; the lake also has an overlooked population of brown trout. Late winter and early spring finds these cold-water exotics in the headwaters of Fontana's many feeder streams.

White bass are another abundant species found in the lake. They make a river-spawning run in the lake's headwaters during April that's popular with anglers. River-spawning whites are aggressive fish that station themselves in the shoals and pools; cast across the current and briskly retrieve your offering.

Catfish flourish in the impoundment; a 40-and-one-half-pound channel cat was taken from Fontana in 1971. These fish readily strike flies and plugs; serious anglers stalking catfish use "stink" baits such as chicken liver or cut shad innards.

Bluegill and redbreast bream are popular vacation-time fish; live crickets or red worms dangled beneath a bobber along almost any shoreline will do the job.

Little Tennessee River

A stretch of the Little Tennessee River between Bryson City and Franklin is world renown for its **smallmouth bass** fishing—and it's on the side of a paved road. From Bryson City, go south on US 19/74 till the four-lane ends and make the first left onto Needmore Road. That's the Little Tennessee following alongside the road. The best smallmouth fishing is in the spring and fall.

—— Bicycling

Road Rides

Burningtown Loop. This is an easy to moderate, 20-mile ride on backroads between Bryson City and Franklin that gives cyclists an inside look at Southern Appalachian life. It's a gently rolling loop ride with only 300 feet of elevation change.

From Bryson City, drive south on US 19/74 and turn left onto Needmore Road, the first turn after the end of the four-lane stretch of road. Follow it for six miles to the end and turn left onto Tellico Road. Next, drive three-tenths of a mile and park at the Burningtown Church of God.

On your bike, ride out Burningtown Creek Road (take the right fork at the "Y" near the church). At mile eight, turn left (look for Bike Route 30) and go another mile and get on Rose Creek Road (Bike Route 35). After another five miles cross Lost Bridge and get on NC 28. Then turn right and go one and a half miles to your car.

Along the way you'll enjoy lots of rolling countryside, light traffic, old churches, tobacco barns, views of big peaks, horse and cattle farms, and lots of pretty streams.

Santeetlah Lake Loop. This moderately difficult, 40-mile ride makes a loop around Santeetlah Lake, near Robbinsville. It features light traffic, great scenery, and plenty of places to go swimming. You also can bring a lock and hike the Big Tree Cove Loop through a virgin forest. Warning: There's one *very* steep climb on the loop.

Start the ride at the Cheoah Ranger District Office on Joyce Kilmer Road, off US 129 north of Robbinsville. From the station, turn left out of the parking lot and follow signs to Joyce Kilmer Memorial Forest. The climb from the turnoff to the Blue Boar Lodge to Santeetlah Gap may reduce the strongest rider to tears.

Descend from the gap and turn right onto the hardpack dirt Forest Service Road 416. The route returns to pavement two miles past Horse Cove Campground. Cross under the aqueduct and turn right toward the dam; stay on the dam road past Cheoah Point Recreation Area. After a climb, the road joins US 129. Turn right and take US 129 south to a right turn on Joyce Kilmer Road and the ranger station.

Mountain Biking

Tsali Recreation Area. The trails along Fontana Lake have earned a national reputation among mountain bikers who love moderately easy single track trails in a gorgeous setting. Tsali (pronounced "SAH lee") is located three and a half miles west of US 19/74, 15 miles west of Bryson City.

On Tuesdays, Thursdays, and Saturdays, riding is restricted to two loops: Thompson (formerly the New) and Mouse Branch. Most riders do Mouse Branch first as a warmup. Total length of the figure-eight ride is about 15 miles. The trails are about 70% rolling single track.

On other days of the week, ride the Left Loop and the Right Loop (in that order) for a total of 23 miles. These are about 95% single track and leave most riders giddy. All the loops offer outstanding scenery, views of the Smokies across Lake Fontana, and lots of big-grin single track.

Whigg Meadow Loop. This spectacular 12-mile ride takes intrepid mountain bikers to the highest ridge on the western edge of the Appalachian Mountains for a stupendous view of several huge river drainages. While most of the riding is in Tennessee, it starts about ten miles from the Joyce Kilmer Memorial Forest near Robbinsville, North Carolina. This ride is rated moderate to strenuous.

From the Forest Service ranger station just off US 129 north of Robbinsville, drive toward Joyce Kilmer. About one and a half miles before the parking lot for Joyce Kilmer, turn left onto Forest Service Road 81 and drive eight miles. When the dirt road turns to pavement, park under the bridge at the North Carolina–Tennessee state line.

On your bike, ride back towards Robbinsville. When you get to the sign for Mud Gap, turn right onto a gated road and start climbing a gravel road that soon starts to deteriorate; even strong riders may have to dismount. After three miles, look for Whigg Meadow on the right. Ride out to the middle and look to the west—there's nothing between you and the Rockies.

A spring is located near the road on the north side of the field where you can fill your water bottles. (Play it safe and treat the water before drinking.) From late July to mid-August, the meadow is full of blueberries. Just keep an eye open for bears; they like blueberries, too. In early June, the meadow is full of wild strawberries.

To complete the loop, ride past the field on the road and start a long, steep descent. Watch out for cars, which can negotiate the road (FS 61), and be careful at the concrete fords over streams—erosion can create huge gaps that can swallow a wheel. At FS 217, turn right and go uphill to your car, about three miles. Hmm, this ride starts *and* finishes with a climb. Local riders say it's worth it.

—— *Horseback Riding*

C&C Stables in Franklin offers one-hour guided rides into the mountains daily starting at 10 A.M. Rates are $20 an hour per person;

small children can ride with adults for $5. By reservation only; call (704) 369-6805.

Nantahala Village Riding Stables, located between Andrews and Bryson City, offers one-hour, two-hour, and two-and-a-half-hour guided tours on horse trails in Nantahala National Forest. Rides leave between 9 A.M. and 5:30 P.M. daily from Easter to Labor Day; the rate is $10 per person/per hour. After Labor Day, tours are available weekends and by appointment. For more information, call (704) 488-9649.

Track Rock Riding Academy in Blairsville, Georgia, offers one- and two-hour guided rides on private property through woods, meadows, and creeks. One-hour rides are $15 per person and leave at 1 P.M., 2:30 P.M., and 4 P.M. daily, year-round; two-hour rides are $28 per person and leave at 10:30 A.M. Reservations are recommended; call (706) 745-5252.

—— *Golf*

The best course in Zone 4 is that of the Mill Creek Country Club in Franklin, North Carolina. This and other quality golf courses in the area are profiled below.

Chatuge Shores Golf Course

Established: 1969

Address: Route 2, Box 145E, Hayesville NC 28904

Phone: (704) 389-8940

Status: Public course

Tees:

>Championship: 6,687 yards, par 72, USGA 71.3, slope 123.
>Men's: 6,269 yards, par 72, USGA 69.9, slope 118.
>Ladies': 4,950 yards, par 72, USGA 68.3, slope 120.

Fees: Green fee and cart per person: $24 for 18 holes, $13.50 for 9 holes. Carts are not mandatory. Club rental per person: $7 for 18 holes, $4 for 9 holes.

Facilities: Pro shop, driving range, putting green, snack bar in clubhouse, tennis courts, and pool.

Cherokee Hills Golf Course

Established: 1969

Address: Harshaw Road, Murphy NC 28906

Phone: (704) 837-5853 or (800) 334-3905

Status: Semiprivate resort course

Tees:

Men's: 6,324 yards, par 72, slope 117.
Ladies': 5,172 yards, par 72, slope 113.

Fees: Green fees: $15 for 18 holes, $8 for 9 holes. Cart fees: $10 for 18 holes, $6 for 9 holes. Carts are required weekends and holidays until 2 P.M. Tee times are required daily until 1 P.M. during season.

Facilities: Putting green, driving range, swimming pool, fitness trail, snack bar, restaurant, and lodging.

Mill Creek Country Club

Established: 1980

Address: 98 Mill Creek Road, P.O. Box 848, Franklin NC 28734

Phone: (704) 524-6458 or (800) 533-3916

Status: Semiprivate course

Tees:

Championship: 6,167 yards, par 72, USGA 69, slope 115.
Men's: 5,775 yards par 72, USGA 68.5, slope 113.
Ladies': 4,485 yards, par 72, USGA 66.4, slope 113.

Fees: Green fees (includes cart): $36 in season, $23 off-season. Golf packages and mountain villa rentals available.

Facilities: Pro shop, putting green, golf lessons, deli-style restaurant, tennis, and lodging.

—— Gem Prospecting in Franklin

Discover the thrill of prospecting for precious stones at a gem mine near Franklin, a town synonymous with rubies and other gems. Put on some old clothes and get your hands dirty rooting through

muddy water in a sluice in search of the elusive Big One that will
make you rich. Before or after your prospecting trip, visit the Franklin Gem and Mineral Museum (see page 322).

Cowee Mountain Ruby Mine is open seven days a week starting at 9
A.M. Prospecting takes place along a 150-foot covered flume. Six ten-
pound bags of dirt cost $5; figure about 30 minutes of sifting to see if
you've struck it rich. For more information, call (704) 369-5271.

Gold City Gem Mine offers six bags of dirt for $5, as well as enriched
buckets from $12–35. Open daily from 9 A.M. The flume is con-
structed for use by folks who are physically disabled. A picnic area,
playground, game room, and gift shop are on the premises. Call (704)
369-3905 for more information.

Jacobs Ruby Mine assures customers each ruby, sapphire, rhodolite,
garnet, or other precious stone they find is a native gem not imported
from outside the area. Admission is $6 for adults and $3 for children
12 and under. Rest rooms, cold snacks and drinks, and changing
rooms are on the premises. For more information, call (704)
524-7022.

Buck Creek Pine Barrens is a delightful place where you can pan for
rubies in a stream that's biological and geologically unique. Not only
that, it's free. This isn't a commercial gem mine.

On US 64 between Franklin and Hayesville, turn right onto Old
US 64, then take a right onto Forest Service Road 350. Drive about a
mile and park near some scrubby pine trees. The stream is on the
right, where you can go out and pan for rubies and rhodolite. On a
sunny day, the stream looks red. It's a really neat spot.

—— Scenic Drives

While both US 74/19 and US 64 provide stunning mountain
vistas, visitors can explore some smaller roads that honeycomb the
Southwestern Foothills for even better back-country scenery.

Robbinsville/Fontana Lake Loop. A few miles north of Andrews
on US 74/19, US 129 heads northwest to Robbinsville. It's a pleasant, two-lane road that winds its way through Nantahala National
Forest on its way to Tennessee. In Robbinsville, follow the signs to

the national forest ranger office on NC 1116 and pick up information on how to make an easy side trip to Joyce Kilmer Memorial Forest.

Past Lake Santeetlah, US 129 follows the Cheoah River to Tapoco. Turn right onto NC 28, which follows Lake Cheoah past a series of dams. On the left is Great Smoky Mountains National Park; look for a sign for Fontana Dam.

Then make a left to enjoy an impressive, up-river view of the massive, 480-foot-tall structure. (Just don't think about what's on the other side.) A couple miles farther east on NC 28, follow signs to the Fontana Dam visitor center, where you can ride an incline car down the face of the dam to visit the huge generators.

NC 28 continues east through the national forest, providing plenty of great views of huge Fontana Lake, Great Smoky on the other side, and mountains. Tsali Recreation Area is on the left, featuring miles of trails popular with hikers, equestrians, and mountain bikers. At US 74/19, turn left to complete the loop, which takes about two hours at a leisurely pace.

US 64.   Between Murphy and Franklin the highway passes through some wildly scenic back country, with numerous overlooks, where you can pull over and soak up the views. Near Hayesville the road passes Lake Chatuge, a TVA impoundment featuring camping, boating, and fishing.

To the south, the Standing Indian Basin (in Zone 5) offers visitors blue-ribbon trout streams, camping, horse trails, waterfalls, and hiking in the Southern Nantahala Wilderness.

North Carolina 294.   A few miles west of Murphy on US 64, NC 294 goes north past Lake Hiwassee. The countryside is rolling, with farms, forests, lake views, and an off-the-beaten-path ambiance.

Eighteen miles west of Murphy is Fields of the Wood, a fundamentalist "theme park" with Biblical inscriptions in marble and stone spread across 200 acres of mountainside. An unusual place, to say the least. Admission is free.

You can make this a loop drive by continuing a short distance into Tennessee, going south on TN 68 to Ducktown, and then heading east on US 64 to Murphy.

Nantahala Gorge via Franklin.   This mountainous route starts in Franklin: Go west on US 64 three miles and turn right at the sign for Wayah Bald; then make a left onto NC 1310 (Wayah Road). After passing through a lush farm valley, the road begins a steep, winding ascent up Wayah Mountain. At the top, a road on the right leads to Wayah Bald; see "Easy Hikes" below for more information on a pleasant walk to this impressive overlook.

NC 1310 connects to US 74/19; turn right and follow the Nantahala River (look for kayakers shooting the rapids). Next, you've got two choices: Either turn right onto NC 28, a curvy road leading to the many gem mines in Cowee Valley and Franklin, or continue straight to Cherokee, the Indian reservation, and Great Smoky Mountains National Park. To make a loop, return to Franklin on US 441 via Dillsboro.

Brasstown Knob. Beautiful Brasstown Knob, Georgia's highest mountain at 4,784 feet, offers spectacular 360-degree views into four states. The visitor information center at the summit features exhibits, video presentations, and interpretive programs. A steep, paved, half-mile-long trail leads to the information center at the summit; a concessionaire operates a shuttle bus for those who would rather ride.

It's a beautiful drive from Blairsville, Georgia, to reach Brasstown Knob, which is located in Chattahoochee National Forest: Take US 19/129 south eight miles and turn left (east) on GA 180. Go nine miles to the GA 180 spur and turn right (north). It's three miles of steep, winding, and narrow roadway to the Brasstown Knob parking lot.

Brasstown Knob is open daily from Memorial Day through October and on weekends in early spring and late fall. For more information, call the visitor center at (706) 896-2556 or the District Ranger's Office at (706) 745-6928.

—— A Scenic Railroad Excursion

Great Smoky Mountains Railway offers excursions through Great Smoky Mountains National Park, across Fontana Lake, and through the Nantahala Gorge from spring through fall.

The diesel-locomotive-pulled trains leave the Dillsboro depot at 9:30 A.M. and 2:30 P.M. and depart the Bryson City depot at 9 A.M. and 2 P.M. From Dillsboro, tickets are $15 for adults and $7 for children for a trip lasting three and a half hours. From Bryson City, it's a four-and-a-half-hour ride; the cost is $17 for adults and $7 for children.

Reservations are required; call (800) 872-4681. Excursions run from mid-April through October on a varying schedule. On Sundays, the train is pulled by a steam locomotive.

Raft 'N Rail

Combine a scenic railroad excursion on the **Great Smoky Mountains Railway** with rafting on the Nantahala River: The trip features a two-hour train trip across Fontana Lake and up the Nantahala Gorge. Then you're bused to the "put-in" (river-runner lingo for where the raft trip starts) for the two-and-a-half-hour, eight-mile guided rafting trip down the river. A picnic lunch is included during the seven-hour trip.

The train departs the Bryson City depot, where rafters are met by professional river guides. Trips leave at 9 A.M. and 2 P.M. from March through October. Schedules vary and reservations are required: Call (800) 872-4681. The cost is $46 for adults and $36 for children ages 2–12; the minimum weight is 60 pounds.

Attractions

Considering its remoteness, the Southern Foothills offer a surprisingly wide range of attractions for visitors looking to do something other than run a river, hike a trail, or fish for trophy smallmouth bass in Fontana Lake. There's much to discover in this corner of the Southern Appalachians.

Places to explore range from a fascinating (and bizarre) fundamentalist "theme park" near the Tennessee border (Fields of the Wood) and a couple of fun-to-browse county historical museums, to some excellent museums that chronicle the sad history—and display the rich culture—of the Cherokee Indians.

Cherokee County Historical Museum

Type of Attraction: A museum with exhibits on Cherokee life during the time of the Cherokee Nation and about the early days of white settlers. A self-guided tour.

Location: 205 Peachtree Street, Murphy, North Carolina.

Admission: Free.

Hours: 9 A.M. to 5 P.M. Monday through Friday.

Phone: (704) 837-6792

When to Go: Any time.

Special Comments: The museum is located over the Murphy police department. A chair lift is available for disabled visitors.

Overall Appeal by Age Group:

Pre-school	Grade School	Teens	Young Adults	Over 30	Senior Citizens
★★	★★¹/₂	★★¹/₂	★★★	★★★	★★★¹/₂

Author's Rating: A small, well-designed museum with some interesting exhibits. ★★★

How Much Time to Allow: One to two hours.

DESCRIPTION AND COMMENTS   Exhibits in this one-floor museum range from items left by 16th-century Spanish explorers and an ancient soapstone carving of a turtle on the front lawn, to a replica of Fort Butler, a stockade near Franklin where the Cherokee were assembled to begin their march on the Trail of Tears in 1838–39. Other exhibits include the interior of a one-room school, guns, tools, minerals, old photos, clothing, and arrowheads. You couldn't ask for more on a rainy afternoon.

TOURING TIPS   Exploration of this eclectic museum reveals some interesting items, including an old crank telephone that once belonged to Joe Cannon, a Speaker of the U.S. House of Representatives from Illinois. (The connection to Cherokee County isn't clear, but that's okay.) A stuffed beaver that weighed in at 60 pounds when trapped looks humongous.

OTHER THINGS TO DO NEARBY   Across the street is the Church of the Messiah, an old clapboard church equipped with blue Tiffany windows. Walk over and take a peek inside.

Cherokee Indian Cyclorama Wax Museum

Type of Attraction: A small museum that tells the story of the
     Cherokee people through dioramas and taped lectures. A tour
     guided by lighting and a taped narrative.

Location: Highway 19 North, Cherokee, North Carolina.

Admission: $2.50 for adults, $1.50 for students ages 13–17, and $1
     for children ages 6–12.

Hours: 9 A.M. to 5 P.M. daily (April, May, September, October); 9
     A.M. to 8 P.M. daily (June through August).

Phone: April through October: (704) 497-4521. November through
     March: (704) 497-2111.

When to Go: Any time.

Special Comments: The cyclorama—a series of dioramas with a taped
     narrative—is on the second floor, up one flight of stairs.

Overall Appeal by Age Group:

Pre-school	Grade School	Teens	Young Adults	Over 30	Senior Citizens
★★	★★½	★★½	★★	★★	★★

Author's Rating: Gloomy and a little frayed around the edges, but its grim historical message packs a punch. ★★

How Much Time to Allow: 30 minutes.

DESCRIPTION AND COMMENTS From the first meeting with De Soto in 1540 to the Trail of Tears, the history of the Cherokee is, well, depressing. So it only figures that this wax museum about the Native Americans is decidedly downbeat.

It doesn't help that the exhibits are right out of the 50s and that the taped narrative is cliche-ridden. But it's a nonsugar-coated telling of one of the most disgraceful chapters in U.S. history: the forced move of 17,000 Cherokees from their home in the Southern Appalachians to Oklahoma. More than 4,000 Cherokees died along the way.

TOURING TIPS A small gallery downstairs—really a waiting room for the cyclorama above—features exhibits of artifacts and techniques used by Cherokees to tan hides and make arrowheads. Look for wax figures of Will Rogers, Andrew Jackson, and De Soto.

OTHER THINGS TO DO NEARBY The town of Cherokee features plenty of tacky roadside shops selling cheap trinkets made in Taiwan and other tourist junk; Oconaluftee Indian Village and the Museum of the Cherokee Indian are classier destinations.

Fields of the Wood

Type of Attraction: A 200-acre biblical "theme park"—actually, a collection of stone markers, the Ten Commandments, and monuments spread over manicured lawns on the sides of two mountains. A self-guided tour.

Location: 18 miles west of Murphy, North Carolina, on NC 294.

Admission: Free.

Hours: Sunrise to sunset daily.

Phone: (704) 494-7855

When to Go: Any time. Skip it during inclement weather.

Special Comments: Billed as one of the "biblical wonders of the 20th century"—and one of the oddest.

Overall Appeal by Age Group:

Pre-school	Grade School	Teens	Young Adults	Over 30	Senior Citizens
★	★★	★★	★★	★★	★★½

Author's Rating: Bizarre. ★¹/₂

How Much Time to Allow: A tough call—anywhere from five minutes (for a quick glance) to half a day.

DESCRIPTION AND COMMENTS Drive through the gates and you're greeted by the sight of dozens of gleaming white religious monuments spread across two mountain slopes. The centerpiece is the world's largest representation of the Ten Commandments: The letters are five feet high, four feet wide, and spread across the side of a mountain.

Almost as odd—though no where near as big—is the enshrined airplane that overlooks the parking lot. This fundamentalist theme park is owned and operated by the Church of God of Prophecy, which is headquartered in Cleveland, Tennessee, about 52 miles away.

TOURING TIPS Expect to get an aerobic workout if you plan to explore all the monuments: Steep stairs lead to the top of the slope facing the Ten Commandments and a "place of prayer" and a so-so view of the mountains at the top. Drive a mile up the mountain to view the world's largest cross. There's also a gift shop, cafe, and bookstore on site.

OTHER THINGS TO DO NEARBY Hiwassee Dam and Lake Hiwassee are close. Otherwise, there's not much to do except take a scenic drive. This is an isolated, yet beautiful, part of the Southern Foothills of North Carolina.

Fontana Dam

Type of Attraction: The highest dam east of the Rocky Mountains and the largest dam in the Tennessee Valley Authority system. Guided and self-guided tours.

Location: 28 miles west of Bryson City, North Carolina, off NC 28.

Admission: Free. The ride on the incline car to view the generators costs $1 per person.

Hours: The visitor center is open 9 A.M. to 8 P.M. daily; the incline car runs on the half hour from 10 A.M. to 5 P.M. daily from May through September.

Phone: (704) 498-2374

When to Go: Any time.

Special Comments: For a heart-stopping view of the dam from the bottom up, follow signs from NC 28 about two miles west of the turnoff to the dam's visitor center. Just don't think about all the water on the other side.

Overall Appeal by Age Group:

Pre-school	Grade School	Teens	Young Adults	Over 30	Senior Citizens
★	★★★	★★★	★★★	★★★	★★★½

Author's Rating: Incredibly massive—and scenic. ★★★

How Much Time to Allow: One hour.

DESCRIPTION AND COMMENTS Fontana Dam is 480 feet high, a half-mile wide, and backs up a lake 40 miles long. The Appalachian Trail crosses the huge structure and an incline car takes visitors down the slope in front of the dam for a 25-minute tour of the three generators that can produce 238,500 kilowatts of electricity. People enthralled by engineering marvels shouldn't miss it.

TOURING TIPS The tour of the generators via the incline car takes about 25 minutes and provides an up-close view of the dam as you descend ("Gee, are those cracks, uh, *serious*?"). For a case of the heebie-jeebies that rivals a ride in Dollywood, walk out on the dam and look down the huge concrete spillways that are used (rarely) to drain high water off the lake: The huge tubes go down for nearly 500 feet. The intakes to the generators, however, are invisible—the 16-foot-wide pipes are located 250 feet below the surface of Fontana Lake.

OTHER THINGS TO DO NEARBY Opportunities for fishing, picnicking, camping, hiking, and boating are located along Fontana Lake for the 3.5 million annual visitors to the area. The old construction village created during World War II when the dam was built is now called Fontana Village, a resort offering boating, golf, horseback riding, and crafts.

Franklin Gem and Mineral Museum

Type of Attraction: A museum featuring mineral specimens from North Carolina, all 50 states, and around the world. A self-guided tour.

Location: Phillips Street, Franklin, North Carolina.

Admission: Free.

Hours: 10 A.M. to 4 P.M. Monday through Saturday; 1 P.M. to 4 P.M. Sundays.

Phone: (704) 369-7831

When to Go: Any time.

Special Comments: The museum is housed in the old Macon County jail, circa 1850. The stairs are steep; there's a bathroom on the second floor.

Overall Appeal by Age Group:

Pre-school	Grade School	Teens	Young Adults	Over 30	Senior Citizens
★	★★	★★½	★★	★★½	★★½

Author's Rating: An old-time museum filled with glass cases jamming the small rooms. Fun stuff, though. ★★½

How Much Time to Allow: One hour.

DESCRIPTION AND COMMENTS   Rock hounds will love this small museum, which is crammed with notable items such as a huge sapphire, a 49-pound corundum crystal, and a fist-sized ruby crystal. The Fluorescent Room (formerly the solitary cell in the old jail) displays the phenomenon of phosphorescence; other attractions include a 346-pound beryl crystal from Brazil and a collection of Indian artifacts.

TOURING TIPS   Even if you're not a rock hound, check out the display of rocks used in the manufacture of glass. It's housed in the old jail's high-security lock up. A small gift shop features minerals and books on gems and rocks.

OTHER THINGS TO DO NEARBY   The Macon County Historical Society Museum is around the corner.

Joyce Kilmer Memorial Forest/ The Big Tree Cove Loop Trail

Type of Attraction: An easy, two-mile-long footpath through a 3,800-acre, old-growth forest with more than 100 species of trees, many more than 300 years old. A self-guided tour.

Location: Off US 29, about ten miles west of Robbinsville, North Carolina.

Admission: Free.

Hours: Sunrise to sunset daily.

Phone: (704) 479-6431

When to Go: Any time. Rhododendron, mountain laurel, and azalea bloom in the late spring and early summer.

Special Comments: Don't hike the trail during high winds and storms; large branches blown off the big trees are called "widow makers" for obvious reasons. During spring, summer, and fall, volunteers often are on hand to direct visitors and answer questions.

Overall Appeal by Age Group:

Pre-school	Grade School	Teens	Young Adults	Over 30	Senior Citizens
★★★	★★★	★★★¹/₂	★★★★	★★★★	★★★★

Author's Rating: A stunning glimpse at how these mountains looked before most of the original trees were cut down. ★★★★¹/₂

How Much Time to Allow: One hour to hike the trail at a brisk pace; longer to savor the ambiance of these ancient woods.

DESCRIPTION AND COMMENTS   After logging access was cut off by the impoundment of Santeetlah Lake, leaving an impressive stand of virgin hardwoods, the area was set aside as a memorial to Joyce Kilmer, the soldier-poet and author who was killed in action in France during World War I.

Kilmer, you may remember, wrote "Trees" ("I think that I shall never see/A poem lovely as a tree . . ."). The two-mile path is moderately easy to hike, with plenty of handholds, stairs, and rustic footbridges across streams. The forest is a knockout; some people say hiking the Big Tree Cove Loop Trail is an almost mystical experience. Some of the specimens are more than 20 feet in circumference and more than 100 feet high.

TOURING TIPS   The trail is a figure-eight-shaped loop, so it doesn't matter which way you hike it. But if you prefer steeper walking in the beginning followed by an easy downhill return to the parking lot, do this: Begin your walk to the right as you face the forest with the parking lot behind you. Then continue in a figure-eight pattern. The largest trees are on the upper loop.

OTHER THINGS TO DO NEARBY   The nearby Joyce Kilmer–Slickrock Wilderness area contains 13,000 acres of forest and primitive hiking trails. The Tsali Recreation Area on NC 28 features camping, hiking trails, and mountain bike routes overlooking Fontana Lake. Fontana

Dam is the largest dam east of the Rockies. The Nantahala River is one of the nation's top whitewater rafting destinations.

Macon County Historical Society Museum

Type of Attraction: Exhibits on Southern Appalachian culture, history, and life styles from the early 1800s to the turn of the century. A self-guided tour.

Location: 6 West Main Street, Franklin, North Carolina.

Admission: Free.

Hours: 10 A.M. to 4 P.M. Monday through Friday, 10 A.M. to noon Saturdays. Closed Thanksgiving through April.

Phone: (704) 524-9758

When to Go: Any time.

Special Comments: The two-story, store-front museum has a long flight of stairs leading to the second floor.

Overall Appeal by Age Group:

Pre-school	Grade School	Teens	Young Adults	Over 30	Senior Citizens
★	★★	★★¹/₂	★★¹/₂	★★★	★★★¹/₂

Author's Rating: Charming. ★★★

How Much Time to Allow: 30 minutes to an hour.

DESCRIPTION AND COMMENTS   This old-fashioned museum recalls the early days of Franklin County—and comes complete with codgers jawing at the cracker barrel just inside the door. Items on display include old photographs, clothing, artifacts from an old pharmacy, ancient typewriters, old books, and quilts. It's an eclectic display of the county's heritage.

TOURING TIPS   Unlike most museums, there are no glass cases between you and the items on display. Wander around and you're sure to find something to pique your interest.

OTHER THINGS TO DO NEARBY   The Franklin Gem and Mineral Museum is around the corner.

Museum of the Cherokee Indian

Type of Attraction: Exhibits on Cherokee ethnicity, archaeology, culture, crafts, and modern history. A self-guided tour.

Location: Cherokee, North Carolina.

Admission: $4 for adults, $2 for children ages 6–12.

Hours: Mid-June through August: 9 A.M. to 8 P.M. Monday through Saturday, 9 A.M. to 5 P.M. Sundays. September through mid-June: 9 A.M. to 5 P.M. daily.

Phone: (704) 497-3481

When to Go: Any time.

Special Comments: The gift shop and gallery offer a wide selection of nontacky items for sale, including books, crafts, and paintings.

Overall Appeal by Age Group:

Pre-school	Grade School	Teens	Young Adults	Over 30	Senior Citizens
★	★★	★★¹/₂	★★¹/₂	★★★	★★★¹/₂

Author's Rating: Small, modern, airy, and informative. ★★★

How Much Time to Allow: One to two hours.

DESCRIPTION AND COMMENTS   The history of Cherokee and U.S. relations is long on betrayal to the Native Americans, as this museum, owned by the Eastern Band of the Cherokee Indians, makes abundantly clear. On a less somber note, the museum features exhibits on Cherokee crafts, clothing, language, and myths of the people who have lived in the Southern Appalachians for at least a thousand years.

TOURING TIPS   A 12-minute film in the museum auditorium provides a glimpse of the present-day Cherokee community. Six video presentations scattered through the museum take visitors through the history of the Cherokees from the prehistoric to the present.

OTHER THINGS TO DO NEARBY   The Oconaluftee Indian Village is less than a mile drive; the town of Cherokee is surpassed only by Gatlinburg for sheer tourist tackiness. The entrance to Great Smoky Mountains National Park is about a mile away.

Oconaluftee Indian Village

Type of Attraction: Re-creation of a Cherokee Indian village depicting Indian life 250 years ago. A guided tour.

Location: Cherokee, North Carolina.

Admission: $8 for adults, $4 for children ages 6–13.

Hours: 9 A.M. to 5:30 P.M. daily, May 15 through October 25. Closed
the rest of the year.

Phone: (704) 497-2315

When to Go: Any time. Skip it during inclement weather.

Special Comments: Summer afternoons are often warm and muggy,
so try to schedule your summer visit during the morning.

Overall Appeal by Age Group:

Pre-school	Grade School	Teens	Young Adults	Over 30	Senior Citizens
★★★	★★★½	★★★½	★★★½	★★★★	★★★★

Author's Rating: Not touristy: The guides are well spoken and
dignified, the village is attractive, and the tour is informative.
★★★★

How Much Time to Allow: Two hours—one hour for the tour, another
hour to wander around and visit the Indian garden.

DESCRIPTION AND COMMENTS   At Oconaluftee Indian Village, visitors
watch Cherokee women string beads, mold ropes of clay into pots,
and weave baskets, while Cherokee men make a dugout canoe with
fire and ax, and demonstrate small-game hunting with a blowgun.

After the leisurely tour of the village, visitors sit in the seven-sid-
ed council house and hear a short, enjoyable lecture about Cherokee
culture, history, society, and rituals. It's an enjoyable, informative
way to spend a morning or afternoon.

TOURING TIPS   After the tour, you're free to return to the village on
your own. Then visit the nearby nature trail and Indian garden for a
pleasant 20-minute stroll.

OTHER THINGS TO DO NEARBY   The Museum of the Cherokee Indian is
only a short drive away. The town of Cherokee is loaded with roadside souvenir stands; the entrance to Great Smoky Mountains National Park is about a mile away.

PART EIGHT:
The Tri-State Mountains of
North Carolina, Georgia, and
South Carolina—Zone 5

A Brief History and Orientation

The beautiful high ridges and valleys along the southern portion of the Blue Ridge Mountains have attracted—and solaced—lowland visitors to the area for more than 100 years. The Tri-State Mountains that surround the area where three states meet—North Carolina, Georgia, and South Carolina—are a vacation mecca of forested highlands, clear waters, and spectacular waterfalls. And in the summer, it's usually 10° or so cooler than the coastal areas to the south and east.

—— North Carolina: Highlands and Cashiers

Near the geographic center of the region is Highlands, North Carolina (elevation 4,118 feet), a resort town with a winter population of 2,000 that swells to over 20,000 during the summer. In addition to the high elevation, the region boasts a distinctive topography: It's an area with terrain that strikes many visitors as a "Yosemite with trees," because of big, granite dome mountains found in an otherwise deeply forested part of the Blue Ridge Mountains.

More dramatic scenery: At escarpment gorges along the North Carolina–South Carolina state line south of the towns, the Blue Ridge Mountains drop away 1,000 feet to the Piedmont below. It's an amazing sight as the Horsepasture, Toxaway, and Thompson rivers turn into waterfalls spilling over the craggy drop-offs.

History

Legend has it Highlands was founded in the late 19th century, when two land developers, Samuel T. Kelsey and C. C. Hutchinson, drew a line on a map between the major population centers of Chicago and Savannah, then another between New Orleans and Baltimore. The lines met near present-day Highlands—and the entrepreneurs were on their way.

Today, affluent visitors come each summer to resorts and summer homes in the rarified atmosphere of the town; many high-powered executives keep second homes here. The small downtown shopping district, crammed with tony shops and restaurants, is crowded with Mercedes and BMWs—and the occasional Rolls—on summer afternoons. Highlands attracts a different kind of tourist.

Four miles west of Highlands on US 64 is Cashiers (pronounced "cashers"), another town distinguished by an upscale summer clientele. Surrounded by high mountains that rise up to 5,000 feet, the town sits on a mountain plateau of the Blue Ridge at an elevation of 3,486 feet.

Its unusual name may have come from a horse named Cash owned by Senator John C. Calhoun, the famous pre–Civil War era politician who had a plantation near present-day Clemson, South Carolina. Legend has it Cash wandered off to a valley pasture and that a search party yelled "Cash's here!" when they found the horse.

Forests

The Highlands District of Nantahala National Forest covers nearly 105,000 acres and provides a wealth of outdoor activities to visitors to the area, including hiking, camping, picnicking, fishing, scenic overlooks along the roads, and many waterfalls to discover. The highest is Whitewater Falls, at 441 feet. Dry Falls got its name because you can walk behind the falling water without getting wet.

Farther west, the Wayah Ranger District contains 134,000 acres of forest. Standing Indian Basin, a remote and popular region, provides an abundance of recreational opportunities: trout fishing in teeming streams, horse trails, backpacking and hiking, and loop trails for day hikers—including a two-mile hike on the Appalachian Trail to Standing Indian Mountain to see the "Standing Indian." Legends say it's the remains of an Indian who neglected his tribal duties.

—— Georgia

History

In May 1777, botanist, naturalist, artist, and explorer William Bartram traveled into the wilderness of northeast Georgia collecting plant specimens and making sketches. In 1791, his journal, *Travels of William Bartram*, was published.

Today, hikers can walk in Bartram's steps as they journey along the Bartram Trail, a National Recreation Trail, dedicated in 1978, that loops through Rabun County, Georgia, for 37 miles. Rabun Bald, which the trail crosses, is a popular spot to watch hawk migrations in the spring and fall. You can see several hundred broad-winged hawks riding the thermals in a single afternoon.

Mountains and Rivers

The county is 60% forested and includes designated wilderness areas such as the famous Chattooga Wild and Scenic River, Tallulah Gorge (called the Grand Canyon of the South), and Rabun Bald, which, at 4,696 feet, is the second highest mountain in Georgia. Nearby Sky Valley is the southernmost downhill ski resort in the United States. The area's natural beauty not only attracts tourists, but is a draw to Hollywood film crews: *Deliverance* was filmed on the Tallulah and Chattooga rivers.

Foxfire, a series of best-selling books, a magazine, a movie, and a national education program that promotes activities between students and their communities, is located outside Clayton, the seat of Rabun County. Visitors can tour the Foxfire Museum or visit the Foxfire Center, a 19th-century mountain community used as an education center for teachers.

To the west, Chattahoochee National Forest and the Georgia portion of the Southern Nantahala Wilderness contain the southern portion of the Blue Ridge Mountains. Elevations range from 2,400 feet to 5,499 feet.

The streams in the 24,515-acre wilderness feed the Nantahala, Tallulah, and Hiwassee rivers. While the Georgia portion of the wilderness has no developed trails, intrepid hikers armed with topographic maps and compass can follow old roadbeds that connect with trails in North Carolina.

—— South Carolina

History

The Cherokees called the Blue Ridge Mountains "the Great Blue Hills of God." But by the 1820s, all that was left of the Lower Cherokee Nation was place and river names such as Seneca, Keowee, Jocassee, and Toxaway. Settlers had replaced traders at the end of the 18th century and then pushed the Indians out.

In the early years of the 19th century, this was cotton country. While cotton is hard on the land, it brought in cotton mills, which sprung up in Greenville (which today calls itself the textile center of the world) and in dozens of small towns as railroads began to connect the communities.

Today, manufacturing is more diversified in the red hills of upland South Carolina as factories produce tires, motor parts, pumps, and cars. And peaches have replaced cotton as the number one crop.

The Uplands

Not surprisingly, the uplands of South Carolina have attracted generations of visitors. One popular destination is pristine, 7,500-acre Lake Jocassee, located 25 miles north of the college town of Clemson. Long fingers of the lake reach into North Carolina, and several waterfalls pour directly into the lake. The 80-mile-long Cherokee Foothills Trail wraps around Jocassee's northern end as it zigzags among ridges, valleys, and waterfalls on the South Carolina–North Carolina border.

Whitewater rafting on the Chattooga, which crashes through Sumter National Forest on the South Carolina side of its border with Georgia, features Class III, Class IV, and Class V rapids—and leaves rafters drenched and pumped with adrenaline.

A number of state parks in spectacular settings provide outdoor recreational opportunities such as fishing, hiking, and camping—and touches of luxury; Devils Fork State Park, for example, features 20 "mountain villas" that overlook the lake from a stand of mixed evergreens and hardwoods. Appointed with cathedral ceilings, central air, screened porches, stone fireplaces, and modern kitchens, they're just too fancy to be called cabins.

The Cherokee Foothills Scenic Highway, a picturesque, 130-mile route, winds its way through South Carolina's upcountry as it links many attractions and historic sites. Native American culture is interpreted at Keowee-Toxaway State Park, whose name is believed to mean in Cherokee "land of mulberry groves" and "no more tomahawks." At Table Rock State Park rustic cabins and campsites sprinkle the woods.

—— A Self-Contained Destination

With its long history as a summer destination for folks from the lowlands—many of them affluent—looking to beat the heat, the Tri-State Mountains region is a place where people come to stay during their vacations; it's not a jumping-off point for, say, Great Smoky Mountains National Park or Asheville. Everything you need for a relaxing mountain vacation is at hand: Great scenery, spectacular waterfalls, hotels and resorts, great restaurants, camping and hiking, rafting on the Chattooga, and shopping.

Yet folks seeking to explore attractions outside the Tri-State Mountains will be pleasantly surprised: World-famous destinations such as Great Smoky Mountains National Park (Zone 1), Nantahala Gorge (Zone 4), Asheville, Shining Rock, and the Blue Ridge Parkway (Zone 6) are all within striking distance for a day trip.

Geographically, the Tri-State Mountains (Zone 5) is bordered by the Southern Foothills of North Carolina (Zone 4) and Asheville and Brevard (Zone 6). The closest major cities are Asheville, North Carolina, to the north and Greenville, South Carolina, to the east.

—— Major Roads

In North Carolina, US 64 enters Highlands from Franklin, then goes east to Cashiers and Sapphire on its way to Brevard and Hendersonville. In Georgia, US 76 cuts across the Blue Ridge Mountains between Hiawassee in the west to Clayton. Then the highway heads southeast on its way to Westminster, South Carolina. US 23/441 goes north out of Clayton toward Franklin, North Carolina.

SC 28 goes north from Seneca to Walhalla, then nips Georgia on its way to Highlands, North Carolina. US 76/123 in South Carolina connects Westminster and Clemson; SC 93 goes east of the home of Clemson University to Central, Norris, and Liberty; US 178 forms the eastern border of the Tri-State Mountains between Easley, South Carolina, and US 64 in North Carolina.

The Cherokee Foothills Parkway (also called SC 11 or Scenic 11), cuts an arc northeast from Westminster to US 178. I-85 passes south of the Tri-State Mountains, connecting Atlanta; Greenville, South Carolina; Charlotte and Raleigh; and Petersburg, Virginia.

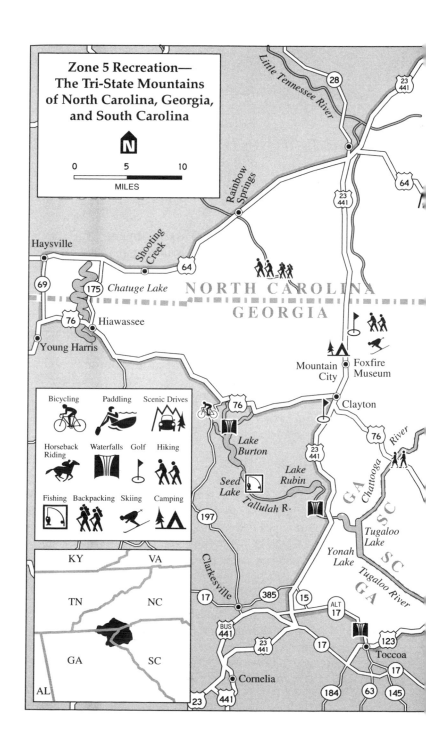

**Zone 5 Recreation—
The Tri-State Mountains
of North Carolina, Georgia,
and South Carolina**

N

0   5   10
MILES

Little Tennessee River

Rainbow Springs

Shooting Creek

Haysville

Chatuge Lake

Hiawassee

Young Harris

NORTH CAROLINA

GEORGIA

Mountain City

Foxfire Museum

Clayton

Chattooga River

Bicycling   Paddling   Scenic Drives

Horseback Riding   Waterfalls   Golf   Hiking

Fishing   Backpacking   Skiing   Camping

Lake Burton

Seed Lake

Lake Rubin

Tallulah R.

Tugaloo Lake

Yonah Lake

Tugaloo River

GA

SC

KY   VA

TN   NC

GA   SC

AL

Clarkesville

Toccoa

Cornelia

Outdoor Recreation and Activities

—— Camping

Black Rock Mountain State Park in Mountain City, Georgia (a few miles north of Clayton), has a terrific campground perched on top of a 3,400-foot mountain. It's a steep, winding two-mile drive into the park, where you'll find 53 wooded sites with water and an electrical hookup.

Section 1 has a new, heated bathhouse—and on our visit the curtains in the showers weren't even moldy. Section 2's bathhouse is older, but the campsites are a bit more private. Camping in either section is $14 a night. For reservations or more information, call (706) 746-2141.

—— Hiking

Easy Walks and Hikes

Sunset Rock.   For a stunning overlook of Highlands and national forest lands, take this easy, 20-minute hike from the Highlands Nature Center on the edge of Highlands. Nearby **Sunrise Rock** features a view of Horse Cove. Don't attempt to drive up the dirt road to the top; the narrow road has few places to pull over when you meet oncoming cars. Park across from the Nature Center.

Whiteside Mountain.   This is a hike that can cause nosebleeds. It's an easy two-mile round trip to some cliffs on the side of the mountain that's nearly 5,000 feet high—and it's 2,000 feet to the valley floor below. Keep children and pets on a leash. Pick up a map from the ranger station on US 64 between Highlands and Cashiers; the road to the trail head (Trail 70) starts in back.

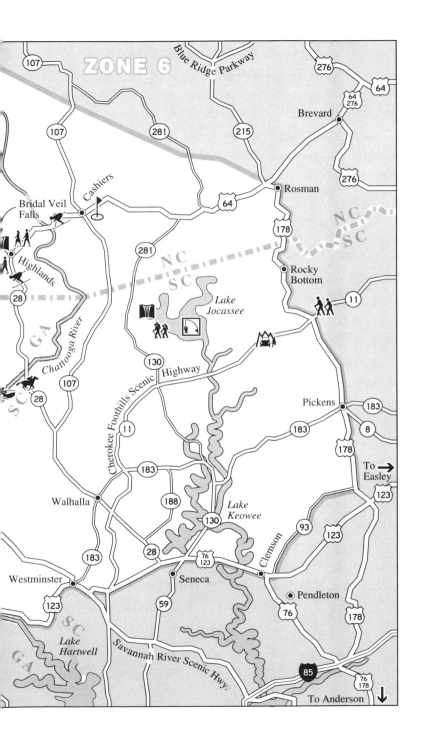

Chattooga River Trail. This half-mile walk features views of a beautiful river—and scenes of carnage as kayaks, canoes, and rafts flip in Bull Sluice Rapid, rated Class V. River guides say the best thing about the rapid is that it's easy to get an ambulance there.

The easy trail features a wide spectrum of humanity, ranging from little old ladies, hippies smoking dope on the rocks, and whitewater wannabes thinking to themselves, "Do I really want to run this thing?" They may not. While the water looks easy, many people have died here. The trail is on US 76, 12 miles east of Clayton, Georgia, on the South Carolina side of the river.

Moderate Hikes/Easy Backpacking Trips

Deep Gap to Standing Indian. This is either a moderate hike on the Appalachian Trail or an easy overnighter that offers great views, especially in winter when the leaves are off the trees.

From Franklin, drive west on US 64 and turn left on Forest Service Road 71. At the split in the road, keep left and drive just under seven miles to the parking area at the end.

Hike the Appalachian Trail north for two and four-tenths miles; the elevation gain is a moderate 1,000 feet of elevation when you reach Standing Indian. It's a small bald where you can camp for the night; there's a shelter and water just below the summit. At sunset, look at the rocks around the bald and you'll see chunks of imbedded garnet. The magnificent view is of the Tallulah River Basin. Retrace your steps back to your car.

Whiteoak Stamp. Starting at Deep Gap, hike south on the Appalachian Trail for four miles to explore a unique biological area called Whiteoak Stamp. It's a huge, flat region that's one of the last remaining highland bogs; it's also a tangle of laurel thickets. There's a spring at Muskrat Creek Shelter, so this can be either a moderate day hike or an easy overnighter. While it's not exactly flat, this section of the Appalachian Trail is one of its easiest stretches, considering the elevation (over 4,000 feet).

Rabun Bald. This moderate, eight-mile hike leads to a stupendous, 360-degree-view from the second-highest point in Georgia (or as local wags like to say, the highest *undeveloped* point in Georgia—

Brasstown Bald's summit is graced by a visitor center). Adding to the drama is the approach through a dense laurel thicket that drops away just before the summit.

To get there: From NC 106 out of Highlands, drive to the Scaly ski center. Two miles after Scaly, turn left onto a gravel road by a white picket fence. Drive for one and one-half miles and park. (Note: Four-wheel-drive vehicles can continue up the primitive road and cut the amount of hiking in half.)

Hike up the road for two miles to another gap and take the yellow-blazed Bartram Trail through the laurel thicket (an incredible walk in mid- to late June when in bloom). It's two miles to the observation tower. Most people are flabbergasted by the view, which stretches to the Smokies, far into South Carolina, and to Whiteside Mountain near Cashiers.

Moccasin Creek Waterfalls. Enjoy two beautiful waterfalls along a pleasant trail and the thrill of gripping a steel cable across a creek while you think about being swept over a waterfall if you screw up! This is either a moderate out-and-back day hike or an easy overnighter where you camp next to a waterfall. It's especially popular in hot weather because of the many stream crossings.

Drive to Moccasin Creek State Park, 15 miles west of Clayton, Georgia, on GA 197. Walk up the dirt road directly across from the entrance to the park. After crossing a gate, the road becomes a trail; at two and one-half miles from the park is the major creek crossing with the cable.

If the weather's cold, it's a great place to hang out. If it's warm, grab the cable and a hiking stick (there are usually a couple laying around) and *carefully* cross the knee-deep stream to the other side: You're wading through a pool but the current is still fairly strong. If you're wearing a backpack, loosen your waist belt so that if you slip you can get out of it.

Walk upstream to the 30-foot waterfall on the left, a huge pool, and campsites. Go farther upstream about a mile, however, and there's an even higher waterfall—maybe 80 feet high—that most people miss. You've got to scramble across the remains of a rock slide to get there, but it's doable.

Strenuous Hikes

Table Rock Trail. This seven-mile round trip hike starts at Table Rock State Park in South Carolina, located five miles east of the junction of the Foothills Parkway (SC 11) and US 178. The hike has many ups and downs but offers incredible views of lakes, Caesars Head, and mountains.

Raven Cliff Falls Trail. This five-mile hike in Caesars Head State Park in South Carolina is rugged, passes through lush vegetation on old jeep roads and trails, and rewards hikers with awesome views of five major waterfalls from an observation deck. Pick up a map at park headquarters; it's easy to wind up on the wrong trail.

—— Backpacking

Dispelling the myth that there are no long backpacking trips in South Carolina is the 85-mile **Foothills Trail.** The trail allows access to the major escarpment gorges of the Eastern Blue Ridge, an area notable for Yosemite-like exposed granite mountains and high waterfalls.

Hiking the trail usually involves setting up a shuttle (leaving a car at the end of the hike *before* you start walking); it is strenuous in some sections, and the trail is not always well maintained. For more information on the Foothills Trail, call or write: the Foothills Trail Conference, P.O. Box 3041, Greenville, South Carolina 29602; phone (803) 232-2681.

Another scenic and relatively easy (considering the elevation) area to backpack is **Deep Gap** in the Nantahala Wilderness. For details on the hikes to Standing Indian and Whiteoak Stamp, see Moderate Hikes, above.

—— Canoeing, Kayaking, and Rafting

Chattooga River

Forming the border between South Carolina and Georgia is the Chattooga National Wild and Scenic River, the most beautiful and pristine of all commercially rafted southeastern rivers. Most people know the Chattooga as the river where the film classic *Deliverance,* with Burt Reynolds and Jon Voight, was filmed. And anyone who has seen the movie knows that the Chattooga means serious whitewater.

A free-flowing stream, the Chattooga usually is discussed in terms of four discrete sections. Section I is the headwaters and essentially is reserved for fishing. Section II is a scenic Class I (II) float that can be enjoyed by beginning and novice canoeists and kayakers. Section III runs 12 miles from Earls Ford to the US 76 bridge and contains Class III (IV) whitewater, with nine major rapids. Exceptionally beautiful, Section III offers everything from riverwide ledges to narrow chutes. Bull Sluice, the last rapid before the US 76 bridge, is one of the most famous rapids in the United States and one of the most difficult.

Section IV is the most challenging section with 12 major rapids. It also is one of the most hauntingly spectacular streams anywhere in the United States. Consider banks flush with ferns, cascading waterfalls tumbling into the Chattooga from tributaries, and exposed rock bluffs. Section IV of the Chattooga is everything a wilderness experience should be. The rapids are tight and technical with big drops. Teamwork and precise boat control are essential.

The U. S. Forest Service closely regulates commercial rafting on the Chattooga to ensure that everyone can enjoy a real wilderness experience. Only three companies are licensed to operate commercial raft trips; and the number of trips offered by each, along with the number of guests allowed on each trip, is kept to a minimum. The objective of the regulation is that guests on a given trip not encounter any other commercial users while they are on the river.

Both Section III and Section IV are rafted commercially. On Section III, some trips run 12 miles from Earls Ford to the US 76 bridge, while others put in at Sandy Ford, shortening the run by three miles. A third option combines part of Section III with the beginning of Section IV, running from the Fall Creek put-in at mile eight of Section III to below Woodall Shoals on Section IV. On Section III trips, including the itinerary that incorporates the first part of Section IV, there is not always a guide in every raft. This does not present a problem for most guests, though the rapids are somewhat more difficult than those on the French Broad or Nantahala Rivers, where guests also captain their own rafts. The outfitters on the Chattooga are sensitive to the anxieties of their customers. If you want to be in a raft with a guide, all you have to do is ask. On trips where there is not a guide in each raft, the trip leader will stop the trip upstream of Bull Sluice, a Class IV (V) rapid located just upstream of the US 76 bridge. Here the guides will take each raft through the rapid, one at a time, walking back up from the bottom of the rapid to join the crews of the guideless rafts and pilot them down. Minimum age for Section III trips is ten years. Section III trips take about six hours, including lunch and shuttle time, with four to five hours on the water depending on the itinerary and the water level.

On Section IV, there is a guide in every raft. Because there are at least four rapids on Section IV that have claimed the lives of paddlers, it is imperative that guests pay attention and work together as a team. Guides on Section IV require a maximum effort from their guests to navigate the more challenging rapids. On Section IV, there are no passengers, only paddlers. The trip begins at the US 76 bridge and increases in difficulty and intensity as it moves downstream. The climax of the trip is the Five Falls, a series of five Class IV–V rapids, one after the other, concentrated in about a third of a mile. Following the Five Falls and a quarter mile of Class II water, the Chattooga flows into Lake Tugaloo. To complete the trip you must paddle two and a half miles of flatwater to the take-out. Some trips tow rafts across the lake with powerboats. If you want to avoid the flatwater paddle, inquire about the tow when you make your reservations. Minimum age for Section IV trips is 13 years. Trips run about seven hours in duration, including lunch and shuttle.

Because the Forest Service limits the number of daily raft guests, it is a good idea to make your reservations as far in advance as possible. Remember also that the Chattooga is a free-flowing stream. While it usually is runnable all summer, you are more certain of good water levels in the spring and early summer. The price per adult for Chattooga trips ranges from $45–80. Weekends are more expensive than weekdays, and Section IV is more expensive than Section III. Group rates are available.

The three licensed commercial outfitters on the Chattooga are:

Nantahala Outdoor Center	(800) 232-7238
Southeastern Expeditions	(800) 868-7238
Wildwater Ltd.	(800) 451-9972

Chauga River

A nearby favorite for whitewater veteran canoeists and kayakers is the Chauga River near Long Creek, South Carolina. Runnable from Blackwell Bridge to Cobbs Bridge during the spring, the Chauga delivers whitewater ranging from Class II to Class V in difficulty, with at least one Class VI mandatory portage which is for expert and advanced canoeists and kayakers only. For detailed information on this and other area rivers, check our list of recommended reading for canoeing, kayaking, and rafting on pages 76–77.

—— Fishing

Georgia

In Northern Georgia, the most popular game fish is the **rainbow trout**—probably due to the spectacular jumps and long runs that mark the species' fighting style. Virtually every stream in the region is stocked with rainbows to supplement the natural population. Rainbows are found mostly in larger, fast-flowing rivers and streams and will strike just about any bait, including crickets, spinner baits, and worms.

The most widespread trout in the region is the wary **brown trout.** It's attracted to flies, spinning lures, and live bait—if you can get one to strike. But if you catch a trophy-size trout, it probably will be a brown; many attain a good size.

Most of Northern Georgia's trout streams are located in Chattahoochee National Forest. The state's official trout season runs from the last Saturday in March to October 31. In addition, there are a number of streams that stay open all year.

The Tallulah River off US 76 and Forest Service Road 79 west of Clayton is both a scenic and popular trout stream that's heavily stocked every week during the season. **Wildcat Creek** is another popular spot located on Forest Service Road 26 off GA 197 north of Clarksville on the Lake Burton Wildlife Management Area. It's stocked weekly during trout season.

South Carolina

At **Lake Jocassee,** some anglers have learned to think like deep-sea fishermen—the lake is 440 feet deep in spots. To reach brown and rainbow trout lurking in the lake's cooler depths, they troll using heavy-duty lines. Visitors without special gear will have better luck in the spring and fall when the trout reside closer to the lake's surface.

Other popular game fish in the lake include largemouth and small-mouth bass, crappie, and bluegill. Anglers must possess either a South Carolina or Georgia fishing license.

In **Sumter National Forest,** popular stocked trout streams include the Chauga River, the East Fork of the Chattooga River, and, for native trout, the Chattooga River's Section 1 (Ellicott Wilderness Area), where hiking trails follow the stream.

Trout fishing is permitted all year in Sumter; out-of-state visitors can buy single or multiday licenses at local businesses.

North Carolina

Outside of Highlands on US 64 toward Franklin is the **Cullasaja River,** the only stocked trout stream in the area. No bait restrictions apply; try red worms, night crawlers, or crickets for a nibble from the brown trout in the stream. A valid North Carolina fishing license is required; out-of-staters can get a one-day license for $15. The trout fishing season is closed in March.

For licenses, fishing gear, or professional guide services, contact **Main Stream Outfitters** in Highlands; phone (704) 526-5649. Half-day guided trips to the best fishing spots are $115 per person.

—— Bicycling

Road Riding

Highlands and Cashiers via Horse Cove is a moderate-to-strenuous, 25-mile loop offering great views of Whiteside Mountain and one long, steep climb. Starting in Cashiers at US 64 and NC 107, ride out NC 107 south for two miles and turn right onto Horse Cove

Road. It's a fast descent through Whiteside Cove (at the church and cemetery) and Grimshaws (look quickly for the old post office the size of a bus stop). You might want to stop to enjoy the views of the cliffs on Whiteside Mountain.

After crossing the county line, stay to the right (follow the main road). After six miles, take the paved road on the right (it's Whiteside Road but the sign gets stolen a lot—look for the pond on the left), and begin the steep, three-mile climb to Highlands.

After you reach Highlands, turn right on US 64 for the ten-mile spin to Cashiers. Careful, though: Traffic is usually heavy. Note: You can make this into a 12-mile, out-and-back ride that eliminates the hard climb and the traffic by turning back at Whiteside Cove (at the cemetery and church). It's a pretty ride through a valley, and worth seeing twice.

Mountain Biking

For bikers in the Tri-State Mountains, the best off-road riding is in nearby **Pisgah National Forest** near Brevard in Zone 6—with one exception: the **Dick's Creek and Wildcat Creek Loop** at Moccasin Creek State Park, 15 miles west of Clayton, Georgia, on GA 197. This 14-mile ride is strenuous and strictly for advanced hammerheads; however, it offers splendid views and a heart-stopping descent.

From the park, go left on GA 197 for two miles and turn right onto Wildcat Creek Road (Forest Service Road 26). Go up a gentle climb, cross Pig Pen Ridge, and descend to a gate where you make a right hand turn. It's about seven miles after the road changes to dirt and is easy to spot.

Ride along the road past some fields for three miles, where you cross Park's Mountain. You're at "The Monster," which descends 500 feet in seven-tenths of a mile—that's a drop! But it's a smooth road surface.

Next, turn right onto Dick's Creek Road (FS 164) and follow it downstream. It's four miles to GA 197, where you turn right, cross the ridge, and descend to your car. Total elevation gain is more than 1,200 feet.

—— Horseback Riding

Dillard House Stables in Dillard, Georgia, features one-hour guided farm rides daily beginning at 9 A.M. and departing every 90 minutes till 6 P.M. The cost is $20 per person; the minimum age is six. Two-hour rides into Warwoman Wildlife Management Area depart at 9:30 A.M. and 4:30 P.M.; the cost is $40 per person. Three-hour rides leave at 12:30 P.M. and cost $55 per person. Reservations are suggested; call (706) 746-5348.

Arrowmont Stables, located between Cashiers and Cullowhee, North Carolina, offers guided tours on six miles of trails on private property, including a high mountain trail, a valley ride, and a level trail without ascents or descents. Rides lasting from 90 minutes to three hours leave at 10 A.M., 1:30 P.M., and 3:30 P.M. Monday through Saturday; costs range from $25–40 per person, depending on the length of the ride. Reservations are required; call (704) 743-2762.

Circle R Trails, located near SC 28 in Mountain Rest, South Carolina, offers guided, one- and two-hour horseback rides daily on the Circle R ranch, and three- and four-hour rides on 27 miles of horse trails in Sumter and Chattahoochee national forests. On the four-hour trips, riders cross the Chattooga River into Georgia—if the water is low enough. Rates are $15 an hour. Children must be 12 and older for the three- and four-hour rides. Reservations required; call (803) 638-0115.

—— Golf

The outstanding courses in Zone 5 are Sky Valley Resort at Sky Valley, Georgia, ranked as the tenth best course in the state, and the course at the High Hampton Inn & Country Club in Cashiers, North Carolina. These and other quality golf courses in the area are profiled below.

Butternut Creek Golf Course

Established: 1962

Address: Recreation Road, Highway 129 North, Blairsville GA 30512

Phone: (706) 745-5153

Status: Public course

Tees:

Men's: 6,539 yards, par 73, USGA 73, slope 121.
Ladies': 4,500 yards, par 75, USGA 75, slope 117.

Fees: Green fees (cart included): $27 for 18 holes, $15 for 9 holes. Senior citizens get $3 off regular price on Wednesday.

Facilities: Pro shop, putting green, snack bar, tennis courts, and swimming pool.

High Hampton Inn and Country Club

Established: 1923

Address: Highway 107 South, Cashiers NC 28717

Phone: (704) 743-2450

Status: Semiprivate course

Tees:

Championship: 6,012 yards, par 71.
Men's: par 71.
Ladies': par 71.

Fees: $34 for visitors, $24 for guests of the inn. Cart fees: $11.66 per person for 18 holes, $5.83 per person for 9 holes. The 900 rule or paths only.

Facilities: Tennis courts, 35-acre lake, hiking trails, fitness trail, meeting rooms, art gallery, and pro and gift shop.

Holly Forest Golf Club

Established: 1982

Address: 50 Slicers Avenue, Sapphire NC 28774

Phone: (704) 743-1174

Status: Semiprivate course

Tees:

Championship: 6,147 yards, par 70, USGA 70, slope 119.
Men's: 5,690 yards, par 70, USGA 70, slope 118.
Ladies': 4,515 yards, par 70, USGA 70, slope 112.

Fees: $40. Cart included.

Facilities: Pro shop, restaurant, pools, tennis courts, and miniature golf.

Piedmont College Golf Course

Established: 1965

Address: Demorest–Mount Airy Highway, Demorest GA 30535

Phone: (706) 778-3000

Status: Private

Tees:

Championship: 5,656 yards, par 72.

Fees: Green fees: $11 weekdays, $13 weekends. Cart fees: $12 per person for 18 holes, $6 per person for 9 holes. Senior citizen rates available weekdays.

Facilities: Putting green.

Rabun County Golf Course

Established: 1940

Address: Old Highway 141 South, Clayton GA 30525

Phone: (706) 782-5500

Status: Municipal course

Tees:

Men's: 5,347 yards, par 70, USGA 65.7, slope 118.
Ladies': 4,194 yards, par 70, USGA 64, slope 109.

Fees: Green fees (cart included): $18 for 18 holes, $11 for 9 holes. Green fees (without cart): $10 for 18 holes, $7 for 9 holes. Cart fees: $4 per 9 holes. Fees subject to change.

Facilities: Pro shop.

Sky Valley Resort

Established: 1970

Address: One Sky Valley, Sky Valley GA 30537

Phone: (706) 746-5303

Status: Resort course

Tees:

Championship: 6,452 yards, par 72, USGA 71.7, slope 128.

Men's: 5,961 yards, par 72, USGA 69.5, slope 123.

Ladies': 5,107 yards, par 72, USGA 69, slope 118.

Fees: Green fees (include cart): $39.50 April 1–November 15, $22 November 16–March 31.

Facilities: Pro shop, driving range, putting green, restaurant, tennis courts, junior Olympic swimming pool, hiking trails, health club, lounge, snack bar on course, snowskiing, rafting, fishing, and horseback riding.

—— *Skiing*

If you don't associate downhill skiing with the South, think again—all it takes is an overnight low of 28° F, and snowmaking equipment takes over for Mother Nature. And sub-freezing temperatures are the norm from mid-December through February in the high Blue Ridge Mountains of North Carolina and Georgia. The slopes, however, offer modest verticals and usually are crowded on weekends.

North Carolina

Ski Scaly Mountain, located south of Highlands on NC 106, is the southernmost ski resort in the state and only two hours from Atlanta. The area features four slopes with a 225-foot vertical drop, one chair lift, and one surface lift. Ski rentals, night skiing, a ski school, and food are all available. For more information, call (704) 526-3737.

Fairfield Sapphire Valley, located near Cashiers, has four slopes with a vertical drop of 425 feet, one chair lift, and two surface lifts. Ski rentals, night skiing, a ski school, and food are available on the premises. For more information, call (704) 743-3441.

Georgia

Sky Valley is the southernmost ski resort in the United States. Downhill skiers can enjoy a 2,400-acre resort with four slopes (plus a bunny slope), a double chair lift, and a rope tow. The vertical drop is 250 feet. The lodge has two dining rooms, a ski school, and a ski shop. Weekday lift tickets are $15 for adults from 9 A.M. to 5 P.M. and $18 till 10 P.M. Weekend rates are $18 and $28 respectively. Sky Valley is located off US 441 on GA 246 east of Dillard. For more information, call Sky Valley Resort at (800) 437-2416.

—— Waterfalls

The Tri-State Mountains are prime waterfall country—and waterfalls make a great excuse to get out of the car, take a walk, and enjoy the view of water crashing and falling over rock in a pristine setting.

Just keep a few simple rules in mind and you'll avoid becoming a statistic: Don't attempt to climb a waterfall or venture near the top or sides. Be especially careful when taking photographs—even dry rocks can be slippery, and wet rocks almost always are.

North Carolina

If you like viewing waterfalls without leaving your car, you'll *love* this one: At **Bridal Veil Falls,** three miles from Highlands on US 64, you can drive your car *under* the falls. The water tumbles from a height of 120 feet.

Only a mile farther on US 64 is **Dry Falls,** an unusual name until you understand how it got it: A path goes behind the falling water, so you can walk behind it without getting wet. The height of the waterfall is 75 feet.

The Kalakaleskies, located on US 64 west two and a half miles northwest of Highlands, consists of 18 small waterfalls within a quarter mile in the river paralleling the roadway. **Lower Cullasaja Falls,** also on US 64 about seven miles from Highlands, is one of the most picturesque in North Carolina as it cascades for 250 feet.

Georgia

Minnehaha Falls, located south of Lake Rabun and the town of Clayton, is rated one of the most beautiful in the area. It's 100 feet high and easily reached on a quarter-mile access trail that gently climbs through dense rhododendron and mountain laurel thickets.

To reach the falls, go south from Clayton on old US 441 and follow the Lake Rabun Road to the west around the north side of the lake. Turn left one mile past the Rabun Beach Recreation Area. Then cross the bridge and follow Bear Gap Road around the lake for one and six-tenths miles. Park and take Fall Branch Trail to the falls.

Toccoa Falls, located on the campus of Toccoa Falls College, is 19 feet higher than Niagara Falls. A meandering stream flows through the lower part of the 1,100-acre, wooded campus from the base of the 186-foot-high falls. The site is open from 9 A.M. to sunset year-round. The college is located on GA 17 north of Toccoa.

It's a three-and-six-tenths-mile, one-way hike to **Panther Creek Falls** on a trail that's hilly in the beginning but then flattens out. The water drops through a series of cascades, which culminate in a beautiful 50-foot fall. Keep an eye peeled for a wide variety of ferns and wildflowers along the trail.

The Panther Creek Trail starts at the western end of the Panther Creek Recreation Area on US 441/23, three miles south of Tallulah Falls.

Tallulah Gorge is the deepest natural gorge in the Eastern United States. Its overlooks provide stunning views of the river and falls below. But the river is dammed, slowing the water to a trickle; try to imagine what it was like when you could feel the ground shake. Tallulah Falls is located on US 441/23 south of Clayton.

South Carolina

Whitewater Falls features two stunning, 400-foot falls located on the South Carolina–North Carolina state line; in fact, the state line passes between the falls. The falls are located off SC 130, ten miles north of Cherokee Foothills Scenic Highway (SC 11), above Salem.

Issaqueena Falls is reached via an easy nature trail; the falls cascade for 200 feet. Nearby is the **Stumphouse Mountain Tunnel,** a 1,600-foot hole in the mountain. The story: In the 1850s, builders went broke trying to build a railroad to the Midwest. No locomotive ever roared through this tunnel; track was never laid. Bring a good flashlight and a picnic lunch. To get to the tunnel and the falls, go five miles north of Walhalla on SC 28.

Lake Jocassee is surrounded by high mountains where streams tumble into the lake—often, from quite a height. If you don't have a boat, consider signing up for the **Waterfall Experience,** led each Thursday (or by appointment any day for groups of six or more) April through October. The nine-hour excursion leaves at 10:30 A.M. and includes short hikes, views of a 440-foot waterfall, a picnic lunch, a steak dinner served on your pontoon boat, and a sunset cruise. The cost is $59.50 per person. Reservations are required; call (800) 451-9972.

—— Scenic Drives

US 64. The 11-mile drive between Franklin (Zone 4) and Highlands is one of the most scenic in the area as it squeezes through the Cullasaja River Gorge—and reminds many people of mountain passes in Europe. The river plunges over falls, tumbles through rapids, and forms deep pools—all within sight of the road. Bridal Veil Falls is a popular photo stop; you can see where the highway once passed behind the falls.

Pull into the parking area for a short hike to Dry Falls, a 75-foot waterfall you actually can walk behind without getting soaked. From Highlands to Cashiers, the curvy highway is lined with rhododendron and tall trees. But along the road is a great view of Whiteside Mountain, which rises up 2,100 feet from the valley floor to a height of 4,930 feet.

US 76. From Hiawassee east to Clayton, Georgia, this four-lane highway crosses the Blue Ridge Mountains. It's a spectacular drive featuring views of mountain ridges fading into the distance. The road has many scenic overlooks where drivers can pull over and enjoy the vistas.

Georgia 246/North Carolina 106. Running between Highlands, North Carolina, and US 23/441 north of Clayton, Georgia, this beautiful mountain road passes through Nantahala National Forest, past the Scaly ski area, and over wooded ridges and valleys. It's a gorgeous drive.

Cherokee Foothills Scenic Highway. While less famous than the Blue Ridge Parkway or Skyline Drive—its high-profile cousins to the north—this road is also a bit different: Instead of looking down from a high ridge, sightseers traveling this road look up from the foothills to the big mountains above. Threading its way through South

Carolina's portion of the Tri-State Mountains, the road (also called Scenic 11) roughly parallels US 123 between Westminster and Greenville.

Sights along the highway include peach orchards, deep forests, the toes of the Blue Ridge Mountains stretching toward the coastal plain, and small towns. Close enough for easy side trips are a slew of state parks: Oconee, Keowee-Toxaway, Devil's Fork, Table Rock, Jones Gap, and Caesars Head.

Attractions

Foxfire Museum/Foxfire Center

Type of Attraction: The museum features handmade household and farm items from the late 19th and early 20th centuries. The center is a 19th-century mountain community used as an education center for teachers. Self-guided tours.

Location: The museum is on US 23/441 in Mountain City, Georgia (three miles north of Clayton), near the turnoff for Black Rock Mountain State Park. The center is off Church Street, which intersects US 23/441 about half a mile south of the museum. Check your odometer when you make the turn onto Church Street and go exactly half a mile and turn left (look for a small sign staked in the ground with an "F"). Park in the small lot on the left at the gate house.

Admission: Free.

Hours: 10 A.M. to 4:30 P.M. Monday through Friday.

Phone: (706) 476-5828

When to Go: Any time.

Special Comments: Both the museum and the center are low-key attractions; don't expect a lot of hand holding. The drive to the center is steep and winding on a dirt road. In the summer, tour guides sometimes are available at the center; check at the museum first.

Overall Appeal by Age Group:

Pre-school	Grade School	Teens	Young Adults	Over 30	Senior Citizens
★★	★★½	★★½	★★★	★★★	★★★½

Author's Rating: An intimate glance into Southern Appalachian mountain culture. ★★★

How Much Time to Allow: One to two hours to see both places.

DESCRIPTION AND COMMENTS   *Foxfire,* a series of books that have sold more than eight million copies since 1972, focuses on Southern Appalachian folklife. The Foxfire Museum houses a collection of fascinating handmade artifacts from the 19th and early 20th century: cornstalk toys, wire puzzles, a "Jud Nelson" wagon, woodworking tools, a toothpuller, a curling iron, a dinner bell, and a complete grist mill, all displayed in an authentic log cabin. Most are detailed items built without glue or fasteners. It's an easy-to-explore, one-room museum with a gift shop next door.

Foxfire is also a nationally recognized, nonprofit educational organization that promotes interaction between students and their communities. The Foxfire Center is located in a 19th-century community consisting of a mill, blacksmith shop, barn, and cabins; it's where Foxfire holds meetings and training seminars for teachers. The center sits in a pretty, shady setting on the side of a mountain, and visitors are welcome to browse.

TOURING TIPS   The museum is easy to find, so stop there first. Then get detailed directions to the center.

OTHER THINGS TO DO NEARBY   Black Rock Mountain State Park has camping, picnicking, hiking, a playground, and terrific views of the Blue Ridge Mountains.

PART NINE: Asheville and Brevard—Zone 6

A Brief History and Orientation

At the heart of North Carolina's Southern Highlands, a mountainous region that stretches from the Great Smokies in the west to the Blue Ridge Mountains in the east, is the thriving city of Asheville. It's the economic and cultural center for the western part of the state.

Geographically, it's a city of 62,000 sitting in a natural bowl surrounded by mountains. As a state of mind, Asheville is where many folks come in search of the good life. The word is out: *Outside* magazine rated the town as one of its top ten cities to live in.

It's easy to see why. Asheville's strong craft tradition, a stunning French Renaissance chateau, historic buildings, a growing selection of quality restaurants and cultural attractions, and its accessibility to world-class outdoor recreation all contribute to its livability. And visitors? The city is a popular base for exploring the Blue Ridge and Great Smoky mountains.

—— The Region

Consider: The 495,000-acre Pisgah National Forest virtually surrounds Asheville, while the Blue Ridge Parkway loops below the city to the south and then skirts Asheville to the east on its way north to Virginia and Shenandoah National Park.

Farther east is Black Mountain, a village famous for its bluegrass festival, and Chimney Rock, a private park on a mountain topped by spectacular rock formations and a waterfall; *The Last of the Mohicans* was filmed here.

Southwest of Asheville is Hendersonville, a popular destination for children off to summer camp, retirees looking for the good life, and fans of poet/historian Carl Sandburg; his nearby home is preserved as a national monument.

Brevard, directly south of Asheville, is another small town popular with retired folks. It's also a jumping-off point for exploring the Shining Rock Wilderness. The Davidson River Area, just outside of Brevard, offers plenty of fantastic scenery and opportunities for hiking, backpacking, mountain biking, fly-fishing, and camping—and it's only minutes from the amenities of town.

To the east, Waynesville is a town that's big on crafts, while Maggie Valley offers skiing, horseback riding, lots of schlocky roadside souvenir stands, and an all-time favorite with the ankle-biter set: Ghost Town in the Sky, an amusement park on top of a mountain. Maggie Valley is also a convenient jumping-off point for visits to Great Smoky Mountains National Park and the Cherokee Indian reservation.

—— *History*

Asheville

Asheville was incorporated in 1797 and was named for Governor Samuel Ashe. For a long time, though, the town was just a stop on the road between Greeneville, Tennessee, and Greenville, South Carolina. Settlers to the area were mostly Scots-Irish immigrants from Northern Ireland who farmed the mountains outside of town. In the early and mid-19th century, the high mountains around Asheville were remote and hard to reach. As a result, a unique Southern Appalachian culture survives in the music and crafts that flourish in and around the city.

The railroad came in the 1880s and started a boom. Rich folks—in some cases, *really* wealthy people—discovered Asheville: George W. Vanderbilt (the grandson of a robber baron), for example, built a 250-room French chateau called Biltmore Estate on the edge of town. Prominent doctors in the East fueled the city's popularity by recommending Asheville to patients with tuberculosis and other ailments that required rest and fresh air.

As a result, many hotels, sanitariums, and boardinghouses were built, and the population grew to around 10,000. For a glimpse of turn-of-the-century life in Asheville, see Thomas Wolfe's *Look Homeward, Angel*. His mother ran a boardinghouse, and the book is a thinly disguised autobiography that scandalized the town. Today, the ramshackle old house is a Wolfe museum.

In the 1920s another boom hit and Art Deco–style buildings went up downtown. The economic upswing ended in the Depression of the 30s: Tourism suffered, modern medicine found better ways to treat tuberculosis than to send patients on "cures," and the town declined.

But today Asheville is on the rebound. Many downtown buildings have been restored, while night life and cultural events are on an upswing. Pack Place (a modern complex of three museums and a theater), restaurants, bars, and clubs create a lively scene downtown. At the end of July each year, Asheville closes off downtown to traffic and throws a huge street party, the Bell Chere Festival, which attracts 300,000 people.

The Biltmore Estate remains Asheville's biggest tourist drawing card, attracting thousands of visitors each year. The Blue Ridge Parkway funnels more visitors to the town, Great Smoky is only 40 miles away, and attractions such as the Thomas Wolfe Memorial, the Western North Carolina Nature Center, the Folk Art Center, and whitewater rafting on the French Broad River make Asheville a tourist destination with many facets to explore.

Hendersonville

Southeast of Asheville, Hendersonville is the main town along the oldest route used by tourists on their way to the mountains. Plantation owners as far back as the 1830s escaped the heat of the lowlands on vacations to the Blue Ridge. Before the Revolutionary War, the rolling countryside was a Cherokee hunting ground.

At an altitude of 2,200 feet and surrounded by mountains, the town is a small tourist destination in its own right—although many people pass it by on their way to other better-known destinations such as Asheville. It's also the summer camp capital of the Smokies, attracting thousands of youngsters each year.

But Hendersonville isn't completely dependent on tourism for revenue: Its economic base includes manufacturing, agriculture, and a thriving retirement community. The surrounding county is also renown for its apple orchards and a popular apple festival each August.

Brevard, Waynesville, Maggie Valley

Brevard, incorporated in 1867, is another town that consistently shows up on lists of "best places to live in the United States"—and has a large retirement community to prove it. The Brevard Music Festival, a world-class music event, draws classical music lovers from all over.

The Cardinal Drive-In is right out of the 50s—except the waitresses don't wear roller skates when they bring hamburgers and shakes to your car. Located in the heart of waterfall country on the edge of Pisgah National Forest, Brevard also is popular with outdoor recreation enthusiasts looking for a taste of civilization.

Located west of Asheville, Waynesville is named for Revolutionary War hero "Mad" Anthony Wayne—though there's no record of the general ever setting foot in town. Major attractions in town include the Museum of North Carolina Handicrafts and the annual North Carolina International Folk Festival.

West of Waynesville, Maggie Valley is a right-out-of-the-50s tourist town. Petting zoos, motels, fast-food restaurants, bumper cars, campgrounds, and gimcrack souvenir stands line the road. A steady flow of tourist traffic along the Blue Ridge Parkway and from Great Smoky fuels the businesses along US 19.

—— *Major Highways*

Zone 6 is easy to get around, with two interstate highways: the scenic Blue Ridge Parkway, and US 74—a major route that dips below Great Smoky Mountains National Park on its way to Bryson City and Murphy (Zone 4) and the Southeast Foothills of Tennessee (Zone 3).

From the east I-40 cuts across the Asheville-Brevard region (Zone 6) through Asheville before swinging northwest around Great Smoky Mountains National Park (Zone 1). The Blue Ridge Parkway crosses US 19 between Cherokee and Maggie Valley, heads south below Waynesville, and then starts its northward journey, passing Asheville to the east and the Blue Ridge Mountains of North Carolina (Zone 7).

I-26 heads north out of Spartanburg, South Carolina, to Hendersonville before ending at I-40 near Asheville. US 64 connects Brevard and Hendersonville, while US 276 goes north out of Brevard to Waynesville. US 74 is the major route from Asheville to Bryson City (Zone 4) and points south. US 19/23 goes north from Asheville toward Johnson City, Tennessee.

—— *Pisgah National Forest*

The half-million-acre Pisgah National Forest got its start when George Vanderbilt, the grandson of railroad robber baron Cornelius Vanderbilt, bought property around his Biltmore Estate at the confluence of the Swannanoa and French Broad rivers—including Mt. Pisgah.

Across the river from his chateau, thousands of acres of forest were managed for timber, water, and other natural resources. Vanderbilt brought in Gifford Pinchot (the first chief of the U.S. Forest Service) and Dr. Carl Alwin Schenck, a German forester, to develop the forests.

Professional Forestry

It was a historic collaboration: They were the first to practice professional forestry in the United States. Today the Cradle of Forestry in America contains Dr. Schenck's reconstructed forestry campus and a visitor center. After Vanderbilt's death in 1914, the land was sold to the federal government and became one of the first tracts in Pisgah National Forest.

Today, this forest is the Pisgah Ranger District, located south of Asheville; other popular attractions include the 18,000-acre Shining Rock Wilderness, renown for its rugged hiking and a big, quartz-topped mountain that the Cherokees say talks; Looking Glass Falls, with a 60-foot sheer drop; and the Pisgah Forest National Fish Hatchery, one of the largest trout hatcheries in the East.

The French Broad Ranger District, which butts up against Great Smoky Mountains National Park, contains 80,000 acres of rugged mountains. The French Broad River, famous for its whitewater river rafting, runs through the district before entering Tennessee. Seventy-four miles of the Appalachian Trail passing through the French Broad Ranger District and Hot Springs is the focal point for hiking in the area. It's an area for those who like rugged and remote back country.

How the Forest Got Its Name

Mount Pisgah, south of Asheville in the Pisgah Ranger District, was the biblical name for the mountain from which Moses saw the promised land after 40 years of wandering in the wilderness. Local legend attributes the naming of the mountain to the Reverend James

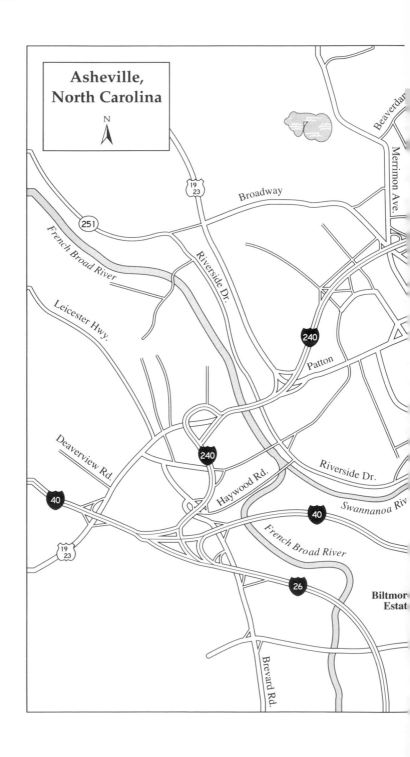

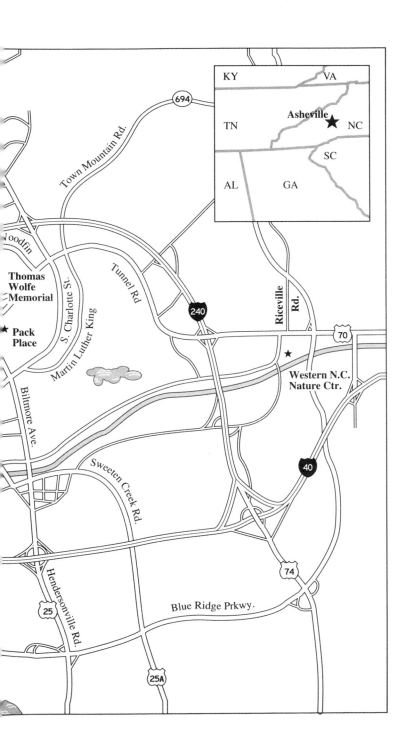

Hall, a Scots-Irish, gun-toting, Indian-fighting Presbyterian minister who accompanied an early expedition into western North Carolina.

Impressed by the bountiful French Broad River basin, visible from the mountain, he drew upon his knowledge of the Bible to name the peak Mt. Pisgah, from which the national forest got its name.

—— *A Self-Contained Region and a Jumping-Off Point*

Visitors stay in Maggie Valley at the western end of Zone 6 for its proximity to Great Smoky Mountains National Park (Zone 1)—and, in the winter, to be close to the ski slopes. But for anyone vacationing in Asheville, Brevard, or Hendersonville, this region offers plenty of things to do and the amenities—lodging, restaurants, things to do outdoors and on a rainy day—to keep them from jumping in the car for a long drive.

Luckily, major attractions outside the region aren't that far away—and anyone staying near Asheville and Brevard should consider a drive to Great Smoky Mountains National Park (Zone 1), Highlands (Zone 5), Nantahala Gorge (Zone 4), Mount Mitchell, Grandfather Mountain, or Linville Falls (all in Zone 7). They're all within an easy striking distance—and well worth the effort.

Outdoor Recreation and Activities

—— Camping

Davidson River Campground.   Located near Brevard, this national forest campground is ideally located near some of the region's best scenery, attractions, trails, waterfalls, and you name it. Tent campers should head toward either the White Oak or River Bend loops, which are reserved for tents and keep you away from noisy RVs. Total number of sites is 162. Amenities include flush toilets and hot showers. For reservations, call (800) 280-2267. For more information, call (704) 877-3265.

Mt. Pisgah Campground.   This campground, operated by the National Park Service, is located just off the Blue Ridge Parkway near The Cradle of Forestry in America at milepost 408. It's a high-elevation campground, so don't expect much shade or shrubbery. But some sites out of the more than 100 available offer some privacy. In addition, there are separate tent and RV loops.

The campground is open from about May 1 through October. Rest rooms are provided, but no showers or laundry facilities. Each campsite has a picnic table and a fireplace, and there's a camp store with a limited amount of supplies for sale.

Sunburst Campground.   Located on NC 215 south of Waynesville on the edge of Pisgah National Forest, this small campground is in a glade across from a popular swimming hole in the bend of a river. The campsites are open, not shaded, and often used by bicycle tourists riding the Blue Ridge Parkway on saddlebag-laden bikes.

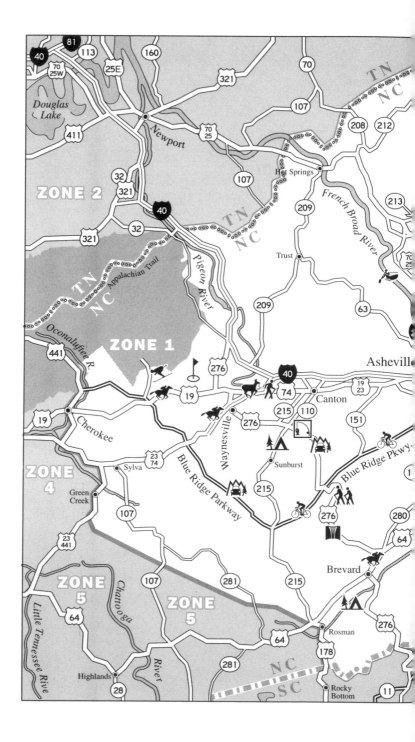

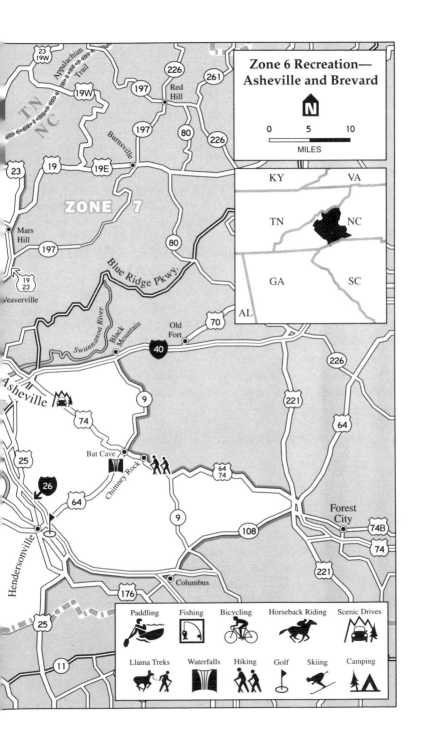

Zone 6 Recreation—
Asheville and Brevard

N

0   5   10
MILES

KY   VA

TN   NC

GA   SC

AL

23
19W

Appalachian Trail

226   261

197   Red
           Hill

19W

197   80   226

Burnsville

23   19   19E   80

ZONE 7

Mars
Hill

197

Blue Ridge Pkwy.

19
23

Weaverville

Swannanoa River

Black
Mountain

Old
Fort   70

40   226

Asheville

221

9

74   64

25   64
                            74

Bat Cave

26   Forest
                            City

64   Chimney Rock   74B

9

108   74

Hendersonville

221

Columbus

176

25

11

| Paddling | Fishing | Bicycling | Horseback Riding | Scenic Drives |
| Llama Treks | Waterfalls | Hiking | Golf | Skiing | Camping |

—— Hiking

Easy Hikes and Walks

Holmes Educational State Forest.   A series of easy trails takes strollers through a rich mixture of mountain hardwoods, rhododendron, flame azaleas, and a variety of wildflowers. The well-marked trails, one three miles long and the other about half a mile long, are accented by exhibits and displays depicting ecology of a managed forest. The Talking Trees Trail features recorded messages about the trees, the site, and the forest's history. The state forest is located between Hendersonville and Brevard on NC 1127 (Kanuga Road).

Mount Pisgah.   This five-mile round trip from the Blue Ridge Parkway is moderately easy and leads to the summit that the national forest is named after. It's located north of the Cradle of Forestry in America at milepost 410; the summit is 5,749 feet high.

The Devils Courthouse.   This rugged, exposed mountaintop is rich in Cherokee legend. The easy, less-than-two-mile walk to the summit reveals a spectacular view of Pisgah National Forest, including Looking Glass Rock. It's at mile post 422 on the Blue Ridge Parkway.

A Moderate Day Hike/Easy Backpacking Trip

Shining Rock Wilderness.   This spectacular, eight-mile round-trip hike leads to Shining Rock, a quartz-topped rock the Cherokee Indians said could talk. Going north on US 276 past the Blue Ridge Parkway, park your car in the area at the first big turn in the road. Then hike up Trail 363 four miles to Shining Rock Gap; from here it's less than a mile to the Shining Rock; make a right on the Art Loeb Trail. Camp around the rock—and keep your ears open. Return via Trail 332, which intersects Trail 363 just above the parking area. Turn left on Trail 363 and walk back to your car.

—— Canoeing, Kayaking, and Rafting

The Appalachian Mountains just east of the Smokies (Zone 6) offer two good commercial rafting opportunities. To the west of Asheville paralleling I-40 is the Pigeon River, sometimes called the

"Big" Pigeon to avoid confusion with the similarly named river that flows though Gatlinburg and Pigeon Forge, Tennessee. To the north of Asheville is the French Broad River; relatively pastoral for much of its length, the French Broad offers a good whitewater section between Barnard and Hot Springs.

Pigeon River

The Pigeon River is similar to the Ocoee in Tennessee: dam controlled with big waves, big rapids, and nonstop action. Badly polluted for many years, the Pigeon only recently has become clean enough to attract paddlers. The stream remains a tea color from years of pollutants now settled on the bottom, but the water quality is vastly improved and the terrible stench is gone. You would not want to drink the water, but otherwise, the river's unfortunate past will not diminish your rafting enjoyment. The Class III (IV) run covers five miles and takes about two to three hours including shuttle. Because the whitewater is so fast and continuous, the actual river time is often as brief as an hour and fifteen minutes. Minimum age for most outfitters is ten years. The cost for most trips is about $35.

Outfitters on the Pigeon include:

Wildwater Ltd.	(800) 451-9972
Rapid Descent River Company	(800) 455-8808

French Broad River

The French Broad is a free-flowing river that meanders past the Biltmore Estate and through Asheville before crossing into Tennessee. The classic whitewater run is the eight-mile, Class III (IV) section between Barnard and Hot Springs, North Carolina. Here the river is wide with many rapids of the ledge/shoal variety separated by moderate stretches of pools or flatwater. There are also some big drops. Islands punctuate the run and provide a varied choice of routes through several rapids. Frank Bell's Rapid, Class IV at higher water, is the highlight of the trip. While the French Broad provides a lot of action, the easy floating between rapids gives you a chance to relax and enjoy the scenery. The French Broad is runnable throughout the spring, summer, and early fall; and both half- and full-day trips are offered. Half-day trips run about $32. Full-day trips cost between $40–50 and include lunch. Minimum age for most outfitters is ten years. Expect to spend about three hours on a half-day trip and about five to seven hours on a full-day trip. There's not much shade on the French Broad, so don't forget to take your sunscreen. Finally, some trips operate without a guide in every raft. If you want a guide in your raft, tell the outfitter when you make your reservations.

Outfitters on the French Broad include:

Carolina Wilderness	(800) 872-7437
Nantahala Outdoor Center	(800) 232-7238
USA Raft	(800) 872-7238
Infiniti Rafting	(800) 442-0386
French Broad Rafting Company	(800) 842-3189

In addition to guided raft trips, canoe, rafts, and duckies can be rented for float trips on the more tranquil sections of the French Broad in the Asheville area. Call Southern Waterways, (800) 849-1970. For detailed information on this and other area rivers, check our list of recommended reading for canoeing, kayaking, and rafting on pages 76–77.

—— *Fishing*

The West Fork of the Pigeon River. This popular and easy-to-access stretch of the river follows NC 215 as it climbs up to the Blue Ridge Parkway from Waynesville. Above the Sunburst Campground it's easy to get to the river, which has a reputation for excellent rainbow trout fishing. Higher up, you may find some brook trout.

Davidson River. This is an excellent trout stream upstream of the Davidson River Campground near Brevard. It follows US 276 north to Looking Glass Falls. Above there, stick with the river for some excellent rainbow trout fishing.

Mills River. North of Brevard, County Road 1345 off of NC 280 provides good access to the Mills River; follow signs to the campground. The stream is renown for its rainbow and brown trout.

—— Bicycling

Road Riding

Biltmore Estate.   While you've got to pay to get in—and it ain't cheap—the roads inside the Biltmore Estate in Asheville offer about 15 miles of easy, scenic riding on paved roads. The grounds were designed by Frederick Law Olmstead, the same guy who designed Central Park in New York and many other municipal parks. The terrain varies from flat to rolling; keep an eye peeled for rubbernecking tourists in cars as you ride. Bring along a strong lock, park your bike, and tour the building after your ride.

Shining Rock Wilderness Loop.   This strenuous, 40-mile ride offers plenty of great views and a stupendous 12-mile, 2,000-foot-altitude-gain climb to the Blue Ridge Parkway. Start at the intersection of US 276 and NC 215 east of Waynesville and take NC 215 south. After the climb to the Parkway, head north. Surprise: The scenic highway isn't really that difficult on this stretch, and traffic is light. Next, go north on US 276 for the return to NC 215.

Mountain Biking

Ivestor Gap.   This easy, dead-flat (though rocky) four miles is an out-and-back ride that rewards you with fantastic views of the Waynesville Valley. To drive to the trail head, get on the Blue Ridge Parkway west of Asheville. At mile post 20 is the only paved road between the intersections with NC 215 and US 276. Drive one and one-half miles to the end and park. Ride out Trail 101 to Ivestor Gap. Be careful not to wander into Shining Rock Wilderness Area, where bikes aren't allowed.

Sycamore and Thrift Cove Loops.   These two loops, only minutes from Pisgah Ranger Station and the town of Brevard, are an easy, scenic, and delightful introduction to a mountain biking destination with a growing reputation. Both routes are virtually all single track, and can be ridden separately or together for a total length of about nine miles.

Sycamore Cove, the first trail you come to as you enter Pisgah National Forest on US 276 from Brevard, passes through a classic cove hardwood forest and offers ridge views, log bridges over streams, and a set of steps that only show-offs will attempt to ride.

Thrift Cove, the next trail up the road toward the ranger station, rewards cyclists with a nice riding surface, fern glades, meadows, rhododendron thickets, and plenty of open woods. Combine the routes by riding either the pavement or Grass Road.

—— Horseback Riding

Pisgah Forest Stables, near Brevard, offers one-hour guided trips into Pisgah National Forest daily on the hour from 10 A.M. to 5 P.M. daily (except 1 P.M.) April through October. Longer trips are available with a minimum of four riders. Two-hour rides are $30, half-day rides are $55, and full-day trips into the back country are $75. Reservations are suggested; call (704) 883-8258.

Smoky Mountain Stables in Waynesville features guided rides on private land that offer views of mountains and big valleys. One-hour trips are $15; also offered are two-hour ($20), two-and-a-half hour ($25), three-and-a-half hour ($30), and four-hour ($35) rides. All-day trips into Great Smoky Mountains National Park are $50 per person; overnight trips are $50 per person per day. For more information, call (704) 452-9579.

A Dude Ranch in the Smokies

Cataloochee Ranch in Maggie Valley offers accommodations for 70 guests in the main ranch house, a lodge, and several cabins on its 1,000-acre ranch. Guided horseback rides let guests take in the ranch's three peaks: Fie Top, Moody Top, and Hemphill Bald. Riders also can explore Great Smoky Mountains National Park on half-day and full-day rides.

Rooms in the ranch house range from $115–160 double occupancy; lodge rooms, from $120–200, including breakfast and dinner (wine and beer are extra). Riding is extra: $60 a person for an all-day trip, or $27 for half a day. For more information, call (800) 868-1401 or (704) 926-1401.

—— *Llama Treks*

Hiking with llamas adds a new dimension to a wilderness experience. Forget about yucky freeze-dried food and 40-pound packs: With a llama toting the load, it's gourmet meals, a choice between red or white wine with dinner, and all the comforts of home.

Windsong Llama Treks in Clyde enlists these intelligent, friendly relatives of the camel on guided overnight hikes and day hikes into Pisgah National Forest. Sure-footed and capable of carrying loads from 60 to 90 pounds, llamas also are kind to the trails as they tread softly on two-toed feet with cushiony underpads. (LeConte Lodge in the national park, connected to the outside world by a five-and-a-half-mile trail that could be ruined by horses, is resupplied throughout its season by llamas who bring in clean sheets and fresh food, and haul out dirty sheets and garbage three times a week.)

Sound like fun? Overnight treks lasting from two to four days are $90 per person per day. Guides prepare gourmet meals on trips that change with the seasons to highlight wildflower blooms and native foliage. A gourmet picnic and day hike is $60 a person. For a schedule and more information, call (704) 627-6986.

—— *Golf*

The two standout courses in Zone 6 are the Maggie Valley Resort & Country Club in Maggie Valley, North Carolina, host of the Professional Golf Schools of America, and Asheville's Grove Park Inn Resort. These and other quality golf courses in the area are profiled below.

Cleghorn Plantation Golf Club

Established: 1969
Address: 200 Golf Circle, Rutherfordton NC 28139
Phone: (704) 286-9117
Status: Public course
Tees:

Championship: 6,903 yards, par 72, USGA 74.6, slope 134.
Men's: 6,313 yards, par 72, USGA 70.5, slope 126.
Ladies': 4,751 yards, par 73, USGA 68.1, slope 111.

Fees: $22 weekdays, $30 weekends. Carts included and mandatory.

Facilities: Pro shop, driving range, putting green, pool, tennis courts, snack bar, and restaurant.

Cummings Cove Golf Community and Country Club

Established: 1986

Address: 3000 Cummings Road, Hendersonville NC 28739

Phone: (704) 891-9412

Status: Semiprivate course

Tees:

Men's: 6,008 yards, par 70.
Ladies': 4,794 yards, par 70.

Fees: Weekdays and weekends: $25 (includes cart), $15 (without cart)

Facilities: Clubhouse, pro shop, snack bar, putting green, pool, tennis courts, and bridge room.

Great Smokies Holiday Inn Sunspree Resort

Established: 1974

Address: 1 Hilton Drive, Asheville NC 28806

Phone: (704) 254-3211

Status: Resort/Public course

Tees:

Championship: 5,700 yards, par 70, USGA 69.5, slope 115.
Men's: 5,300 yards, par 70, USGA 68.6, slope 112.
Ladies': 4,800 yards, par 70, USGA 68.6, slope 112.

Fees: $30 hotel guests, $36 visitors. Carts included.

Facilities: 280-room resort, indoor and outdoor tennis courts, two pools, three lounges, and two restaurants.

The Grove Park Inn Resort

Established: 1895

Address: 290 Macon Avenue, Asheville NC 28804-3799

Phone: (800) 438-0050

Status: Resort course

Tees:

Championship: 6,520 yards, par 71, USGA 71.7, slope 125.
Men's: 6,039 yards, par 71, USGA 69.4, slope 119.
Ladies': 4,687 yards, par 71, USGA 68.6, slope 111.

Fees: April–November: $44 (18 holes), $22.50 (9 holes); December–March: $20 (18 holes), $12.50 (9 holes). Cart fee: $16 per player (18 holes), $7.95 per player (9 holes).

Facilities: Pro shop, putting greens, snack bar, tennis courts, golf clinics, and lessons.

Maggie Valley Resort and Country Club

Established: 1961

Address: 340 Country Club Road, Maggie Valley NC 28751

Phone: (704) 926-1616

Status: Semiprivate resort course

Tees:

Championship: 6,336 yards, par 72, USGA 69.8, slope 121.
Men's: 6,031 yards, par 72, USGA 68.5, slope 118.
Ladies': 5,195 yards, par 73, USGA 69.4, slope 117.

Fees: $30 per player. Cart fee, $14.50

Facilities: Restaurant, lounge, snack bar, meeting and banquet facilities, pro shop, putting green, driving range, golf clinics, tennis courts, and pool.

Reems Creek Golf Club

Established: 1989

Address: Pink Fox Cove Road, Weaverville NC 28787

Phone: (704) 645-4393

Status: Semiprivate course

Tees:

Championship: 6,477 yards, par 72, USGA 71.6, slope 133.
Men's: 6,106 yards, par 72, USGA 70.1, slope 126.
Ladies': 4,605 yards, par 72, USGA 66.9, slope 114.

Fees: $37 weekdays, $40 weekends and holidays. Carts included and mandatory.

Facilities: Pro shop, driving range, pool, tennis courts, putting green, bar, and grill.

Waynesville Country Club Inn

Established: 1926

Address: Country Club Drive, Waynesville NC 28786

Phone: (800) 627-6250

Status: Resort course

Tees:

Championship: 6,000 yards, par 70, USGA 66.8, slope 105.
Men's: 5,500 yards, par 70, USGA 64.8, slope 100.
Ladies': 5,000 yards, par 70, USGA 67, slope 104.

Fees: $22 guests, $27 visitors. Cart fee, $13 per player.

Facilities: Pro shop, putting green, restaurant, snack bar, tennis courts, and outdoor heated pool.

—— Skiing

Cataloochee Ski Area. Located in Maggie Valley, this downhill ski resort offers nine slopes with a vertical drop of 740 feet, one chair lift, and two surface lifts. On site, skiers will find rentals, instruction, day care, a kids' ski school, food, and a lounge. For more information, call (800) 768-3588 or (704) 926-3588.

—— Waterfalls

The Southern Highlands get more than 80 inches of rain a year in higher elevations. Throw in spectacular mountain scenery, and it adds up to a region renown for its waterfalls. Here are some of the best.

Looking Glass Falls. Located on US 276 in Pisgah National Forest a few miles south of The Cradle of Forestry in America is one of the best-known waterfalls in the East: Looking Glass Falls. This picture of classic beauty, an unbroken rush of white water, is 30 feet wide and drops vertically more than 60 feet over sheer rock to the pool below. A massive overhanging shelf of rock towering above the walls on the far side adds an aspect of rugged grandeur.

Hickory Nut Falls. Famous as a backdrop for the climactic scenes in the movie *The Last of the Mohicans,* Hickory Nut Falls drops more than 440 feet off the face of the mountain. Located in Chimney Rock Park (which is private and charges $9 per person admission), the hike to the top of the falls takes two hours. If you just want to see it from afar, pull over along US 64/74, south of Bat Cave, and look up; the view is free.

Sliding Rock. Bring your swim suit—this isn't really a waterfall, but a cascade over rocks where it's OK to enjoy the natural water slide created by Mother Nature. There's also a bathhouse and, in the summer, a lifeguard. Sliding Rock is located on US 276 in Pisgah National Forest south of the Cradle of Forestry in America. And it's free.

—— *Scenic Drives*

The Blue Ridge Parkway. The premier scenic drive in the region is the Blue Ridge Parkway, which comes in from the west near Maggie Valley, loops below Waynesville and through Pisgah National Forest, and passes east of Asheville.

A popular drive from Asheville is **Town Mountain Road,** which heads northeast out of the city to the Blue Ridge Parkway. Take the scenic highway north to the Folk Art Center, then return to town on US 70 (Tunnel Road) to complete the drive. Along the way you'll be treated to interesting architecture on Town Mountain Road and incredible views of the mountains on the rest of the trip.

Waynesville/Shining Rock Wilderness. From Waynesville, take US 276 east to NC 215 and turn right. Pass Lake Logan and Sunburst Campground, and follow the West Fork of the Pigeon River. Before getting on the Blue Ridge Parkway at Beech Gap (it's a left), you'll see Sam Knob and Little Sam Knob to the left and the Middle Prong Wilderness to the right.

At US 276, turn left and follow the road north back to Waynesville. The scenery doesn't let up. Back in town, be sure to stop at the Mast General Store, which is done up in turn-of-the-century fashion.

Asheville/Chimney Rock/Hendersonville/Brevard.   This can be an all-day drive starting in Asheville that goes through some of the best scenery in the region. Go east on I-40 to US 76 south toward Bat Cave. At Bat Cave, continue straight to Chimney Rock, where *The Last of the Mohicans* was filmed. (If you don't feel like dropping big bucks to visit this pricey attraction, pull over and look to your right for a great—and free—view of Hickory Nut Falls from the side of the road.)

Backtrack to Bat Cave and turn left on to US 64, which leads to Hendersonville. In town, you can take a side trip two miles south to Flat Rock and visit the home of poet and biographer Carl Sandburg.

From Hendersonville, continue west on US 64 toward Brevard. At the intersection with NC 280, US 64 makes a left into Brevard. Continue straight and you're on US 276, which cuts through the center of Pisgah National Forest. Along the way are Looking Glass Falls, Sliding Rock, and the Cradle of Forestry in America—and they're all worth exploring. Just past the Cradle of Forestry is the Blue Ridge Parkway. Take it north for more spectacular scenery and the return to Asheville.

Attractions

Reflecting the wide diversity of the Asheville-Brevard region, its best tourist attractions range from world-class art in a modern gallery and a 250-room French chateau to a mountaintop amusement park where youngsters witness the thrill of "live" gunfights. And everything in between.

Asheville Art Museum

Type of Attraction: An art gallery featuring a collection of American paintings and sculpture. A self-guided tour.

Location: Pack Place, 2 South Pack Square, Asheville, North Carolina 28801.

Admission: $3 for adults, $2.50 for seniors 62 and over and students, $2 for children ages 4–15. One-day passes for admission to all four Pack Place Museums are $5.50 for adults, $4.50 for seniors and students, and $3.50 for children.

Hours: 10 A.M. to 5 P.M. Tuesday through Saturday, 1–5 P.M. Sundays from June to October. Pack Place museums are closed on Mondays.

Phone: (704) 257-4500

When to Go: Any time.

Special Comments: Elevators are available for physically disabled visitors.

Overall Appeal by Age Group:

Pre-school	Grade School	Teens	Young Adults	Over 30	Senior Citizens
★	★★	★★½	★★★	★★★	★★★

Author's Rating: Small, airy, modern, and comfortable. ★★★

How Much Time to Allow: One to two hours.

DESCRIPTION AND COMMENTS   This small, three-level art gallery has two permanent collections featuring modern works by Jasper Johns,

Frank Stella, and Romare Bearden. Nineteenth-century works include paintings by Thomas Hart Benton and other masters. But most of the art is from the 20th century.

TOURING TIPS   The third level features temporary exhibits.

OTHER THINGS TO DO NEARBY   Three other museums share quarters at Pack Place: The Health Adventure, the Colburn Gem & Mineral Museum, and the YMI Cultural Center.

Biltmore Estate

Type of Attraction: A 250-room mansion that's the largest private home in the United States. A self-guided tour.

Location: On US 25 north of exit 50 or 50B on I-40 in Asheville, North Carolina.

Admission: $24.95 adult (16 and over), $18.75 youth (10-15).

Hours: 9 A.M. to 5 P.M. daily. Closed Thanksgiving, Christmas, and New Year's days.

Phone: (800) 543-2961 or (704) 255-1700

When to Go: Weekdays.

Overall Appeal by Age Group:

Pre-school	Grade School	Teens	Young Adults	Over 30	Senior Citizens
★	★★	★★★	★★★¹/₂	★★★★¹/₂	★★★★¹/₂

Author's Rating: ★★★★

How Much Time to Allow: Four to six hours.

DESCRIPTION AND COMMENTS   George Vanderbilt commissioned architect Richard Morris Hunt to design this French Renaissance chateau modeled after the great French chateaux of the Loire Valley in 1888. Today, the Biltmore House appears much as it did 100 years ago, showcasing George Vanderbilt's original collection (50,000 objects) of furnishings, art, and antiques. The ten acres of gardens, designed by Frederick Law Olmsted, are as spectacular as the mansion itself. The blooming season at Biltmore begins in early spring and continues until the first frost. Visitors also are invited to tour the winery, located in the Estate's original dairy barns. Here guests may view a brief slide presentation of the winemaking process, visit the fermentation and bottling rooms and cellars, and sample the finished product.

In addition to the self-guided tour, Biltmore Estate offers a Behind-the-Scenes Guided Tour for an additional fee ($10 per adult, $7.50 per youth). This tour features 25 rooms that are not part of the regular tour, including the sub basement, which houses the engineering systems of the house, servants' quarters, and Mrs. Vanderbilt's art studio. You will often witness preservation work in progress on this tour. The regular and Behind-the-Scenes tours involve approximately 350 stairs. Handicap access is provided; please ask for information.

TOURING TIPS We don't recommend taking children on the guided tour, as they become restless early in the tour. Also, don't be surprised if you feel rushed when you bring children on the regular self-guided tour. Since the gardens are such an integral part of the Biltmore Estate, try to plan your visit for a sunny day.

OTHER THINGS TO DO NEARBY Downtown Asheville features museums, restaurants, shopping, and the Thomas Wolfe Memorial. The Western North Carolina Nature Center, a sure-fire hit for both children and adults, is off exit 53B on I-40.

Chimney Rock Park

Type of Attraction: A 1,000-acre, privately owned park featuring impressive rock formations, trails and picnicking, and mountaintop views of Lake Lure and distant mountains.

Location: Highway 64/74, Chimney Rock, North Carolina 28720

Admission: $9 for adults, $4.50 for children ages 6–15.

Hours: Ticket office: 8:30 A.M. to 4:30 P.M. (5:30 P.M. daylight savings time). Access to trails is closed a half hour after the ticket office closes.

Phone: (704) 625-9611, (800) 277-9611

When to Go: Any time. Skip it in inclement weather.

Special Comments: The three-mile drive from the park entrance to the parking area near the elevator is steep and twisty.

Overall Appeal by Age Group:

Pre-school	Grade School	Teens	Young Adults	Over 30	Senior Citizens
★★★	★★★★	★★★★	★★★★	★★★½	★★★

Author's Rating: The view is great, but so are many vistas along the Blue Ridge Parkway—and they're free. ★★½

How Much Time to Allow: One hour to savor the view, half a day or longer to explore the many trails and see more vistas, waterfalls, and rock formations.

DESCRIPTION AND COMMENTS Chimney Rock provided many sets and backdrops for the 1993 film, *The Last of the Mohicans,* and it's easy to see why: The striking rock formations, lush forests, and spectacular waterfalls evoke an earlier, less-developed America. In addition to the 30-second elevator ride to the top of Chimney Rock (which ends, unfortunately, in the back of a tacky gift and T-shirt shop), visitors can hike trails to view 404-foot Hickory Nut Falls and other natural sights.

TOURING TIPS The Skyline Trail to the top of Hickory Nut Falls is a moderate to strenuous, 45-minute (one way) hike and starts at Chimney Rock. Other trails leave from the parking lot at the base of the big rock: The Cliff Trail is a 45-minute (one way) hike to the top of the falls that passes Nature's Showerbath, recognizable to moviegoers who have seen *The Last of the Mohicans.* The Forest Stroll is an easier, 30-minute hike (one way) that leads to the bottom of Hickory Nut Falls.

OTHER THINGS TO DO NEARBY Sixty-minute boat tours of nearby Lake Lure depart on the hour from 9 A.M. to 7 P.M. daily, April through November. Rates are $6 for adults and $4 for children ages 6–15. For more information, contact Lake Lure Tours, P.O. Box 541, Lake Lure, North Carolina 28746; (704) 625-0077.

Carl Sandburg Home National Historic Site

Type of Attraction: The house and farm where the two-time Pulitzer Prize–winning historian and poet lived for the last 22 years of his life. Guided tours of the house and self-guided tours of the grounds.

Location: Little River Road, Flat Rock, North Carolina (three miles south of Hendersonville).

Admission: $2 for the house tours, free for children under 16. Visiting the grounds is free.

Hours: Tours are given from 9 A.M. to 5 P.M. daily on the half hour. The park is closed Christmas Day.

Phone: (704) 693-4178

When to Go: House tours fill up quickly, so plan to arrive early and reserve a place on a tour later in the day.

Special Comments: The best way to enjoy this popular destination is to bring a lunch and spend the day exploring the farm, walking its trails, and taking the house tour.

Overall Appeal by Age Group:

Pre-school	Grade School	Teens	Young Adults	Over 30	Senior Citizens
★★★	★★★	★★	★★★	★★★½	★★★★

Author's Rating: A delightful setting and an interesting slice of American literary history. ★★★½

How Much Time to Allow: One to two hours to explore the farm and tour the house—if you arrive before the tour buses, which can signal a half-day wait for a guided house tour.

DESCRIPTION AND COMMENTS   The Sandburg home is much the way it was when the poet and historian died on July 22, 1967. The 240-acre working goat farm offers panoramic views of the rolling countryside, mountain lakes and ponds, and the Blue Ridge Mountains beyond.

TOURING TIPS   Every 30 minutes a video on Sandburg is shown in the basement of the house that gives a perspective on his life and works. It's a good introduction to the site, which is operated by the National Park Service. House tours fill up fast and reservations are good for that day only—so arrive early in the day or risk being disappointed. In the summer, dramatic presentations of Sandburg's works are performed under the trees at 11 A.M. Tuesday through Saturday.

OTHER THINGS TO DO NEARBY   Hendersonville, with plenty of shops, restaurants, and lodging, is three miles away. The Flat Rock Playhouse is across the street; call (704) 693-0731 for more information.

Colburn Gem & Mineral Museum

Type of Attraction: A museum displaying the wide diversity of geologic wealth in North Carolina. A self-guided tour.

Location: Pack Place, 2 South Pack Square, Asheville, North Carolina 28801.

Admission: $3 for adults, $2.50 for seniors 62 and over and students, $2 for children ages 4–15. One-day passes for admission to all four Pack Place Museums are $5.50 for adults, $4.50 for seniors and students, and $3.50 for children.

Hours: 10 A.M. to 5 P.M. Tuesday through Saturday, 1–5 P.M. Sundays
from June to October. Pack Place museums are closed on
Mondays.

Phone: (704) 257-4500

When to Go: Any time.

Special Comments: The small museum is located on the lower level.

Overall Appeal by Age Group:

Pre-school	Grade School	Teens	Young Adults	Over 30	Senior Citizens
★★★	★★★½	★★★	★★½	★★½	★★½

Author's Rating: Well-arranged exhibits in a carpeted, quiet setting.
★★½

How Much Time to Allow: One hour, although dedicated rock hounds
could linger here for half a day.

DESCRIPTION AND COMMENTS   This small, modern museum showcases
North Carolina's mineral wealth using exhibits, videos, interactive
computers, and displays of gems and minerals. It's a kid-friendly
place.

TOURING TIPS   The small gift shop is well stocked with items that will
interest rock hounds.

OTHER THINGS TO DO NEARBY   The Asheville Museum of Art and the
Health Adventure are upstairs. Downtown Asheville has plenty of
places to eat and drink.

The Cradle of Forestry in America

Type of Attraction: A 6,500-acre National Historic Site within Pisgah
National Forest that commemorates the beginning of forestry
conservation in the United States. Guided and self-guided tours.

Location: 1002 Pisgah Highway (US 276), Pisgah National Forest,
North Carolina 28768 (between Waynesville and Brevard, off the
Blue Ridge Parkway at Milepost 412).

Admission: $2 for adults, $1 for children under 16 and seniors over 62.

Hours: 10 A.M. to 6 P.M.

Phone: (704) 877-3130, (704) 884-5713

When to Go: Any time.

Special Comments: While the trails are fairly easy, they're not
  completely flat.

Overall Appeal by Age Group:

Pre-school	Grade School	Teens	Young Adults	Over 30	Senior Citizens
★★½	★★★	★★★	★★★	★★★½	★★★★

Author's Rating: A fascinating look at a period when the Industrial
  Revolution met the Southern Appalachians. ★★★★

How Much Time to Allow: Two hours to half a day.

DESCRIPTION AND COMMENTS   Three pioneers of American forestry—
George Vanderbilt, Gifford Pinchot, and Dr. Carl Schenck—worked
at the turn of the 20th century to create a vast estate where forest resources could be conserved for a continual supply of goods. A visitor
center and exhibit room tell the story of forest conservation and its
advances over the last century.

Sound dull? It's not. Small children can enjoy a Forest Fun exhibit
with puppets, puzzles, and costumes, while older folks can get more
information on conservation via touch-screen video monitors. One-
hour guided tours of the restored, turn-of-the-century Biltmore Campus allows visitors to watch and talk with spinners, weavers, quil-
ters, woodsmen, and blacksmiths as they work.

TOURING TIPS   An 18-minute film is shown in the visitor center on the
hour and half-hour throughout the day. But for a better insight into
what the Cradle of Forestry in America is all about, take one of the
guided tours that are led by well-informed, friendly tour guides. The
tours depart at 10:50 A.M., 12:20 P.M., 1:50 P.M., 3:20 P.M. and 4:40 P.M.

OTHER THINGS TO DO NEARBY   Hike or picnic in Pisgah National Forest or car tour on the Blue Ridge Parkway. Sliding Rock, where a
mountain stream cascades over huge rocks forming a natural water
slide, is south on US 276; bring a bathing suit. A lifeguard is on duty
in the summer and a bathhouse is provided courtesy of the U.S. Forest Service.

A little farther south is Looking Glass Falls. At 30 feet wide and 60
feet high, it's one of the most scenic—and best-known—falls in the
East. Brevard, ten miles away, and Hendersonville, about 20 miles
away, offer all the amenities: restaurants, lodging, and shopping.

Ghost Town in the Sky

Type of Attraction: A mile-high carnival/amusement park/country-music emporium in an outrageously beautiful mountaintop setting. A self-guided tour.

Location: US 19 in Maggie Valley, North Carolina.

Admission: $15.40 for adults and children 10 and over, $12.31 for children ages 3–9.

Hours: Weekdays and Sundays 9:30 A.M. to 4 P.M.; Saturdays 9 A.M. to 5 P.M. The park opens the first Saturday in May and closes the last Sunday in October.

Phone: (800) 446-7886, (704) 926-1140

When to Go: Expect long lines at the most popular rides on weekend afternoons; mornings early in the week are almost dead.

Special Comments: Visitors have three choices to reach the mountaintop Western theme park: a ski lift, a mountainside tram, or a shuttle van. The ski lift is the most scenic.

Overall Appeal by Age Group:

Pre-school	Grade School	Teens	Young Adults	Over 30	Senior Citizens
★★★★★	★★★★¹/₂	★★★★	★★★	★★	★

Author's Rating: Right out of the 50s—and a real treat for the younger set. ★★

How Much Time to Allow: At least half a day.

DESCRIPTION AND COMMENTS   It's like a visit to the set of a Grade B Western movie: Bank robbers stick up the bank on Main Street, gunslingers shoot it out with the marshall, and the Silver Dollar Saloon features dancers kicking the cancan. The place is hokey and unashamedly corny—and kids love it.

More than 30 rides and activities, including the Red Devil Roller Coaster, are free and can be ridden over and over—although the lines get long on busy afternoons. Figure a 20-minute wait for each 100 people in front of you for the popular roller coaster, which features a 360-degree loop.

TOURING TIPS   Open-air buses transport visitors from the top of the chair lift to the Ghost Town, where you then walk to Kiddieland (featuring games and rides for younger children), Fort Cherokee, and, at the top, the Mile-High Ride Area. Gunfights, saloon shows, country-and-western music shows, and Indian dances take place in various locations throughout the park every 30 to 45 minutes.

OTHER THINGS TO DO NEARBY   Maggie Valley is midway between Asheville and Cherokee, and close to Great Smoky Mountains National Park.

The Health Adventure

Type of Attraction: A two-story health education facility that's geared to children. A self-guided tour.

Location: Pack Place, 2 South Pack Square, Asheville, North Carolina 28801.

Admission: $3 for adults, $2.50 for seniors 62 and over and students, $2 for children ages 4–15. One-day passes for admission to all four Pack Place Museums are $5.50 for adults, $4.50 for seniors and students, and $3.50 for children.

Hours: 10 A.M. to 5 P.M. Tuesday through Saturday, 1–5 P.M. Sundays from June to October. Pack Place museums are closed on Mondays.

Phone: (704) 257-4500

When to Go: Any time.

Special Comments: An elevator is available to reach the second floor.

Overall Appeal by Age Group:

Pre-school	Grade School	Teens	Young Adults	Over 30	Senior Citizens
★★★★	★★★★	★★★	★★½	★★	★★

Author's Rating: A bright and colorful collection of small galleries that's nothing like a visit to the doctor. ★★½

How Much Time to Allow: One to two hours.

DESCRIPTION AND COMMENTS   Step through the double glass doors to visit dozens of small exhibits featuring health and science information, photographs of the human body, and hands-on exhibits. Classrooms and a theater do a good job of making the subjects of health and biology appealing to youngsters.

TOURING TIPS   Creative PlaySpace is designed for children age eight and younger. Older children and adults can discover which part of the brain sends messages to the eyes, ears, mouth, and skin—and much more.

OTHER THINGS TO DO NEARBY   Other museums in Pack Place are the Asheville Museum of Art, the Colburn Gem & Mineral Museum, and the YMI Cultural Center.

Pack Place

This 92,000-square-foot complex on Pack Square in downtown Asheville features four museums, performance spaces, courtyards, a cafe, and a theater. For specific information on its major attractions, see listings for the Asheville Art Museum, Colburn Gem & Mineral Museum, the Health Adventure, and the YMI Cultural Center.

Smith-McDowell House

Type of Attraction: Asheville's oldest brick residence, circa 1840. A guided tour.

Location: 283 Victoria Road, Asheville, North Carolina 28801.

Admission: $3 for adults, $1.50 for children.

Hours: March 1 through October 31: 10 A.M. to 4 P.M., Tuesday–Saturday; Sunday 1–4 P.M. November 1 through April 30: 10 A.M. to 2 P.M., Tuesday–Friday.

Phone: (704) 253-9231

When to Go: Any time.

Special Comments: The tour requires climbing two sets of stairs.

Overall Appeal by Age Group:

Pre-school	Grade School	Teens	Young Adults	Over 30	Senior Citizens
★	★¹/₂	★¹/₂	★★	★★¹/₂	★★★

Author's Rating: An interesting peek at the home of a wealthy 19th-century Asheville family. ★★★

How Much Time to Allow: One hour.

DESCRIPTION AND COMMENTS   This stately old home is a museum illustrating 19th-century life-styles from the 1840s through the Victorian period. The basement houses a rustic, dirt-floor kitchen, while upstairs the parlor and dining room are decorated with heavy and ornate furnishings from the 1860–1880s. The upstairs bedrooms feature a rope bed, a flintlock rifle that pre-dates the house by 60 years, and books and a secretary owned by the original owners. The guides are knowledgeable, friendly, and eager to discuss the antiques and decorative art on display.

TOURING TIPS   The gift shop features items with a Victorian theme.

OTHER THINGS TO DO NEARBY   Downtown Asheville is only a few minutes away by car; the Western North Carolina Nature Center, a place children and adults will love, is east of Asheville off NC 81 (Swannanoa River Road).

Thomas Wolfe Memorial

Type of Attraction: The early home of a major American novelist and the setting for his most famous novel. A guided tour.

Location: 48 Spruce Street, Asheville, North Carolina 28807.

Admission: $1 for adults, $.50 for children.

Hours: April 1 through October 31: Monday–Saturday, 9 A.M. to 5 P.M.; Sunday, 1–5 P.M. November 1 through March 31: Tuesday–Saturday, 10 A.M. to 4 P.M.; Sunday, 1–4 P.M., closed Monday.

Phone: (704) 253-8304

When to Go: Any time. Tours leave on the half hour.

Special Comments: One set of stairs leads to the second floor.

Overall Appeal by Age Group:

Pre-school	Grade School	Teens	Young Adults	Over 30	Senior Citizens
★	★	★¹/₂	★★¹/₂	★★★¹/₂	★★★★

Author's Rating: It's like walking inside a novel. ★★★★

How Much Time to Allow: One hour.

DESCRIPTION AND COMMENTS   In Wolfe's most famous novel, *Look Homeward, Angel,* the ramshackle old boardinghouse was called "Dixieland." In reality it was known as "The Old Kentucky Home," where Wolfe spent the first 16 years of his life. The old house has been preserved in its ramshackle seediness without renovation—99% of the furnishings are original. For fans of the lyric writer who died at age 38, a visit to this Victorian boardinghouse is pure literary bliss.

TOURING TIPS   Look for Wolfe's college degrees on the wall (a B.A.

from the University of North Carolina in Chapel Hill and a master's from Harvard). Other interesting sights in the house include the room where Wolfe's brother died (a key scene in *Look Homeward, Angel*), original kitchen utensils, family books, and the furnishings of the author's last New York apartment, including his writing table and typewriter.

OTHER THINGS TO DO NEARBY   Pack Place, a modern cultural center with three small museums and a theater, is only a few blocks away.

Western North Carolina Nature Center

Type of Attraction: A zoo and "living museum" featuring a wide array of woodland animals and exhibits on geology, biology, and other sciences. A self-guided tour.

Location: 75 Gashes Creek Road, Asheville, North Carolina 28805. Follow signs from I-40 (exit 53B) and I-240 (exit 8).

Admission: $4 for adults, $3 for seniors, $2 for children ages 3–14.

Hours: June through August: 10 A.M. to 5 P.M. daily. September through May: 10 A.M. to 5 P.M., Tuesday through Saturday; 1–5 P.M., Sunday; closed Monday.

Phone: (704) 298-5600

When to Go: Any time.

Special Comments: Exploring the center requires a lot of walking on wood chip paths through the woods.

Overall Appeal by Age Group:

Pre-school	Grade School	Teens	Young Adults	Over 30	Senior Citizens
★★★★★	★★★★★	★★★★	★★★★	★★★★	★★★★

Author's Rating: Educational, beautiful, fun. ★★★★★

How Much Time to Allow: Half a day or longer, depending on your ability to absorb information on science.

DESCRIPTION AND COMMENTS   This combination museum/zoo features a wide array of woodland animals indigenous to the North Carolina mountains (such as deer and bobcats) and formerly indigenous (such as the red wolf and river otters). Other animals on display include black bears, a mountain lion, deer, wild turkey (which look almost as big as an ostrich), snakes, turtles, eagles. . . .

Inside, young scientists (and their parents) will find excellent exhibits and displays on the sciences, including a fascinating glimpse of animals that are active at night. Younger children will enjoy the petting zoo and barn. This is a great place for young and old alike.

TOURING TIPS   Don't miss the outdoor enclosures containing raccoons, river otters, a bobcat, and a mountain lion. The two-thirds-mile Trillium Glen Nature Trail gives visitors a chance to see native Appalachian plants in natural surroundings.

OTHER THINGS TO DO NEARBY   Buncombe County Recreation Park, which is next door, features carnival rides.

YMI Cultural Center

Type of Attraction: A collection of African artifacts and a cultural center for African-American art, culture, and history. A self-guided tour.

Location: A block behind Pack Place, 2 South Pack Square, Asheville, North Carolina 28801.

Admission: $3 for adults, $2.50 for seniors 62 and over and students, $2 for children ages 4–15. One-day passes for admission to all four Pack Place Museums are $5.50 for adults, $4.50 for seniors and students, and $3.50 for children.

Hours: June through October: 10 A.M. to 5 P.M., Tuesday through Saturday; 1–5 P.M., Sunday. Pack Place museums are closed on Monday.

Phone: (704) 257-4500

When to Go: Any time.

Special Comments: To get there from Pack Place, walk out the front doors, turn right, then turn right again at the first street. The YMI Cultural Center is the brick building diagonally across the street at the end of the block.

Overall Appeal by Age Group:

Pre-school	Grade School	Teens	Young Adults	Over 30	Senior Citizens
★★	★★½	★★½	★★½	★★	★★

Author's Rating: Interesting stuff, but it's a small collection that's not convenient to the rest of Pack Place. A letdown. ★★

How Much Time to Allow: 30 minutes.

DESCRIPTION AND COMMENTS   The former Young Men's Institute was commissioned by George Vanderbilt in 1893 and the Tudor building is considered a historical landmark. The newly refurbished gallery features a small collection of African art and artifacts.

TOURING TIPS   If you parked in the garage adjacent to Pack Place, make the YMI Cultural Center either the first or last stop on your tour and save some steps.

OTHER THINGS TO DO NEARBY   Pack Place features an art museum, a health education facility, and a gem and mineral museum. There are plenty of places to eat and drink in downtown Asheville.

PART TEN:
The Blue Ridge Mountains
of North Carolina—Zone 7

A Brief History and Orientation

The section of the Blue Ridge Mountains stretching to the northeast from Asheville toward Virginia is known locally as the High Country. The popular tourist destinations of Boone, Banner Elk, Spruce Pine, and Burnsville are small communities close to the Blue Ridge Parkway, which threads its way northeast through the center of the region.

While renowned for its spectacular mountain scenery—here you'll find Mt. Mitchell, the highest mountain east of the Rockies—this part of the Blue Ridge Mountains offers a year-round variety of recreational options, including children's attractions, an annual Scottish festival, and some of the best downhill ski resorts in the Southeast.

Tourism in these mountains is a booming industry, but visitors won't feel squeezed for their tourist bucks the way they do in Gatlinburg or Cherokee. Maybe it's because of tradition: Quite a few of North Carolina's oldest travel attractions are found here—Grandfather Mountain, a private park and the highest peak in the Blue Ridge Mountains; Blowing Rock, another private tourist attraction that's been packing them in since the 1920s; Linville Gorge, a spectacular wilderness canyon; and Linville Caverns, North Carolina's only commercial cave.

Aside from enjoying scenic vistas, popular activities include panning for gems in mines near Little Switzerland, attending the outdoor drama *Horn in the West* in Boone, or taking the children for a ride on the old steam train at the Tweetsie Railroad amusement park (outside Boone). Hiking, backpacking, whitewater rafting and kayaking, mountain and road biking, and fishing draw visitors to Pisgah National Forest, which stretches northeast from Asheville to Blowing Rock.

—— *History*

The town of Boone, the economic and cultural center of the region, was named for Daniel Boone. Legends say the renowned Indian fighter roamed the area from 1760 through 1769 and camped on the site of the town. Sparsely settled until well into the 20th century, this part of the Blue Ridge Mountains has suffered its ups and downs over the decades, but mostly downs.

The Depression

While the Roaring 20s were a time of prosperity for most Americans, it wasn't true for many High Country families. As one old-timer put it, "When the Depression came, we didn't know anything had happened."

Yet things managed to get worse in the 1930s as tax revenues fell, some schools closed, markets for botanicals and crafts dried up, and local governments fell into debt. Just as the Depression was coming to a close, a flood in 1940 killed dozens of people around the Blue Ridge and destroyed hundreds of homes.

The Second World War

The impact of World War II on the Blue Ridge was immense. Everyone in the region had a family member in the service or knew dozens of people who did. There had been nothing like it since the Civil War.

The war also introduced a new sense of unity that extended to the mountains. In 1917 during World War I, France could have been on another planet, and some recruiters who ventured out into the mountains met with gunfire that year. In 1941, however, support for the war effort was nearly 100%.

More Decline

The end of the conflict brought rapid change as veterans returned home with government benefits that enabled them to get a college education and buy a home.

More decline, however, followed the war. Many families that had left the area for war work didn't return. Young veterans found few jobs awaiting them. The population got smaller and grew older, and formerly prosperous rural communities shrank.

Turnaround

Then in 1952 the development of Grandfather Mountain began, turning around the region's economy. Over the next few years the mountain evolved into a popular tourist stop. By 1957, almost 200,000 people a year took the road to the top of the highest mountain in the Blue Ridge.

In the 1960s, it was skis, not protest signs, that marked a revolution in the Blue Ridge Mountains. The first commercial slopes, led by Appalachian Ski Mountain, marked the beginning of a tremendous turnaround in tourism: Now the season no longer extended from Memorial Day and ended in mid-October. That translated to more jobs for young people and an incentive to stay in the mountains.

Before and during the Vietnam War, a generation of urban Americans discovered these mountains. Some came for the music and folklore, while others wanted to carve out a simpler life. The newcomers' politics often didn't mesh well with that of the old-timers. But the two sides came to coexist.

Another major development came in 1972, when Appalachian State Teachers College in Boone joined the University of North Carolina system and became Appalachian State University. The school exploded in size and influence—as did Boone.

The Tourism Roller Coaster

The trickle of newcomers, however, changed into a flood after 1970. Some wore overalls and headed back to the land. Others brought plans for multimillion dollar resort developments. It was the fastest era of change to hit the mountains as the economic boom raised property values—and local residents saw their tax bills soar. The decade of the 70s evolved into a boom and bust cycle that followed the price—and availability—of gasoline.

By the early 80s, the cycle had slowed and put a sharp halt to the rapid growth of the 70s. While tourism continued to grow, retail sales soared and housing prices shot up. In addition, residents and local government wrestled with a new problem: quality of life.

The hot topics were air, water, and land. The area's growth meant that the days of unregulated use of property were ending. Rising congestion in Boone made some people in the town say, "We don't want to be another Gatlinburg." Many in the smaller towns outside of Boone chimed in, "We don't want to be another Boone."

Pollution, congestion, development: In the 90s, the problems in this once remote part of the Southern Appalachians aren't much different from most other parts of the country.

—— *Major Highways*

While two superhighways, I-40 and I-77, skirt Zone 7, the Blue Ridge region doesn't have many straight roads that get you where you're going fast. The terrain is just too rugged. A look at a map reveals a lot of white space—a sure sign of big mountains and valleys.

The Blue Ridge Parkway runs through the center of the Blue Ridge, forming a curving spine through the region that's a beautiful drive but not efficient if you're trying to get somewhere in a hurry. US 19 heads north out of Asheville, then veers east toward Burnsville and Spruce Pine. From Spruce Pine, US 19E heads north toward Banner Elk. I-40 forms the southern border of the region east of Asheville.

US 221 roughly parallels the Blue Ridge Parkway from Linville Falls, Blowing Rock, Boone, Jefferson, and, near the Virginia state line, Twin Oaks. US 321 cuts across the region from Lenoir and Boone on its way to Johnson City, Tennessee.

US 421 out of Winston-Salem, North Carolina, heads west to North Wilkesboro and Boone before crossing into Tennessee on its way to Bristol. US 21 drops down from Virginia, cutting across the northern end of the region from Twin Oaks to I-77, which is the northeastern border of Zone 7.

—— *Geographic Location*

Zone 7 is roughly rectangular, its long sides pointing northeast along the crest of the Blue Ridge Mountains. The region is bordered on the south by Zone 6 (Asheville and Brevard) and to the north by Zone 8 (Virginia's Blue Ridge.)

The closest major cities are Asheville (Zone 6) to the south, Johnson City and Bristol, Tennessee, to the west, and Hickory and Winston-Salem, North Carolina, to the east.

—— Pisgah National Forest

With more than 300,000 acres scattered along the eastern edge of the mountains of western North Carolina, Pisgah National Forest offers much to visitors looking for outdoor recreation in a rugged setting. In Pisgah they'll find more than 600 miles of hiking and nature trails, scenic views of cascading waterfalls, mile-high mountains and deep valleys, and fast-flowing rivers for whitewater rafting and canoeing.

But it's not just a recreation area. The Pisgah is primarily a hardwood forest producing some of the best timber in the United States. Many woody plants and vines found in the national forest aren't found anywhere else in the country.

Two Ranger Districts

Toecane Ranger District. This area is named after the Toe and Cane rivers, the two main streams that flow through the district. The area contains 76,000 acres, including Mt. Mitchell, which, at 6,684 feet, is the highest point in the East.

Mt. Mitchell is one of the Black Mountains, nine peaks over 6,000 feet. Along the ridge of the mountains is a virgin stand of Fraser fir and red spruce. It's a rugged and inaccessible range of peaks, except for a foot trail along the mountain crest.

Roan Mountain Gardens, at over 6,000 feet of elevation, is renowned for outstanding displays of wild purple rhododendron blooms during June. It's a popular spot for hiking, cross-country skiing, and picnicking. Craggy Mountain Scenic Area is 950 acres of rugged, roadless terrain popular with hikers.

Douglas Falls provides a scenic and rustic water setting in the area. Virgin timber, hemlock, poplar, spruce, and oaks grow abundantly in this rugged terrain. The Carolina Hemlock Area offers swimming and tubing in the South Toe River.

Grandfather Ranger District. Located northeast of the Toecane District, this area includes the first tract of land purchased for Pisgah National Forest. It contains 187,000 acres of land sitting on the eastern edge of the Blue Ridge Mountains.

The Linville Gorge Wilderness is a 7,600-acre wilderness with a wild torrent of water and steep mountain slopes that soar more than a thousand feet up from the river's bed. It's one of the most scenic and rugged gorges in the United States.

The gorge is ideal for primitive recreation such as hiking, backpacking, fishing, and rock climbing. Trees in the gorge include mountain laurel, yellow root, and sand myrtle. Linville Gorge is so popular that a visitor permit is required.

The Wilson Creek Area is popular for its hunting and fishing. Among the animal life found in Wilson Creek are bear, wild turkey, deer, squirrel, and grouse. Wilson Creek also is a well-regarded destination for backpackers, hikers, and mountain bikers.

Bordered by Grandfather Mountain on the west, Linville Gorge on the southwest, and Brown Mountain on the east, the Wilson Creek Area has elevations from 1,100 feet to 3,700 feet and is thick with beautiful thickets of mountain laurel and rhododendron.

Brown Mountain is renowned for an unexplained phenomena: flickering and darting lights that have intrigued nearby residents and visitors for hundreds of years. The lights often seen on Brown Mountain are mentioned in local Indian mythology and in accounts by settlers from before Civil War days.

Swamp gas? Visitors from another galaxy? Check it out for yourself. Popular viewing spots for a glimpse of the Brown Mountain Lights are from the overlook south of Jonas Ridge on NC 181 and Wiseman's View on the Kistler Memorial Highway.

—— A Self-Contained Region

Visitors who come to this part of the Blue Ridge Mountains don't really have to leave it during their vacation. There's a wide range of outdoor activities—hiking, rafting, cycling, fishing, skiing—and a wide selection of lodging, restaurants, shopping, and tourist attractions to satisfy their needs.

There is another reason why most visitors aren't jumping in their cars to visit Asheville or Great Smoky Mountains National Park. The main towns that tourists visit—Boone, Blowing Rock, Banner Elk, Linville Falls, and Spruce Pine—are close together, making it easy to visit the region's cornucopia of attractions.

But that doesn't mean everyone should rule out visits beyond the borders of the Blue Ridge region. Asheville, featuring museums, night life, and a 250-room French chateau, is an easy jaunt. Great Smoky is only 40 miles farther, and other attractions within an easy day's drive include the Shining Rock Wilderness, the Cradle of Forestry in America (both in Zone 6), the upscale resort of Highlands (Zone 5), and whitewater rafting on Nantahala Gorge (Zone 4).

Outdoor Recreation and Activities

—— Camping

Mount Mitchell.   Nine sites with spectacular views are available from May 1 through October 31 (weather permitting), not far from the highest point east of the Rockies. (The elevation at the campground is 6,320 feet.) Each site offers plenty of privacy—it's like having your very own room with a view. Modern rest rooms are on-site, but no hot showers. No reservations accepted. Bring a warm sleeping bag.

Mortimer Campground.   Located in the Wilson Creek Area, this pretty campground is located in a forest of hemlocks and pine. It makes an excellent base for hikers, anglers, and mountain bikers who want to explore the area. The campground is located beneath Grandfather Mountain in the Linville Gorge. Facilities, however, are primitive.

—— Hiking

This part of the Blue Ridge is a hiker's paradise that offers an overwhelming number of trails. Major trail systems include the 2,100-mile Appalachian Trail, which follows the North Carolina–Tennessee border through the area.

The Linville Gorge Wilderness Area covers 10,975 acres of some of the most rugged and awesomely beautiful terrain in the eastern United States. It's a favorite destination for hikers, rock climbers, and backpackers. It's also one of the most dangerous spots outdoor enthusiasts can visit; many people get lost here each year, and some have died. Be sure to leave a detailed itinerary of your hike and when you plan to return with a responsible person.

The Wilson Creek Area, located in Pisgah National Forest, is crisscrossed with challenging trails through dense vegetation, over rugged rock formations, and along scenic waterfalls.

Roan Mountain State Park, located about a 45-minute drive southwest of Boone on the North Carolina–Tennessee border, boasts the world's largest rhododendron gardens, which offer peak blooms in mid-June. The park also offers camping, hiking and backpacking on the Appalachian Trail, picnicking, and a visitor center.

Remember that no guidebook can offer the detailed, up-to-date information you need to navigate the back country. Make sure you pick up trail maps of the region you plan to explore—and take them with you on a hike. Also, check with a ranger for the latest information on trail conditions before you leave.

Easy Hikes and Walks

Mount Mitchell.   A five-mile access road from the Blue Ridge Parkway takes visitors to the tallest point in the East. It's an easy walk on a paved path to the stone observation tower and spectacular views—up to 70 miles on a clear day. (Alas, the peak is often socked in by clouds.) Bring a jacket: The summit is usually windy and several degrees cooler than lower elevations. The Balsam Trail is an easy, three-quarter-mile self-guided nature trail at the summit.

Moses Cone Memorial Park.   Near Blowing Rock on the Blue Ridge Parkway at milepost 294, Cone Park offers 25 miles of easy, graded paths that are popular with casual walkers and, in the winter after it snows, cross-country skiers. A map is available at the Manor House Visitor Center from May through October.

Julian Price Memorial Park.   Located on the Blue Ridge Parkway at milepost 297 near Blowing Rock, the park offers several easy walks, including the Price Lake Trail, which circles the lake (popular with joggers), and the two-mile Green Knob Trail, which passes through pastures and a section of blackberry briars.

Moderate Hikes

Linville Falls Trails.   The Erwin Falls Trail is a moderate hike with four overlooks, each revealing a different aspect of the Linville Falls area. Round trip is one and six-tenths miles. The Linville Falls Visitor Center is off NC 183, near the community of Linville Falls.

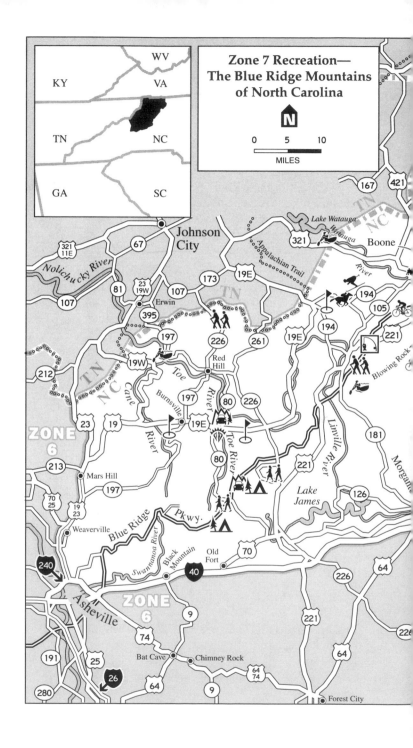

Zone 7 Recreation—
The Blue Ridge Mountains
of North Carolina

N

0   5   10
MILES

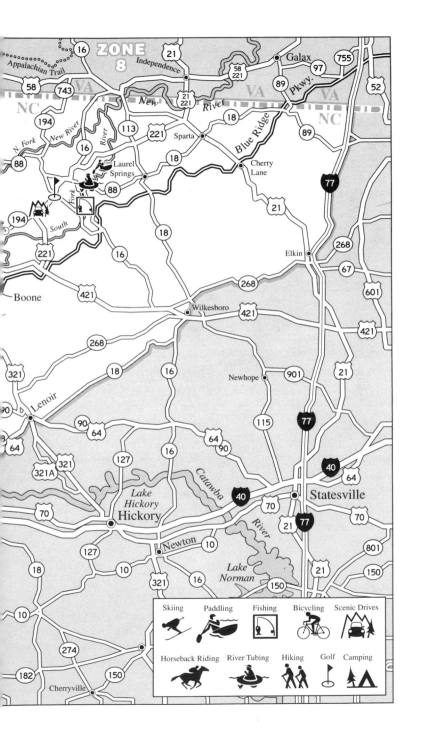

Wilson Creek Trails.   This section of Pisgah National Forest is bordered by Grandfather Mountain to the west, the Linville Gorge Wilderness to the south, and Brown Mountain to the east. The two-and-four-tenths-mile Woodruff Ridge Trail is one of many popular trails in this rugged area. The trail head is on NC 1362.

The Boone Fork Trail.   Located in Julian Price Park at milepost 297 on the Blue Ridge Parkway, this popular trail is a five-mile hike through an area filled with wildflowers all year (fall is best, however). The trail also passes some interesting rock formations and a series of rapids in a stream.

The trail begins in the picnic area as a wide, graveled path and quickly turns into a well-defined hiking trail. Along its length, the Boone Fork Trail weaves through deep forests, around towering rock formations, alongside a river, and across pastures.

Strenuous Hikes

Linville Gorge.   Several trails drop sharply into the gorge, making the climb out rugged and difficult. The Linville River descends 2,000 feet in only 12 miles as it plunges through the mountains. Access to the trails is along Forest Service roads off US 221. A permit is required and can be picked up at the U.S. Forest Service District Ranger office in Marion.

Appalachian Trail.   The Appalachian Trail passes to the west along the North Carolina–Tennessee border, crossing Roan Mountain, Hump Mountain, and Yellow Mountain. It's a stretch of the Maine-to-Georgia trail that passes through an area known for its large expanses of mountaintop meadows and spectacular views. The trail heads are in Elk Park and at Carvers Gap on Roan Mountain.

—— Canoeing, Kayaking, and Rafting

Because most of the whitewater streams in the North Carolina Blue Ridge are free flowing, commercial rafting tends to be seasonal. In March, April, May, and early June, spring rains provide ample water for trips on the Class III–IV Nolichucky Gorge, and the steep Watauga Gorge and Wilson Creek.

Nolichucky River

The upper Nolichucky has the longest season, stretching into June for Class III–IV rafting and providing low-water ducky fun later in the summer. Along with the Chattooga, the gorge section of the Nolichucky offers a remote wilderness experience. While the Chattooga is totally isolated, a railroad runs along the river through the Nolichucky Gorge. The put-in is at Poplar, North Carolina, southwest of Boone near the Tennessee border. The take-out is near Erwin, Tennessee.

Trips on the upper Chucky get off to an intense start with ten Class III (IV) rapids in the first five miles. At about mile 5.5, the river eases up and most of the action is mellow Class II and straightforward Class III on down to the take-out. Though the duration of the nine-mile trip varies with water levels, most runs average five to seven hours including shuttle time and a lunch break. On the Nolichucky Gorge, there is almost always a guide in each raft. Minimum age for most outfitters is 13 years. Cost per person ranges from $55–65.

Outfitters who run the Nolichucky include:

Carolina Wilderness	(800) 872-7437
Cherokee Adventures	(800) 445-7238
High Mountain Expeditions	(800) 262-9036
Nantahala Outdoor Center	(800) 232-7238
USA Raft	(800) 872-7238
Wahoo's Adventures	(800) 444-7238

Watauga Gorge and Wilson Creek

If you are looking for an adrenaline rush, consider the Watauga Gorge or Wilson Creek runs. Runnable in the spring (and occasionally into early June), these steep creek runs push commercial rafting to its limits. These boulder-clogged streams have huge, blind drops; tight, technical chutes; and grabby hydraulics. Both demand good conditioning, experience, and teamwork. Wilson Creek trips cover five miles of Class III–V water, while the Watauga Gorge serves up six miles of Class III–V action with 15 rapids rated Class IV or higher. While the Watauga drops through a remote gorge, a road runs alongside Wilson Creek. Our advice to anyone contemplating either of these runs is to take a good look at Wilson Creek from the road before signing up.

Wilson Creek is south of the Blue Ridge Parkway, near Lenoir, North Carolina. Guided raft trips run $65–75 and can take up to six hours depending on the water level, the scouting required, and how the outfitters set up their safety. The Watauga Gorge is north of the Blue Ridge Parkway near where US 321 crosses from North Carolina into Tennessee. The run begins at the S.R. 1200 bridge northwest of Boone, and ends at Watauga Lake just over the state line in Tennessee. Watauga Gorge trips also vary in length. To be safe, allocate five to seven hours for the trip, including shuttle time. Watauga Gorge trips cost anywhere from $90–150.

Outfitters who run the Watauga include:

Wahoo's Adventures	(800) 444-7238
High Mountain Expeditions	(800) 262-9036
Edge of the World Outfitters	(704) 898-9550

Outfitters who run Wilson Creek include:

Wahoo's Adventures	(800) 444-7238

Trips for Families

The Nolichucky and Watauga rivers both have milder sections that are appropriate for families and inexperienced rafters. Below Erwin, Tennessee, the Nolichucky has a broad, rocky bottom, frequent ripples, and an occasional Class II (III) rapid. Known as the lower Nolichucky by commercial rafters, both guided and unguided trips are available. Trip length can vary from five to ten miles depending on the put-in and take-out used.

Similarly, family trips are offered on the Watauga River, below Wilbur Dam in Tennessee. The river features a swift current and a lot of small waves. The scenery is pleasant as the river winds through fertile farm plains and beneath limestone bluffs. Below Elizabethton, Tennessee, the Watauga enters a scenic lower gorge with mellow Class I–II water. Once again, trip lengths vary.

New River

In addition to commercial rafting, scenic canoeing is offered on the New River, northeast of Boone, near Jefferson, North Carolina. One of the oldest rivers in the world in spite of its name, the New flows gently for more than 100 miles through forested mountains and fertile, pastoral valleys. Both one-day and overnight trips—guided and unguided—are available mid-April through mid-October.

For detailed information on this and other area rivers, check our list of recommended reading for canoeing, kayaking, and rafting on pages 76–77.

Canoe outfitters on the North Carolina New River include:

New River Outfitters	(919) 982-9192
Zaloo's Canoes	(919) 246-3066

—— *Tubing*

Enjoy a cool and refreshing float down the New River, geologically the oldest river in the United States. It's a gentle stream that flows by banks lined with blooming wildflowers in May and early June and an explosion of color in the fall.

Zaloo's Canoes (it rhymes) near Jefferson offers tube trips on the South Fork of the New River weekends from April 1 through October 31, and weekdays from mid-May through mid-September. Two-hour and four-hour float trips are offered for $8 a tube. Depending on the trip, tubers are either shuttled to the put-in or shuttled from the take-out. Reservations are suggested; call (910) 246-3066.

—— *Fishing*

Along the Blue Ridge Parkway, trout streams and lakes are stocked annually and offer excellent fishing. At Cone Park, **Bass Lake** has bass and blue gill, while **Trout Lake** is designated as native trout waters. Most mountain streams in the area are stocked with trout in addition to their own population of native trout.

The **Watauga River** and the various forks of the **New River** have smallmouth bass, red-eye bass, catfish, and in a few areas, large muskies. Other streams and lakes in the Blue Ridge famous for good fishing are **Wilsons Creek, Elk River** (between Banner Elk and Old Park on NC 194), **Howards Creek** (off NC 194 north of Boone), **Boone's Fork** (off the Watauga River above Hounds Ears), the Globe section of the **Johns River Gorge** (eight miles south of Blowing Rock off US 321 on Globe Road), **Anthony Creek, Johns River,** and **Big Horse Creek** (upstream from the bridge on NC 1361 to the Virginia state line).

Regulations

Streams and lakes on the Blue Ridge Parkway are game fish waters under federal regulation. North Carolina state fishing licenses are required for all anglers 16 years or older; state trout stamps are not required on Parkway waters. Comprehensive nonresident licenses are $15 a day and $25 for three days. For residents, an annual license is $25. The season runs all year except for March, when streams and lakes are stocked.

If you want a sure catch, try fishing at one of many **commercial trout ponds** in the area. You're only charged for what you catch, typically $3 a pound undressed. The trout pond season generally runs from the first Saturday in April through mid-November. And you don't need a license.

—— Bicycling

Road Riding

The region's premier road-riding attraction is the lightly traveled, pot-hole free, and scenic **Blue Ridge Parkway**. For a double whammy of great vistas, intermediate to advanced riders can ride a loop on **US 221 from Blowing Rock to Linville**. Starting in Linville, it's a steep two-mile climb to the Blue Ridge Parkway, where you turn left. It's about ten miles to Blowing Rock, where you exit and turn right onto US 221 for the spin back to Linville. Local riders say the road surfaces are good, the traffic is moderate, and the views are incredible.

For an easy, out-and-back ride along a river, go north of Boone to Todd and park at the **Todd General Store** (but not too close to the building, please). Then spin the cranks for ten easy miles along the river to Fleetwood, turn around and come back. It's beautiful—and easy.

Mountain Biking

The high country in the Wilson Creek Area of Pisgah National Forest is gaining a national reputation for its single-track trails. Strong riders with good handling skills will want to try the Wilson Ridge Trail, a forested and technical single track that's 15 miles in length—one way. Climbs are straight up in a few places, and it ends with a 2,000-foot vertical gain. You can either loop back on paved roads on a screaming descent for a 30-mile ride or take the easier, dirt Forest Service roads to the trail head. Either way it's a challenging ride.

Another—and much easier—alternative in the Wilson Creek Area is the **Woodruff Ridge Trail.** The stream crossings along the two-and-four-tenths-mile single-track trail are welcome on hot summer rides, while ferns and wildflowers line the side of the trail.

Bikers intent on exploring Pisgah National Forest should enlist some local help: Regulations regarding mountain bikes are evolving, and bikes aren't allowed on some hiking trails. The local experts in Boone are **Rock & Roll Sports** on East King Street. Stop by to pick up some maps and the latest trail information, or call them at (704) 264-0765.

For an in-depth look at off-road cycling in Pisgah National Forest, get a copy of Lori Finley's *Mountain Biking the Appalachians: Northwest North Carolina/Southwest Virginia.* It's a guide to the trails in the region published by John F. Blair Publisher, (800) 222-9796.

—— *Horseback Riding*

Banner Elk Riding Stables, off NC 194 in Banner Elk, offers one-hour guided rides on mountain trails on the hour from 10 A.M. to 5 P.M. daily. The rate is $12 per horse, and reservations are required. For more information, call (704) 898-5424.

Smith's Quarter Horse Farm in Banner Elk offers 90-minute guided rides on this 200-acre farm. The stables specialize in rides for families and children; the maximum group size is ten. Three guides go along on a scenic ride that offers views into three states. Rides leave daily at 10 A.M., noon, 2 P.M., and 4 P.M. year-round; the rate is $12 per horse. Reservations are required; call (704) 898-4932 for more information.

—— *Golf*

The best course in the North Carolina Blue Ridge is the Mount Mitchell Golf Club in Burnsville. This and other quality golf courses in the area are profiled below.

Black Mountain Golf Club

Address: 1 Ross Drive, Black Mountain NC 28711

Phone: (704) 669-2710

Status: Municipal course

Tees:

> Championship: 6,200 yards, par 71, USGA 71, slope 116.
> Men's: 5,800 yards, par 71, USGA 71, slope 113.
> Ladies': 5,000 yards, par 71, USGA 71, slope 109.

Fees: April–October, $20; November–March, $15. Cart, $10.

Facilities: Putting green, snack bar, and pro shop.

Boone Golf Club

Established: 1959

Address: 433 Fairway Drive, Boone NC 28607

Phone: (704) 264-8760

Status: Semiprivate course

Tees:

> Championship: 6,401 yards, par 71, USGA 70.1, slope 120.
> Men's: 5,859 yards, par 71, USGA 67.4, slope 112.
> Ladies': 5,172 yards, par 75, USGA 69.1, slope 113.

Fees: $25 weekday and weekend. Cart fee, $9.

Facilities: Pro shop, putting green, restaurant, and locker rooms.

Crestview Golf Course

Established: 1982

Address: HCR 1, Box 19A, Ennice NC 28623

Phone: (910) 657-3471

Status: Public course

Tees:

>Championship: 5,905 yards, par 72.
>Men's: 5,713 yards, par 72
>Ladies': 4,385 yards, par 72.

Fees: $7 weekday and weekend. Cart fee, $8 per player.

Facilities: Snack bar, putting green, and pro shop.

Jefferson Landing

Established: 1989

Address: Highway 16/88, Jefferson NC 28640

Phone: (800) 292-6274

Status: Semiprivate course

Tees:

>Championship: 6,424 yards, par 72, USGA 69.4, slope 115.
>Men's: 5,720 yards, par 72, USGA 66.2, slope 109.
>Ladies': 4,960 yards, par 72, USGA 66, slope 103.

Fees: $25 weekday, $35 weekend. Cart fee, $10.

Facilities: Pro shop, snack bar, driving range, putting green, tennis courts, pool, lodge, and manor house.

Mount Mitchell Golf Club

Established: 1975

Address: 7590 Highway 80 South, Burnsville NC 28714

Phone: (704) 675-5454

Status: Resort course

Tees:

>Championship: 6,475 yards, par 72, USGA 70, slope 121.
>Men's: 6,110 yards, par 72, USGA 68, slope 116.
>Ladies': 5,455 yards, par 72, USGA 69.5, slope 117.

Fees: $39 weekdays, $44 weekends and holidays. Carts included.

Facilities: Clubhouse, pro shop, snack bar, dining room, and putting green.

Sugar Mountain Golf Course

Address: Sugar Mountain Drive, Banner Elk NC 28604

Phone: (704) 898-6464

Status: Municipal course

Tees:

Championship: 4,488 yards, par 64, USGA 61.1, slope 94.
Men's: 4,198 yards, par 64, USGA 59.9, slope 91.
Ladies': 3,470 yards, par 64, USGA 60.1, slope 90.

Fees: $17 weekday, $19 weekend. Cart fee, $10 per player.

Facilities: Pro shop, putting green, and snack bar.

—— Skiing

This is premier North Carolina ski country: The highest, steepest slopes in the state are here, and this is where the serious skiers come. Ski Beech and Sugar Mountain Resort are the giants of the North Carolina ski industry. The ski season typically runs from Thanksgiving through March, but varies from year to year according to weather conditions. Weekends typically are crowded at all the ski resorts.

Sugar Mountain Resort. Located in Banner Elk, Sugar Mountain features the state's highest vertical drop—1,200 feet. Skiers can choose from 18 slopes after a mile-long chair lift ride deposits them on top of Sugar Mountain. For more information, call (704) 898-5256.

Ski Beech. Located near Banner Elk, Ski Beech boasts a vertical drop of 830 feet, 15 slopes, 9 chair lifts, and 2 surface lifts. Rentals, ski schools, food, a lounge, and lodging are all on the premises. For more information, call (800) 438-2093 (Eastern United States) or (704) 387-2011.

Hawksnest Golf and Ski Resort. This ski area, near Banner Elk, features 7 slopes, 2 chair lifts, 2 surface lifts, and a vertical drop of 619 feet. Rentals, a ski school, food, and a lounge are on the site, but no lodging. For more information, call (704) 963-6561.

Appalachian Ski Mountain. Located near Blowing Rock, this resort offers 8 slopes with a vertical drop of 365 feet. The slopes are serviced by three chair lifts and three surface lifts. Lift hours are 9 A.M. to 4 P.M. daily and 6–10 P.M. nightly. Note: The resort markets itself heavily through bus tours and often is extremely crowded on weekends. For more information, call (800) 322-2373 or (704) 295-7828.

—— Scenic Drives

The Blue Ridge Parkway.   Writhing for 150 miles through spectacular mountains of North Carolina's Blue Ridge, the Blue Ridge Parkway is a stretch of scenic highway with few equals in the world. Popular destinations along the two-lane, noncommercial road include the Lin Cove Viaduct (milepost 304), an engineering marvel that skirts Grandfather Mountain and was the final link in the 469-mile highway. It was completed in 1987.

Places to get out and stretch your legs include Mount Mitchell State Park (milepost 355), where it's an easy walk to the highest point in the East, and Linville Falls (milepost 316), where paved trails lead to overlooks into a wild gorge. The Folk Art Center (milepost 383) offers a look at traditional and contemporary crafts of the Southern Appalachians through interpretive programs, a museum, and a library.

Boone to Jefferson.   This scenic ramble on narrow, two-lane roads north of Boone takes visitors into the rolling agricultural areas north of town and to the towns of Jefferson and West Jefferson, thriving communities with a growing population of retired residents. Some of the roads were on the route of 1994's Tour Dupont, an international bicycle stage race; look for the kilometer readings painted on the roadway to let the (mostly) European racers know how far they were from the finish line.

From Boone, drive out US 421E and turn left onto NC 194 (at the Hardees). It's 13 miles to Todd; continue straight and get on the US 221 Bypass around Jefferson and West Jefferson (or stay on the business route and explore the two towns). Continue on US 221 and turn right on either NC 113 or NC 93; both routes go south to the Blue Ridge Parkway, where you head south toward Boone and complete the loop.

Linville to Blowing Rock on US 221. This stretch of federal highway paralleling the Blue Ridge Parkway has fantastic views, huge rock formations, and light traffic. You can create a loop ride by returning to your starting point on the Blue Ridge Parkway.

US 19. From Asheville this road parallels the Blue Ridge Mountains to the west as it winds its way through pretty countryside and the towns of Burnsville and Spruce Pine. At NC 194, turn right and go to Linville, where you can get on US 221 going north to Boone for some fantastic mountain scenery. Create a loop by returning to Asheville on the Blue Ridge Parkway.

South Toe—Blue Ridge Parkway—Crabtree Meadows. One of the highlights on this drive is the scenic South Toe River Valley; the road follows the river for 15 miles. Starting in Burnsville, take US 19E to Micaville and turn right on NC 80 south. As you follow the river, the massive Black Mountains are on one side and Seven Mile Ridge is on the other. When you reach the Blue Ridge Parkway at Buck Creek Gap, you have the option of taking it south to Mount Mitchell.

Turn north, however, and you'll pass several sweeping overlooks and Crabtree Meadows, where there is a coffee shop and campground. Next is the summer colony of Little Switzerland; check out the specialty shops. From Little Switzerland come back under the Parkway and follow Crabtree Creek Road down the mountain.

The road brings you back to US 19E. (Along the way you pass two mines where you can stop to mine for gems.) Turn left to return to Micaville and Burnsville. The drive is about 40 miles, not counting the optional side trip to Mount Mitchell.

Attractions

For such a formerly remote region in the Blue Ridge Mountains, the High Country offers a surprising array of tourist destinations. Attractions range from a topnotch museum on life in the Appalachians, a train pulled by a steam locomotive that the children will love, spectacular overlooks and natural scenery, and magnificent waterfalls.

Appalachian Cultural Museum

Type of Attraction: A wide ranging collection of exhibits and artifacts on Appalachian life and its people. A self-guided tour.

Location: University Hall Drive, off U.S. 221/231, in Boone, North Carolina.

Admission: $2 for adults, $1.75 for seniors, $1 for children ages 12–18; free admission on Tuesdays.

Hours: 10 A.M. to 5 P.M. Tuesday through Saturday, 1–5 P.M. Sunday.

Phone: (704) 262-3117

When to Go: Any time.

Special Comments: This remarkable museum is buried along Boone's main commercial strip south of downtown and easy to miss; look for the Scotsman gas station and a sign for University Hall.

Overall Appeal by Age Group:

Pre-school	Grade School	Teens	Young Adults	Over 30	Senior Citizens
★	★★½	★★★	★★★½	★★★★	★★★★½

Author's Rating: An undiscovered gem; don't miss it. ★★★★½

How Much Time to Allow: One to two hours.

DESCRIPTION AND COMMENTS   Like most museums that focus on North Carolina's cultural heritage, the Appalachian Cultural Museum covers some familiar ground: geology, handicrafts, Native Americans, early farm life in the mountains. And this museum, part of Appalachian State University, does that job well.

What sets it apart—and makes it a lot of fun—is the museum's focus on popular culture, ranging from exhibits on an early theme park called the Wizard of Oz (an effort to attract tourists during the off-season that closed in 1980) to a display on stock cars (including an exhibit on legendary racer Junior Johnson, who journalist Tom Wolfe called "the last American hero"). What can you say about a museum that displays two real stock cars? Don't miss it.

TOURING TIPS   Many of the exhibits are thought-provoking. Not only will you learn about, say, an early attempt to attract tourists to the mountains after the snow melts, but also about how the entire tourist industry affects the state's culture and economy. It's the same with the stock-car racing exhibits. Dangerous, glamorous, rewarding for a few—and an unusual career path for young men desperate to escape the grinding poverty of farm life.

OTHER THINGS TO DO NEARBY   The Daniel Boone Native Gardens, next to *The Horn in the West* outdoor theater off US 321, is an oasis of tranquillity in this busy little town. The gardens feature a collection of North Carolina native plants arranged in an informal landscape design. Open May through September 10 A.M. to 6 P.M. daily and on weekends in October. Admission is $2.

Next to the gardens, the Hickory Ridge Homestead offers visitors a glimpse of an authentic 18th-century homestead. On weekends May through October, the homestead is open from 9 A.M. to 4 P.M. Saturday and 1–4 P.M. Sunday. Admission is $2 for adults and $1 for children ages 7–12. A gift shop sells local arts and crafts.

The Blowing Rock

Type of Attraction: An overlook with a magnificent vista of North Carolina's tallest mountains. A self-guided tour.

Location: Highway 321 South, Blowing Rock, North Carolina 28605.

Admission: $4 for adults, $3 for seniors and AAA members, $2 for children ages 6–11.

Hours: 8 A.M. to 8 P.M. daily, March through November; weekends only during the winter. Closed during inclement weather.

Phone: (704) 295-7111

When to Go: Any time. Skip it in cloudy, windy, or icy weather.

Special Comments: Bring binoculars.

Overall Appeal by Age Group:

Pre-school	Grade School	Teens	Young Adults	Over 30	Senior Citizens
★★★	★★★	★★★	★★★	★★★★	★★★¹/₂

Author's Rating: A great view—but there's no shortage of those in the area, and most are free. ★★¹/₂

How Much Time to Allow: 30 minutes.

DESCRIPTION AND COMMENTS   This immense cliff 4,000 feet above sea level overhangs the Johns River Gorge 3,000 feet below, creating an air current that can return light objects thrown over the cliff. We didn't have any "light objects" with us the morning we visited Blowing Rock and didn't test it out. But the view was impressive: Mount Mitchell, Grandfather Mountain, Grandmother Mountain, and Table Rock are visible on the horizon. The setting, as befits North Carolina's oldest tourist attraction, is pleasant, with rock walls, gardens, a miniature waterfall, a picnic table, and paths leading to the wooden observation deck. A large gift shop, rest rooms, and a snack bar round it out.

TOURING TIPS   Bring a jacket; the paths and observation deck are usually breezy. And keep this legend in mind as you savor the view: An Indian brave who leaped to his death was returned to the arms of his heart-broken maiden by the upward drafts that mark this spot. Ever since, it's been said that if you speak words of love from the top of Blowing Rock, the wind carries them to your beloved.

OTHER THINGS TO DO NEARBY   Boone, a college town featuring lodging, shopping, the Tweetsie Railroad, and restaurants, is about ten miles away.

Emerald Village and the North Carolina Mining Museum

Type of Attraction: A self-guided tour of an old mine; prospecting for gems along shaded flumes.

Location: McKinney Mine Road and Crabtree Creek Road, Little Switzerland, North Carolina 28749 (two miles west of the Blue Ridge Parkway between Boone and Asheville).

Admission: Underground mine museum: $3.50 for adults, $2.50 for students, $3 for seniors; other above-ground exhibits are free. Gemstone buckets for prospecting range in price from $5–100.

Hours: 9 A.M. to 6 P.M. daily from April 1 through November 30.

Phone: (704) 765-6463

When to Go: Any time.

Special Comments: Wear boots or thick-soled shoes when exploring the underground mine; the ground is uneven and often wet. Wear old clothes you don't mind getting dirty if you're panning for gems.

Overall Appeal by Age Group:

Pre-school	Grade School	Teens	Young Adults	Over 30	Senior Citizens
★	★★	★★½	★★★	★★★	★★★½

Author's Rating: An informative museum tour—and afterwards you can pan for gems. ★★★

How Much Time to Allow: One hour for the museum; pan for gems until you strike it rich—or as long as your patience and lust for discovery lasts.

DESCRIPTION AND COMMENTS   Authentic mining equipment and displays in a real mine show the heritage—and, often, the hardship—of mining in the mountains of western North Carolina. This mine yielded feldspar, a mineral used in Bon Ami polishing cleaner. A small museum outside the mine features old photos, including one of child miners who worked below ground until 1938, when child labor was outlawed. Many of the children look prematurely aged and perhaps blind.

A nearby company store is an early example of a shopping mall, featuring several shops, an assay office, and a post office—all stocked with original items. Across the road visitors can stand along flumes and pan for gems; employees stand by to help you identify your finds.

TOURING TIPS   Upstairs above the museum is an interesting exhibit of old—and quaint—Bon Ami magazine ads.

OTHER THINGS TO DO NEARBY   The Little Switzerland Mine Company, on Highway 226 near the Blue Ridge Parkway, offers half-day and full-day tours of a historic mine; call (704) 765-8687 for more information.

Grandfather Mountain Park

Type of Attraction: A private park encompassing Grandfather Mountain, at 5,964 feet the highest peak in the Blue Ridge Mountains. A self-guided tour.

Location: Two miles northwest of Linville on US 211; the closest exit on the Blue Ridge Parkway is at milepost 305.

Admission: $9 for adults, $5 for children ages 4–12.

Hours: 8 A.M. to 7 P.M. daily in the summer. In the winter the park closes at 5 P.M., and at 6 P.M. in the spring and fall. Closed Thanksgiving and Christmas days.

Phone: (800) 468-7325, (704) 733-4337

When to Go: Any time. Skip it in inclement weather.

Special Comments: Be prepared for lower temperatures and high winds at the summit (which you can drive to).

Overall Appeal by Age Group:

Pre-school	Grade School	Teens	Young Adults	Over 30	Senior Citizens
★★★★	★★★★	★★★¹/₂	★★★	★★★	★★★

Author's Rating: It's more than a view: With the Nature Museum, small zoo, and nature movies, visitors get a decent return on the rather steep entrance fee. ★★★

How Much Time to Allow: Two hours to see the sights; an entire day to explore some hiking trails and enjoy a picnic.

DESCRIPTION AND COMMENTS   The highlight of this private park near the Blue Ridge Parkway is the mile-high, 228-foot-long suspension bridge at the summit of Grandfather Mountain that rewards visitors with impressive views of the surrounding mountains and valleys—if it's not raining.

There's more: The Nature Museum, while small, is in a large, airy building and features exhibits on geology, wildlife, and geography. The Wildlife Habitat contains several outdoor enclosures holding bears, cougars, bald eagles, and white-tail deer. In the background are nice views of the mountains; there's a snack bar at the bear enclosure.

For hikers, Grandfather Mountain offers 30 miles of hiking. Moderate trails include the Black Rock Cliffs Cave Trail (one and three-tenths miles, fine views) and the Grandfather Trail Extension (two and a half miles, round trip). Followed farther, most of the trails become challenging, with ladders over cliff faces and rocky summits. Detailed hiking maps are available at the Entrance Gate, Visitor's Center, or Nature Museum.

TOURING TIPS   The Nature Museum is where you'll find a fast-food restaurant, rest rooms, a 165-seat theater that presents 28-minute movies on the hour between 9 A.M. and 5 P.M., and a large gift shop.

OTHER THINGS TO DO NEARBY   Linville Falls is south of Linville on US 221; Blowing Rock is north on US 221; Boone is a college town offering lodging, shopping, and restaurants.

Linville Falls

Type of Attraction: Beautiful falls that cascade 90 feet into Linville Gorge, a national wilderness preserve that's second only to the Grand Canyon in length and depth. A self-guided tour.

Location: Off milepost 317 on the Blue Ridge Parkway. From the community of Linville Falls on US 221, take NC 183 to the spur road leading to the visitor center.

Admission: Free.

Hours: Always open.

Phone: (704) 298-0398

When to Go: Any time.

Special Comments: Wear sturdy, flat or rubber-soled shoes, even on trails marked "easy." Hiking boots are recommended on more challenging trails.

Overall Appeal by Age Group:

Pre-school	Grade School	Teens	Young Adults	Over 30	Senior Citizens
★★	★★★	★★★½	★★★★	★★★★	★★★★

Author's Rating: Beautiful views of the falls and remnants of a virgin forest. ★★★★

How Much Time to Allow: Two hours to half a day.

DESCRIPTION AND COMMENTS   Most folks will want to explore the Erwins View Trail, a moderate, one-and-six-tenths-mile round trip with four overlooks. Chimney View, seven-tenths of a mile from the visitor center, is the first point on the trail where the lower falls can be seen. At Gorge View Overlook, hikers can see the Linville River cutting its way through the Linville Gorge Wilderness Area.

TOURING TIPS   Sudden changes in weather are common in these mountains. Before setting out on a hike to see the falls, stuff rain gear and some extra clothing in a day pack or fanny pack. And don't drink the water in the river or springs: Bacterial diseases or the dreaded *giardia* can be contracted by drinking "wild" water.

OTHER THINGS TO DO NEARBY   Grandfather Mountain, a private park featuring the highest point in the Blue Ridge Mountains, is two miles north of the town of Linville. Linville Caverns, the only commercial caverns in North Carolina, are located on US 221 between Linville and Marion, four miles south of the Blue Ridge Parkway at milepost 317. The caverns are open daily spring, summer, and fall and weekends only in the winter; call (704) 756-4171 for more information.

Mount Mitchell State Park

Type of Attraction: North Carolina's first state park and, at 6,684 feet, the highest peak east of the Mississippi. A self-guided tour.

Location: Five miles north of the Blue Ridge Parkway on NC 128, 30 miles northeast of Asheville.

Admission: Free.

Hours: The park and trails to Mount Mitchell always are open.

Phone: (704) 675-4611

When to Go: Any time, but don't bother in inclement weather. Mount Mitchell is covered in clouds and fog eight out of ten days.

Special Comments: Be ready for air temperatures about ten degrees cooler than on the Parkway—and it's usually a lot windier. Dress appropriately.

Overall Appeal by Age Group:

Pre-school	Grade School	Teens	Young Adults	Over 30	Senior Citizens
★★★	★★★★	★★★★	★★★★	★★★★	★★★★

Author's Rating: A spectacular view (if it's not cloudy) and the dubious satisfaction of driving—not hiking—to the highest point in the eastern United States. ★★★★

How Much Time to Allow: One hour to explore the summit, observation tower, and a small museum.

DESCRIPTION AND COMMENTS   In 1835, Dr. Elisha Mitchell, a science professor at the University of North Carolina, visited this mountain and measured its height at 6,476 feet—off by a few hundred feet, but enough to verify that the mountain is higher than Grandfather Mountain, which until then was assumed to be the highest peak in North Carolina.

Subsequently, Dr. Mitchell honed his estimate to within 12 feet of the mountain's actual height. Today, the peak offers outstanding views of the western North Carolina mountains—and a lesson on the effects of air pollution on trees: Many of the trees on Mount Mitchell are dying.

TOURING TIPS   Bundle up; the summit usually is cold and windy. A concession stand offering light snacks, crafts, and books is open daily from June 1 through Labor Day and on weekends through late October. The grave of Dr. Mitchell is at the foot of the stone observation tower.

OTHER THINGS TO DO NEARBY   A restaurant is located about a mile from the summit and is open from mid-May through late October. For some unusual tent camping, try the campground, also about a mile below the summit. Nine sites with spectacular views are available from May 1 through October 31, weather permitting. Modern rest rooms are on-site, but no hot showers. No reservations accepted. See our section on camping for more information.

The Tweetsie Railroad

Type of Attraction: A train pulled by a coal-fired steam locomotive that will delight youngsters; a Wild West theme park. A self-guided tour.

Location: Blowing Rock, North Carolina 28605.

Admission: $12.95 for adults; $10.95 for seniors and children ages 4–12. After September 4 through October 31, rates are reduced to $10 for adults and $8 for children and seniors; some rides and entertainment may not be available weekdays in the fall.

Hours: 9 A.M. to 6 P.M. daily from May 21 through September 4; 9 A.M. to 6 P.M. on weekends and 9 A.M. to 5 P.M. weekdays September 5 through October 31. Closed in the winter.

Phone: (800) 526-5740, (704) 264-9061

When to Go: Any time. During afternoons in the first two weeks of July, visitors may have to wait up to 30 minutes to board the train.

Special Comments: Folks who arrive after 3 P.M. can tour the park the next day without buying another ticket.

Overall Appeal by Age Group:

Pre-school	Grade School	Teens	Young Adults	Over 30	Senior Citizens
★★★★★	★★★★★	★★★	★★	★	★

Author's Rating: Pure bliss for the ankle-biter set; pure corn for everyone else. ★

How Much Time to Allow: A half day or longer.

DESCRIPTION AND COMMENTS   A 20-minute ride on a train pulled by a steam locomotive, Indian attacks, and gun fights are the main events at this western theme park. Other activities in the kid-oriented park include a ski lift ride to Mouse Mountain, featuring kiddy rides, a petting zoo, face painting, gold panning, a snack bar, and a carnival with rides and an arcade. There's also live entertainment, a small railroad museum, and crafts offered for sale. The admission price covers the cost of all activities.

TOURING TIPS   If it's peak tourist season, try to arrive in the morning and ride the train first. Small children may be frightened by the "gunfire" during the comic gun battles that take place along the ride, and the huffing and loud whistle of the train.

OTHER THINGS TO DO NEARBY   Boone is a college town with lodging, restaurants, and shopping. Blowing Rock, a scenic overlook billed as North Carolina's oldest tourist attraction, is a few miles south on US 321.

Just down the road (within sight of the Tweetsie Railroad) are three minor attractions: **Mystery Hill**, a roadside carnival attraction featuring a bunch of optical illusions and a disconcerting room built on a slant; the **Appalachian Heritage Museum,** an interesting, but small, peek at the life of a wealthy Boone family at the turn of the century; and the **Military Museum,** a tasteless and sloppy collection of military firepower and ammo boxes for sale. Admission to all three attractions is $5.99 for adults, $4.99 for seniors, and $3.99 for children ages 6–11.

PART ELEVEN:
The Blue Ridge Mountains
of Virginia—Zone 8

A Brief History and Orientation

From Front Royal, just over an hour's drive west of Washington, D.C., to the North Carolina state line more than 300 miles to the south, the Blue Ridge Mountains form the eastern rampart of the great Appalachian Mountains in Virginia.

With its close proximity to the megalopolis on the East Coast, this long, slender mountain range is a popular outdoor recreation mecca *par excellance* that separates Virginia's rolling Piedmont from the lush Shenandoah Valley beyond. The Piedmont, the mountains, and the valley have a worldwide reputation for their natural beauty; they entice visitors to enjoy scenic drives, hiking, bicycling, river rafting, and just about anything that's fun to do outdoors.

The Blue Ridge's most famous man-made feature is Skyline Drive, a 105-mile scenic highway that follows the high mountain ridge from Front Royal to Waynesboro, where it meets the Blue Ridge Parkway. From there, the road continues south along the mountain crest for 469 miles to Great Smoky Mountains National Park on the Tennessee–North Carolina state line.

Designed for relaxed motor touring, the two-lane road is lined with scenic overlooks, visitor centers, restaurants and coffee bars, and lodging. Administered by the National Park Service, both roads are decidedly noncommercial routes: No billboards get in the way to mar the views.

A National Park

South of Front Royal is Shenandoah National Park, which lies astride a beautiful section of the Blue Ridge. Providing vistas of the spectacular landscape is Skyline Drive, which winds along the Blue Ridge for the length of the park. Many parking overlooks present panoramas of the Piedmont to the east and the Shenandoah Valley to the west.

Park visitor centers at Dickey Ridge (milepost 4) and Big Meadows (milepost 50) provide visitors with information, interpretive exhibits, and ranger programs such as campfire talks, hikes, and demonstrations. Family campgrounds are located at Big Meadows, Lewis Mountain (milepost 57), and Loft Mountain (milepost 79). More than 500 miles of hiking trails await those willing to leave their cars and explore the lush woodlands that carpet the mountains.

Unlike amenity-less Smoky Mountain National Park, visitors don't have to rough it when staying overnight in Shenandoah. Comfortable lodging and restaurants are located at Skyland Lodge (milepost 41–43) and at Big Meadows Lodge (milepost 51). In addition, cottages are available for rent at Lewis Mountain (milepost 57).

Daytrippers

Shenandoah also attracts hordes of daytrippers from Washington, D.C., and its suburbs, as well as Richmond and Baltimore. While it makes for a long day, folks living two to three hours from the park can enjoy some of the prettiest mountain scenery in the United States and still sleep in their own beds.

One-day visitors from Washington and points north should take I-66 to the Front Royal entrance to the park; visitors from D.C.'s Virginia suburbs and points south can enter the park at Thornton Gap on US 211, west of Warrenton. From Richmond, take I-64 west to Waynesboro and enter the park at its southern entrance.

Two National Forests

South of Shenandoah National Park, the Blue Ridge Parkway enters George Washington National Forest for more mountain vistas. The St. Mary's Wilderness is 6,700 acres of solitude and spectacular scenery for hikers, campers, and anglers. Crabtree Falls consists of five cascading waterfalls that are the highest in Virginia's Blue Ridge. Sherando Lake, four and a half miles from the Parkway, offers swimming, boating, and hiking in a beautiful mountain setting.

Between Roanoke and Lexington, the Parkway passes through a segment of Jefferson National Forest containing the James River Face Wilderness, an 8,703-acre area set aside and managed to retain its wilderness character. It's closed to vehicles and only accessible by foot.

At the Peaks of Otter, a popular tourist spot since the days of Thomas Jefferson, visitors can ride a shuttle bus to Sharp Top and a splendid mountain vista. South of Roanoke on the Blue Ridge Parkway, motorists can explore Mabry Mill on a short trail that takes them to a gristmill, sawmill, blacksmith shop, and other outdoor exhibits. In the summer and fall, old-time skills are demonstrated.

Off the Ridge

There's more to a visit to the Blue Ridge Mountains than scenic drives, hiking, and fresh mountain air. Both the Piedmont to the east and the Shenandoah Valley to the west offer visitors a wide variety of things to do and see. Not only that, sometimes it's nice to break up a long drive along the mountains' crest with a side trip off the ridge.

Luray Caverns in Luray offer some spectacular scenery below ground, while whitewater rafters can get an adrenaline high in the Shenandoah River. In New Market you can explore a Civil War battlefield and museum, while Staunton (pronounced "Stanton") features the birthplace of Woodrow Wilson and the Museum of American Frontier Culture.

East of the Blue Ridge, Charlottesville offers visitors a taste of sophistication. Here you'll find Monticello (the neoclassical home of Thomas Jefferson) and the University of Virginia, which the United States' third president founded. The city also hosts upscale restaurants, lodging, and shopping.

Charlottesville has been discovered. The area's combination of beautiful countryside and a cosmopolitan atmosphere attracts celebrity residents such as Sissy Spacek, Jessica Lange and Sam Shepard, and Rita Mae Brown.

Lexington, the location of Washington and Lee University and the Virginia Military Institute (VMI), is a charming town on the other side of the mountains that is awash in history. General Stonewall Jackson taught at VMI before joining the Confederate army and embarking on his successful Shenandoah Valley Campaign of 1862. You can visit the house he lived in and his grave.

Natural Bridge, one of the Seven Natural Wonders of the World, is a short drive south of Lexington. It's a piece of real estate with an impressive pedigree: George Washington surveyed the property, and

Thomas Jefferson once owned it. Nearby is a wax museum, caverns, and a zoo.

Roanoke is the largest city close to the Blue Ridge Parkway and offers plenty of excuses to get off the ridge. Museums, a wide array of restaurants, a mountaintop zoo, and Virginia's oldest farmers market are some of the attractions to this modern, upbeat city.

Below Roanoke, the Blue Ridge Parkway continues for 90 miles or so on its way to North Carolina. Due to its relative remoteness, this stretch is one of the least visited sections of the scenic highway. It's also one of the most beautiful, and worth the time and effort to do a leisurely exploration.

—— *History*

Early Settlers

It took more than 100 years for Virginia's first settlers to cast their eyes westward away from the flat Tidewater to the rolling Piedmont and the Blue Ridge Mountains. While explorers first penetrated the Shenandoah Valley in the late 1600s, settlers didn't arrive until the early 1700s. While some of them entered the valley through passes in the high mountains, the majority came southwestward from Pennsylvania and Maryland through the parallel ridges that define the valley.

They came to a valley that virtually was uninhabited. Native Americans had lived in the Shenandoah Valley for at least 10,000 years, but had abandoned it about the time the Europeans arrived. English settlers from Virginia, as well as German-speaking and Scots-Irish immigrants, bought cheap land and brought with them an Old World heritage reflected in specific housing styles and farming methods.

War

In the early years, frontier life was often violent. The French and Indian War of 1754–63 allied settlers with British redcoats fighting the French and their Native American allies in their quest for controlling the North American continent.

George Washington helped train a local militia. (You can see his colonial office in Winchester.) More than 100 people were killed in

Indian raids, and the population of the valley dropped as some settlers fled for safer country east of the Blue Ridge.

While no major engagements of the War of American Independence took place in the Shenandoah Valley or in the Blue Ridge Mountains, the people who lived in the valley had been agitating for independence since before the Declaration of Independence was signed in 1776. More than 500 commissioned officers from the valley served in the Continental Army, while wagon trains and cattle drives from the valley kept the army supplied throughout the war with flour and grain.

Place names in the Shenandoah Valley also reflect its involvement in the American revolution. Lexington is named in honor of Lexington, Massachusetts, where the Revolutionary War began, while Waynesboro was named for General "Mad" Anthony Wayne.

The Civil War

During the Civil War, soldiers who didn't agree with the conflict hid out in the Blue Ridge Mountains. One small battle occurred in today's Shenandoah National Park at Overall Run (milepost 22).

To the west, the Shenandoah Valley played a vital role in the Confederacy's success or failure in the war as a supplier of food and of iron for munitions. Its close proximity to Washington, D.C., and the rebel capital in Richmond also added to its strategic importance.

One of the greatest campaigns of the war occurred in 1862 when General Stonewall Jackson defeated an army ten times larger than his, securing the valley's resources—only temporarily, it turned out—and diverting Union pressure from Richmond. Less than a year later, Jackson was killed accidentally by friendly fire at the Battle of Chancellorsville and died on May 10, 1863.

Later, the Shenandoah Valley was ravaged by invading Union armies in 1864. The "Breadbasket of the Confederacy" was plundered and burned, and Union General Philip Sheridan reported to his superiors that "a crow would perish in the valley."

Following the war, the valley recovered and returned to its primary economic strength: agriculture. In the mountains, however, things were different. By 1900, many of their natural resources were depleted following an active period of mining of manganese, iron, and copper, as well as timbering.

A National Park

The soil in the Blue Ridge was badly eroded, and people kept moving up the slopes in search of arable land. By 1925, about half the people had moved off the ridge, and plans were begun for establishing a national park, which was dedicated in July 1936 by President Franklin D. Roosevelt. Since then, the wilderness has returned with a surprising swiftness, making Shenandoah one of the most popular parks in the national park system.

To the east and west of the Blue Ridge, the Piedmont and Shenandoah Valley are bustling regions with mixed economies relying on agriculture, manufacturing, and tourism. It's a country of century-old barns standing next to superhighways, small villages that virtually look unchanged since Civil War days, and rolling horse farms crowding growing thriving cities such as Roanoke, Harrisonburg, Charlottesville, and Staunton.

—— Major Roads

For those not in a rush and looking for lots of scenery, Skyline Drive and the Blue Ridge Parkway are the *crème de la crème* roads in the area. More than 300 miles of serpentine mountaintop roadway follow the Blue Ridge in Virginia as it links Shenandoah National Park to Great Smoky Mountains National Park to the south.

When planning a drive along the roads, keep in mind that the toll is $5 to get on Skyline Drive and there are only four exits; the Blue Ridge Parkway is free and is intersected by many state roads and highways.

Paralleling the Blue Ridge Mountains to the west is I-81, which drops down from Maryland and Pennsylvania (and a tiny slice of West Virginia) through the Shenandoah Valley on its way to Tennessee; this is the fast route to Great Smoky. The old Valley Turnpike, US 11, shadows the interstate as it passes through the Shenandoah Valley.

I-66 connects Washington's Capital Beltway with I-81 just past Front Royal, where Skyline Drive begins. US 29 parallels the mountains in the east from Warrenton to Lynchburg; US 340 follows the ridge on the west from Front Royal, Luray, and Elkton to Waynesboro.

I-64 connects Richmond, the state capital, with Charlottesville, Waynesboro, and Staunton, where it meets I-81. From there, I-64 doubles up with I-81 south to Lexington, where I-64 hangs a right and heads west to Clifton Forge and into West Virginia.

Roads that cross the Blue Ridge from east to west include VA 7, which connects Washington's Northern Virginia suburbs to Leesburg and Winchester. Farther south, US 211 connects Warrenton in the Piedmont to Luray and New Market in Shenandoah Valley; it crosses Skyline Drive at Thornton Gap, one of four entrance stations to Shenandoah National Park.

US 460 runs west from Lynchburg to Roanoke, before continuing to Blacksburg and into West Virginia. I-77 crosses the Blue Ridge Parkway just above the North Carolina state line midway between Charlotte, North Carolina, and Charleston, West Virginia.

—— *A Self-Contained Region*

Virginia's Blue Ridge Mountains and the adjacent Piedmont and Shenandoah Valley offer visitors enough amenities to qualify as a completely self-contained region. Unlike amenity-less Great Smoky Mountains National Park to the south, Shenandoah National Park offers lodging, food, gasoline, and limited shopping right on Skyline Drive.

And if the lodges on Skyline Drive are booked? Nearby towns such as Front Royal, Luray, Harrisonburg, Staunton, Charlottesville, Lexington, and Roanoke offer plenty of lodging, places to eat, and things to do and see. The geography of the mountains and the Shenandoah Valley work to the visitor's advantage: Both are long and skinny, making it quick and easy to jump on or off the ridge.

Zone 8 is northeast of Zone 7 (North Carolina's Blue Ridge Mountains). The stretch of the Blue Ridge Parkway from Roanoke to Boone is relatively remote and isolated, with lots of views of high-altitude farmland—and no major attractions. As a result, just about the only people who make the jump between Zones 7 and 8 are folks on a long tour of the scenic highway. The nearest major cities to Zone 8 are Washington, D.C. and Richmond to the east, and Roanoke, which sits in the shadow of the Blue Ridge to the west.

Outdoor Recreation and Activities

—— Camping

Shenandoah National Park

Three developed campgrounds are in the park, all located along Skyline Drive: **Big Meadows** (milepost 51), **Lewis Mountain** (milepost 57), and **Loft Mountain** (milepost 79). All the campgrounds are open from late May through October and feature separate tent and RV areas (but no hookups), flush toilets and showers, and a 14-day limit. The fee is $12 a night. Note: The showers aren't free; it's $1 for five minutes. Bring lots of quarters.

Big Meadows is the most popular campground by far and the only one requiring reservations; call (800) 365-CAMP up to eight weeks in advance. Our favorite, however, is Loft Mountain, which boasts private, wooded tent sites along the perimeter of the campground.

George Washington National Forest

Sherando Lake Recreation Area features a lovely campground for tent campers. One loop with 37 sites is wooded; some have stone-bordered tent sites and stone stairs built by the Civilian Conservation Corps in the 1930s. Two smaller loops have open sites along a tumbling mountain stream. The recreation area, which includes a swimming beach on a mountain lake, fishing, and hiking is located four and a half miles off the Blue Ridge Parkway at milepost 16 (turn onto VA 814 and follow the signs).

The U.S. Forest Service campground is open from April through October; camping is $10 a night. Hot showers are available at the bathhouse near the lake (not convenient, but free).

—— *Hiking*

From Front Royal south to Roanoke, the Appalachian Trail is the central link to hundreds of miles of trails in the Blue Ridge Mountains. On longer hikes and backpacking trips in Shenandoah National Forest, the high trail that follows the ridge makes it possible to create circuit loops through the forests.

In addition, folks looking for short walks, strolls to overlooks, and nature trails will find plenty of each in Shenandoah National Park, George Washington National Forest, and Jefferson National Forest.

In Shenandoah, the color of the blazes painted on trees to mark the trails indicates the trail type. *Red-orange blazes* indicate the park boundary. *White blazes* are used on the Appalachian Trail. *Yellow blazes* are used to indicate trails open to both hikers and horseback riders. *Blue blazes* are for hikers only; unblazed trails are not maintained and may be difficult to follow. Leave them to experienced hikers.

With the exception of self-guided nature trails, we recommend picking up a trail map at one of the visitor centers before attempting a hike; it's beyond the scope of any guidebook to provide the detailed information you need to navigate the back country. You also can find out about local conditions, such as temporary trail closures and storm damage that might make a hike longer or more difficult.

Short Hikes and Walks

The Dickey Ridge Nature Trail at milepost four on Skyline Drive leads to an old homesite where you can see the remnants of old farm fences and a cemetery. The self-guided trail gains 310 feet of elevation in a little over one mile.

The Stony Man Nature Trail is a one-and-six-tenths-mile, self-guided hike to the second highest peak in Shenandoah (at milepost 47) on a portion of the Appalachian Trail. The elevation gain, however, is only 340 feet.

The Massanutten Story Trail is a four-tenths-mile interpretive trail suitable for wheelchairs that tells the story of Massanutten's geologic history and features an overlook of Page Valley and the Blue Ridge Mountains. From US 211 and the Massanutten Visitor Center (west

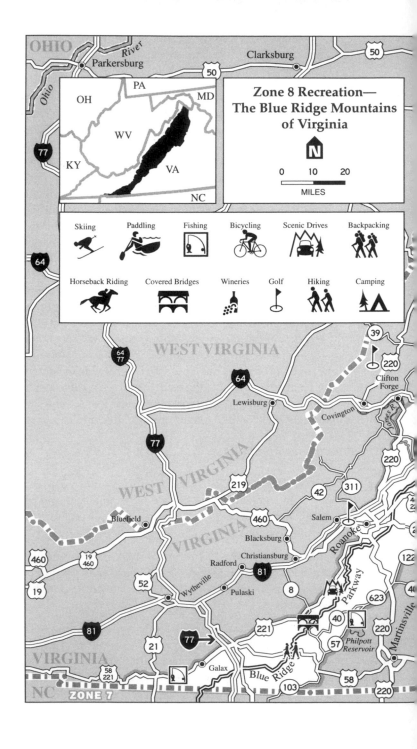

**Zone 8 Recreation—
The Blue Ridge Mountains
of Virginia**

Ⓝ

0   10   20
MILES

Skiing   Paddling   Fishing   Bicycling   Scenic Drives   Backpacking

Horseback Riding   Covered Bridges   Wineries   Golf   Hiking   Camping

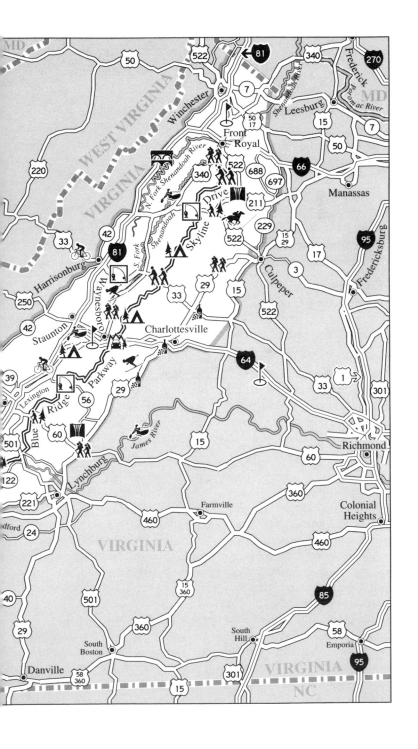

of Shenandoah National Park), take Forest Service Road 274 for one and one-half miles.

Humpback Rocks Trail at milepost 6 on the Blue Ridge Parkway adjoins the Appalachian Trail. It's a steep but well-graded trail with lots of benches along the way. The one-mile trail leads to a terrific view of the Shenandoah Valley.

Moderate Hikes

Hawksbill Mountain Summit (at milepost 45 on Skyline Drive) is a steep hike to the park's highest point, 4049 feet—and a great view. This hike is one and seven-tenths miles, and the elevation gain is 690 feet.

Dark Hollow Falls, at milepost 50, is the shortest trail in Shenandoah National Park leading to a waterfall. Dark Hollow Falls cascade 70 feet over a series of terraced drops. The hike is one and a half miles with an elevation gain of 440 feet.

Crabtree Falls Trail features a series of five major cascades and a number of smaller ones that fall a total of 1,200 feet. Hikers are treated to scenic views of the falls from overlooks that start only 700 feet from the lower parking lot. The peak season for viewing the falls is winter through spring, when water levels are high. The trail is nearly three miles one-way and reached from VA 56, near milepost 30 on the Blue Ridge Parkway.

Strenuous Hikes

Little Devils Stairs.   This aptly named trail is a steep scramble up a narrow canyon lined with sheer cliffs; it's also dangerously slippery in wet and icy weather. We suggest doing a five-and-a-half-mile hike starting outside the park that gets the hard work out of the way first so you can descend to your car. Hikers who enjoy a challenge in spectacular settings will love this one.

To reach the foot of the Little Devils Stair Trail, take US 211 two miles northeast of Sperryville (on the eastern approach to Shenandoah National Park) and turn left on VA 622. Go two miles and turn left on VA 614. The parking area is about three miles ahead on the right; the blue-blazed trail starts from the lot.

Whiteoak Canyon. This is one of the most popular and wildly scenic hikes in Shenandoah National Park (at milepost 42, across from Skyland). The trail features spectacular waterfall views and the ancient Limberlost hemlocks, the largest stand of virgin hemlock in the park. Whiteoak Run cuts a steep canyon on its way to Old Rag Valley and includes six waterfalls (all more than 50 feet high) in a stretch of one and three-tenths miles. The trail drops 2,000 feet before reaching the last waterfall. The total distance is a little over seven miles.

Rip Rap Trail. Located at milepost 90 in Shenandoah National Park, this is a circular trail to Rip Rap Hollow, a wild, picturesque ravine west of the main ridge. You can start a circuit hike, which runs nine and three-tenths miles with a total elevation change of 2,030 feet, from the Rip Rap Parking Area at milepost 90 on Skyline Drive.

Take the Appalachian Trail north for four-tenths of a mile and turn left onto the blue-blazed Rip Rap Trail. Then turn left onto Wildcat Ridge Trail and meet the Appalachian Trail again, a little over six miles into the hike. Then turn left onto the Appalachian Trail (north) and hike back to your car.

Old Rag Mountain Circuit. Old Rag (altitude 3,291 feet) is the single most spectacular peak in Virginia's Blue Ridge and rewards hikers with outstanding panoramic views of the Blue Ridge Mountains to the west. Two trails lead to the summit, making a circuit hike possible.

The Ridge Trail follows the mountain's ridge for a mile. It's steep and strenuous, requiring the use of handholds and a lot of scrambling across bare rock. After enjoying the view from the summit, return on the Saddle Trail and the Weakley Hollow Fire Road. Note: This is an extremely popular hike and the mountain gets positively crowded on weekends. For the most enjoyment, hike Old Rag on a weekday.

The hike starts in Nethers, on the eastern edge of the park. Directions: Take VA 522 south from Sperryville (on US 211 east of Thornton Gap); in eight-tenths of a mile, turn right onto VA 231. At eight and three-tenths miles, cross the Hughes River and turn right onto VA 602. The road will change route numbers several times; just remember not to cross the Hughes River again and you'll be okay.

Look for the overflow parking lot; if it's a weekend, park here. During the week, continue another eight-tenths of a mile where there's a lot at the beginning of the circuit hike. The blue-blazed Ridge Trail starts at the end of the road, to the left.

—— Backpacking

Shenandoah National Park

Free back-country permits are required for overnight treks along the 500 miles of trails inside the park. Pick one up at the park headquarters in Luray, visitor centers along Skyline Drive, the Thornton Gap Information Center (where US 211 crosses Skyline Drive), or an entrance station.

Things to see and explore along the trails include the crumbling remains of old mountain cabins from the days before the mountains became a park, Camp Hoover (the weekend White House of President Herbert Hoover, located at the end of the Mill Prong Trail at milepost 52), and more than 100 cemeteries scattered throughout the park.

For more than an overnighter, the central and southern sections of the park offer more possibilities for multiday hikes. The northern section, while pretty, is steeper and narrower than the rest of the park, which limits your choices of trails to explore.

In the central section, a maze of trails that include Whiteoak Canyon, Nicholson Hollow, Catlett Mountain, Hazel Mountain, and Hot-Short Mountain trails can be linked together to provide nearly endless opportunities for multiday backpacking treks. Near Big Meadows, intrepid backpackers can explore Dark Hollow, Mill Prong, the Appalachian, and Lewis Spring Falls trails.

The southern section has a wilder, more remote feel than the rest of the park. Rip Rap Hollow, Trayfoot Mountain, and Rockytop trails are all linked by the Appalachian Trail and offer plenty of miles to stretch your legs on long—and strenuous—backpacking trips.

George Washington National Forest

The St. Mary's Wilderness (9,385 acres) is the largest designated wilderness in Virginia, offering a number of possibilities for overnight hikes. To avoid heavy traffic (both foot and car), enter the area from the Blue Ridge Parkway at the Fork Mountain Overlook near milepost 23; take either the Mine Bank Trail or Bald Mountain Trail. The Green Pond Trail has some nice camping spots.

—— *Canoeing, Kayaking, and Rafting*

While canoe rentals are available on the Maury, the upper James, and the Shenandoah rivers in the Virginia Blue Ridge (Zone 8), there are no guided raft trips. These rivers are free flowing and can be run most of the year, but probably are best in the late spring through the end of June. Though there is some mild whitewater on the sections served by canoe liveries, the trips can best be characterized as scenic Class I–II floats, running past cliffs and through scenic woodlands and farms. The outfitter rents you equipment, transports you to the put-in (launching site), and then picks you up at the take-out when you have completed your run.

Both day trips and overnights are available. You can choose a trip ranging from one and a half miles to more than 50 miles. For detailed information on these and other area rivers, check our list of recommended reading for canoeing, kayaking, and rafting on pages 76–77.

The upper James and the Maury rivers are situated in western Virginia in the area where I-64 and I-81 intersect. The middle James is about 65 miles west of Richmond near Scottville, Virginia. The Shenandoah is west of Washington, D.C., and roughly parallels (but does not run next to) the Blue Ridge Parkway and I-81.

Outfitters on the James and Maury include:

James River Basin Canoe Livery	(703) 261-7334
James River Runners, Inc.	(804) 286-2338

Outfitters on the Shenandoah include:

Blue Ridge Outfitters	(304) 725-3444
Downriver Canoe Company	(703) 635-5526
Front Royal Canoe Company	(703) 635-5440
Massanutten Canoe Company	(703) 636-4724
River & Trail Outfitters	(301) 695-5177
Shenandoah River Outfitters	(703) 743-4159
River Rental & Outfitters	(703) 635-5050
River Riders	(304) 535-2663

——— *Fishing*

Trout Fishing

As many as 40 trout streams are open for fishing from the third Saturday in March through October 15 in **Shenandoah National Park,** where anglers can fish one of the last completely protected strongholds of the native eastern brook trout. Anglers between 16 and 65 must possess a valid Virginia fishing license, which costs $30 a year for nonresidents or $6 for five consecutive days.

Licenses are available at Panorama, Big Meadows, and Loft Mountain along Skyline Drive, or in local sporting goods stores off the ridge. More restrictions: Only artificial lures with a single hook may be used, and the limit is five trout per day; each must be at least eight inches in length. Check with park authorities to see which streams are open on your visit.

All the streams in the park feature steep gradients and alternating rapids and pools. Most are remote, requiring hikes of various lengths. Usually, the more effort it takes to reach a stream, the less fishing pressure; be prepared for strenuous hikes of one to three hours to reach the really good spots.

Spring draws many people to Shenandoah, and they're rarely disappointed; it's not uncommon to catch 30 or 40 fish in a day. After May, the stream levels drop and the fishing gets tougher.

The better known streams in the park are the Rapidan (where President Herbert Hoover kept a camp and regularly fished the stream), Staunton, Rose, Hughes, Conway, and Thornton rivers, as well as Hawksbill Creek, Big Run, Jeremy's Run, and Ivy Creek.

For the inside scoop on fly-fishing in Shenandoah, contact Harry Murray, a pharmacist in Edinburg, Virginia, who is also a fishing author and guide. His book, *Trout Fishing in Shenandoah National Park,* provides locations and access points, as well as discussions on successful angling techniques. He also offers fly-fishing clinics through the year. Contact him at P.O. Box 156, Edinburg, VA 22824; phone (703) 984-4212.

Lake Fishing

Lake Sherando, four and a half miles from the Blue Ridge Parkway at milepost 16, has been stocked with walleyes since 1988, while bluegill and red-ear sunfish angling is steady. You'll also find channel catfish and grass carp, which have been introduced to control aquatic vegetation.

Lake Shenandoah is a 37-acre lake six miles east of Harrisonburg loaded with largemouth bass, bluegills, pumpkinseed sunfish, crappie, channel catfish, and muskie. Anglers will find an abundance of small sunfish ready to bite almost anything. Fishing for largemouth bass can be difficult, but a few big ones are landed each year. Channel catfish and muskie are stocked in the lake, and many are growing to trophy size.

Smith Mountain Lake, east of Roanoke and the Blue Ridge Parkway, is one of Virginia's most popular fishing lakes. The 20,000-acre lake yields catfish, crappie, largemouth bass, muskie, smallmouth bass, striped bass, sunfish, walleye, white bass, and yellow perch.

Philpott Reservoir, a 2,880-acre lake located east of the Blue Ridge Parkway and south of Roanoke, is stocked with trout, as well as catfish, crappie, largemouth and smallmouth bass, sunfish, and walleye. Trout can be caught throughout the lake during spring, fall, and winter, but during the summer you've got to fish deep at night. Philpott has a reputation for producing some of the larger rainbow trout taken each year in Virginia, with catches of up to seven or eight pounds.

River Fishing

The **South Fork of the Shenandoah River** contains smallmouth and largemouth bass, rock bass, redbreast sunfish, bluegill, muskie, and channel catfish. Bass are abundant, and catch rates are high. Panfishing, local anglers report, is excellent.

The **Maury River** is excellent for float fishing from Rockbridge Baths downstream to Glasgow (south of Lexington). There's a ramp at Buena Vista under old US 60 and public access at various parks and waysides for cartops and canoes. The dam at Lexington has excellent smallmouth bass and redbreast sunfish opportunities.

Muskie is the highlight of **New River** angling near the Virginia–North Carolina state line. The state record, 45 pounds, came out of the New in 1989. Walleyes run up the river out of Claytor Lake as early as February, as do white bass in April and May. Virginia and North Carolina state fishing licenses and permits are honored on the mainstream portion of the river between the confluence of the North and South forks of the New River in North Carolina downstream to the confluence of the New and Little rivers in Virginia.

—— Bicycling

Road Riding

In Shenandoah National Park, it's one of those good news/bad news scenarios. The good news: The 105-mile **Skyline Drive** is a delightful spin for fit riders who love cranking out the miles on smooth asphalt and savoring great mountain scenery.

The bad news: Traffic is really heavy during warm weather, and, while it's still legal to bike the highway, park officials would just as soon you wouldn't. We agree. There is a solution: Go south and spin your cranks on the **Blue Ridge Parkway.** The traffic is significantly lighter, and the scenery is just as good.

Waynesboro Loop. A popular 40-mile ride (for strong riders only) starts in Waynesboro: Climb Afton Mountain on US 250 (a 580-foot vertical climb in three miles) and turn right onto the Blue Ridge Parkway. Continue for about 17 miles of fantastic scenery and turn right onto VA 814 for a three-and-eight-tenths-mile descent; check your brakes first.

VA 814 becomes VA 664; continue straight. You can stop for a swim at Sherando Lake Recreation Area. Eight miles later, bear right at a bend in the road onto VA 624, which takes you back into Waynesboro.

Rides off the Ridge. To the west of the Blue Ridge Mountains is the **Shenandoah Valley**, offering some of the most gorgeous road riding in the United States. But there's not much flat riding to be found; local cyclists say the rolling, sometimes steep, hills in the valley lend to its unique character. Keep that in mind if you're a novice or it's early in the season.

South River Out-and-Back. That doesn't mean there aren't *any* flat rides. In Lexington, you can pack a lunch from the South River Market and head north along VA 608 for eight and seven-tenths miles to the village of Marlbrook; it's one of the longest flat stretches of roadway in the valley. Find a shady spot along the South River and have a picnic. Then turn around and ride back.

Dayton Loop. Dayton, a small town west of Harrisonburg, features a moderate loop through Mennonite countryside and a view of the former home of Daniel Harrison (1749), brother of Harrisonburg's founder Thomas Harrison.

The 12-mile ride starts at the entrance to Hillandale Park on Hillandale Avenue, south of Harrisonburg. Ride east on Hillandale and turn right onto US 42 south. A half-mile after that, turn right on to VA 726; this begins a loop. Turn right onto US 33, then left onto US 726. Next is a left onto VA 701 at Cooks Creek Presbyterian Church.

In Dayton (settled in the mid-1700s), continue straight on VA 702 through town. Turn left at the stop sign onto Main Street; the Dayton Farmers Market is open Thursday through Saturday and features all kinds of Mennonite treats. Continue straight on Business 42. Cross US 42 south (be careful) and turn left onto US 42 north. In about two miles, turn left onto Hillandale Avenue to complete the ride.

Lexington Loop. More experienced riders will enjoy a 60–70 mile spin along US 39 going north out of Lexington. Then take VA 252 towards Brownsburg. To close the loop, take a left on any paved road and ride up over a ridge (the only significant climb) to VA 602. Then pick up US 39 again for the ride back into town. It's a pleasant ride, traffic is light with vistas of rolling hills and open countryside—and the road was recently repaved.

Bikers looking to explore more riding in Shenandoah should get a copy of *A Cyclist's Guide to the Shenandoah Valley* by Randy Porter and Nancy Sorrells (Shenandoah Odysseys). The book includes detailed directions on 28 rides, as well as lots of local history and flavor.

Mountain Biking

In Shenandoah National Park, it's all bad news for fat-tire cyclists: As in all national parks, bikes are banned from all trails and fire roads, with the exception of some short bike paths around Big Meadows.

George Washington National Forest. Luckily, there is plenty of riding in nearby George Washington National Forest. Between Steeles Tavern and Sherando Lake, Fire Road 42 encircles a huge area of forest containing loads of single-track trails and fire roads; just remember to keep turning right and you won't get lost. FR 42 hits FR 664 near Sherando Lake, where you can pick up the St.

Mary's Trail to a waterfall; from there, continue on the trail back to Steeles Tavern. Do the whole loop and it's about 20 miles of riding.

Goshen-Little North Mountain Wildlife Management Area. North of Lexington, this area offers plenty of easy to challenging single-track trails to explore. Take US 11 to US 39 to Lake Merriweather and park. Then explore the marked trails on Little North Mountain, located east of the lake and north of the Maury River.

For more information on mountain biking around Lexington, call R. Wane Schneiter at **Rockbridge Outfitters** in Lexington at (703) 463-1947. He's the local expert on off-road riding in the area. The shop also rents bikes and does repairs.

Massanutten Resort. A downhill ski area east of Harrisonburg off US 33, Massanutten Resort lets knob-heads bike for free on 2,000 acres of woods loaded with miles of challenging single-track trails. Don't have a bike? Then rent one from the ski resort's bike shop. Rentals are $5 an hour, $8 for two hours, $10 for four hours, and $18 hours for 24 hours. For more information, call (703) 289-9441.

—— *Horseback Riding*

In Shenandoah National Park, guided horseback rides are available at **Skyland Stables,** located at milepost 42. The rides follow designated horse trails on one-hour ($18) and two-and-a-half hour rides ($36) that depart five times daily from April through October. Half-hour pony rides for smaller children are $5. Reservations are recommended; call (703) 999-2210.

—— *Golf*

The Virginia Blue Ridge is home to the best golf in the southeastern mountains. Outstanding courses include The Homestead in Hot Springs; the Wintergreen Resort in Wintergreen, the site of the 1995 Virginia state amateur championship; the Hanging Rock Golf Club in Salem; and the Royal Virginia Golf Club in Hadensville. These and other quality golf courses in the area are profiled below.

Caverns Country Club Resort

Established: 1976
Address: US Highway 211 Bypass, Luray VA 22835
Phone: (703) 743-6551
Status: Resort course
Tees:

Championship: 6,499 yards, par 72, USGA 72, slope 117.
Men's: 6,307 yards, par 72, USGA 72, slope 115.
Ladies': 5,499 yards, par 72, USGA 72, slope 120.

Fees: $18 weekdays, $24 weekends. Cart fee, $10 per player.
Facilities: Pro shop, putting green, snack bar, tennis courts, pools, and lodging.

Countryside Golf Course

Established: 1967
Address: 1 Countryside Road, Roanoke VA 24017
Phone: (703) 563-0391
Status: Public course
Tees:

Championship: 6,852 yards, par 71, USGA 72.6, slope 118.
Men's: 6,028 yards, par 71, USGA 68.6, slope 114.
Ladies': 5,193 yards, par 71, USGA 69.8, slope 114.

Fees: $30 weekday, $35 weekend.
Facilities: Pro shop, driving range, putting green, snack bar and grill, and tennis courts.

Hanging Rock Golf Club

Established: 1990
Address: 1500 Red Lane, Salem VA 24153
Phone: (703) 389-7275
Status: Public course
Tees:

Championship: 6,828 yards, par 73, USGA 72.3, slope 125.
Men's: 6,216 yards, par 73, USGA 69.5, slope 120.

Ladies' Championship: 5,664 yards, par 73, USGA 67, slope 115.
Ladies': 4,463 yards, par 72, USGA 62.6, slope 106.

Fees: $11.50 (18 holes), $8.36 (9 holes). Carts mandatory on weekends and holidays until 1 P.M.

Facilities: Pro shop, driving range, putting green, and lessons.

The Homestead

Established: 1766

Address: P.O. Box 2000, Hot Springs VA 24445

Phone: (703) 839-5500

Status: Resort course

Tees:

Homestead Course
Men's: 6,200 yards, par 72, slope 115.
Ladies': 5,150 yards, par 72, slope 108.

Cascades Course
Championship: 6,566 yards, par 70, slope 136.
Men's: 6,280 yards, par 70, , slope 134.
Ladies': 5,448 yards, par 70, slope 137.

Lower Cascades Course
Championship: 6,619 yards, par 72, slope 127.
Men's: 6,240 yards, par 72, slope 124.
Ladies': 4,726 yards, par 72, slope 116.

Fees: $60 Homestead Course, $60 Lower Cascades Course, $85 Cascades Course. Carts mandatory.

Facilities: Pro shop, driving range, putting green, tennis courts, pools, horseback riding, health spa, and restaurant.

Mariners Landing Golf and Country Club

Established: 1993

Address: Smith Mountain Lake, Route 1, Box 119, Huddleston VA 24104

Phone: (703) 297-7882

Status: Semiprivate course

Tees:

> Championship: 6,905 yards, par 72, USGA 72.8, slope 125.
> Men's: 6,394 yards, par 72, USGA 70.8, slope 120.
> Ladies': 5,120 yards, par 72.

Fees: $15 weekdays, $18 weekends. Cart fee, $11.

Facilities: Pro shop, driving range, and snack bar.

Royal Virginia Golf Club

Established: 1993

Address: 3181 Dukes Road, Hadensville VA 23093

Phone: (804) 457-2041

Status: Public course

Tees:

> Championship: 7,104 yards, par 72, USGA 72, slope 131.
> Men's: 6,789 yards, par 72, USGA 72, slope 127.
> Ladies': 6,422 yards, par 72, USGA 72, slope 124.

Fees: $13.50 weekdays, $19.50 weekends. Cart fee, $10.50.

Facilities: Clubhouse, pro shop, snack bar, and lessons.

Shenandoah Valley Golf Club

Established: 1935

Address: Route 2, Box 1240, Front Royal VA 22630

Phone: (703) 636-4653

Status: Semiprivate course

Tees:

> Championship: 3,095 yards, par 36, USGA 69, slope 115.
> Men's: 2,911 yards, par 36, USGA 67.8, slope 113.
> Ladies': 2,454 yards, par 37, USGA 66.3, slope 114.

Fees: $22 Tuesday–Thursday, $30 Monday and Friday, $42 weekends and holidays. Carts included.

Facilities: Driving range, putting green, snack bar, conference and banquet facilities, and lodging.

Skyland Lakes Golf Course & Resort

Established: 1989
Address: Route 1, Box 178, Fancy Gap VA 24328
Phone: (703) 728-4923
Status: Public course
Tees:

Championship: 6,520 yards, par 71.
Men's: 5,955 yards, par 71.
Ladies': 5,118 yards, par 71.

Fees: $20.50 Monday–Wednesday, $21.50 Thursday and Friday, $24.50 weekends and holidays. Carts included.
Facilities: Pro shop, putting green, and snack bar.

Wintergreen Resort

Established: 1976
Address: P.O. Box 706, Wintergreen VA 22958
Phone: (804) 325-2200
Status: Resort course
Tees:

Devils Knob
Championship: 6,576 yards, par 70, USGA 72.4, slope 126.
Men's: 6,003 yards, par 70, USGA 69.8, slope 119.
Ladies': 5,101 yards, par 70, USGA 68.6, slope 118.
Stoney Creek
Championship: 7,005 yards, par 72, USGA 74, slope 132.
Men's: 6,341 yards, par 72, USGA 71.6, slope 121.
Ladies': 5,500 yards, par 72, USGA 71, slope 125.

Fees: Guests: $60.50 weekdays, $70.50 weekends. Visitors: $70.50 weekdays, $80.50 weekends. Cart included.
Facilities: Pro shop, driving range, putting green, restaurant, snack bar, tennis courts, and indoor and outdoor pools.

—— Skiing

Wintergreen Resort. Located 43 miles from Charlottesville and only 12 miles from Waynesboro and the Blue Ridge Parkway, this upscale ski resort draws downhillers from Washington, D.C., and Richmond because of its convenience and a reputation for fine skiing. Wintergreen offers 17 slopes and trails, ranging from a vast beginner's area to a three-slope complex designed for advanced skiers only. The highest vertical drop is 1,003 *continuous* feet, and the resort operates five chair lifts. Lessons, rentals, accommodations, restaurants, and shops are on site. For more information, call (800) 325-2200.

Massanutten Resort. Located ten miles east of Harrisonburg off US 33, this resort features 14 slopes on 68 acres on the southern end of Massanutten Mountain, once a haven for moonshiners. The highest vertical drop is 1,110 feet, and the resort offers snowmaking, night skiing, rentals, and instructions. One quad lift and three double lifts haul skiers up the mountain; a J-bar surface lift takes snowboarders to the top of the resort's snowboard park.

Weekday ski lift tickets are $24, and $36 on weekends and holidays. Lodging is available at Massanutten's chalets, villas, and hotels, as well as in motels ten miles away in Harrisonburg. For more information, call the resort at (703) 289-9441.

—— Covered Bridges

A few side roads in Virginia feature some covered bridges, which evoke the past. But hurry—their numbers are dwindling fast. A survey in 1936 revealed that 50 of the spans were still in use. Today, that number is down to nine; three are on private property. Three of the bridges accessible to visitors are close to the Blue Ridge Mountains.

The best known of the surviving covered bridges in the state is the **Meems Bottom Bridge** in the Shenandoah Valley. The long, 204-foot span over the North Fork of the Shenandoah River carried traffic for more than 80 years before being destroyed by vandals on Halloween 1976. After salvaging the original timbers, the bridge was reconstructed and undergirded with steel beams and concrete piers—and reopened to traffic.

The bridge is easy to reach from I-81 at exit 68 between New Market and Mount Jackson. Take VA 730 four-tenths of a mile to US 11, then go north another nine-tenths of a mile to VA 720. Then go west a short distance to the river.

The **Bob White Bridge** and the **Jack's Creek Bridge** are located near the Blue Ridge Parkway off VA 8 near milepost 165. The Bob White span is an 80-foot bridge over the Smith River built in 1921. Directions: From Woolwine on VA 8, go south one and a half miles, then east one mile on VA 618 to VA 869. Then go south a tenth of a mile to the bridge. Jack's Creek Bridge, two miles south of Woolwine, is a 48-foot span that also crosses the Smith River. It can be seen from VA 8 at its intersection with VA 615.

—— *Wineries*

Virginia wines have been a tradition since 1607, when the Jamestown settlers fermented native American grapes and made the first wine in the New World. But the real father of the state's thriving wine industry was none other than Thomas Jefferson, who, as ambassador to France for the fledgling U.S. republic, recognized the similarity of Virginia's soil and climate to the great winegrowing regions of Europe. Today the state boasts more than 42 wineries.

Folks interested in embarking on a winery tour should use centrally located, upscale Charlottesville as a base. Amenities found at many of the wineries include tours, picnic areas, tastings, and, of course, sales. Here's a list of the closest wineries to town:

Jefferson Vineyards in Charlottesville offers tastings of the largest selection of vinefera variety wines in the state. Tours are available from March through November, 11 A.M. to 5 P.M. daily, holidays excepted. For more information, call (804) 977-3042.

Totier Creek Vineyard in Charlottesville suggests you bring a picnic lunch and enjoy it on their deck. Wines from the vineyard include chardonnay, riesling, blush, merlot, and cabernet sauvignon. Tours are offered from 11 A.M. to 5 P.M. Wednesday through Sunday from March through December. Call (804) 979-7105 for more information.

Located outside Charlottesville, **Oakencroft Vineyard & Winery** produces chardonnay, sweet Virginia, cabernet sauvignon, and white-seyval wines. Free tours and tastings are offered April through December daily 11 A.M. to 5 P.M., holidays excepted. For more information, call (804) 296-4188.

Burnley Vineyards in Barboursville (15 miles northeast of Charlottesville) offers tastings and banquet rooms overlooking the Virginia countryside. The vineyard produces nine wines, including cabernet sauvignon, chardonnay, rivanna sunset (a blush), and Daniel Cellars somerset. Tours and tastings are offered Thursday through Monday, March through December, from 11 A.M. to 5 P.M. Call (703) 832-2828 for directions and more information.

Also in Barboursville is **Barboursville Vineyards**, located in the historic ruins of Governor Barbour's mansion, which was designed by Thomas Jefferson. Tours are offered Saturdays 10 A.M. to 4:30 P.M. Tastings and sales are Monday through Saturday from 10 A.M. to 5 P.M. Call (703) 832-3824 for more information.

Visitors traveling the Blue Ridge Parkway easily can jump off the scenic road and visit these convenient wineries:

Afton Mountain Vineyards touts itself as "Virginia's most beautiful farm winery." It's open from 10 A.M. to 6 P.M. daily except Tuesday; it closes at 5 P.M. in the winter and on major holidays. The winery is located a few miles southeast of Waynesboro. For more information, call (703) 456-8667.

Wintergreen Vineyards & Winery is located on a historic plantation on the South Fork of the Rockfish River adjoining Wintergreen ski resort. The winery is open daily 10 A.M. to 6 P.M. Winter hours are noon to 5 P.M.; closed Tuesdays. From the Blue Ridge Parkway, exit on VA 664 east at milepost 13; the winery is five miles on the left. Call (804) 361-2519 for more information.

—— *Scenic Drives*

Skyline Drive in Shenandoah National Park and the Blue Ridge Parkway (which follows the crest of the Blue Ridge south of Waynesboro) constitute one of the most beautiful stretches of highway in the world. But they're not fast: The speed limit in the national park is 35 mph, and 45 mph on the Blue Ridge Parkway. Often, though, it's difficult to maintain even that modest speed when you're caught behind a lumbering RV on a long grade.

While Skyline Drive and the Blue Ridge Parkway are, in fact, one continuous stretch of highway, there are more differences between them than speed limits, the status of the lands they pass through (national park and national forest), and a toll ($5 per car to get on Skyline Drive).

For one thing, Skyline Drive can be accessed only in four places: Front Royal, Thornton Gap (US 211), Swift Run Gap (US 33), and

Waynesboro. The distance from Front Royal to Thornton Gap is about 30 miles; from there to Swift Run Gap is another 30 miles; the southern entrance at Rockfish Gap is 40 miles farther. The entrance stations effectively divide the park into three sections: northern, central, and southern.

On the Blue Ridge Parkway, however, many small county and state roads, as well as federal highways and interstates, intersect the scenic road along its length. That's why jumping on the Parkway doesn't require the commitment of time required for a jaunt on Skyline Drive.

Beating the Traffic in the Fall

Another difference between the two roads is the level of traffic you'll encounter. Skyline Drive sees heavy use, especially on weekends in warm weather. In early October, it's usually bumper to bumper as Washingtonians by the thousands jump in their cars for a one-day trek to ogle the fall colors in Shenandoah National Park.

Is there any way to escape the autumn traffic jams? You bet. Shenandoah's southern section (from Swift Run Gap to Waynesboro) gets less traffic than the stretch of highway to the north. Of course, for most folks it's a longer drive, which explains the southern section's lighter use.

But if you really hate traffic and want to enjoy the fall colors without breathing exhaust fumes the whole way, go even farther south to the Blue Ridge Parkway. The road south of Waynesboro gets significantly less traffic than Skyline Drive—and the views are just as good.

Loop Drives Off Skyline Drive

While most travelers drive the scenic highways in an out-and-back configuration, it's possible to get off the high ridge and drive a loop that brings you back to your starting place without backtracking. A side trip through the Shenandoah Valley will take you past plenty of fine Virginia scenery, old farms, and quaint villages.

US 340, which parallels Skyline Drive in Shenandoah Valley, can be used as a loop all along the length of the scenic highway. Depending on where you entered Skyline Drive, drive south or north to the next entrance station and take that road west to US 340 (they all intersect with it). Then take the highway in the appropriate direction to complete your loop.

For example, if you started your loop in Waynesboro, go north on Skyline to US 33 at Swift Run Gap. Go west on US 33 until intersecting US 340 in Elkton. Then go south on US 340 and you'll come back to Waynesboro. You can get back onto Skyline Drive without paying the entrance fee for up to five days; just be sure to save your receipt.

Massanutten

Another alternative is to drive south on Skyline Drive from Front Royal and exit the park at Thornton Gap. Then take US 211 to the Massanutten Visitor Center. Massanutten is the big mountain sitting in the Shenandoah Valley that parallels the Blue Ridge in the west.

Stop in the visitor center and pick up information on George Washington National Forest, which covers almost a million acres to the west and south of Shenandoah National Park. Then take Forest Service Road 274 north for a tour of the mountain. Nature trails, interpretative trails that accommodate wheelchairs, a wildflower trail, and recreation areas for picnicking and hiking are all along the road, which starts off as gravel and changes to pavement. The road surface, by the way, is fine for passenger cars.

Along the way is Camp Roosevelt, a recreation area constructed at the site of the first Civilian Conservation Corps Camp in America; you can explore the ruins. Then continue straight into Fort Valley on VA 678. Along the way is Elizabeth Furnace, the ruins of a pig iron furnace left over from the region's flourishing iron industry a century ago. The road ends at VA 55; turn right and return to Front Royal.

The Valley Road

As beautiful and breathtakingly scenic as Skyline Drive and the Blue Ridge Parkway are, sometimes you must get off. After a while the overlooks all start looking the same.

For a change of pace, consider a drive down US 11, the main, mostly two-lane highway through the Shenandoah Valley before I-81 was built. Its history goes back to before the settlers came to the valley. The approximate route of today's US 11 was an Indian road controlled by the Iroquois nation. Then it evolved into the Great Wagon Road of the 1740s as German-speaking settlers funneled in from Pennsylvania.

Road improvements continued when a Valley Turnpike Company was formed in the 1830s. A packed-gravel road ran from Winchester 95 miles south to Staunton with toll booths every five miles. By the mid-1840s, the road was a major north-south stagecoach route. Today, a lot of history remains along US 11 as it winds through old stagecoach stops such as Greenville, Mt. Sidney, Mt. Crawford, and New Market. Traffic is light, and the countryside is gorgeous.

Loops from the Blue Ridge Parkway

South of Waynesboro, VA 56 takes a breathtaking plunge off the ridge as it switchbacks west on its way to Steeles Tavern; don't try this in a Winnebago. Just past Steeles Tavern is the Cyrus McCormick Farm, the site of an interesting slice of Shenandoah Valley history and a terrific picnic spot.

The pretty town of Lexington easily is accessible from US 60, which crosses the Blue Ridge Parkway near milepost 45. Then go south on US 11 to Natural Bridge and you'll understand why the Shenandoah Valley is famous for its natural beauty.

From Natural Bridge you can either get back on the Parkway by going east on VA 130 or continuing south on US 11 (you'll drive over Natural Bridge if you do) to Buchanan, where VA 43 takes you back up to the scenic highway.

Attractions

Abram's Delight Museum

Type of Attraction: A house built in 1754 that illustrates the rapid cultural and social evolution of early settlers of the Shenandoah Valley. A guided tour.

Location: 1340 Pleasant Valley Road, Winchester, Virginia 22601 (near the visitor center).

Admission: $3.50 for adults, $1.75 for children, $8.75 for families. Combination tickets to Abram's Delight, Stonewall Jackson's Headquarters, and George Washington's Office are $7.50 for adults over 21, $6.50 for students ages 13–21, $6.50 for seniors 60 and over, $4 for children ages 6–12, and $20 for families.

Hours: 9 A.M. to 5 P.M. daily April 1 through October.

Phone: (703) 662-6519

When to Go: Any time.

Special Comments: Two sets of stairs on the tour. The last tour is at 4:15 P.M.

Overall Appeal by Age Group:

Pre-school	Grade School	Teens	Young Adults	Over 30	Senior Citizens
★	★½	★★	★★	★★½	★★½

Author's Rating: An interesting, yet narrow, slice of early Americana. ★★½

How Much Time to Allow: One hour.

DESCRIPTION AND COMMENTS   The oldest standing house in Winchester—called the first city west of the Blue Ridge Mountains—is Abram's Delight, with two-and-a-half-foot-thick walls of native limestone. Today it's restored and furnished in colonial and Victorian style. Clothing (lots of early wedding gowns), quilts, furniture, and artifacts from the late 18th century and early 19th century fill the house.

TOURING TIPS   Tours begin anytime. Combine a visit to Abram's Delight with two other nearby Winchester destinations: Stonewall Jackson's Headquarters and George Washington's Office.

OTHER THINGS TO DO NEARBY   Downtown Winchester features a pedestrian shopping mall full of shops and restaurants. Belle Grove Plantation in Middletown, Virginia (about ten miles south of Winchester on US 11; take Exit 302 from I-81), is a restored 18th-century plantation. Thomas Jefferson helped design Belle Grove, which was completed in 1797.

Art Museum of Western Virginia

Type of Attraction: An art gallery featuring permanent and temporary exhibits of 19th-century and modern artists.

Location: First and second floors of Center in the Square, downtown Roanoke, Virginia.

Admission: Free.

Hours: 10 A.M. to 5 P.M.

Phone: (703) 342-5760

When to Go: Any time.

Special Comments: The permanent collection is on the second floor, which connects to the temporary exhibits on the first floor via stairs or elevator.

Overall Appeal by Age Group:

Pre-school	Grade School	Teens	Young Adults	Over 30	Senior Citizens
★	★★	★★¹/₂	★★★	★★★¹/₂	★★★¹/₂

Author's Rating: An attractive, but small, gallery of mostly 20th-century art. ★★★¹/₂

How Much Time to Allow: One hour.

DESCRIPTION AND COMMENTS   The collection of art on display ranges from large 19th-century landscapes, primitive folk art, and works by students, to 20th-century paintings by masters such as Rauschenberg and Johns. It's a comfortable, well-designed museum that features a few surprises, such as ancient Egyptian treasures and handmade Appalachian furniture.

TOURING TIPS   Start your visit on the second floor, where the permanent collection is on display. It's not necessary to exit to get to the first-floor, temporary exhibit; there's a staircase in the middle of the museum.

OTHER THINGS TO DO NEARBY   The Science Museum of Western Virginia and the Roanoke Valley History Museum also are located in Center in the Square. Downtown Roanoke offers a wide diversity of restaurants and shops.

Ash Lawn—Highland

Type of Attraction: A 535-acre estate that was the home of James Monroe, fifth president of the United States. A guided tour.

Location: On VA 795, two and a half miles past Monticello (three miles from Charlottesville, Virginia).

Admission: $6 for adults, $5.50 for seniors over 60, $3 for children ages 6–11. Combination discount tickets are available for touring Monticello, Ash Lawn, and Historic Michie Tavern at the Thomas Jefferson Visitors Center on Route 20 south and I-81: $17 for adults, $15.50 for seniors. The combination tickets also save you a buck on the entrance fee at Montpelier, another presidential home north of Charlottesville.

Hours: 9 A.M. to 6 P.M. March through October; 10 A.M. to 5 P.M. November through February. Closed Thanksgiving, Christmas, and New Year's days.

Phone: (804) 293-9539

When to Go: Any time. While on busy days Ash Lawn gets the overflow crowds from nearby Monticello, the wait in line for the house tour never exceeds 30 minutes.

Special Comments: There's a short set of stairs on the tour.

Overall Appeal by Age Group:

Pre-school	Grade School	Teens	Young Adults	Over 30	Senior Citizens
★	★★½	★★★	★★★½	★★★★	★★★★

Author's Rating: A refreshing contrast to overwhelming Monticello— and a fascinating glimpse of early-19th-century plantation life. ★★★★

How Much Time to Allow: 30 to 45 minutes for the house tour; another 30 minutes to explore the grounds on your own.

DESCRIPTION AND COMMENTS   James Monroe was a protege and colleague of Thomas Jefferson, and moved to this plantation to be close to his illustrious friend. (On a clear day, Monticello can be seen from the Monroe porch.) Frequent guests of the Monroes at Ash Lawn included James and Dolly Madison.

The house, unlike Jefferson-designed (and classically inspired) Monticello, grew organically, room by room. As a result, the scale of Ash Lawn is more human than the Big Guy on the Hill. Yet the building reflects federal-style elegance and design. In cool weather, costumed interpreters prepare colonial-style meals in the downstairs kitchen.

TOURING TIPS   Tours of the house, which last about 30 minutes, start every 15 minutes; groups are limited to 20. Most tours end with a demonstration of a plantation-era craft—it's really neat. Afterwards, explore the outbuildings and formal gardens in front of the house. During the summer, Ash Lawn—Highland presents evening concerts of opera and musical theater, as well as a variety of classical music, jazz, folk, and contemporary music. Call Ash Lawn—Highland for a schedule and ticket prices.

OTHER THINGS TO DO NEARBY   Monticello is two and a half miles from Ash Lawn; Michie Tavern Museum is another half mile away. Nearby Charlottesville offers restaurants, shops, and the beautiful campus of the University of Virginia (founded by Jefferson in 1819).

Confederate Museum

Type of Attraction: An old-fashioned museum of glass cases filled with personal and domestic items from the Civil War period. A self-guided tour.

Location: 95 Chester Street, Front Royal, Virginia 22630.

Admission: $2 for those 12 and over.

Hours: April 15 through November 1: 9 A.M. to 5 P.M., Monday through Saturday; noon to 5 P.M., Sunday. Open by appointment only the rest of the year.

Phone: (703) 636-6982, (703) 635-2478

When to Go: Any time.

Special Comments: A real find for both Civil War buffs and folks interested in the human side of the conflict.

Overall Appeal by Age Group:

Pre-school	Grade School	Teens	Young Adults	Over 30	Senior Citizens
★	★★	★★½	★★★	★★★★	★★★★

Author's Rating: Not just another collection of firearms. ★★★★

How Much Time to Allow: One hour.

DESCRIPTION AND COMMENTS   Browse long enough through this tiny, one-room museum crammed with display cases and you're sure to find something interesting—or even alarming.

An example: a handkerchief stained with the first blood spilled in the Civil War. When Union troops seized Alexandria, Virginia, on May 24, 1861, a small skirmish broke out as the troops took over a house still flying a Confederate flag. The proprietor was killed after firing a shotgun at a Union sergeant—and later a bystander dipped his handkerchief in the blood on the floor.

Other interesting artifacts include spurs worn by Colonel John Singleton Mosby (of Mosby's Raiders fame), authentic Civil War uniforms, a sterling silver chatelaine owned by Confederate spy Belle Boyd, a United States flag captured by Stonewall Jackson's army at the Battle of Front Royal on May 23, 1862, and faded documents and letters of participants in the conflict. This is a rewarding stop for those who take the time to nose around.

TOURING TIPS   Strike up a conversation with a staff member, who may be a descendent of a Confederate soldier: The museum is owned and operated by the Warren Rifles Chapter of the United Daughters of the Confederacy.

OTHER THINGS TO DO NEARBY   Up the street at the intersection of Royal and Chester streets is the Royal Dairy, an ice cream bar and restaurant right out of the 40s, complete with a high ceiling, a large oval counter surrounded by low stools and booths, and hustling waitresses who call you "hon." The food is cheap and good. Skyline Caverns and the northern entrance to Skyline Drive and Shenandoah National Park are located just outside Luray.

George C. Marshall Museum

Type of Attraction: A museum focusing on the life and career of America's top general in World War II.

Location: On the south end of the parade grounds on the campus of VMI.

Admission: $3 for adults, $2 for seniors, $1 for children.

Hours: 9 A.M. to 5 P.M. daily. Closed Thanksgiving, Christmas, and New Year's days. The museum closes at 4 P.M. November 1 through March 1.

Phone: (703) 463-7103

When to Go: Any time.

Special Comments: One set of steps leads to the lower level.

Overall Appeal by Age Group:

Pre-school	Grade School	Teens	Young Adults	Over 30	Senior Citizens
★	★½	★★	★★½	★★★	★★★★

Author's Rating: An interesting look at a famous American who is often overlooked. ★★★

How Much Time to Allow: One hour.

DESCRIPTION AND COMMENTS   The real jeep just inside the door will bring a smile to the faces of most folks. Yet the rest of this museum/memorial to this hero of World War II (who later served as secretary of state and defense under President Harry Truman) is distinctly serious.

The East Wing exhibits items associated with the general's early days, from his birth in 1890 to his appointment as chief of staff in 1939. The West Wing is dominated by an electric map and a taped narration on the campaigns of the Second World War. The lower level focuses on the Marshall Plan, his program for post-war European recovery. The lobby is dominated by a bronze bust of General Marshall.

TOURING TIPS   For a good overview of the impact of this noteworthy American (and winner of the Nobel Peace Prize in 1953), turn right inside the entrance and take a seat in front of the electric map. As the narration progresses, the map illuminates the theater of operation under discussion.

OTHER THINGS TO DO NEARBY   The VMI Museum is located on the northeast corner of the parade grounds. The Lee Chapel is next door on the Washington and Lee University campus. Downtown Lexington offers shopping and restaurants.

George Washington's Office Museum

Type of Attraction: A small log building used by a young George Washington from September 1755 to December 1756. Self-guided or guided tours.

Location: The corner of Braddock and Cork streets in downtown Winchester, Virginia.

Admission: $3.50 for adults, $1.75 for children, $8.75 for families. Combination tickets to Abram's Delight, Stonewall Jackson's Headquarters, and George Washington's Office are $7.50 for adults over 21, $6.50 for students ages 13–21, $6.50 for seniors 60 and over, $4 for children ages 6–12, and $20 for families.

Hours: 9 A.M. to 5 P.M. daily April 1 through October.

Phone: (703) 662-4412

When to Go: Any time.

Special Comments: The last tour of the day is at 4:30 P.M.

Overall Appeal by Age Group:

Pre-school	Grade School	Teens	Young Adults	Over 30	Senior Citizens
★	★★	★★	★★	★★	★★

Author's Rating: A minor attraction. ★★

How Much Time to Allow: 30 minutes.

DESCRIPTION AND COMMENTS Colonel George Washington, a 24-year-old officer in the Virginia Militia, served in the Winchester area for almost ten years. This crude cabin served as his office during the construction of Fort Loudoun on the highest hill in what is today Winchester (the fort is long gone). Today the only remnant of Washington's Winchester days is this cabin. Other items on display in this tiny museum include a model of Fort Loudoun, an original land grant from the British crown, a "Brown Bess" musket and bayonet, and some Civil War artifacts.

TOURING TIPS Look for a lock of Washington's reddish hair in one of the glass display cases.

OTHER THINGS TO DO NEARBY Downtown Winchester features a pedestrian shopping mall full of shops and restaurants. Belle Grove Plantation in Middletown, Virginia (about ten miles south of Winchester on US 11; take Exit 302 from I-81), is a restored 18th-century plantation. Thomas Jefferson helped design Belle Grove, which was completed in 1797.

Historic Michie Tavern Museum

Type of Attraction: An authentic 18th-century inn that shows how ordinary people lived in early Virginia. A guided tour.

Location: Three miles south of Charlottesville, Virginia, on VA 53 (half a mile before Monticello).

Admission: $5 for adults; $4.50 for seniors, students, and military personnel; $1.50 for children. Combination discount tickets are available for touring Monticello, Ash Lawn, and Historic Michie Tavern at the Thomas Jefferson Visitors Center at Route 20 South and I-81: $17 for adults, $15.50 for seniors. The combination tickets also save you a buck on the entrance fee at Montpelier, a presidential estate north of Charlottesville.

Hours: 9 A.M. to 5 P.M. daily.

Phone: (804) 977-1234

When to Go: Any time.

Special Comments: Lots of steep stairs in the tavern and steep, narrow paths lead to and from the outbuildings.

Overall Appeal by Age Group:

Pre-school	Grade School	Teens	Young Adults	Over 30	Senior Citizens
★	★★	★★½	★★½	★★★	★★★

Author's Rating: An interesting look at how lesser mortals than Jefferson, Monroe, and Madison worked and lived in the early days of America. ★★★

How Much Time to Allow: 30-minute tours start every eight minutes; allow another 30 minutes to explore the gristmill and shop.

DESCRIPTION AND COMMENTS   In 1927 Michie (pronounced "mickey") Tavern was transported piece by piece from a site 17 miles to the northwest and reconstructed on this location near Monticello. Four furnished rooms illustrate how the tavern served as the center of an early American community. Many artifacts and furniture on display are more than 200 years old. Outside the tavern, visitors may peek into a variety of dependent outbuildings, then move to the basement to view an exhibit on Virginia winemaking.

TOURING TIPS   While visitors are greeted by a museum employee in period dress as they wait for the start of their tour, regrettably the tour itself is guideless: A taped narrative in each room explains its functions and artifacts. It's disconcerting and makes you long for the human touch of a living, breathing tour guide. After the tour, you're free to visit the gristmill and the gift shop, which features a wide variety of local foods, wines, beers, and ales.

OTHER THINGS TO DO NEARBY   "The Ordinary," a restaurant in a 200-year-old log cabin next door, serves a luncheon buffet daily from 11:30 A.M. to 3 P.M. The bill of fare features typical (and bland) dishes of the colonial period. The price is $8.95 for adults and $3.50 for children, not including beverage, dessert, tax, and tip. Monticello and Ash Lawn are only minutes away by car.

Lee Chapel and Museum

Type of Attraction: A lovely Victorian chapel on the campus of Washington and Lee University; the Lee family crypt containing the remains of Robert E. Lee; a small museum and the office of Lee, who, after the Civil War, served as the university's president until his death in 1870. A self-guided tour.

Location: On the campus of Washington and Lee University, Lexington, Virginia.

Admission: Free.

Hours: 9 A.M. to 5 P.M. Monday through Saturday, 2–5 P.M. Sunday.

Phone: (703) 463-8768

When to Go: Any time.

Special Comments: Two sets of stairs.

Overall Appeal by Age Group:

Pre-school	Grade School	Teens	Young Adults	Over 30	Senior Citizens
★	★★	★★½	★★½	★★★	★★★

Author's Rating: A beautiful chapel; a small, tasteful museum. ★★★
How Much Time to Allow: One hour.

DESCRIPTION AND COMMENTS   Lee Chapel, built at the request of the former leader of the Confederate armies in 1868, is located on the beautiful, shaded campus of Washington and Lee University. The chapel features plain lines and pleasing proportions, and is dominated by the famous statue of Lee by Edward Valentine. Downstairs is the family crypt containing Lee's remains, his office (much as he left it on September 28, 1870), and a small museum containing artwork and items belonging to Lee and his family.

TOURING TIPS Combine a visit to the Lee Chapel with a pleasant stroll of the campus of Washington and Lee University.

OTHER THINGS TO DO NEARBY Downtown Lexington offers shopping and restaurants. The adjacent campus of VMI features the VMI Museum and the George C. Marshall Museum.

Luray Caverns

Type of Attraction: The largest known cave on the East Coast. A guided tour.

Location: On the US 211 Luray By-Pass, Luray, Virginia.

Admission: $11 for adults, $9 for seniors 62 and over, $9 for armed forces personnel on active duty, $5 for children ages 7–13.

Hours: 9 A.M. to 6 P.M. March 15 through June 14 and the day after Labor Day through October 31; 9 A.M. to 7 P.M. June 15 through Labor Day; 9 A.M. to 4 P.M. November 1 through March 14 (except weekends, when the last tour leaves at 5 P.M.). Open every day of the year.

Phone: (703) 743-6551

When to Go: Any time.

Special Comments: Be prepared to walk about a mile and a quarter on paved walkways.

Overall Appeal by Age Group:

Pre-school	Grade School	Teens	Young Adults	Over 30	Senior Citizens
★★★★	★★★★★	★★★★★	★★★★★	★★★★★	★★★★★

Author's Rating: The first underground room, where your tour assembles, contains more spectacular formations than you'll see in other commercial caves—and that's just the start. ★★★★★

How Much Time to Allow: One hour for the tour, another half hour or so to explore the Historic Car and Carriage Caravan (a car museum that's included in the price of your ticket) and the gift shop.

DESCRIPTION AND COMMENTS   The most visited caverns in cave-laden Shenandoah Valley are also the best. This cave features an unending succession of spectacular underground formations created over millions of years. If you plan to visit only one commercial cave on your visit to the Blue Ridge area, make it Luray Caverns.

Not only is the cave filled with weird and beautiful formations—some in natural underground rooms more than 140 feet high—it also features a man-made oddity as well. The Stalacpipe Organ uses electrical solenoids to strike tuned stalactites (the formations that hang from the ceilings of caves) with rubber-tipped plungers to produce organlike tones.

TOURING TIPS   Tours leave every 10 to 20 minutes, so waiting in long lines isn't a problem. Wear comfortable shoes and bring a sweater or light jacket—the temperature in the cave is in the mid-50s year-round.

OTHER THINGS TO DO NEARBY   The Historic Car and Carriage Caravan, located in the Luray Cavern complex, features a collection of antique cars, carriages, coaches, and period costumes from 1625 to the 1930s. Across US 211 is the Luray Singing Tower, a carillon of 47 bells. Dining, lodging, and campgrounds are located in and around Luray, as well as fishing and boating on the Shenandoah River. The central entrance to Skyline Drive and Shenandoah National Park is a ten-minute drive to the east.

McCormick Farm

Type of Attraction: A 654-acre farm that was the home of Cyrus McCormick, inventor of the world's first mechanical grain reaper. A self-guided tour.

Location: Near Steeles Tavern, about 15 miles northeast of Lexington, Virginia; Exit 54 off I-81.

Admission: Free.

Hours: 8:30 A.M. to 5 P.M. daily.

Phone: (703) 377-2255

When to Go: Any time.

Special Comments: Keep an eye on children when inside the gristmill.

Overall Appeal by Age Group:

Pre-school	Grade School	Teens	Young Adults	Over 30	Senior Citizens
★★	★★¹/₂	★★¹/₂	★★¹/₂	★★¹/₂	★★¹/₂

Author's Rating: A small, but interesting, slice of American history—and it's got nothing to do with the Civil War! ★★¹/₂

How Much Time to Allow: 30 minutes.

DESCRIPTION AND COMMENTS This is where 22-year-old Cyrus McCormick changed the face of agriculture—and the world—in 1831, when the young inventor demonstrated the world's first successful mechanical reaper to a crowd of local farmers and onlookers on a hot July afternoon.

For centuries, grain had been harvested with a long knife (and a strong back). McCormick's invention harvested wheat five times faster, and with a fraction of the physical effort. Over the decades, as fewer and fewer people produced more food on America's farms, the country was freed to turn its efforts to industry, science, and the arts.

The site includes McCormick's blacksmith shop, gristmill, a small museum, and a view of beautiful, rolling Virginia countryside.

TOURING TIPS This is a small attraction located in a gorgeous, rural setting. Picnic tables are on the grounds around the stone buildings; bring a picnic lunch.

OTHER THINGS TO DO NEARBY Lexington is about 15 miles south on I-81; the Blue Ridge Parkway is to the east on windy and steep VA 56. Crabtree Falls, the highest waterfall in the Blue Ridge, is on VA 56 on the other side of the Parkway. Steeles Tavern offers gas, food, and a few tacky roadside souvenir stands.

Mill Mountain Zoo

Type of Attraction: A ten-acre zoo on top of a mountain.

Location: Near the Blue Ridge Parkway in Roanoke, Virginia.

Admission: $3.50 for adults, $2 for children ages 2–11.

Hours: 10 A.M. to 6 P.M. mid-April through September; 10 A.M. to 5 P.M. October through mid-April.

Phone: (703) 343-3241

When to Go: Any time.

Special Comments: The walk from the parking lot to the entrance is about a quarter mile; handicapped visitors, however, can park near the entrance.

Overall Appeal by Age Group:

Pre-school	Grade School	Teens	Young Adults	Over 30	Senior Citizens
★★★★★	★★★★★	★★★★	★★★	★★★	★★★

Author's Rating: Pleasant, not spectacular—except for the view.
★★★

How Much Time to Allow: One to two hours.

DESCRIPTION AND COMMENTS   It's a zoo with a view—and while you won't find any elephants or rhinos in this mountaintop park, there *is* a Siberian tiger. About 45 species of exotic and native animals are on hand for viewing in cages and enclosures along winding pathways. Small children can get up close to goats and other small mammals.

TOURING TIPS   During the summer, visitors can enjoy programs in the zoo's amphitheater on Tuesdays, Thursdays, and weekends.

OTHER THINGS TO DO NEARBY   Roanoke, the largest city in southwest Virginia, is only a few minutes away. Restaurants, lodging, and shopping are all found downtown, as are a wide selection of museums at Center in the Square (the Science Museum of Western Virginia/Hopkins Planetarium, the Art Museum of Western Virginia, and the Roanoke Valley History Museum).

Monticello

Type of Attraction: The neoclassical mansion on a mountaintop that was the home of Thomas Jefferson. Guided and self-guided tours.

Location: Three miles southeast of Charlottesville, off VA 20 on VA 53.

Admission: $8 for adults, $7 for seniors, $4 for children ages 6–11. Combination discount tickets are available for touring Monticello, Ash Lawn, and Historic Michie Tavern at the Thomas Jefferson Visitors Center at Route 20 South and I-81: $17 for adults, $15.50 for seniors. The combination tickets also save you a buck on the entrance fee at Montpelier, another presidential estate north of Charlottesville.

Hours: 8 A.M. to 5 P.M. daily March through October; 9 A.M. to 4:30 P.M. November through February. Closed Christmas Day. Guided house tours are given continuously throughout the day. The grounds can be explored on your own or on optional guided tours of the gardens (daily, April through October; times are posted by the fish pond on the west lawn and at the ticket office).

Plantation tours are offered April through October at 11 A.M., noon, 2 P.M., and 3 P.M. daily. Museum shops are open from 9 A.M. to 5:30 P.M. March through October and from 9 A.M. to 5 P.M. November through February. The entrance gates to Monticello close at 5 P.M. March through October and at 4:30 P.M. the rest of the year. The grounds close one hour later.

Phone: (804) 295-8181

When to Go: Before 10 A.M. from April through October and on holiday weekends.

Special Comments: The house tour is on one level.

Overall Appeal by Age Group:

Pre-school	Grade School	Teens	Young Adults	Over 30	Senior Citizens
★★★	★★★★	★★★★★	★★★★★	★★★★★	★★★★★

Author's Rating: You can feel the presence of genius. ★★★★★

How Much Time to Allow: Two hours; four hours or longer when it's crowded.

Average Wait in Line per 100 People in Front of You: 30 minutes (house tour only).

DESCRIPTION AND COMMENTS   Best remembered as the author of the Declaration of Independence, Thomas Jefferson was also a delegate to the Virginia General Assembly and to Congress, governor of Virginia, minister to France, first secretary of state, second vice president, and third president of the United States. He was also one of the towering geniuses of the Enlightenment, the 18th-century movement that emphasized reason and scientific inquiry.

Yet the center of Jefferson's private life was Monticello (Italian for "little mountain"), located on 5,000 acres he inherited from his father when he was 14. Visitors to this beautiful house with a stunning view of surrounding mountains and valleys learn about the other, nonpublic side of Jefferson: inventor, scholar, scientist, architect, linguist, and art and book collector.

Jefferson was involved in virtually every detail of the design and construction of Monticello, including the famous dome (the first of its kind built on an American house). Other Jeffersonian touches include his astronomical clock, a dumbwaiter, and a wide-ranging collection of artifacts that reflected his interests: mastodon bones, the stuffed head of an American big horn sheep, and Indian artifacts brought back by Lewis and Clark from their exploration of the Louisiana Purchase (a smart buy made by President Jefferson that doubled the size of the United States).

Outside, visitors can explore on their own the former self-contained plantation, including a 1,000-foot-long vegetable garden, a roundabout walk, all-weather passageways, and many flower gardens and outbuildings. The family graveyard, laid out by Jefferson in 1773, contains his grave and continues as the family burial grounds for Jefferson's many descendants. After touring the house and grounds, make it your final stop on a pleasant, downhill walk on a shady, wood-chip path back to the parking lot. (You can also take the bus down the mountain.)

TOURING TIPS   Visitors park below the mountaintop and are shuttled by bus to the front of the mansion; the buses, which transport 25 people at a time, leave every five minutes. Thirty-minute guided tour groups of 25 enter the house every ten minutes—and on busy holiday and summer weekends, the wait can be as long as four hours. Our advice: Arrive early—say, 8 A.M.—April through October, and on holiday weekends the rest of the year.

When the wait exceeds an hour (about 200 people in line), time tickets are handed out as visitors disembark the bus, telling them when to assemble for their tour. That way visitors can explore the grounds—and avoid heat stroke on summer afternoons—before the house tour. Alas, while Monticello is an interesting place to explore, two or three hours is too long a wait: Arrive early and beat the long line. Good news for summertime visitors: Inside, Monticello is air-conditioned.

OTHER THINGS TO DO NEARBY   About two miles away is Ash Lawn, the plantation home of President James Monroe. Even closer is Historic Michie Tavern, a museum, restaurant, gristmill, and general store. The Thomas Jefferson Visitors Center (two miles west of Monticello on VA 20 at I-81) features an exhibition, "Thomas Jefferson at

Monticello," with more than 400 artifacts from his life, including the seat from his self-designed phaeton (a two-horse carriage that Jefferson drove himself); there's also a short film. It's a good warmup visit before stopping at Monticello.

Montpelier

Type of Attraction: The home of James Madison, the fourth president of the United States and "Father of the Constitution." A guided tour.

Location: On VA 20, four miles southeast of Orange, Virginia; 25 miles northeast of Charlottesville and 70 miles south of Washington, D.C.

Admission: $6 for adults, $5 for seniors over 60 and AAA members, $1 for children ages 6–11.

Hours: 10 A.M. to 4 P.M. daily March through December; weekends only in January and February. Closed Thanksgiving, Christmas and New Year's days, and the first Saturday in November.

Phone: (703) 672-2728

When to Go: Any time. During summer hot spells, go early: The mansion isn't air-conditioned.

Special Comments: The tour of the mansion is on one floor; the formal gardens have several sets of steps.

Overall Appeal by Age Group:

Pre-school	Grade School	Teens	Young Adults	Over 30	Senior Citizens
★	★★	★★½	★★½	★★★	★★★½

Author's Rating: Fascinating history and a behind-the-scenes look at how historic preservation unfolds. ★★★½

How Much Time to Allow: The complete tour takes about 90 minutes, including a stroll through the garden and grounds. Shuttle buses returning to the ticket office also take visitors on a short driving tour of the plantation; the shuttles run on the hour and half hour. Figure on two hours, minimum.

DESCRIPTION AND COMMENTS Montpelier, a 2,700-acre estate owned by generations of Madisons, isn't a typical presidential property. Rather, it's a largely unfurnished and as yet unrestored research project in progress involving constitutional studies, architectural research, and archaeology. For visitors who don't mind visiting a historic house that is different, it's a chance to see the process of historic restoration unfold.

The property was sold following Madison's death in 1836, and the property changed hands six times until it was purchased in 1900 by William and Anna Rogers duPont (heirs to the huge duPont chemical empire). They enlarged the house, added horse barns, greenhouses, a dairy—and even a railroad station. (William duPont commuted to his office in Wilmington, Delaware, by train.)

A daughter of the duPonts donated the property to the National Trust for Historic Preservation in 1983 and it opened to the public in 1986. The process of restoration, both of the additions made by the duPonts and the older part of the mansion that was modified by its many previous owners, is still underway.

Exhibits inside the mansion include exposed brickwork showing different styles of bricks used over the decades, and the positions of walls, doorways, and windows long removed. The interior isn't all neat and pretty—although in a few decades it will be—but it gives an interesting glimpse at how other historic Virginia houses were restored to their former glory.

Outside, visitors may stroll a walled formal garden with the Blue Ridge Mountains as a backdrop, watch university students on an archaeological dig, and visit the garden temple built by Madison around 1811 as a decorative cover for an ice house.

TOURING TIPS   On the house tour, keep your eyes peeled for the unusual, round silver electrical outlets located in the newer, duPont section of the house: The aristocrats generated their own power on the estate that required special outlets. (You'll see the generating station on the bus tour.) After the guided house tour, grab a free brochure and take a self-guided tour of the grounds, which features 40 species of trees from all over the world.

OTHER THINGS TO DO NEARBY   Drive south on Route 20 about a mile, turn left and follow the signs to the James Madison Cemetery, where the president, his wife Dolley, and other family members are buried. The charming walled burial ground is surrounded by rolling pasture and forests.

Museum of American Frontier Culture

Type of Attraction: Four authentic farmsteads representing the dominant cultures in the settlement of the Shenandoah Valley and colonial America. A self-guided tour.

Location: On US 250 W (Exit 222 off I-81) in Staunton, Virginia.

Admission: $7 for adults, $6.50 for seniors, $3 for children ages 6–12.

Hours: 9 A.M. to 5 P.M. daily; 10 A.M. to 4 P.M. December 1 through March 15. Closed Thanksgiving, Christmas, and New Year's days.

Phone: (703) 332-7850

When to Go: Any time. Skip it in inclement or cold weather.

Special Comments: Wear comfortable walking shoes—there's more than a half mile of walking. Bring rainwear or an umbrella on summer afternoons in case of a thunderstorm. And don't feed or pet the animals; some may bite.

Overall Appeal by Age Group:

Pre-school	Grade School	Teens	Young Adults	Over 30	Senior Citizens
★★★★	★★★★	★★★½	★★★½	★★★★	★★★★

Author's Rating: An interesting idea for a museum—and a beautiful and informative place. ★★★★

How Much Time to Allow: Two hours.

DESCRIPTION AND COMMENTS   What is American culture? Go back far enough in search for an answer and you'll come to the American farm. Go back further and you'll reach Europe. That's why this unique museum imported three European farms built in the 17th and 18th centuries (a 1688 "townfarm" from Germany, an 18th-century farm from Northern Ireland, and a 17th-century house from the West Midlands of England) to the rolling Virginia countryside, stocked them with animals, and staffed them with costumed interpreters performing day-to-day activities. The last stop is a 19th-century farm from Botetourt County, Virginia, depicting the lifestyle of a Shenandoah farmer in 1860—and showing the influences of European farm cultures.

TOURING TIPS   Don't miss the 14-minute film in the visitor center that explains what visitors are about to see on the walking tour. The museum shop features crafts and books on cooking, farm animals, and ethnic food.

OTHER THINGS TO DO NEARBY   The Woodrow Wilson Birthplace & Museum, as well as restaurants and shops, are located in nearby Staunton. Country music fans will want to visit the Statler Brothers Complex at 501 Thornrose Avenue, Staunton. In nearby Waynesboro, fans of artist/illustrator P. Buckley Moss should stop by her museum, near I-64 and US 340. It's free.

Natural Bridge

Type of Attraction: A self-guided tour of a 21-story natural rock formation surveyed by George Washington and once owned by Thomas Jefferson.

Location: 15 miles south of Lexington, Virginia, on US 11.

Admission: $8 for adults, $4 for children ages 6–15. Tickets for all three attractions at the site (Natural Bridge, Natural Bridge Wax Museum, and Natural Bridge Caverns) are $13 for adults and $7.50 for children. Admission for any two attractions is $10.50 for adults and $5.50 for children.

Hours: 9 A.M. to 9 P.M. daily.

Phone: (800) 533-1410, (703) 291-2121

When to Go: Any time.

Special Comments: A free shuttle bus is available just beyond the gate house for folks who would rather avoid the steps leading down to Cedar Creek, the stream that flows under Natural Bridge. From there, it's an easy stroll to the bridge. You also can grab a ride for the return trip.

Overall Appeal by Age Group:

Pre-school	Grade School	Teens	Young Adults	Over 30	Senior Citizens
★★★	★★★★	★★★★	★★★★	★★★★	★★★★

Author's Rating: An awesome sight in a beautiful setting. ★★★★
How Much Time to Allow: One to two hours.

DESCRIPTION AND COMMENTS   Natural Bridge is one of the Seven Natural Wonders of the World—and it's easy to see why. The magnificent rock formation soars over a tumbling mountain stream and an easy footpath that allows visitors to walk under and past the bridge. There are plenty of places to sit and enjoy the view.

TOURING TIPS   To get your money's worth from this rather pricey attraction, take the time to enjoy the Glen Trail, an easy, stone-walled gravel path which passes beneath Natural Bridge. It leads upstream to the entrance to an old saltpeter mine and a small waterfall. At the bridge, look for the initials "GW" carved on the bridge across the stream. Legend has it the letters were placed there by the Father of Our Country—and one of its first graffiti artists. For folks staying in the area, "The Drama of Creation," a classical music and light show, takes place every night at the bridge.

OTHER THINGS TO DO NEARBY   The Natural Bridge Wax Museum is next door to the Natural Bridge entrance building. Natural Bridge Caverns are a short drive away. The Gatehouse Deli, a small cafeteria located in the entrance building, is open from 11:30 A.M. to 2:30 P.M. daily. The Summerhouse Cafe, located at the bottom of the steps leading to Natural Bridge, is open in warm weather from 11 A.M. to 9 P.M. Both offer fast-food fare. A mile north on US 11, Enchanted Castle will intrigue children and amuse adults on a guided tour featuring life-size dinosaurs and action heroes.

Natural Bridge Caverns

Type of Attraction: Limestone caverns that go 347 feet underground. A guided tour.

Location: Near Natural Bridge, 15 miles south of Lexington, Virginia, on US 11.

Admission: $7 for adults, $3.50 for children ages 6–15. Tickets for all three attractions at the site (Natural Bridge, Natural Bridge Wax Museum, and Natural Bridge Caverns) are $13 for adults and $7.50 for children. Admission for any two attractions is $10.50 for adults and $5.50 for children.

Hours: 9 A.M. to 9 P.M. daily. Closed from late November through mid-March.

Phone: (800) 533-1410, (703) 291-2121

When to Go: Any time.

Special Comments: Wear comfortable shoes with nonskid soles that you don't mind getting wet. This cavern contains steep stairs, narrow passages, and a few low overhangs.

Overall Appeal by Age Group:

Pre-school	Grade School	Teens	Young Adults	Over 30	Senior Citizens
★★★	★★★★	★★★★	★★★	★★½	★★

Author's Rating: As commercial caves go, rather ho-hum. ★★¹/₂

How Much Time to Allow: 40-minute tours leave every 20 minutes.

DESCRIPTION AND COMMENTS   This isn't an elaborate cave full of breathtaking formations. Furthermore, it's basically an in-and-out, noncircular trip, so you see much of the cave twice. While a ghost legend spices up the tour somewhat, the best sight is looking up 100 feet through a narrow fault line—and knowing that the surface is another 200 feet up.

TOURING TIPS   Wear skid-proof shoes, since the floors are often wet and occasionally irregular. The temperature in the cave is a constant 54 degrees, so consider wearing a light jacket or sweater—although touring the caverns on a hot summer day in shorts and T-shirt feels great.

OTHER THINGS TO DO NEARBY   Natural Bridge and Natural Bridge Wax Museum are a short drive away. Natural Bridge Zoo is about a mile north. A mile north on US 11, Enchanted Castle will intrigue children and amuse adults on a guided tour featuring life-size dinosaurs and action heroes.

Natural Bridge Wax Museum and Factory Tour

Type of Attraction: More than 150 wax figures in scenes depicting the history of Virginia's Shenandoah Valley. A self-guided tour.

Location: Next door to Natural Bridge, 15 miles south of Lexington, Virginia, on US 11.

Admission: $7 for adults, $3.50 for children ages 6–15. Tickets for all three attractions at the site (Natural Bridge, Natural Bridge Wax Museum, and Natural Bridge Caverns) are $13 for adults and $7.50 for children. Admission for any two attractions is $10.50 for adults and $5.50 for children.

Hours: 9 A.M. to 9 P.M. daily.

Phone: (800) 323-8843, (703) 291-2426

When to Go: Any time.

Special Comments: NonChristians—and some Christians not from the Bible Belt—may be puzzled by the incongruous Last Supper presentation that ends the self-guided tour.

Overall Appeal by Age Group:

Pre-school	Grade School	Teens	Young Adults	Over 30	Senior Citizens
★★★	★★★¹/₂	★★★¹/₂	★★★	★★¹/₂	★★¹/₂

Author's Rating: An okay destination—if it's raining. ★★

How Much Time to Allow: 30 minutes to an hour.

DESCRIPTION AND COMMENTS   Wax figures are arranged in scenes from Virginia's past, including a display of presidents from the state, early tourism at Natural Bridge (an "elevator"—actually, a basket—that lowered visitors down the side of the bridge), and historical presentations of the Civil War. Children seem to enjoy the diorama showing all of America's living presidents.

TOURING TIPS   After the tour, go downstairs and visit the factory where the wax figures are made. Visitors can see how they are made, finished, and stored, as well as watch videos on the manufacturing process.

OTHER THINGS TO DO NEARBY   The entrance to Natural Bridge is across the parking lot; Natural Bridge Caverns is a short drive away. A mile north on US 11, Enchanted Castle will intrigue children and amuse adults on a guided tour featuring life-size dinosaurs and action heroes.

Natural Bridge Zoo

Type of Attraction: A small, roadside zoo featuring a large petting area and elephant rides for the kiddies. A self-guided tour.

Location: On US 11, about a mile north of Natural Bridge.

Admission: $6 for adults, $5 for seniors, $4 for children ages 3–12.

Hours: 9 A.M. to 6 P.M. daily. Closed November through April.

Phone: (703) 291-2420

When to Go: Any time. Skip it in inclement weather.

Special Comments: Elephant rides are offered on Saturday and Sunday.

Overall Appeal by Age Group:

Pre-school	Grade School	Teens	Young Adults	Over 30	Senior Citizens
★★★★★	★★★★	★★★	★★¹/₂	★★	★★

Author's Rating: Best for families with small children. ★★

How Much Time to Allow: One hour.

DESCRIPTION AND COMMENTS   Animals on hand at this 25-acre zoo include pygmy goats, a Siberian tiger, llamas, camels, bears, and ring-tailed lemurs. Everything's outside, and gravel paths connect the cages and fenced-off areas containing animals. But don't expect the level of magnificence found at many big-city zoos.

TOURING TIPS   The large petting area—a major attraction for youngsters—is located up the hill at the rear of the zoo. Since the entire zoo is outdoors, keep an eye peeled for gathering clouds on steamy summer afternoons. Or consider touring in the morning before the heat and humidity approach triple digits.

OTHER THINGS TO DO NEARBY   Natural Bridge is a mile south on US 11. Nearby Enchanted Castle will intrigue children and amuse adults on a guided tour featuring life-size dinosaurs and action heroes.

New Market Battlefield Historical Park

Type of Attraction: A Civil War battlefield, museum, and a restored 19th-century farm. Guided and self-guided tours.

Location: VA 305 (George Collins Memorial Parkway), New Market, Virginia (Exit 264 off I-81).

Admission: $5 for adults, $2 for children ages 7–15.

Hours: 9 A.M. to 5 P.M. daily. Closed Thanksgiving, Christmas, and New Year's days.

Phone: (703) 740-3101

When to Go: Any time.

Special Comments: This is the *third* museum on George Collins Memorial Parkway (which parallels I-81). It's easy to confuse with the New Market Battlefield Military Museum (the second museum on the drive).

Overall Appeal by Age Group:

Pre-school	Grade School	Teens	Young Adults	Over 30	Senior Citizens
★	★★	★★★	★★★	★★★¹/₂	★★★¹/₂

Author's Rating: An attractive museum, informative films, a restored farm, and the battlefield is outside the door. Too bad noisy I-81 is so close, though. ★★★¹/₂

How Much Time to Allow: Two hours.

DESCRIPTION AND COMMENTS   This modern museum complex, operated by the Virginia Military Institute, features exhibits, graphics, and artifacts on Stonewall Jackson's Shenandoah Valley Campaign of 1862 and the Battle of New Market in 1864, and a theater showing two short films that give an overview of the two events. Almost 250 VMI cadets participated in the Battle of New Market, and the Hall of Valor Museum inside the complex is their memorial.

Outside, visitors can tour the section of battlefield where the cadets successfully charged Union lines. The Bushong Farm is restored to its 1864 condition. The house is surrounded by outbuildings, including an oven, an older farmhouse, a summer kitchen and wash house, an ice house, and a blacksmith shop.

The one-mile-long walking tour of the battlefield follows the steps of the cadets as they charged the Union position on a hill. On the return, two overlooks feature views of the North Fork of the Shenandoah River.

TOURING TIPS   The two films, which last 30 minutes and start on the hour, give a good overview of the events that happened here in 1864, as well as Stonewall Jackson's 1862 Valley Campaign. Guided walking tours of the battlefield begin at 10:15 A.M. and 3 P.M., weather permitting, and last about 45 minutes. A half hour tour of the Bushong home begins at 1:30 P.M. daily. Both optional tours are included in the price of admission and are the only way visitors can see the inside of the farmhouse.

OTHER THINGS TO DO NEARBY   The New Market Battlefield Museum is next door. New Market, on the other side of I-81, features food, lodging, and shops. Bedrooms of America Museum and Pottery (two blocks from I-81 in New Market) features 11 bedrooms furnished in antiques that date from 1650 through the 1930s.

New Market Battlefield Military Museum

Type of Attraction: A privately owned museum containing more than 2,000 Civil War military artifacts, as well as 500 more military items dating from 1750 to the present. A self-guided tour.

Location: VA 305 (George Collins Memorial Parkway), Exit 264 off I-81, New Market, Virginia.

Admission: $5 for adults, $4 for seniors, $2.50 for children.

Hours: 9 A.M. to 5 P.M. daily March 15 through December 1. Open by appointment only the rest of the year.

Phone: (703) 740-8065

When to Go: Any time.

Special Comments: This museum (distinguished by its white columns) is often confused with the state-operated New Market Historical Park, located next door.

Overall Appeal by Age Group:

Pre-school	Grade School	Teens	Young Adults	Over 30	Senior Citizens
★	★★½	★★½	★★★	★★★	★★★

Author's Rating: A narrower, deeper focus on military artifacts—mostly firepower—than the state-operated facility next door, which presents a broader picture of the events of 1864. ★★½

How Much Time to Allow: One hour.

DESCRIPTION AND COMMENTS   The museum (modeled after Robert E. Lee's mansion in Arlington, Virginia) features more than 2,000 authentic military objects chronologically arranged in 108 displays. Items include guns, uniforms, medals, tents, and other items associated with the 1864 Battle of New Market. That's not all: Also displayed are some other interesting items, including a Springfield rifle recovered from the battlefield at Little Big Horn, spurs belonging to General George Armstrong Custer (who left his boots behind when fleeing capture by Confederate troops only a few miles away), and Stonewall Jackson's family Bible.

TOURING TIPS   The gift shop contains a large selection of books on the Civil War and on military history. Outside the museum visitors can take a self-guided tour of the battlefield. Fifteen monuments mark the positions of the first Union line of defense and the Confederate second line of advance.

OTHER THINGS TO DO NEARBY   The New Market Battlefield Historical Park is next door. New Market, located on the other side of I-81, offers restaurants, lodging, and shopping. Bedrooms of America Museum and Pottery (two blocks from I-81 in New Market) features 11 bedrooms furnished in antiques dating from 1650 through the 1930s.

Roanoke Valley History Museum

Type of Attraction: Galleries displaying Roanoke Valley's heritage, from prehistoric days to the present.

Location: Third floor, Center in the Square, downtown Roanoke, Virginia.

Admission: $2 for adults, $1 for seniors and children ages 6–12.

Hours: 10 A.M. to 4 P.M. Tuesday through Friday, 10 A.M. to 5 P.M. Saturday, and 1–5 P.M. Sunday.

Phone: (703) 342-5770

When to Go: Any time.

Special Comments: Admission is free between 3 P.M. and 4 P.M. on the second Friday of each month.

Overall Appeal by Age Group:

Pre-school	Grade School	Teens	Young Adults	Over 30	Senior Citizens
★★★★	★★★★	★★★½	★★★	★★★	★★★

Author's Rating: Lots of neat things to see, from a moonshine still to a car wreck (no kidding). ★★★

How Much Time to Allow: One to two hours.

DESCRIPTION AND COMMENTS This small museum covers a lot of ground, from exhibits on prehistoric artifacts, the frontier days, the railroad boom days of the late 19th century, D-Day in Normandy, and so on up to the present. The most arresting—and informative—exhibit is "To The Rescue," the history of volunteer rescue and emergency medical services in the United States. (That's where the car wreck is found.) Roanoke, by the way, is the birthplace of the international volunteer rescue squad movement.

TOURING TIPS Make this your second stop on a tour of Center in the Square museums. Combine a visit to this cultural emporium with a stroll through the farmers market held daily outside the doors of Center in the Square. It's the oldest continuing farmers market in Virginia.

OTHER THINGS TO DO NEARBY The Art Museum of Western Virginia and the Science Museum of Western Virginia also are located in Center in the Square. A wide array of shops and restaurants are located in downtown Roanoke.

The Rotunda at the University of Virginia

Type of Attraction: A building completed in 1826 designed by
   Thomas Jefferson as the architectural and academic heart of the
   university he founded. Guided and self-guided tours.

Location: Campus of the University of Virginia, Charlottesville,
   Virginia.

Admission: Free.

Hours: 9 A.M. to 4:45 P.M. daily. Optional, 45-minute guided tours
   begin at 10 A.M., 11 A.M., 2 P.M., 3 P.M., and 4 P.M.; free.

Phone: (804) 924-7969

When to Go: Any time.

Special Comments: Visitors must climb and descend two long sets of
   stairs. Guided tours are accessible to those in wheelchairs, and
   interpreters are available for the hearing impaired (call first).
   With advance notice, special tours can be arranged with a guide
   fluent in Spanish, German, or French.

Overall Appeal by Age Group:

Pre-school	Grade School	Teens	Young Adults	Over 30	Senior Citizens
★	★★	★★¹/₂	★★★	★★★¹/₂	★★★★

Author's Rating: Definitely worth a look, but rather cold and austere.
   ★★★

How Much Time to Allow: 30 minutes.

DESCRIPTION AND COMMENTS   The Rotunda is the focal point of the
"academic village" envisioned by Jefferson, and it's modeled after
the Pantheon in Rome. The domed building sits at the north end of a
long lawn flanked by pavilions, which houses faculty and student
rooms. Behind the low buildings are formal gardens.

   Lower rooms in the Rotunda contain artifacts in displays along
walls and on tables. The upper entrance hall offers an excellent view
of the lawn, and curving stairs lead to the Dome Room, which is illu-
minated by a Plexiglas and aluminum skylight in the white, domed
ceiling. The building, restored in 1976 at a cost of $2.3 million, is in
excellent condition.

TOURING TIPS   From the lower entrance hall, visit the lower east and
west oval rooms, formerly used as classrooms. Then go up the stairs
to the upper entrance hall to see a life-size statue of Jefferson sculpted

by Alexander Galt. The east and west oval rooms serve as a meeting chamber of the university's governing body and the official reception room for UVA's president. The north oval room is where doctoral students defend their dissertations. Then take the stairs to the Dome Room, encircled by pairs of columns and featuring a lovely view of the academic village below.

OTHER THINGS TO DO NEARBY   The Bayly Art Museum of the University of Virginia features art from around the world dating from ancient times to the present. The museum is located a block north of the Rotunda on the UVA campus; hours are 1–5 P.M. Tuesday through Sunday. Call (804) 924-3592.

Downtown Charlottesville abounds with many trendy shops and restaurants (many are directly across the street from the Rotunda). Monticello, Historic Michie Tavern, and Ash Lawn are about a 20-minute drive away.

Science Museum of Western Virginia/ Hopkins Planetarium

Type of Attraction: A science education museum and a planetarium aimed at children. A self-guided tour.

Location: 4th floor, Center in the Square, downtown Roanoke, Virginia.

Admission: $4 for adults, $2.50 for children and seniors. Planetarium admission is $1 with museum admission, $2.25 without. Admission is free on the second Friday of each month from 3:30–8 P.M.

Hours: 10 A.M. to 5 P.M. Monday through Saturday; 1–5 P.M. Sunday. Thirty-five minute planetarium shows are at 1 P.M., 2 P.M., and 3 P.M. on weekends.

Phone: (703) 343-7876

When to Go: Any time.

Special Comments: To see a planetarium show during the week, call first; school groups often are scheduled on weekdays.

Overall Appeal by Age Group:

Pre-school	Grade School	Teens	Young Adults	Over 30	Senior Citizens
★★★★★	★★★★★	★★★★	★★★	★★	★★

Author's Rating: Bright, fun, kid-oriented. ★★

How Much Time to Allow: One to two hours.

DESCRIPTION AND COMMENTS   Youngsters get a lot of hands-on, interactive learning time at this shiny new museum. Exhibits on topics ranging from ecology, communications, the weather, biology, physics, and astronomy will keep young scientists-to-be occupied for hours.

TOURING TIPS   Younger children will enjoy the Chesapeake Bay touch tank, where they can handle small, live specimens of marine life such as sea urchins, starfish, and crabs.

OTHER THINGS TO DO NEARBY   The Art Museum of Western Virginia and the Roanoke Valley History Museum also are located in Center in the Square. Downtown Roanoke features a wide selection of restaurants and shops.

Skyline Caverns

Type of Attraction: 60-million-year-old caverns in the foothills of the Blue Ridge Mountains. A guided tour.

Location: One mile from the northern entrance to Skyline Drive on US 340, just outside Front Royal, Virginia.

Admission: $9 for adults, $8 for seniors and armed forces personnel, $4 for children ages 6–12.

Hours: 9 A.M. to 5 P.M. March 15 through June 14 and Labor Day through November 14 (until 6 P.M. on weekends); 9 A.M. to 6 P.M. June 15 through Labor Day; 9 A.M. to 4 P.M. November 15 through March 14. Open every day of the year.

Phone: (800) 296-4545, (703) 635-4545

When to Go: Any time.

Special Comments: Wear comfortable shoes; there's about a mile of walking on the tour. There's one steep set of stairs going in and coming out of the cavern.

Overall Appeal by Age Group:

Pre-school	Grade School	Teens	Young Adults	Over 30	Senior Citizens
★★★	★★★½	★★★½	★★★½	★★★	★★½

Author's Rating: Lots of bare rock walls and not as many spectacular formations as other caverns. ★★

How Much Time to Allow: One hour.

DESCRIPTION AND COMMENTS   Skyline Caverns' claim to fame are unique formations called anthodites, delicate white spikes that spread in all directions from many locations in the cave's ceiling. Other sights include trout living in a stream (they get fed vitamin supplements to make up for the lack of vitamin D usually supplied by the sun), three underground streams, and a lighting system that aids the imagination when viewing some of the formations. Yet a lot of the walls are bare, the tour is paced slowly (often there's not much for the tour guide to say), and the narrow passages evoke images of Tom and Becky in the cave in *Tom Sawyer.*

TOURING TIPS   Bring a sweater or light jacket: The temperature in the cave is a constant 54°F.

OTHER THINGS TO DO NEARBY   The Confederate Museum is located in Luray, while the entrance to Skyline Drive is a mile away. Downtown Luray features shopping, lodging, and restaurants.

Stonewall Jackson House

Type of Attraction: The house, built in 1801, where Thomas "Stonewall" Jackson lived for two years when he was a professor at nearby Virginia Military Institute. A guided tour.

Location: 8 East Washington Street, Lexington, Virginia 24450.

Admission: $4 for adults, $2 for children ages 6–12.

Hours: 9 A.M. to 5 P.M. Monday through Saturday; 1–5 P.M. Sunday. Open until 6 P.M. June through August.

Phone: (703) 463-2552

When to Go: Any time.

Special Comments: There is one flight of steep stairs on the tour.

Overall Appeal by Age Group:

Pre-school	Grade School	Teens	Young Adults	Over 30	Senior Citizens
★	★★	★★½	★★★	★★★	★★★½

Author's Rating: An inside look at life in pre–Civil War Lexington. ★★★½

How Much Time to Allow: One hour.

DESCRIPTION AND COMMENTS   This tour gives an intimate glimpse into a middle-class Victorian home, as well as insight into the life of a famous American soldier. While the Confederate general is best known for his brilliant leadership in the Shenandoah Valley Campaign of 1862, Jackson was a professor at nearby VMI when he lived in this house from 1859 to 1861. Restored in 1979, the house is furnished with many of Jackson's possessions (including his standing desk, a piano, a settee, a couch, his bed, and a dining room table) and period pieces. The leisurely tour is given by guides who talk about the Civil War as if it just happened.

TOURING TIPS   Tours are given on the hour and half hour. Afterward, take a walk through the restored garden behind the house and browse through the museum shop, which specializes in books, prints, and Victoriana.

OTHER THINGS TO DO NEARBY   Stonewall Jackson is buried in Lexington in a lovely cemetery on Main Street, about four blocks to the south. Other nearby sights include the Lee Chapel on the campus of Washington and Lee University and the George C. Marshall and VMI museums on the campus of the Virginia Military Institute. Downtown Lexington, while small, features shopping, restaurants, and a movie theater.

Stonewall Jackson's Headquarters (1861–1862)

Type of Attraction: An 1854 Hudson River Gothic Revival–style house that served as headquarters by General "Stonewall" Jackson before his famous Shenandoah Valley Campaign of 1862.

Location: 415 North Braddock Street, Winchester, Virginia 22601.

Admission: $3.50 for adults, $1.75 for children, $8.75 for families. Combination tickets to Abram's Delight, Stonewall Jackson's Headquarters, and George Washington's Office are $7.50 for adults over 21, $6.50 for students ages 13–21, $6.50 for seniors 60 and over, $4 for children ages 6–12, and $20 for families.

Hours: 9 A.M. to 5 P.M. daily April 1 through October.

Phone: (703) 667-3242

When to Go: Any time.

Special Comments: One set of stairs to the second floor. The last tour is at 4:15 P.M.

Overall Appeal by Age Group:

Pre-school	Grade School	Teens	Young Adults	Over 30	Senior Citizens
★	★★	★★★	★★★½	★★★	★★★½

Author's Rating: Pleasant, slightly offbeat—and interesting. ★★★

How Much Time to Allow: 30 minutes.

DESCRIPTION AND COMMENTS   Lieutenant Colonel Lewis T. Moore invited General Jackson to use his home as headquarters, and today Jackson's office is much as it was during his stay. Many items were restored with money donated by a descendant of Lieutenant Colonel Moore—actress Mary Tyler Moore. Things to look for on the tour include Jackson's saber, stirrup, camp fork, binoculars, lock of hair, prayer book, and cuff links.

TOURING TIPS   Tours begin on the quarter hour from 9:15 A.M. to 4:15 P.M. The volunteer tour guides are often quaint and unpolished—a welcome relief from the canned spiels recited in most museums. These guides know a heck of a lot of local history. (Expect to be quizzed on your Civil War knowledge.) After the tour step around the side of the house to view its handsome facade, which today faces away from the street.

OTHER THINGS TO DO NEARBY   Downtown Winchester features a pedestrian shopping mall full of shops and restaurants. Belle Grove Plantation in Middletown, Virginia (about 10 miles south of Winchester on US 11; take Exit 302 from I-81), is a restored 18th-century plantation. Thomas Jefferson helped design Belle Grove, which was completed in 1797.

Virginia Museum of Transportation

Type of Attraction: A museum dedicated to transportation—mostly railroads—that's located in a former freight station.

Location: 303 Norfolk Avenue, Roanoke, Virginia 24016.

Admission: $4.20 for adults, $3.15 for seniors, $2.10 for children ages 13–18, and $1.85 for children ages 3–12.

Hours: 10 A.M. to 5 P.M. Monday through Saturday and noon to 5 P.M. on Sundays. Closed Mondays in January and February.

Phone: (703) 342-5670

When to Go: Any time. Skip it in inclement weather—most of the exhibits are outside.

Special Comments: Wear comfortable shoes—there's a lot of walking to do at this spread-out museum.

Overall Appeal by Age Group:

Pre-school	Grade School	Teens	Young Adults	Over 30	Senior Citizens
★★★★	★★★★★	★★★★	★★★★	★★★★	★★★★

Author's Rating: Many of the exhibits are the real thing: huge locomotives, airplanes, fire trucks, buses, cars. For railroad buffs, this place is pure bliss. ★★★★

How Much Time to Allow: One to two hours.

DESCRIPTION AND COMMENTS   Inside this restored freight depot visitors can explore exhibits on early cars, hands-on demos that graphically demonstrate the effect of friction on moving a large mass, a 1950 Studebaker, and displays on airplanes that include a hand-built monoplane. Outside the huge depot is where the real action is: a railway yard full of locomotives, including a Norfolk & Western steam model from 1897; diesel electrics; switchers; and cabooses.

TOURING TIPS   Many of the locomotives are equipped with wooden stairs and platforms so visitors can clamber on board. The yard also features a wide array of buses, fire trucks, streetcars, and rolling freight. During the summer, avoid hot, humid afternoons and visit in the morning.

OTHER THINGS TO DO NEARBY   Downtown Roanoke, with restaurants, shops, and more museums, is only a few minutes away by car.

VMI Museum

Type of Attraction: A museum containing exhibits chronicling the history of America's oldest military college. A self-guided tour.

Location: In Jackson Memorial Hall, on the northeast corner of the parade grounds on the campus of the Virginia Military Institute, Lexington, Virginia.

Admission: Free.

Hours: 9 A.M. to 5 P.M. Monday through Saturday, 2–5 P.M. Sunday.

Phone: (703) 464-7232

When to Go: Any time.

Special Comments: One flight of stairs leads down to the museum in Jackson Memorial Hall.

Overall Appeal by Age Group:

Pre-school	Grade School	Teens	Young Adults	Over 30	Senior Citizens
★	★★	★★¹/₂	★★¹/₂	★★¹/₂	★★★

Author's Rating: While this small museum contains some interesting stuff, it's mainly for avid fans of military history and the Civil War—and for VMI buffs. ★★¹/₂

How Much Time to Allow: One hour.

DESCRIPTION AND COMMENTS   This basement museum gives visitors insight into this unusual institution: While it's not a service academy, all cadets are enrolled in Reserve Officers Training Corps programs and about 15% go on to full-time military careers. Exhibits include military uniforms, weapons (including an antique firearms collection), items used by illustrious alumni and faculty (including George C. Marshall, George Patton, and Stonewall Jackson), and last, but not least, Stonewall Jackson's horse, Little Sorrel (stuffed). There's no mention, however, of the current controversy at VMI: admitting women cadets.

TOURING TIPS   Before or after visiting the museum, take a walking tour of the VMI campus and the adjacent campus of Washington and Lee University.

OTHER THINGS TO DO NEARBY   The George C. Marshall Museum is at the other end of the parade grounds. The Stonewall Jackson House is located in downtown Lexington, where you'll also find restaurants and shops.

Woodrow Wilson Birthplace & Museum

Type of Attraction: The birthplace of the 28th president of the United States. Guided house tours and self-guided museum tours.

Location: 18–24 North Coalter Street, Staunton, Virginia 24401.

Admission: $6 for adults, $4 for students over 12, $2 for children ages 6–12.

Hours: 9 A.M. to 5 P.M. daily. Closed Thanksgiving, Christmas, and New Year's days.

Phone: (703) 885-0897

When to Go: Any time.

Special Comments: Visitors on the house tour ascend and descend one steep flight of stairs, and another set of stairs to the basement. Handicapped parking is reserved on Coalter Street in front of the museum.

Overall Appeal by Age Group:

Pre-school	Grade School	Teens	Young Adults	Over 30	Senior Citizens
★	★★	★★½	★★½	★★★	★★★★

Author's Rating: A fascinating glimpse into middle-class life in the 1850s; a small, well-organized, and interesting museum. ★★★★

How Much Time to Allow: Two hours.

DESCRIPTION AND COMMENTS   The Greek Revival house is restored to its 1856 condition, the year Woodrow Wilson was born. Since the future president of Princeton University and the United States only lived in the house two years, the house tour emphasizes mid-19th-century living over presidential trivia.

An example: The well-paced tour gives insight into how mass-manufacturing was affecting Americans during the period. Items formerly associated with the wealthy, such as silver flatware and matching dining room furniture, were finding their way into middle-class homes. In the basement family room, look for the Singer sewing machine, an example of one of the first, big-ticket home appliances made available to homemakers on credit. Spoon feeding this information are tour guides who are precise and often witty. The museum features bright, informative exhibits giving a chronological history of this author, scholar, university president, governor, and statesman.

TOURING TIPS   Try to time your arrival so you can visit the museum before taking the house tour: You'll gain a good perspective on this controversial and underappreciated United States president. For most visitors, the highlight is Wilson's restored 1919 Pierce-Arrow limousine. After the house tour, explore the beautiful formal gardens and the small gift shop.

OTHER THINGS TO DO NEARBY   The Museum of American Frontier Culture is on US 250, east of town toward I-81. Downtown Staunton features shops and restaurants. Country music fans will want to stop by the Statler Brothers Complex at 501 Thornrose Avenue, Staunton. In nearby Waynesboro, fans of artist/illustrator P. Buckley Moss should stop by her museum, near I-64 and US 340. Admission is free.

PART TWELVE:

Dining and Restaurants

Dining in the Smoky and Blue Ridge Mountains

Dining in the mountains is hearty—hefty even—with a decided emphasis on large portions, which as every ad promises, "will stick to your ribs." The culinary buzzwords in the mountains are "Country Cooking," sometimes rendered even more rural by various intentional misspellings as in "Kountry Kookin" and "Maw's Kuntry Kichen." Because the label is applied to everything from chili dogs to beef stroganoff, nobody really understands what "country cooking" means, except possibly, that if you eat enough of it you will founder or explode.

The specialties of the mountains include steak, beef and pork ribs, ham (both sugar and salt or country cured), fried chicken, catfish, and trout. Biscuits figure prominently into the cuisine as do mammoth "farmhand" breakfasts with enough "flapjacks, hen aigs, ham, and grits" to ensure the farmhand's collapse on the way to his tractor.

While there is a plethora of lackluster restaurants in the mountains, and a passable number of good restaurants, there are few great restaurants (perhaps only one: The Inn at Little Washington, Washington, Virginia, in Zone 8). Likewise, there is little variation from the country cooking theme. Many restaurants serve family style. Some, like the Dillard House in Dillard, Georgia (Zone 5), don't even bother with menus, preferring instead to trot out platters of everything in the kitchen the moment a patron sits down. Also, there is not much in the way of ethnic dining, unless you include pizza, which is abundant.

If you enjoy wine, beer, or a mixed drink with your dinner, be sure to check out local alcoholic beverage laws before you sit down. The southeastern mountains are a patchwork of "wet" and "dry" counties, towns, and other jurisdictions. Restaurants in Pigeon Forge, Tennessee (Zone 2), for example, are dry, but five miles away in Gatlinburg (Zone 2), liquor flows freely. In many dry counties, happily, you can bring your own wine or beer.

501

In resort communities, many establishments close for the winter, and even during the tourist season, a lot of restaurants lock up by 10 P.M. or earlier. When ordering, keep it simple: Try to stick to the restaurant's specialties. Because portions generally are large, go easy on the appetizers. Always have a couple bottles of wine stashed in your trunk (along with a corkscrew) in case you forget what county you're in.

Below is a zone by zone rundown of our favorite restaurants. The name of the establishment, along with the entree range, should give you an idea of how fancy the place is. On weekends, make reservations if the restaurant accepts them, and try to eat early or late to beat the crowd. (Most locals and tourists seem dead set on eating between 6:30–8:30 P.M.)

—— *Zone 1: The Great Smoky Mountains National Park*

In the Great Smoky Mountains National Park (Zone 1), the only restaurant is at the LeConte Lodge, and the only way to reach the LeConte Lodge is to hike 3,000 feet up Mount LeConte, the third highest mountain in the eastern United States. Because there is no electricity at the lodge, the fare consists of meat and vegetables from cans, which after your climb will taste like haute cuisine. Reservations are a must, and overnight lodging is included.

—— *Zone 2: The Northern Foothills of Tennessee*

If people ate coal, Gatlinburg and Pigeon Forge would be the tipples of the east (Las Vegas is the tipple of the west). Professional eaters, dressed in bib overalls or moomoos, can be observed night and day training for their next cruise. Buffets, pancake palaces, and family eateries reign. Fortunately, the majority of these human feed lots serve palatable food at quite reasonable prices. Among our favorites are the Pancake Pantry in Gatlinburg for big breakfasts, Pop's Catfish House in Pigeon Forge for big catfish, and Teagues Mill (13 miles from Gatlinburg) for big trout. The best restaurant in the area for an upscale meal is the Peddler in Gatlinburg. Listed below are these and other Zone 2 restaurants worthy of your attention.

Gatlinburg

Bennett's
Address: 714 River Road, Gatlinburg
Phone: (615) 436-2400
Cuisine: Barbecue
Entree range: $3–15.99

Burning Bush
Address: Parkway (at the entrance to Great Smoky Mountains
    National Park), Gatlinburg
Phone: (615) 436-4669
Cuisine: American
Entree range: $12.95–19.95

Heidelberg
Address: 148 North Parkway, Gatlinburg
Phone: (615) 430-3094
Cuisine: German/American
Entree range: $12–22

Mountain Smoke Barbecue
Address: Winer Square, Highway 321 North, Gatlinburg
Phone: (615) 436-9643
Cuisine: Barbecue
Entree range: $2.25–8.95

The Open Hearth
Address: 1138 Parkway, Gatlinburg
Phone: (615) 436-5648
Cuisine: American
Entree range: $12.95–32.95

Pancake Pantry
Address: Parkway, Gatlinburg
Phone: (615) 436-4724
Cuisine: American
Entree range: $3–7.50

The Peddler
Address: River Road, Gatlinburg
Phone: (615) 436-5794

Cuisine: Steak/American
Entree range: $15.95–29.95

Rio Grande
Address: 459 Parkway, Gatlinburg
Phone: (615) 436-0380
Cuisine: Mexican
Entree range: $6.50–7.50

Smoky Mountain Trout House
Address: 410 Parkway, Gatlinburg
Phone: (615) 436-5416
Cuisine: Trout
Entree range: $10.95–16.50

Teagues Mill
Address: 321 North (13 miles from downtown Gatlinburg)
Phone: (615) 436-8869
Cuisine: Trout/Southern regional
Entree range: $8–12

Pigeon Forge

Bennett's
Address: 2910 Parkway, Pigeon Forge
Phone: (615) 429-2200
Cuisine: Barbecue
Entree range: $3–15.99

Cornflour Restaurant
Address: 2934 Middle Creek Road, Pigeon Forge
Phone: (615) 429-3463
Cuisine: American
Entree range: $10.50–17.95

Mel's Diner
Address: Wears Valley Road, Pigeon Forge
Phone: (615) 429-2184
Cuisine: American
Entree range: $3.50–9.95

Pop's Catfish Shack
Address: 3516 Parkway, Pigeon Forge
Cuisine: American
Entree range: $5.95–11.95

Santo's
Address: 3270 North Parkway, Pigeon Forge
Phone: (615) 428-5840
Cuisine: Italian
Entree range: $5.95–14.95

Sevierville

Five Oaks Inn
Address: 1625 Parkway, Sevierville
Phone: (615) 453-5994
Cuisine: Continental
Entree range: $8.95–16.95

—— Zone 3: The Southwest Foothills of Tennessee

Zone 3, to the southwest of the national park in the Tennessee foothills, is pretty much a culinary wasteland. Our favorite restaurant, and it ain't nothin' fancy, is the Ocoee Inn on Lake Ocoee east of Cleveland. Be sure to save room for the homemade pies. Listed below is the Ocoee Inn and other Zone 3 restaurants worthy of your attention.

Ocoee

Ocoee Inn
Address: Highway 64, Ocoee
Phone: (615) 338-2064
Cuisine: American
Entree range: $6–12

Cleveland

Gondolier
Address: 3300 Keith Street, Cleveland

Phone: (615) 472-4998
Cuisine: Italian/Greek
Entree range: $3.25–7

Jenkin's
Address: 88 Mousecreek Road, Cleveland
Phone: (615) 478-1648
Cuisine: American
Entree range: $5.50–8.50

Willy's
Address: 45 North Ocoee Street, Cleveland
Phone: (615) 472-1130
Cuisine: American
Entree range: $5–9

—— *Zone 4: The Southern Foothills of North Carolina*

In western North Carolina (Zone 4), a few stellar restaurants elevate regional fare to a new high, demonstrating how extraordinary the specialties of the southeastern mountains can be when prepared with skill and imagination. For menu creativity and delicious preparations in a stunning mountain setting, try Relia's Garden at the Nantahala Outdoor Center in Wesser, North Carolina, on US 19. A couple miles north of Relia's Garden, we like the Nantahala Village Restaurant; and in Bryson City, the Hemlock Inn and the Fryemont Inn; both serve family style. Listed below are these and other Zone 4 restaurants worthy of your attention.

Andrews, NC

China Hut
Address: 795 Highway 19-129, Andrews
Phone: (704) 321-3326
Cuisine: Chinese
Entree range: $5.95–8.95

Bryson City, NC

Anthony's
Address: 103 Depot Street, Bryson City

Phone: (704) 488-8898
Cuisine: Italian
Entree range: $4–6.95

Fryemont Inn
Address: Fryemont Road, Bryson City
Phone: (704) 488-2159
Cuisine: American/Family style
Entree range: $13.95–16.95

Hemlock Inn & Restaurant
Address: Galbarth Creek Road, Bryson City
Phone: (704) 488-2885
Cuisine: Family style
Entree range: $12.50

Nantahala Village Restaurant
Address: 9400 Highway 19 West, Bryson City
Phone: (704) 488-2826
Cuisine: American
Entree range: $5–12

Randolph House
Address: Fryemont Road, Bryson City
Phone: (704) 488-3472
Cuisine: American
Entree range: $10.95–16.95

Relia's Garden
Address: 13077 Highway 19 West, Bryson City
Phone: (704) 488-9186
Cuisine: American
Entree range: $6.95–13.95

Cherokee, NC

Tee Pee Restaurant
Address: Highway 441 North, Cherokee
Phone: (704) 497-5141
Cuisine: American/Trout
Entree range: $5.95–7.95

Franklin, NC

Lucio's
Address: 150 Highlands Road, Bellavista Square, Franklin
Phone: (704) 369-6670
Cuisine: Italian
Entree range: $4.95–9.95

Mi Casa
Address: Heritage Shopping Village, 75 Porter Street, Franklin
Phone: (704) 369-5444
Cuisine: Mexican/American
Entree range: $5.25–9.25

—— *Zone 5: The Tri-State Mountains of North Carolina, Georgia, and South Carolina*

A food critic friend says that the way to find good restaurants is to "follow the money." In the Smokies, the money is in Cashiers and Highlands, North Carolina (Zone 5): So are the best restaurants. These mountain communities serve as a summer refuge for southern Florida's affluent. If you drive along US 64, which connects the two towns, most of the cars will be expensive, and almost all will bear license tags from Dade, Broward, and Palm Beach counties in Florida. Fortunately for all of us, the Floridians have reasonably discriminating taste when it comes to restaurants. If you have just come off the Appalachian Trail and are hankering for a nice cordon bleu, osso bucco, or bouillabaisse, give thanks to the Floridians and head for Highlands or Cashiers.

Our favorites for upscale dining in Zone 5 are The Frog & Owl Cafe, featuring European preparations, Hildegard's (Austrian, Swiss, German), and Louis Michaud's for steaks, seafood, and Sunday brunch. All three are pricey, and all three are in Highlands. A half hour to the west in Dillard, Georgia, is the Dillard House, the all-time Smokies favorite for family dining. The ultimate no-brainer, all you do is sit down. Moments later, someone will arrive with platters of chicken, ham, pork chops, or whatever, accompanied by bowls of every vegetable known to man. If you are into bulk loading, a meal at the Dillard House probably will be the high point of your life.

For a good meal and a dining adventure, try the Earthshine Mountain Lodge, open weekends only in Lake Toxaway, North Carolina. Specializing in what they call "mountain gourmet dining," the lodge offers one seating a night, kicking off with hors-d'oeuvres (at the ridiculous hour of 5:30 P.M.), and wrapping up several courses later with sing-alongs, mountain dancing, and an introduction to some of the friendlier animals living on the property.

Listed below are these and other Zone 5 restaurants worthy of your attention.

Hayesville, NC

Broadax Inn & Restaurant
Address: Route 1, Box 289 A, Hayesville
Phone: (704) 389-6987
Cuisine: American
Entree range: $7.95–18.95

Hiawassee, GA

Fieldstone Inn
Address: Off US 76, on Lake Chatuge, Hiawassee
Phone: (706) 896-2262
Cuisine: American
Entree range: $6.95–14.95

Clayton and Dillard, GA

John and Earl Dillards
Address: Highway 441 North, Clayton
Phone: (706) 746-5321
Cuisine: American/Barbecue
Entree range: $3.95–9

Julia's Southern Nights
Address: Highway 441 South, Clayton
Phone: (706) 782-2052
Cuisine: American/Seafood
Entree range: $6.95–14.95

Stonebrook Restaurant
Address: Highway 441 South, Clayton

Phone: (706) 782-6789
Cuisine: American
Entree range: $7.50–15.95

Stockton House
Address: Warwoman Road, Clayton
Phone: (706) 782-6175
Cuisine: American
Entree range: $4–7

The Dillard House
Address: Highway 441 (14 miles south of Franklin), Dillard
Phone: (706) 746-5348
Cuisine: Family style
Entree range: fixed price, $12.95

Clarkesville, GA

Glen-Ella Springs Restaurant
Address: Bear Gap Road, Route 3, Box 3304, Clarkesville
Phone: (706) 754-7295
Cuisine: Continental
Entree range: $14.50–21.50

Highlands and Cashiers, NC

Central House Restaurant
Address: Main Street (part of Old Edward's Inn), Highlands
Phone: (704) 526-5026
Cuisine: American
Entree range: $12.95–17.50

Frog & Owl Cafe
Address: Buck Creek Road, Highlands
Phone: (704) 526-5500
Cuisine: French
Entree range: $18.95–27.95

Hildegard's
Address: Main Street, Highlands
Phone: (704) 526-3807
Cuisine: German
Entree range: $10–20

Louie Michaud's Place for Steaks
Address: Mountain Brook Center, Highlands
Phone: (704) 526-3573
Cuisine: Continental
Entree range: $12.95–20.50

The Mountaineer
Address: Main Street, Highlands
Phone: (704) 526-3368
Cuisine: American/Southern regional
Entree range: $7.95–12.95

Nick's
Address: NC 28 at Satulah Road, Highlands
Phone: (704) 526-2706
Cuisine: American
Entree range: $7–18

On the Veranda
Address: Highway 64 West, Highlands
Phone: (704) 526-2338
Cuisine: American
Entree range: $11–24

Patriccio's
Address: 16 Spring Street, Highlands
Phone: (704) 526-2626
Cuisine: Italian
Entree range: $6.95–22.95

Carolina Smokehouse
Address: Highway 64 West, Cashiers
Phone: (704) 743-3200
Cuisine: Barbecue
Entree range: $1.75–11.95

Cornucopia
Address: Highway 107 South, Cashiers
Phone: (704) 743-3750
Cuisine: American
Entree range: $7–16

Lake Toxaway and Sapphire, NC

October's End (open April 1–October 31)
Address: Highway 64 West, Lake Toxaway
Phone: (704) 966-9226
Cuisine: Italian
Entree range: $9.95–17.95

Earthshine Mountain Lodge (weekends only)
Address: Route 1, Golden Lane, Lake Toxaway
Phone: (704) 862-4207
Cuisine: American/Mountain gourmet
Entree range: fixed price, $20 adults/$10 children

Restaurant Vienna
Address: Highway 64 West, Sapphire
Phone: (704) 884-9727
Cuisine: International
Entree range: $12.95–26.95

—— *Zone 6: Asheville and Brevard*

In Zone 6 is Asheville, the largest city in the five-state mountain area covered in this guide. While Asheville offers more ethnic dining options than other mountain destinations, it is hardly a bastion of culinary accomplishment. Still, Asheville has its rising stars, and they are among the better restaurants in the mountains. Vegetarians will enjoy the creative dishes of The Laughing Seed Cafe. Gabrielle's at Richmond Hill uses regional fish and fowl in continental specialties, and Cafe on the Square serves excellent California nouvelle cuisine pasta and seafood dishes. For more continental North Carolina–style, try The Market Place.

Outside of Asheville, we enjoy Lulu's Cafe in Sylva, 40 minutes southwest. If you like eclectic, there's no place better. In the Brevard/ Hendersonville area south of Asheville, Expressions, a Carolina/continental eatery, is your best bet for fine dining. For good food with a knockout view, we also recommend the Echo Mountain Inn, again in Hendersonville.

Listed below are these and other Zone 6 restaurants worthy of your attention.

Asheville/Arden

All Good Things (lunch)
Address: 7 Pack Square, Asheville
Phone: (704) 255-8197
Cuisine: Deli
Entree range: $4.25–5.95

Blue Moon Bakery (lunch)
Address: 60 Biltmore Avenue, Asheville
Phone: (704) 252-6063
Cuisine: American
Entree range: $3–5

Bosco's Italian Eatery
Address: 2310 Hendersonville Road, Arden
Phone: (704) 684-1024
Cuisine: Italian
Entree range: $12.95–24.95

Cafe on the Square
Address: One Biltmore Avenue, Asheville
Phone: (704) 251-5564
Cuisine: New American
Entree range: $3.50–14.50

Gabrielle's at Richmond Hill
Address: 87 Richmond Hill Drive, Asheville
Phone: (704) 252-7313 or (800) 545-9238
Cuisine: Continental
Entree range: $22–28

Greenery
Address: 148 Tunnel Road, Asheville
Phone: (704) 253-2809
Cuisine: Continental
Entree range: $13.75–24

Grove Park Inn
Address: 290 Macon Avenue, Asheville
Phone: (704) 252-2711

Blue Ridge Dining Room
  Cuisine: American
  Entree range: $16–25
Horizons
  Cuisine: New American
  Entree range: $19–29
Carolina Cafe
  Cuisine: American
  Entree range: $7–15

The Laughing Seed Cafe
Address: 40 Wall Street, Asheville
Phone: (704) 252-5445
Cuisine: Vegetarian
Entree range: $4.50–10

The Market Place
Address: 10 North Market Street, Asheville
Phone: (704) 252-4162
Cuisine: Continental
Entree range: $11.50–25

McGuffey's
Address: 13 Kenilworth Knoll, Asheville
Phone: (704) 252-0956
Cuisine: American
Entree range: $5.50–14

Outback Steakhouse
Address: 30 Tunnel Road, Asheville
Phone: (704) 252-4510
Cuisine: Steak
Entree range: $7.95–17.95

Pedro's Porch
Address: One Lodge Street, Asheville
Phone: (704) 274-9388
Cuisine: Mexican
Entree range: $5–8

23 Page at Haywood Park
Address: One Battery Park Avenue, Asheville

Phone: (704) 252-3685
Cuisine: New American
Entree range: $14.25–21.50

Black Mountain

H.T. Papas
Address: East State Street, Black Mountain
Phone: (704) 669-2823
Cuisine: American/Southern regional
Entree range: $3.95–5.50

Monte Vista Hotel
Address: 308 West State Street, Black Mountain
Phone: (704) 669-2119
Cuisine: Buffet/American/Southern regional
Entree range: fixed price, $6.95

Olympic Flame
Address: East State Street, Black Mountain
Phone: (704) 669-9799
Cuisine: Italian/Greek
Entree range: $5.25–6.50

Red Rocker Inn
Address: 136 North Dougherty Street, Black Mountain
Phone: (704) 669-5991
Cuisine: Family style
Entree range: fixed price, $14.95

State Street Cafe
Address: 203 East State Street, Black Mountain
Phone: (704) 669-1006
Cuisine: American
Entree range: $4.75–16

Tong Sing
Address: East State Street, Black Mountain
Phone: (704) 669-5049
Cuisine: Chinese
Entree range: $6–12

Brevard

Wedge & Keg
Address: 10 McLean Road, Brevard
Phone: (704) 884-4050
Cuisine: American
Entree range: $9.95–14

Falls Landing
Address: 23 East Main Street, Brevard
Phone: (704) 884-2835
Cuisine: Seafood
Entree range: $10.25–13.75

Oh! Susanna's
Address: 230 West Main Street, Brevard
Phone: (704) 883-3289
Cuisine: American
Entree range: $6.95–13.95

Twin Dragon
Address: 108 Chestnut Street, Brevard
Phone: (704) 883-3197
Cuisine: Chinese
Entree range: $5–10

Chimney Rock

Esmerelda Inn
Address: Box 57, Highway 74, Chimney Rock
Phone: (704) 625-9105
Cuisine: Continental
Entree range: $10.95–17.95

Hendersonville, Flat Rock, Saluda, Tryon

Echo Mountain Inn
Address: 2849 Laurel Park Highway, Hendersonville
Phone: (704) 692-4008
Cuisine: American
Entree range: $9.95–19.95

Expressions
Address: 114 North Main Street, Hendersonville
Phone: (704) 693-8516
Cuisine: Continental
Entree range: $13.95–24.50

Hubert's
Address: Laurel Park Shopping Center, Highway 64 West,
    Hendersonville
Phone: (704) 693-0856
Cuisine: Continental
Entree range: $8.95–27

Park Deli Cafe (lunch)
Address: 437 Main Street, Hendersonville
Phone: (704) 696-3663
Cuisine: American
Entree range: $5.25–8.95

Sinbad
Address: 133 4th Avenue East, Hendersonville
Phone: (704) 696-2039
Cuisine: Middle Eastern
Entree range: $9.50–13.95

Highland Lake Inn
Address: Highland Lake Road, Flat Rock
Phone: (704) 696-9094
Cuisine: Continental
Entree range: $12.95–21

Green River BBQ
Address: Highway 176, Saluda
Phone: (704) 749-9892
Cuisine: American
Entree range: $3.25–7

Stone Hedge Inn
Address: 300 Howard Gap Road, Tryon
Phone: (704) 859-9114
Cuisine: American/German/Seafood
Entree range: $9.95–17.95

Pine Crest Inn
Address: Pine Crest Lane, Tryon
Phone: (704) 859-9135
Cuisine: Continental
Entree range: $17–24

Maggie Valley

Arf's
Address: 1316 Soco Road, Maggie Valley
Phone: (704) 926-1566
Cuisine: American
Entree range: $7.95–17.95

J. Arthur's
Address: 801 Soco Road, Maggie Valley
Phone: (704) 926-1817
Cuisine: American
Entree range: $8.95–22.95

Joey's Pancake House
Address: Soco Road, Maggie Valley
Phone: (704) 926-0212
Cuisine: Breakfast
Entree range: $1.50–4.50

Maggie Valley Resort & Country Club
Address: 340 Country Club Road, Maggie Valley
Phone: (704) 926-1616
Cuisine: American
Entree range: $10.95–20

Mountaineer Buffet
Address: Highway 19 (one and a half miles west of Ghost Town in the Sky), Maggie Valley
Phone: (704) 926-1730
Cuisine: American/Southern regional
Entree range: $6.95 (drink and dessert not included)

Smokey Shadows Lodge
Address: Fie Top Road, Maggie Valley
Phone: (704) 926-0001

Cuisine: American/Family style
Entree range: $15.50

Snappy's
Address: Eagle Shopping Plaza, Highway 19, Maggie Valley
Phone: (704) 926-6126
Cuisine: Italian
Entree range: $5.95–8.95

Waynesville, Balsam, Pisgah Forest, Sylva

Bogart's
Address: 222 South Main Street, Waynesville
Phone: (704) 452-1313
Cuisine: American
Entree range: $7.25–12.95

Guadalahara's
Address: 1105 Balsam Road, Waynesville
Phone: (704) 452-3224
Cuisine: Mexican
Entree range: $4–8.50

O'Malley's On Main
Address: 295 North Main Street, Waynesville
Phone: (704) 452-4228
Cuisine: American
Entree range: $8.95–13.95

Whitman's
Address: 113 North Main Street, Waynesville
Phone: (704) 456-8271
Cuisine: Bakery/Deli
Entree range: $2–4

Balsam Mountain Inn
Address: Off Highway 74 South (toward Sylva), Balsam
Phone: (704) 456-9498
Cuisine: American
Entree range: $10.95–15.95

Chiantis
Address: 10 New Hendersonville Highway, Pisgah Forest
Phone: (704) 862-5683
Cuisine: Italian
Entree range: $7–18

Lulu's Cafe
Address: 18 West Main Street, Sylva
Phone: (704) 586-8989
Cuisine: American
Entree range: $8.95–15

Meatball's
Address: Corner of Back and Main streets, Sylva
Phone: (704) 586-9808
Cuisine: Italian/Pizza
Entree range: $2.75–15

Merriweathers
Address: 11 West Main Street, Sylva
Phone: (704) 586-4409
Cuisine: American
Entree range: $4–13

—— *Zone 7: The Blue Ridge Mountains of North Carolina*

Restaurants in the North Carolina Blue Ridge (Zone 7) are the most hip and trendy in the mountains. For nouvelle cuisine, try Best Cellar in Blowing Rock. For jazzed-up Mexican, its the Tumbleweed Grill in Boone, a funky place that brews its own beer. Also in Boone is the happily misplaced Caribbean Cafe. Morel's in Banner Elk features competent bistro-style continental cuisine. In Linville, the French/New American Eseeola Lodge is expensive and a little stuffy, but good. A prix-fixe menu is offered. Finally, for superb family-style dining, the Mast Farm Inn at Valle Crucis will blow you away. There are two seatings nightly, and you must have reservations.

Listed below are these and other Zone 7 restaurants worthy of your attention.

Banner Elk, Beech Mountain, Linville

The Louisiana Purchase
Address: Banner Elk (downtown)
Phone: (704) 963-5087
Cuisine: Cajun/Creole/French
Entree range: $12.95–22

Morels Restaurant
Address: One Banner Street, Banner Elk
Phone: (704) 898-6866
Cuisine: Continental
Entree range: $17.95 and up

Nick's
Address: Shoppes at Tynecastle (at the junction of US 105 and NC 184), Banner Elk
Phone: (704) 898-9613
Cuisine: American
Entree range: $4.95–5.95

Smoke Tree Lodge Restaurant
Address: Highway 105 between Seven Devils and Banner Elk
Phone: (704) 963-6505
Cuisine: American
Entree range: $8.95–15.95

Stone Walls
Address: NC 184, Banner Elk
Phone: (704) 898-5550
Cuisine: American
Entree range: $8–16

Villa Sorrento
Address: NC 194, Banner Elk
Phone: (704) 898-5214
Cuisine: Italian
Entree range: $8.95–13.95

Fred's Deli
Address: Beech Mountain Parkway (in Fred's General Mercantile Company), Beech Mountain

Phone: (704) 387-4838
Cuisine: American
Entree range: $2–5

Vasarely
Address: Beech Mountain
Phone: (704) 387-4900
Cuisine: American
Entree range: $10-15

The Eseeola Lodge
Address: Near intersection of US 421 and NC 181, Linville
Phone: (704) 733-4311
Cuisine: French/New American
Entree range: fixed price, $29

Blowing Rock

Green Park Inn
Address: US 321, Blowing Rock
Phone: (704) 295-3141
Cuisine: Continental
Entree range: $13.95–19.95

Stephen's Restaurant
Address: 1190 Sunset Drive, Blowing Rock
Phone: (704) 295-4344
Cuisine: Continental
Entree range: $5.95–15.95

Village Cafe
Address: Main Street, Blowing Rock
Phone: (704) 295-3769
Cuisine: American
Entree range: $3.95–9.95

Buchanan's
Address: North Main Street, Blowing Rock
Phone: (704) 295-3869
Cuisine: American
Entree range: $4.95–11.95

Woodland's
Address: US 321 Bypass, Blowing Rock
Phone: (704) 295-3651
Cuisine: Barbecue
Entree range: $5–7

Gamekeeper's
Address: Yonahlossee Resort, Blowing Rock
Phone: (704) 963-7400
Cuisine: American
Entree range: $11–25

Best Cellar
Address: Off Highway 321 (They share an entrance with
    Foodline), Blowing Rock
Phone: (704) 295-3466
Cuisine: Continental
Entree range: $10.95–15.95

Boone and Valle Crucis

Dan'l Boone Inn
Address: 105 Hardin Street, Boone
Phone: (704) 264-8657
Cuisine: Family style
Entree range: fixed price, $10.95

Red Onion Cafe
Address: 227 Hardin Street, Boone
Phone: (704) 264-5470
Cuisine: American
Entree range: $6–14

Tumbleweed Grille and Micro-Brewery
Address: Blowing Rock Road across from the ASU baseball field,
    Boone
Phone: (704) 264-7111
Cuisine: Tex-Mex
Entree range: $5.50–13.50

Pepper's
Address: Blowing Rock Road, Boone

Phone: (704) 262-1250
Cuisine: American
Entree range: $5–16

The Caribbean Cafe
Address: 489 B West King Street, Boone
Phone: (704) 265-2233
Cuisine: Caribbean
Entree range: $6.75–9.95

Mast Farm Inn
Address: S.R. 1112, Valle Crucis
Phone: (704) 963-5857
Cuisine: Family style
Entree range: fixed price, $14.80

Jefferson and West Jefferson

Greenfield Restaurant
Address: Just off US 221 between Jefferson and West Jefferson
Phone: (910) 246-9671
Cuisine: American
Entree range: $4.50–10.95

Shatley Springs Inn
Address: Five miles north of Jefferson on NC 16
Phone: (910) 982-2236
Cuisine: Family style/Southern regional
Entree range: Family style, $11.50; plate lunches, $5.50–8

Little Switzerland, Spruce Pine, Burnsville

The Chalet Restaurant
Address: Switzerland Inn, Little Switzerland
Phone: (704) 765-4089
Cuisine: Continental
Entree range: $9.95–15.95

Beam's
Address: US 19 East, Spruce Pine
Phone: (704) 765-6191
Cuisine: Chinese/American
Entree range: $4–8

Nu-Wray Inn
Address: Town Square, Burnsville
Phone: (704) 682-2329
Cuisine: Family style
Entree range: fixed price, $12.67

—— *Zone 8: The Blue Ridge Mountains of Virginia*

Virginia is known for its rural patricians, even in the mountains. Here, history, universities, and a proximity to the American locus of power combine to ensure sophisticated country fare for discriminating palates. Some of the best food in Zone 8 is served at country inns and bed-and-breakfasts, much of it before noon.

The only five star restaurant in all of the territory covered in this guide is The Inn at Little Washington, located at Washington, Virginia, not far from Skyline Drive. Though the service is not always the best, and the attitude of staff and management vacillates between haughty and tolerant, the food is unbelievable. Try the black-eyed peas and Smithfield ham topped with fois gras as an appetizer, followed by seafood and wild mushroom risotto, beef tenderloin, or home-smoked trout. It's expensive, but think of the Inn at Little Washington as the pot of gold at the end of the Skyline Drive rainbow.

Other favorites in the Virginia Blue Ridge area include the Belle Grae Inn in Staunton, Virginia. The Belle Grae offers upscale New American cuisine in a restored Victorian inn setting. At the Joshua Wilton House in Harrisonburg, Virginia, you will enjoy California-style cuisine with a European flair. And don't miss the innovative New American fare at Memory & Company in Charlottesville, Virginia.

Listed below are these and other Zone 8 restaurants worthy of your attention.

Charlottesville

Boar's Head Inn
Address: Route 250 West, Charlottesville
Phone: (804) 972-2230
Cuisine: Regional
Entree range: $13–24

Brasa
Address: 215 Water Street, Charlottesville
Phone: (804) 296-4343
Cuisine: Mediterranean
Entree range: $13–16

Hardware Store Restaurant
Address: Downtown Historic District, 316 East Main Street, Charlottesville
Phone: (804) 977-1518
Cuisine: American
Entree range: $7.95–13.95

Hotcakes
Address: Barracks Road Shopping Center, Emmett Street, Charlottesville
Phone: (804) 295-6037
Cuisine: Gourmet Deli
Entree range: $6–10

Memory & Company Restaurant
Address: 213 2nd Street SW, Charlottesville
Phone: (804) 296-3539
Cuisine: New American
Entree range: fixed price, $27.50

Metropolitan
Address: 119 West Main Street, Charlottesville
Phone: (804) 977-1043
Cuisine: French/American
Entree range: $15-21

Oregano Joe's
Address: 1252 Emmett Street, Charlottesville
Phone: (804) 971-9308
Cuisine: Italian
Entree range: $5.95–12.95

Silver Thatch
Address: 3001 Hollymead Drive, Charlottesville
Phone: (804) 978-4686
Cuisine: American
Entree range: $20–24

Taiwan Gardens
Address: Route 250 West, University Shopping Center, 9 Ivy
　Plaza, Charlottesville
Phone: (804) 295-0081
Cuisine: Chinese
Entree range: $5.50–16

Tastings
Address: 502 East Market Street, Charlottesville
Phone: (804) 293-3663
Cuisine: American/French
Entree range: $12.95–21.95

Front Royal, Flint Hill, Middletown, Strasburg, Washington

Four-and-Twenty Black Birds
Address: Route 522 at Route 647, Flint Hill
Phone: (703) 675-1111
Cuisine: New American/International
Entree range: $13–18

Dean's Steak House
Address: 708 South Royal Avenue, Front Royal
Phone: (703) 635-1780
Cuisine: Steak
Entree range: $8–25

Feed Mill Restaurant
Address: 500 East Main Street, Front Royal
Phone: (703) 636-3123
Cuisine: American
Entree range: $9–14

Ruffino's
Address: 1516 Shenandoah Avenue, Front Royal
Phone: (703) 636-1155
Cuisine: Italian
Entree range: $4.95–8.95

Stadt Cafe
Address: 300 East Main Street, Front Royal

Phone: (703) 635-8300
Cuisine: German
Entree range: $7.50–10.50

Sweet Time (lunch only)
Address: North Royal Avenue, Front Royal
Phone: (703) 636-4256
Cuisine: American
Entree range: $3–6

Wayside Inn
Address: 7738 Main Street, Middletown
Phone: (703) 869-1797
Cuisine: American
Entree range: $13.95–21.95

Hotel Strasburg
Address: 201 South Holliday Street, Strasburg
Phone: (703) 465-9191
Cuisine: American
Entree range: $7.95–18.95

Inn at Little Washington
Address: Washington
Phone: (703) 675-3800
Cuisine: American
Entree range: fixed price, $78 per person weekday, $98 weekend

Harrisonburg

Bluestone Inn
Address: Route 2, Box 246, Harrisonburg
Phone: (703) 434-0535
Cuisine: American
Entree range: $12–14

BBQ Ranch
Address: Highway North 11, Harrisonburg
Phone: (703) 434-3296
Cuisine: Barbecue
Entree range: $3.25–9.50

The Different Drummer
Address: 1 Pleasant Valley Road, Harrisonburg
Phone: (703) 432-0016
Cuisine: American/International
Entree range: $5.95–16.95

The Joshua Wilton House
Address: 412 South Main Street, Harrisonburg
Phone: (703) 434-4464
Cuisine: Continental
Entree range: $14.95–19.95

Nestor
Address: Neff Avenue, Harrisonburg
Phone: (703) 564-2900
Cuisine: Italian
Entree range: $6.95–14.95

Lexington

Harbs' Bistro
Address: 19 West Washington Street, Lexington
Phone: (703) 464-1900
Cuisine: American
Entree range: $5.95–13

Il Palazzo
Address: 24 North Main Street, Lexington
Phone: (703) 464-5800
Cuisine: Italian
Entree range: $7.25–15.95

The Palms
Address: 101 West Nelson Street, Lexington
Phone: (703) 463-7911
Cuisine: American
Entree range: $9.75–14.95

Southern Inn
Address: 37 South Main Street, Lexington
Phone: (703) 463-3612

Cuisine: American
Entree range: $7.95–15.95

Willson-Walker House
Address: 30 North Main Street, Lexington
Phone: (703) 463-3020
Cuisine: American
Entree range: $10–18

Luray

The Mimslyn Inn Restaurant
Address: 401 West Main Street, Luray
Phone: (703) 743-5105
Cuisine: American
Entree range: $7.95–19.95

Brookside Restaurant
Address: Route 4, Box 346, Luray
Phone: (703) 743-5698
Cuisine: American/Southern regional
Entree range: $3–13.95

River's Bend Cafe
Address: 42 East Main Street, Luray
Phone: (703) 743-5881
Cuisine: Steak/American
Entree range: $5.25–12.95

Roanoke and Salem

Alexander's
Address: 105 South Jefferson Street, Roanoke
Phone: (703) 982-6983
Cuisine: Continental
Entree range: $12.95–21.95

Buck Mountain Grill
Address: US 220 South, Roanoke
Phone: (703) 776-1830
Cuisine: American
Entree range: $9.95–17.95

Carlos
Address: 312 Market Street SE, Roanoke
Phone: (703) 345-7661
Cuisine: Brazilian/International
Entree range: $7.95–16.95

La Maison
Address: 5732 Airport Road, Roanoke
Phone: (703) 366-2444
Cuisine: Continental
Entree range: $9.95–29.95

The Library
Address: 3117 Franklin Road, Roanoke
Phone: (703) 985-0811
Cuisine: Continental
Entree range: $18.95–24.95

Longhorn Steaks
Address: 4490 Electric Road, Tanglewood Mall, Roanoke
Phone: (703) 776-3011
Cuisine: American
Entree range: $10.95–17.95

Stephen's
Address: 2926 Franklin Road, Roanoke
Phone: (703) 344-7203
Cuisine: Seafood/American
Entree range: $9.95–19.95

Vanucci's
Address: 315 Market Street, Roanoke
Phone: (703) 981-0000
Cuisine: Italian
Entree range: $7.50–14.95

Three Lil' Pigs Barbecue
Address: Market Square Building, Roanoke
Phone: (703) 345-7447
Cuisine: Barbecue
Entree range: $2.25–4

The Homeplace
Address: Catawba (near Salem)

Phone: (703) 384-7252
Cuisine: Family style
Entree range: fixed price, $7.95

Mac 'N' Bob's

Address: 316 East Main Street, Salem
Phone: (703) 389-5999
Cuisine: American
Entree range: $5–13.95

Macado's

Address: East Main Street, Salem
Phone: (703) 387-2686
Cuisine: Deli
Entree range: $3.50–5.25

Shanghai

Address: 219 Apperson Drive, Salem
Phone: (703) 389-4151
Cuisine: Chinese
Entree range: $4.95–8.95

Staunton and Waynesboro

The Belle Grae Inn

Address: 515 West Frederick Street, Staunton
Phone: (703) 886-5151
Cuisine: American
Entree range: $6.95–22

The Beverley Restaurant

Address: 12 East Beverley Street, Staunton
Phone: (703) 886-4317
Cuisine: American/Southern regional
Entree range: $2–4

Cafe on the Green

Address: Holiday Inn, Route 275 at I-81, Staunton
Phone: (703) 248-6020
Cuisine: International
Entree range: $7.95–18.95

El Puerto
Address: 830 Greenville Avenue, Staunton
Phone: (703) 886-3578
Cuisine: Tex Mex
Entree range: $5–8

The Depot Grille
Address: 42 Middlebrook Avenue, Staunton
Phone: (703) 885-7332
Cuisine: American
Entree range: $7.95–13.95

J. Rugles Warehouse
Address: 18 Byers Street, Staunton
Phone: (703) 886-4399
Cuisine: American
Entree range: $4–10.95

The Pullman Restaurant (located in the C & O Train Station)
Address: 36 Middlebrook Avenue, Staunton
Phone: (703) 885-6612
Cuisine: American
Entree range: $4–20

Wong's
Address: 812 Spring Hill Road, Staunton
Phone: (703) 886-6955
Cuisine: Chinese
Entree range: $5–11

The Fox & Hounds Pub & Restaurant
Address: 533 West Main Street, Waynesboro
Phone: (703) 946-9200
Cuisine: American
Entree range: $8.95–21.95

Purple Foot (lunch only)
Address: 1035 West Broad Street, Waynesboro
Phone: (703) 942-9463
Cuisine: American/German
Entree range: $3–6

Scotto's
Address: 1412 West Broad Street, Waynesboro
Phone: (703) 942-8715
Cuisine: Italian
Entree range: $4.99–9.99

South River Restaurant
Address: 2910 West Main Street, Waynesboro
Phone: (703) 9-GALLOP
Cuisine: American
Entree range: $8.95–15.95

Winchester

Castiglia's
Address: 2100 South Pleasant Valley Road, Winchester
Phone: (703) 722-6084
Cuisine: Italian
Entree range: $6.25–10.95

China Gourmet
Address: 210 Millwood Avenue, Winchester
Phone: (703) 722-3333
Cuisine: Chinese
Entree range: $5.95–9.25

Coalie Harry's
Address: 28 East Picadilly Street, Winchester
Phone: (703) 665-0616
Cuisine: English
Entree range: $5–10

The Continental
Address: Highway 522 North, Winchester
Phone: (703) 667-9797
Cuisine: Continental
Entree range: $10.95–15.95

Karrow's
Address: 12 South Braddock Street, Winchester
Phone: (703) 722-4557
Cuisine: Brazilian/International
Entree range: $7.95–12

L'Auberge
Address: Route 340 (seven miles east of Winchester), Winchester
Phone: (703) 837-1375
Cuisine: French Provençal
Entree range: fixed price, $53 per person

The Old Post Office
Address: 200 North Braddock Street, Winchester
Phone: (703) 722-9881
Cuisine: Continental
Entree range: $10–20

Venice Restaurant
Address: Highway 522 North, Winchester
Phone: (703) 722-0992
Cuisine: Italian
Entree range: $6.25–14.95

Index

Unofficial Guide Reader Survey

If you would like to express your opinion about the Smoky and Blue Ridge Mountains or this guidebook, complete the following survey and mail it to:

Unofficial Guide Reader Survey
P.O. Box 43059
Birmingham, AL 35243

Inclusive dates of your visit: _____

How did you travel to the mountains? ❑ Air ❑ Car ❑ Bus

Did you have a car during your stay? ❑ Yes ❑ No

Hometown: _____ State: _____

Number of Adults: _____ Minors: _____

Your age: _____ and Gender: M   F

The primary purpose of your visit: _____

Have you been to the Smoky and Blue Ridge Mountains before?
❑ Yes ❑ No

Where did you stay on your most recent visit? _____

Concerning your accomodations, on a scale with 100 the best and 0 the worst, how would you rate:

The quality of your room: _____
The value for the money: _____
Staff helpfulness: _____
How long did you wait to check in? _____ Check out? _____

Please list the restaurants where you ate, and rate your overall dining experience at each. Use the 100 = best, 0 = worst scale:

_____
_____
_____

Other comments about your visit to the mountains? _____
_____
_____
_____